Understanding Gender, Crime and Justice

Understanding Gender, Crime and Justice

Sebrina Conner

Larsen & Keller
www.larsen-keller.com

Understanding Gender, Crime and Justice
Sebrina Conner
ISBN: 979-8-88836-036-1 (Hardback)

Larsen & Keller
Published by Larsen and Keller Education,
5 Penn Plaza,
19th Floor,
New York, NY 10001, USA

Cataloging-in-Publication Data

Understanding gender, crime and justice / Sebrina Conner.
p. cm.
Includes bibliographical references and index.
ISBN 979-8-88836-036-1
1. Criminal justice, Administration of. 2. Sex role. 3. Women--Crimes against.
4. Sex discrimination in criminal justice administration. 5. Sex and law.
6. Gays--Crimes against. 7. Female offenders. 8. Women prisoners.
I. Conner, Sebrina.
HV7419 .U53 2023
364--dc23

For more information regarding Larsen and Keller Education and its products, please visit the publisher's website www.larsen-keller.com

Table of Contents

Preface

Criminal justice refers to the system of practices and organizations, which are used for maintaining social control, discouraging and controlling crime, and punishing those who break the laws. Gender is considered to be an important factor which affects not only the rate of crime but also the manner in which it is dealt with, in a criminal justice system. The proportion of crime committed by a particular gender has a significant impact on criminological thinking as well as the criminal justice policies. The degree to which this impact is visible in a society varies with time, and has been observed to shift with changes in gender roles. The readers would gain knowledge that would broaden their perspective about gender, crime and justice through this book. For all those who are interested in this subject, it can prove to be an essential guide.

This book unites the global concepts and researches in an organized manner for a comprehensive understanding of the subject. It is a ripe text for all researchers, students, scientists or anyone else who is interested in acquiring a better knowledge of this dynamic field.

I extend my sincere thanks to the contributors for such eloquent research chapters. Finally, I thank my family for being a source of support and help.

Sebrina Conner

1

An Overview of Crime, Gender and Justice

On 5 February 1755, married spinner Barbara Lambertini had to be treated in one of Bologna's hospitals for a serious head wound.[1] Under one of Bologna's many *porticos* near her house she had got into a fight with her neighbour, Ursula Bagliardi, who had been angry with Barbara because Barbara had disciplined Ursula's young daughter for throwing a pebble at her 16-month-old son's face. After hearing about the disciplining, Ursula sought out Barbara and threw a bed warmer still full of fire (*pieno di fuoco*) at her face. Consequently, Barbara ended up with serious and what the surgeon called life-threatening wounds all the way from her mouth to her stomach. Despite the fact that the gravity of the wounds meant that this altercation was formally categorised as a serious crime, the case appears to have been halted before a sentence was pronounced.

Cases such as these speak to various particularities of crime and criminal justice in early modern Italy. First, the violence central to many of these cases has caught the attention of scholars who noticed Italy – not rarely as a representative of 'southern Europe' – for its persistently high rates of violence all throughout the early modern period as well as its comparatively late decline.[2] Second, the fact that no sentence was recorded alludes to the pervasive culture and judicial indulgence of reconciliation. While criminal bylaws officially prescribed harsh sentences for crimes, the authorities' goal was often to reconcile the two parties, to reintegrate the culprit into society, and to re-establish social peace. According to some scholars, the resulting very moderate deterrent power of the judicial system actually contributed to Italy's particularly violent culture.[3]

Far less expected from a historiographical perspective was that the perpetrator of this aggression was a woman. After all, cases such as these are in stark contrast to the constraints, seclusion and enclosure of demure southern women's lives often emphasised in general discussions or syntheses.[4] Especially

1 Archivio di Stato di Bologna (hereafter ASBO), Tribunale del Torrone (hereafter Torrone), Atti e processi, 8166-2, fasc. 50.

2 M. Eisner, 'Long-term historical trends in violent crime,' *Crime and justice* 30 (2003) 83-142.

3 D. Boschi, 'Knife fighting in Rome, 1845-1914,' in P. Spierenburg (ed.), *Men and violence. Gender, honor and rituals in modern Europe and America* (Columbus: Ohio State University Press, 1998) 150-153, especially 152.

4 For a good overview of the interpretations of various sources that have led to these assumptions, see E.S. Cohen, 'To pray, to work, to hear, to speak: Women in Roman streets, c.1600,' *Journal of early modern history* 12 (2008) 292-293.

when contrasted to a 'freer' northern culture, the strict gender norms as well as Italy's persistent honour culture appear to have left little normative space for women's agency, whether legal or illegal. This oversimplified characterisation has been subject to substantial criticism from scholars of Italian history, not in the least place because what women *should* not do does not necessarily represent what women *could* or *did* not do.

Recorded crimes attest to the discrepancy between norms and practice by their very nature, yet the criminal endeavours of Italian women have to this day received little scholarly scrutiny. This silence exists despite a wealth of sources available, as well as indications of several important differences in recorded crimes between Italy and other parts of Europe – not only for men but also for women. This book about women's crimes in early modern Bologna therefore seeks to address the gendered dynamics of their crimes and their treatment by the criminal court. This introductory chapter examines the state of current historical research: what has scholarship taught us about women in crime in early modern Europe, and how has Italian scholarship engaged with this topic? Looking at Bologna as a case study it furthermore poses the question central to this book: how can its legal and socioeconomic circumstances explain the patterns of female involvement in recorded crime?

1 Historical Involvement of Women in Crime in Early Modern Europe

The roots of current studies of women's historical involvement in crime must be sought in the late 1970s and 1980s. Influenced by the 'new social history,' two new disciplines emerged alongside one another: modern criminal justice history and women's history.[5] Though initially not in an integrated manner, these disciplines introduced a focus both on the impact of criminal justice processes on daily life, on the lived experiences, and on women as important historical actors. With the notable exception of scholars such as John Beattie and Barbara Hanawalt, historians of crime have for a long time paid little attention

5 P. Knepper, *Writing the history of crime* (Bloomsbury: London/New York, 2016) 173; M.L. Arnot and C. Usborne, 'Why gender and crime? Aspects of an international debate,' in M.L. Arnot and C. Usborne (eds.), *Crime and gender in modern Europe* (London: UCL Press, 1999) 3; G. Walker and J. Kermode, 'Introduction,' in J. Kermode and G. Walker (eds.), *Women, crime and the courts in early modern England* (New York and London 1994) 1-2; P. Lawrence, 'The historiography of crime and criminal justice,' in P. Knepper and A. Johansen (eds.), *The Oxford Handbook of the History of Crime and Criminal Justice* (Oxford: Oxford University Press, 2016) 18.

to women's involvement in crime.[6] If the topic was discussed, it was either in the sense of women as victims of crime, or in the context of women's involvement in so-called 'female' crimes, such as witchcraft, infanticide and scolding.[7] The prevalent focus on discerning long-term trends through the quantitative method among crime historians in England, France, Germany and Holland contributed to the lack of attention for women as criminal actors.[8] After all, statistically women generally constituted only a minority of the individuals officially prosecuted by criminal courts.

This traditional approach to crime history has increasingly been criticised from the 1990s onwards, particularly for its inability to enhance our understanding of the nature of women's criminality in the past. Jenny Kermode and Garthine Walker importantly argued that the emphasis on the quantification of a particular type of source material (the indictments) has led to women "being duly counted and then discounted" due to their statistical insignificance.[9] In their eyes, this unjustly denied agency to women as historical actors in the legal process, particularly because other types of approaches and sources revealed that women were far less passive than traditional interpretations let on to believe. More and more scholars also incorporated cultural approaches, analysing the discourses, perceptions, representation and narratives concerning women's behaviours in early modern Europe. Various important German scholars have, for example, revealed women as active users of justice, and demonstrated how women were able to employ expectations surrounding gender norms to further their cases before criminal and ecclesiastical courts.[10]

6 J.M. Beattie, 'The criminality of women in eighteenth-century England,' *Journal of social history* 8:4 (1975) 80-116; B. Hanawalt, 'The female felon in fourteenth-century England,' *Viator* 5 (1974) 253-268.

7 For a discussion of this historiography, see Walker and Kermode, 'Introduction,' 5-6.

8 A good review of this literature is offered by A. Schmidt and M. Pluskota, 'Gevaarlijke vrouwen, gewelddadige mannen? Een review van het historisch onderzoek naar criminaliteit en gender in Europese steden, 1600-1900,' *Stadsgeschiedenis* 8:1 (2013) 61; Walker and Kermode, 'Introduction,' 4.

9 Walker and Kermode, 'Introduction,' 4.

10 J. Eibach, 'Böse Weiber und grobe Kerle. Delinquenz, Geslecht und soziokulturelle Räume in der frühneuzeitlichen Stadt,' in A. Blauert and G. Schwerhoff (eds.), *Kriminalitätsgeschichte. Beiträge zur Sozial- und Kulturgeschichte der Vormoderne* (Konstanz: UVK Universitätsverlag Konstanz, 2000) 672; H.R. Schmidt, 'Hausväter vor Gericht. Der Patriarchalismus als zweischneidiges Schwert,' in M. Dinges (ed.), *Hausväter, Priester, Kastraten. Zur Konstruktion von Männlichkeit in Spätmittelalter und Früher Neuzeit* (Göttingen: Vandenhoeck & Ruprecht, 1998) 213-236. For a comparable argument made by a scholar of Italian history, see J.M. Ferraro, *Marriage wars in late Renaissance Venice* (Oxford: Oxford University Press, 2001) 157; J.M. Ferraro, 'The power to decide. Battered wives in early modern Venice,' *Renaissance Quarterly* 48:3 (1995) 492-512. For early modern Normandy,

Since then several social histories of women and crime in England, France, Germany and Holland have shown that different choices of sources reveal considerably higher proportions of women in crime before the twentieth century, especially when the lower courts are considered.[11] For various towns in early modern Holland, it has been calculated that women made up around 30 per cent of the criminal offenders, and at times even reached levels as high as 50 per cent.[12] Similarly, in seventeenth- and eighteenth-century Frankfurt and Surrey, women accounted for 22 and 21 per cent respectively of all suspects investigated.[13] Examinations furthermore revealed significant differences between rural and urban areas: numbers and shares of female crime were much higher in cities.[14] This has prompted scholars to consider which elements or characteristics of the urban environment engendered criminal behaviour or prosecution, underpinning the importance of cities' wider range of social and economic opportunities, higher levels of institutionalised forms of control, and a lack of the communal social control and support networks that kept rural women away from crime or out of the hands of the criminal justice system. The combination of women's relative independence and vulnerability meant that their crime was above all an urban phenomenon.[15] In a more general

see Z.A. Schneider, 'Women before the bench: Female litigants in early modern Normandy,' *French historical studies* 23:1 (2000) 1-32.

11 M.M. Feeley and D. Little, 'The vanishing female: The decline of women in the criminal process, 1687-1912,' *Law & society review* 25:4 (1991) 719-757; R. Jütte, 'Geslechtsspezifische Kriminalität im Späten Mittelalter und in der Frühen Neuzeit,' *Zeitschrift der Savigny-Stiftung für Rechtsgeschichte* 108 (1991) 93; J.M. Kamp, 'Female crime and household control in early modern Frankfurt am Main,' *The history of the family* 21:4 (2016) 640; M. van der Heijden, 'Criminaliteit en sexe in 18e-eeuws Rotterdam,' *Tijdschrift voor sociale geschiedenis* 21:1 (1995) 1-36; Farge, *Délinquance et criminalitè. Le vol d'aliments à Paris au XVIIIe siècle* (Paris: Plon, 1974).

12 M. van der Heijden, *Women and crime in early modern Holland* (Leiden: Brill, 2016) 4-9; M. van der Heijden, 'Women and Crime 1750-2000,' in P. Knepper and A. Johansen (eds.), *The Oxford Handbook of the History of Crime and Criminal Justice* (Oxford: Oxford University Press, 2016) 251-252; A. Schmidt, *Prosecuting women. A comparative perspective on crime and gender* (Leiden: Brill, 2020) 68. *Before the Dutch Criminal Courts, c. 1600-1810*

13 J. Kamp, *Crime, gender and social control in early modern Frankfurt am Main* (Leiden: Brill, 2019) 67; Beattie, 'The criminality of women,' 81.

14 Beattie, 'The criminality of women,' 80-116; N. Castan, *Les criminels de Languedoc. Les exigences d'ordre et les voies du ressentiment dans un société pré-révolutionnaire (1750-1790)* (Toulouse: Association des publications de l'université de Toulouse-Le Mirail, 1980) 27; Van der Heijden, *Women and crime*, 17-18; P. King, *Crime and law in England, 1750-1840* (Cambridge : Cambridge University Press, 2006) 207-208.

15 A recent, explicit mention of the independence and vulnerability thesis is proposed by A. Schmidt and M. van der Heijden, 'Women alone in early modern Dutch towns: opportunities and strategies to survive,' *Journal of urban history* 42:1 (2016) 22.

sense, notions that women were 'naturally' less likely to commit crimes than men, and that gender differences were static over time, have increasingly been discredited.[16]

In Italy an interest in the social history of criminal justice also emerged during the 1980s, developing in a strong dialogue with the micro-historical approach. This, for one, meant that the quantitative method did not gain a lot of ground among Italian scholars. Responding to the dominant institutional historiography that examined power structures through the actions of jurists and magistrates, micro-historians focussed on the networks of relationships within social groups through accounts of single crimes. In their eyes, a focus on aggregate trends, large-scale processes and overarching categories and groups was unable to grasp these complexities.[17]

Emblematic for the development of Italian crime history was the discussion between Edoardo Grendi and Mario Sbriccoli during the 1980s and 1990s, both strongly advocating other approaches than a quantitative one. In a range of articles and special issues of *Quaderni Storici*, Grendi proposed a qualitative, socio-cultural approach to criminal court records that allowed individual or comparable groups of cases to be understood within their specific contexts.[18] Sbriccoli responded to these publications by warning against a naive understanding of criminal court records as reflections of criminality. As historical products of law, they should be viewed not as reflections of histories of criminality, but as measures of criminal justice.[19] Grendi, in turn, rejected such a reduction of criminal court sources. He contended that the criminal court records were not only the product of the central authorities' concerns, but also of other forms of social control by individuals and the wider community, especially when taking the different (earlier or lower) levels and facets of the criminal justice process into consideration. In his opinion, recorded crime was formed both by criminal justice *and* social relations, and he therefore called for

---

16 For an overview of this literature, see M. van der Heijden and A. Schmidt, 'Theorizing crime and gender in long term perspective,' in E.M. Dermineur, A.K. Sjögren and V. Langum (eds.), *Revisiting gender in European history, 1400-1800* (Routledge: New York, 2018) 52-77; Schmidt and Pluskota, 'Gevaarlijke vrouwen, gewelddadige mannen?,' 60-77.

17 A discussion of the historiographical developments is presented by C. Casanova, *Crimini nascosti. La sanzione penale dei reati "senza vittima" e nelle relazioni private (Bologna, XVII secolo)* (Bologna: CLUEB, 2007) 16; M. Cavarzere, 'At the crossroads of feud and law: Settling disputes in early modern Tuscany,' in S. Cummins and L. Kounine (eds.), *Cultures of conflict resolution in early modern Europe* (Surrey: Ashgate, 2016) 52-53.

18 E. Grendi, 'Premessa,' *Quaderni Storici* 66:3 (1987) 696.

19 M. Sbriccoli, 'Fonti giudiziarie e fonti giuridiche. Riflessioni sulla fase attuale degli studi di storia del crimine e delle giustizia criminale,' *Studi storici* 29:2 (1988) 494.

the use of criminal court records to better understand the relations between, for example, different age groups and genders.[20]

The emergence of women's history and the birth of gender studies in Italy in the 1980s did put women, the meaning of their gendered role in social relations, and changes across historical periods into the centre of analysis. Ever since Joan Kelly's famous essay about the place of women in society, the historiography on premodern Italy has been enriched by important works on the family, on marriage, labour, and migration.[21] Cultural experiences (of networks of relationships, the family, and the body) often constituted dominant reference points in these studies, but, as recent works on the field of labour and economic property highlight, there is also increasing attention for Italian women's active manipulation of rule systems, and their ability to negotiate flexible interpretations of otherwise rigid legal rules.[22] Unfortunately, however, a historiographical cross-fertilisation between gender history and crime history is largely lacking in the Italian scholarship up to the present day.[23]

Instead, the image of premodern Italian criminality and criminal justice is dominated by the topics of violence by the nobility and rural banditry. Viewed as crimes against the Pope's sovereignty, these violent behaviours

20 E. Grendi, 'Sulla storia criminale: Risposta a Mario Sbriccoli,' *Quaderni Storici* 73 (1990) 270; Grendi, 'Premessa,' 699.

21 J. Kelly, 'Did women have a Renaissance?,' in J. Kelly (ed.), *Women, history & theory: the essays of Joan Kelly* (Chicago: University of Chicago Press, 1984) 19-50. Good overviews of the developments within and contributions to the field of women's history and gender studies are provided by S. Mantini, 'Women's history in Italy: Cultural itineraries and new proposals in current historiographical trends,' *Journal of women's history* 12:2 (2000) 170-198; E.S. Cohen, 'Evolving the history of women in early modern Italy: Subordination and agency,' in T.J. Dandelet and J.A. Marino (eds.), *Spain in Italy. Politics, society and religion 1500-1700* (Leiden: Brill, 2007); I. Fazio, 'Storia delle donne e microstoria,' in M. Caffiero, M.P. Donato and G. Fiume (eds.), *Donne, potere, religione. Studi per Sara Cabibbo* (Milan: FrancoAngeli, 2017) 81-94; J.C. Brown, 'Introduction,' in J.C. Brown and R.C. Davis (eds.), *Gender and society in Renaissance Italy* (London/New York: Longman 1998) 1-16.

22 A. Bellavitis, *Il lavoro delle donne nelle città dell'Europa moderna* ((Rome: Viella, 2016); B. Zucca Micheletto, 'Reconsidering the southern Europe model: Dowry, women's work and marriage patterns in pre-industrial urban Italy (Turin, second half of the 18th century),' *The history of the family* 16 (2011) 354-370.

23 L. Tedoldi, *La spada e la bilancia. La giustizia penale nell'Europa moderna* (secc. XVI-XVIII) (Rome: Carocci editore, 2008) 128. A notable exception is the work of Trevor Dean, who has published several articles on gender dynamics of particular crimes. See, for example, T. Dean, 'Theft and gender in late medieval Bologna,' *Gender & History* 20:2 (2008) 399-415; T. Dean, 'Gender and insult in an Italian city: Bologna in the later Middle Ages,' *Social history* 29:2 (2004) 217-231. Also see the important (more cultural historical) works of Elizabeth Cohen, such as E.S. Cohen, 'Honor and gender in the streets of early modern Rome,' *Journal of interdisciplinary history* 22:4 (1992) 597-625.

were regarded major scourges throughout the early modern period.[24] The prevalence of these violent behaviours is often connected to the important role of an honour culture and notions of masculinity in premodern Italy. In an honour-based culture, one's honour was public property and violence was considered both legitimate and sometimes obligatory to assert, defend, and win masculine honour and escape shame.[25] Another important framework towards understanding these violent phenomena was provided by the process of state formation, as archaic patterns collided with the states' new ambitions and strengthening judicial institutions.[26] Women are traditionally viewed as having limited (and mainly passive) roles in either of these contexts. It is therefore hardly surprising that a recent historiographical assessment of early Italian modern criminal justice stated that "the complexities of the relationship between the world of women and criminal justice are still to be uncovered."[27]

When women have been discussed in relation to crime, two familiar assumptions have taken centre stage; the first being the low levels of Italian women's involvement in crime. In an important reference work on women and gender in social history, Elisabeth Crouzet-Pavan summarised that Italian women are believed to have had a marginal criminal presence in the early modern period, and are therefore commonly overlooked in the study of crime.[28] Samuel Cohn observed that women constituted just over one-fifth of all offenders in fourteenth-century Florence, a share similar to those observed in many premodern cities across Europe, but noted a deterioration throughout the century.[29] He contended that the decline in the number and share of women among those accused of crime reflected the newly introduced social and legal constraints on women's ability to perform public roles, commit crimes, and gain access to justice. Female criminals played no significant role in John

24 I. Fosi, *Papal justice. Subjects and the courts in the Papal State, 1500-1750* (Washington: Catholic University of America Press, 2011) 79; E.S. Cohen and T.V. Cohen, *Daily life in Renaissance Italy* (Westport/London: Greenwood Publishing Group, 2001) 49.

25 S. Carroll, 'Introduction,' in S. Carroll (ed.), *Cultures of violence. Interpersonal violence in historical perspective* (Basingstoke: Palgrave, 2007) 23, 27; J.C. Wood, 'Conceptualizing cultures of violence and cultural change,' in S. Carroll (ed.), *Cultures of violence. Interpersonal violence in historical perspective* (Basingstoke: Palgrave, 2007) 87.

26 Fosi, *Papal justice*, 79.

27 Tedoldi, *La spada e la bilancia*, 128.

28 E. Crouzet-Pavan, 'Crimine e giustizia,' in G. Calvi (ed.), *Innesti. Donne e genere nella storia sociale* (Rome: Viella, 2004) 56. A similar arguments have been made by Tedoldi, *La spade e la bilancia*, 128.

29 S.K. Cohn, 'Women in the streets, women in the courts, in early Renaissance Florence,' in S.K. Cohn (ed.), *Women in the streets. Essays on sex and power in Renaissance Italy* (Baltimore 1996) 24, 29.

Brackett's work on criminal justice in sixteenth-century Florence, who instead contended that a combination of the ethics of honour, gender roles and restricted political and economic opportunities "militated against women being equal partners with men in crime."[30]

A second assumption pertains to the likening of women's crimes to acts such as infanticide, sexual deviance, and witchcraft. Italian scholarship's predilection toward the micro-historical perspective evoked scrutiny of the more sensational stories of individual women's dealings with the judiciary.[31] While these singular cases are interesting in their own right, the lack of accompanying serial analyses has rendered it difficult to assess the extent to which particular criminal cases represented exceptional events or broader phenomena. Based on larger numbers of court records, the traditional characterisation of the aforementioned crimes as distinct 'feminine crimes' has been contested in English-language historiography. Walker and others contended that these supposedly feminine crimes were neither typical of female behaviour nor of the criminal prosecutions of women.[32] Women, in fact, participated in most categories of crime and were far more likely to take part in non-'feminine' offences such as theft and violence.

Evidence from the Italian peninsula also shakes up the idea of the crimes of men and women as a dichotomy. For late medieval Bologna, Trevor Dean contended that the real difference between the crimes of men and women was

30 J.K. Brackett, *Criminal justice and crime in late Renaissance Florence, 1537-1609* (Cambridge: Cambridge University Press, 1992) 134; D. Zuliani, 'Reati e pene nel vicariato di Prato prima e dopo la «Leopoldina» (1781-1790),' in L. Berlinguer and F. Colao (eds.), *Criminalità e società in età moderna* (Milan: Giuffrè, 1991) 312.

31 T. Dean, *Crime and justice in late medieval Italy* (Cambridge: Cambridge University Press, 2007) 1. For good examples of insightful micro historical accounts based on trials, see T.V. Cohen, *Love and death in Renaissance Italy* (Chicago: University of Chicago Press, 2004); E.S. Cohen and T.V. Cohen, *Words and deeds in Renaissance Rome. Trials before the papal magistrates* (Toronto: University of Toronto Press, 1993); E. Muir and G. Ruggiero (eds.), *History from crime* (Baltimore: Johns Hopkins University Press, 1994) and the contributions in the special issue 'Difendersi in tribunale' of *Quaderni Storici* 47:3 (2012).

32 G. Walker, *Crime, gender and social order in early modern England* (Cambridge: Cambridge University Press, 2003) 4; M. van der Heijden, 'Women, violence and urban justice in Holland, 1600-1838,' *Crime, history & societies* 17:2 (2013) 72; A.M. Kilday, *Women and violent crime in Enlightenment Scotland* (Woodbridge: Boydell Press, 2007); J. Hurl-Eamon, *Gender and petty violence in London, 1680-1720* (Columbus: Ohio State Press, 2005); O. Ruitenbeek, 'Niet zonder kleerscheuren. Criminaliteitspatroon, eergevoel en het gebruik van fysiek geweld door Amsterdamse volksvrouwen, 1811-1838,' *Jaarboek Amstelodamum* 102 (Amsterdam 2010) 62-85; K. Jones, *Gender and petty crime in late medieval England. The local courts in Kent, 1450-1560* (Suffolk: The Boydell Press, 2006) 8.

probably quantitative rather than qualitative.[33] Even the data from restrictive Florence backs up this assessment. Women were indeed disproportionally accused of crimes of immorality compared to men before the Florentine court, yet these crimes made up only one-eighth of their total caseload.[34] Moral crimes can thus by no means be said to be representative of women's crimes. Therefore, it is not unreasonable to assume that Italian women's crimes were probably more alike than different from those of their male counterparts; an important premise for a female population whose roles in urban life have often been undervalued in general or synthesising discussions.

While there were important ways in which characteristics of Italian female crime patterns appear to converge with those from northern Europe, a re-evaluation of the existing literature allows us to tease out various significant differences. Female crime shares in Bologna, Rome, Siena, and Prato also appear to have been lower than what we may expect based on assumptions about urban life's singular fostering of women's crimes.[35] Moreover, studies of fourteenth- and fifteenth-century Florence, sixteenth-century Rome, and sixteenth- to eighteenth-century Bologna indicate that the criminal courts' casebooks were above all filled with acts of physical violence.[36] This does not only contradict normative notions restricting aggression to men, but also runs counter to what is known for much of northern Europe, where theft and other property offences provided the bulk of criminal prosecutions for both male and female offenders.[37] The mechanisms underlying these significant characteristics of

---

33 T. Dean and K. Lowe, 'Writing the history of crime,' in T. Dean and K. Lowe (eds.), *Crime, society and the law in Renaissance Italy* (Cambridge: Cambridge University Press, 1994) 4; T. Dean, *Crime in medieval Europe, 1200-1550* (Harlow: Longman, 2001) 77-78; Dean, 'Theft and gender,' 405.

34 Cohn, 'Women in the streets, women in the courts,' 26.

35 G. Angelozzi and C. Casanova, *Donne criminali. Il genere nella storia della giustizia* (Bologna 2014) 68; C. Vasta, 'Criminal women. Women's violence in sixteenth and seventeenth-century Rome' (Unpublished Conference paper 61th Annual Meeting of the RSA, Berlin, 26-28 March 2015) 6; L.C. Sardi, 'Analisi statistica sulla criminalità nel 1700 (reati e pene) con riguardo allo Stato senese,' in L. Berlinguer and F. Colao (eds.), *Criminalità e società in età moderna* (Milan: Giuffrè, 1991) 396, 439; L. Asta, La violenza femminile nella Roma del primo ottocento,' *Rivista storica del Lazio* 13-14 (2000-2001) 17-19.

36 Cohn, 'Women in the streets, women in the courts,' 26; P. Blastenbrei, *Kriminalität in Rom 1560-1585* (Tübingen: Niemeyer, 1995) 284; Vasta, 'Criminal women,' 6; Angelozzi and Casanova, *Donne criminali*, 73, 79.

37 D.J. Noordam, 'Strafrechtspleging en criminaliteit in Delft in de vroeg-moderne tijd,' *Tijdschrift voor sociale geschiedenis* 15 (1989) 228; *Old Bailey Proceedings Online* (www.oldbaileyonline.org, version 7.2, March 2015), Tabulating offence category, between 1674 and 1800. Counting by defendant; G. Schwerhoff, *Historische Kriminalitätsforschung* (Frankfurt/New York: Campus Verlag, 2011) 116; M.M. Feeley. and H. Aviram, 'Social

Italian women's crimes have not been subject to substantial inquiry, nor have they been considered in a broader European context. For a more solid understanding of the assorted manifestations of urban crime across early modern Europe, a closer examination of the structures and circumstances that influenced Italian women's encounter with the criminal justice system is therefore imperative.

2 Crime and Gender in an Early Modern Italian City

Language barriers as well as divergent historiographical traditions have meant that the various striking features of the Italian case – a preponderance of violence on its courts' dockets, and a comparatively low share of formally investigated female offenders – have by and large escaped scholarly attention. Informed by the findings from international discussions on the social histories of crime and gender, this book addresses this lacuna by providing an in-depth examination of the gender dynamics of recorded crime in one early modern Italian town: Bologna. Were Bolognese women less criminal than their northern European counterparts? Should we understand their comparatively low shares from the context of strict gender norms and an honour culture, or a culture of violence? Or, as this book argues, do the mechanisms withdrawing women from the criminal court records also allow for a more nuanced and generous interpretation of women's licit and illicit scope of action?

Bologna has been the subject of various historical investigations of crime and criminal justice. Sarah Rubin Blanshei, Massimo Vallerani, and Trevor Dean have analysed the evolution of criminal justice from a forum for private accusations to a more public, deterrent-oriented inquisitorial system between the thirteenth and fifteenth centuries.[38] Together with the important works on the sixteenth to the eighteenth centuries by Giancarlo Angelozzi, Cesarina Casanova, and Colin Rose, they allow us to trace the advancements of judicial state powers through, for example, the annexation of the court's jurisdiction over Bologna's dependent territory, the appointment of constables, and the emergence of additional instruments (such as the denunciation through dis-

historical studies on women, crime and courts,' *Annual review of law and social science* 6 (2010) 153.

38 S.R. Blanshei, 'Crime and law enforcement in medieval Bologna,' *Journal of social history* 16:1 (1982) 121-138; M. Vallerani, *Medieval public justice* (Washington: The Catholic University of America Press, 2012); T. Dean, 'Criminal justice in mid-fifteenth-century Bologna,' in T. Dean and K. Lowe (eds.), *Crime, society and the law in Renaissance Italy* (Cambridge: Cambridge University Press, 1994) 16-39, particularly 17-18, 30-31.

trict officials) to bring crimes within the court's purview.[39] Moreover, these works delineate how negotiated and hegemonic justice continued to complement each other throughout the early modern period.

This scholarship also touched on the important role of gender in Bologna's criminal justice system. For the late Middle Ages, Dean methodically scrutinised the gendered nature and shape of particular crimes, discerning, for example, a highly gendered repertoire of insults, but also found that men's and women's thieving was much more congruent than commonly believed.[40] Dean concluded that the gender differences were above all quantitative rather than qualitative, but explicitly rejected explanatory schemata concerning women's limited normative and practical scope of action.[41] Angelozzi and Casanova's recent study offered the first extensive quantitative account of early modern criminal women between the sixteenth and eighteenth centuries.[42] Their foundational work confirmed the persistence of a quantitative gender gap in crime during this time period. Whereas Dean refrained from offering an explanation for women's low crime shares, Angelozzi and Casanova carefully reconstructed the important role that Bologna's paternalistic legal culture played in the underrepresentation of deviant women's behaviours before the court. The court magistrates' discretion to halt prosecutions for reasons of irrelevancy disproportionally affected women's transgressions, contributing towards their relative invisibility among the trial dossiers.

Each of these works have provided important insights upon which this books builds. Dean's work bears witness to the fruitfulness of a gender analysis of criminal behaviours regardless of the period under scrutiny, by weighing characteristics of crimes committed by women and men to distinguish differences *and* similarities between them. By contrast, Angelozzi and Casanova's study only examined female criminal offenders in detail, but they did establish judicial paternalism as an explanatory factor of importance, though existing in tandem with additional "disparities of opportunity, biology, and culture."[43]

39 G. Angelozzi and C. Casanova, *La giustizia in una città di antico regime. Il tribunale del Torrone di Bologna (secc. XVI-XVII)* (Bologna: CLUEB, 2008); G. Angelozzi and C. Casanova, *La giustizia criminale a Bologna nel XVIII secolo e le riforme di Benedetto XIV* (Bologna: CLUEB, 2010); C.S. Rose, 'Violence and the centralization of criminal justice in early modern Bologna,' in S.R. Blanshei (ed.), *Violence and justice in Bologna: 1250-1700* (Lanham: Lexington Books, 2018) 101-122.

40 Dean, 'Gender and insult,' 217-231; Dean, 'Theft and gender in late medieval Bologna,' 399-415.

41 Dean, 'Theft and gender in late medieval Bologna,' 411-412.

42 Angelozzi and Casanova, *Donne criminali*, 55; C. Casanova, 'Crimini di donne, giudici benevoli (Bologna XVI-XVIII secolo,' *Historia et ius* 9 (2016) 1-11.

43 Casanova, 'Crimini di donne, giudici benevoli,' 11.

While significant, this single facet of judicial culture can indeed not account for the full spectrum of women's experiences in crime and before the court. To understand gender dynamics in early modern women's crimes, we must therefore take a broader range of socioeconomic and legal factors into consideration, considering judicial paternalism in tandem with the institutionalisation of problematic women as well as widespread culture of peacemaking.

This book teases out how a gendered socioeconomic and legal regime brought about differences and similarities between the ways in which crimes were committed and adjudicated in early modern Bologna. The overall share of women involved in recorded crime was an important outcome, but more subtle qualitative differences between the characteristics of the recorded crimes of male and female offenders can also be observed. The nature of the men and women's public lives, their labour opportunities, and their social relationships did to a certain degree determine the extent to which, why, how and when crimes were committed. Important theories have focussed on socioeconomic characteristics of the urban environment that were conducive to women's criminality, such as higher levels of policing in lieu of more informal forms of social control, women's vaster labour opportunities and their broader social horizons. But not all cities were alike, nor does this generalising theory explain regional variations across Western Europe.[44] Labour and guild restrictions for women varied across Europe, as did other legislation regulating women's movement in cities. The municipal decrees of many early modern Italian towns included an official curfew for (unescorted) women after sunset's *Ave Maria* bell, which undoubtedly affected their mobility – at the very least in a normative sense – and possibly their opportunities for night-time offending.[45] These are just a few examples of the ways in which socioeconomic realities could affect women's crimes.

Early modern Italy's legal culture was furthermore of importance to the understanding of women's involvement in recorded crime. Its judicial culture – shaped by legal doctrine, court magistrates, civic rulers, and administrators of civic institutions – determined which misdeeds were considered crimes, and which were not. According to legal historians, the law and criminal justice in Italy were essentially masculine until the twentieth century.[46] Not only was the

44 For two excellent recent works elaborating on these themes for the Dutch Republic and Frankfurt am Main, see Schmidt, *Prosecuting women*; Kamp, *Crime, gender and social control*.

45 Cohen, 'To pray, to work, to hear, to speak,' 303.

46 M. Sbriccoli, '"Deterior est condicio foeminarum." La storia della giustizia penale alla prova dell'approccio di genere,' in G. Calvi (ed.), *Innesti. Donne e genere nella storia sociale* (Rome: Viella, 2004) 81-84.

judicial system based on male behaviours, it also actively categorised many of women's deviant behaviours as censorable anomalies subject to institutionalisation rather than to criminal justice. Women's dealings with the criminal court must therefore always be viewed as part of a broader network of formal and informal control mechanisms.[47] This was especially true for the Italian peninsula, which is known for the early proliferation of integrated networks of semi-public charitable institutions seeking to help and correct an array of 'problematic' women and girls, often through custody.[48]

The female offenders whose transgressions did come within the criminal court's purview faced certain gendered prejudice. It is known that gender differences could arise from biased criminal procedures.[49] Expectations regarding women's less criminal and more law-abiding nature could lead to leniency in sentencing for certain types of cases, while others (particularly in the moral and religious context) were subject to more rigorous control when committed by women.[50] The notion of the *fragilitas* or *infirmitas sexus*, derived from Roman law, provided ample space for judicial discretion by likening (in the eyes of Renaissance jurists, at least) a woman's legal capacity to that of a child or handicapped person.[51] The practical and day-to-day effects of this concept on the administration of justice are difficult to discern from the historical court records, though Angelozzi and Casanova have argued convincingly that the

47 M. Dinges, 'The uses of justice as a form of social control in early modern Europe,' in H. Roodenburg and P. Spierenburg (eds.), *Social control in Europe. Volume 1, 1500-1800* (Columbus: Ohio State University Press, 2004) 167-168.

48 N. Terpstra, *Cultures of charity. Women, politics and the reform of poor relief in Renaissance Italy* (Cambridge: Harvard University Press, 2013) 2; S. Cohen, *The evolution of women's asylums since 1500. From refuges for ex-prostitutes to shelters for battered women* (Oxford University Press, 1992) 3.

49 R.B. Shoemaker, *Gender in English society 1650-1850. The emergence of separate spheres?* (London: Longman, 1998); L. Zedner, *Women, crime and custody in Victorian England* (Oxford: Clarendon Press, 1991); G. Schwerhoff, *Köln im Kreuzverhör: Kriminalität, Herrschaft und Gesellschaft in einer frühneuzeitlichen Stadt* (Bonn: Bouvier, 1991); U. Rublack, *The crimes of women in early modern Germany* (Oxford: Oxford University Press, 1999); D. Palk, *Gender, crime and judicial discretion, 1780-1830* (Woodbridge: Boydell Press, 2006); King, *Crime and law in England.*

50 Schmidt and Pluskota, 'Gevaarlijke vrouwen, gewelddadige mannen?,' 66.

51 T. Kuehn, 'Daughters, mothers, wives and widows. Women as legal persons,' in A. Jacobson Schutte, T. Kuehn and S. Seidel Menchi (eds.), *Time, space and women's lives in early modern Europe* (Kirksville: Truman State University Press, 2001) 99; M. Graziosi, '"Fragilitas sexus." Alle origine della costruzione giuridica dell'inferiorità delle donne,' in N.M. Filippini, T. Plebani and A. Scattigno (eds), *Corpi e storia. Donne e uomini dal mondo antico all'età contemporanea* (Rome: Viella, 2002) 20; L. Buttex, 'L'indulgence des juges? La femme incriminée à Genève au siècle des Lumières. Genre et répression pénale (1767-1792),' *Crime, history & societies* 19:1 (2015) 41-65.

dominant judicial paternalism towards female offenders could not only result in lesser sentencing, but also in women not being prosecuted at all.[52]

Underneath these low shares of women among indicted crimes lay a hidden iceberg of misbehaviour and judicial activity. Examinations of lower levels or earlier phases of criminal justice allow us to tell a more subtle story about women's practical scope of action, whether licit or illicit. In a general sense, this book hypothesises that women's criminal contributions largely adhered to broader 'regional' patterns of crime and criminal justice. While the communal textures of everyday life was conducive to chronic violence among most pre-modern Western societies, *antico regime* Italy has been described as particularly violent.[53] Its 'culture of violence' is often portrayed as essentially masculine, related to the highly gendered cultural ideology of honour. However, a closer scrutiny of the Bolognese records will reveal that violent encounters featured prominently in the lives of both sexes. Notions of female honour and gender expectations bore heavily on women's everyday lives, being frequently cited by plaintiffs, witnesses and judicial officials. The court records reveal that this did not mean that women refrained from responding violently to challenges, but they merely did so at different rates, and perhaps under different circumstances.[54] A high degree of institutionalised peacemaking drew many of these violent conflicts into the criminal courts, filling the casebooks now bearing witness to the crimes of the past.

These extensive peacemaking practices reveal ways in which women tried to advance their positions, while also contributing towards their relative invisibility among recorded crime in early modern Italy. The integral role of reconciliation and conflict resolution for the functioning of early modern Italian criminal courts is widely recognised, though its impact on the everyday lives and scope of action of women have rarely been taken into account, whether as defendants or plaintiffs.[55] As will be argued in this book, this litigation provided

52 Angelozzi and Casanova, *Donne criminali*, 55.

53 J. Davies, 'Introduction,' in J. Davies (ed.), *Aspects of violence in Renaissance Europe* (Surrey: Ashgate, 2013) 1; Blastenbrei, *Kriminalität in Rom*, 284; M. Calzolari, 'Delitti e castighi,' in M. Calzolari, M. Di Sivo and E. Grantaliano (eds.), *Giustizia e criminalità nello stato pontificio* (Rome: Gangemi Editore, 2001) 55.

54 A similar argument was made by Trevor Dean for medieval Europe, see Dean, *Crime in medieval Europe*, 77.

55 For an excellent summary of the intertwined nature of criminal justice and conflict resolution from the medieval period onwards, see S.R. Blanshei and S. Cucini, 'Criminal justice and conflict resolution,' in S.R. Blanshei (ed.), *A companion to medieval and Renaissance Bologna* (Leiden: Brill, 2018) 335-360. Also see S. Cummins and L. Kounine, 'Introduction. Confronting conflict in early modern Europe,' in S. Cummins and L. Kounine (eds.), *Cultures of conflict resolution in early modern Europe* (Surrey: Ashgate, 2016) 9;

women with real leverage in the negotiation of their everyday conflicts, regardless of the judiciary's paternalism. Female victims did not necessarily seek out litigation to pursue their complaints to a full criminal trial, but instead used the criminal tribunal as a public and socially sanctioned forum in which to air grievances, spread shame, exert pressure, and to enhance their social bargaining power in extrajudicial conflict resolution. It was a composite of these diverse elements – the institutionalisation of problematic women, a paternalistic judicial culture, and extensive peacemaking – from the same system that 'withdrew' women from the later stages of criminal justice process, and produced specific patterns of their involvement in recorded crime in early modern Italian towns like Bologna.

The city of Bologna offers a fruitful setting for an analysis of these gender dynamics in crime and criminal justice. Although Bologna cannot be said to represent a typical Italian city, neither was it as unusual as some others. As a provincial capital, Bologna was the second largest city in the Papal States after Rome and served as an important economic, cultural and administrative centre for both the city itself and its surrounding 4,000 square kilometres of surrounding countryside.[56] While being home to one of Europe's oldest universities, Bologna was first and foremost an industrial town, relying economically on its textile industry that employed large segments of the urban population.[57]

Compared to the more frequently studied Florence and Venice that are seen as opposites in the spectrum of women's scope of action (Florence representing the most restrictions and Venice the least), Bologna probably falls somewhere in the middle in terms of social and economic resources.[58] Women's legal capacity was normatively and culturally circumscribed by the dowry system as well as interpretations of Roman law in Bologna like elsewhere on the Italian peninsula, but there is little evidence to assume that its local statutes

---

P. Broggio and S. Caroll, 'Introduction. Violence and peacemaking in early modern Europe,' *Krypton* 3:5/6 (2015) 5; O. Niccoli, *Perdonare. Idee, pratiche, rituali in Italia tra cinque e seicento* (Rome: Editori Laterza, 2007) 38-39; S. Carroll, 'Peace-making in early modern Europe. Towards a comparative history,' in P. Broggio and M.P. Paoli (eds.), *Stringere la pace. Teorie e pratiche della conciliazione nell'Europea moderna (secoli XV-XVIII)* (Rome: Viella, 2011) 75-92.

56 Angelozzi and Casanova, *La giustizia in una città di antico regime*, 111-115.

57 A. Guenzi, 'L'identità industriale d'una città e del suo territorio,' in A. Prosperi (ed.), *Storia di Bologna nell'età moderna (secoli XVI-XVIII)* (Bologna: Bononia University Press, 2008) 464-465.

58 T. Kuehn, 'Gender and law in Milan,' in A. Gamberini (ed.), *A companion to late medieval and early modern Milan. The distinctive features of an Italian state* (Leiden/Boston: Brill, 2015) 406-407.

were as restrictive as, for example, Florence's were.[59] The casebooks of Bologna's early modern criminal court – the *Tribunale del Torrone* – regularly feature women as defendants, plaintiffs, as witnesses and as occasional representatives of male family members, echoing their active quotidian roles in most arenas of social and economic public life.[60]The functioning of the *Torrone*, its procedures, as well as its reforms during the early modern period have been documented in various detailed works based on normative, legislative and trial sources.[61] As one of Italy's many textile towns with one of most long-term, best-preserved criminal court archives both within and outside of Italy, Bologna provides an opportune setting to trace women's involvement in criminal behaviour throughout the judicial process.[62]

The principal period under investigation in this book is the mid-seventeenth to the mid-eighteenth century. Recently designated the 'no longer forgotten centuries,' this period has been underrepresented in Italian scholarship, which has traditionally concentrated heavily on the Renaissance.[63] In relation to women, an important and on-going subject of debate has been the question of whether or not women's legal, social and economic positions declined after the Middle Ages.[64] Various works, particularly those on Florence, tended to paint a rather bleak picture of the increasing restrictions imposed on women in the light of a reorganizing society. The Florentine legal requirement to be represented in court by a guardian (*mundualdus*) has been linked to women's

59 According to Shona Kelly Wray, there was for example no legal requirement of a *mundualdus* (male guardian) for women to draw up a legal contract in Bologna as there was in Florence. S.K. Wray, *Communities in crisis. Bologna during the Black Death* (Brill: Leiden, 2009) 15.

60 Angelozzi and Casanova, *La giustizia in una città di antico regime,* 463. For discussions about the scope of action of non-elite women in Italy, see Bellavitis, *Il lavoro delle donne*, 8; A. Groppi, 'A matter of fact rather than principle. Women, work and property in papal Rome (eighteenth-nineteenth centuries), *Journal of modern Italian studies* 7:1 (2002) 46; Kuehn, 'Gender and law in Milan,' 406; E.S. Cohen, 'Open city. An introduction to gender in early modern Rome,' *I Tatti studies in the Italian Renaissance* 17:1 (2014) 44, 48.

61 The most prominent for the seventeenth and eighteenth century being Angelozzi and Casanova, *La giustizia in una città di antico regime*; Angelozzi and Casanova, *La giustizia criminale a Bologna nel XVIII secolo.*

62 Casanova, *Crimini nascosti,* 10; S.R. Blanshei, 'Introduction,' in S.R. Blanshei (ed.), *Violence and justice in Bologna 1250-1700* (Lanham: Lexington Books, 2018) xvi; V. Rizzo, 'Donne e criminalità a Viterbo nel XV secolo,' *Rivista storica del Lazio* 12 (2000) 11; Angelozzi and Casanova, *Donne criminali,* 54.

63 For an overview see E. Muir, 'Italy in the no longer forgotten centuries,' *I Tatti Studies in the Italian Renaissance* 16:1/2 (2013) 5-11.

64 Kelly, 'Did women have a Renaissance?,' 19-50; Brown, 'Introduction,' 1-16; T. Coletti, 'Did women have a Renaissance? A medievalist reads Joan Kelly and Aemilia Lanyer,' *Early modern women. An interdisciplinary journal* 8 (2013) 249-259.

reduced ability to access the criminal court and to perform public roles from the fourteenth century onwards.[65] Although this decline theory has continued to shape dominant conceptions of premodern Italy – also for the centuries after the Renaissance – it has become clear that the Renaissance Florentine culture of constraint was neither absolute nor invariable over time, space and class.[66] The focus in this book on women's licit and illicit behaviours as reflected by the criminal court records in seventeenth- and eighteenth-century Bologna thus allows us to better understand women's scope of action in these recently 'rediscovered' centuries.

3 Criminal Court Records as Sources for Social History

The criminal court records of Bologna's *Tribunale del Torrone* constitute the main source for this research. This secular criminal court was established in around 1530, following the annexation of Bologna to the Papal States, and was dissolved in 1796 after the French invasion. As the papal government sought to claim a monopoly over criminal justice, the *Torrone* replaced the medieval communal court of the *podestà* and gradually expanded its judicial authority from the city to over some 4,000 square kilometres of the surrounding countryside.[67] Its judges were directly appointed by the Pope and dealt with grave crimes such as homicide, counterfeiting and lèse majesté, but also oversaw myriad minor brawls and infractions of the city's decrees on public order. Both these serious crimes and misdemeanours left a significant trail of judicial paper. Not all of the sources once in existence have survived the passing of time: the peacemaking and surety books, the monthly reports on the income notaries received for their work, as well as the dedicated sentence books have for example been lost. Nevertheless, the *Torrone*'s documentary legacy is overwhelming in size. It is estimated that approximately 11,000 registers from the early modern period survive, consisting of about a million criminal cases.[68] Especially when combined with its medieval predecessor, it is considered one of the most long-term, best-preserved and systematic criminal court archives both within and outside Italy.[69]

65 Cohn, 'Women in the streets, women in the courts,' 24, 29.
66 Brown, 'Introduction,' 2-5; Cohen, 'Evolving the history of women,' 348-354.
67 Angelozzi and Casanova, *La giustizia in una città di antico regime*, 111-115.
68 Angelozzi and Casanova, *Donne criminali*, 66.
69 Ibidem; Blanshei, 'Introduction,' xvi; Angelozzi and Casanova, *Donne criminali*, 54; Rizzo, 'Donne e criminalità,' 11;

The archive of the *Torrone* consists of different types of sources. Each year, the criminal court produced records for between 2,000 and 3,000 denunciations – the initial complaint about a crime to a local official of the court – and some 300 to 400 *processi*, which were formal investigation dossiers.[70] In form and spirit these *processi* fell somewhere between an inquest and a trial in the Anglo-Saxon tradition, as it included the first deposition, all of the forensic and other evidence gathered, the verbatim transcripts of witness testimonies and suspect interrogations, but did not necessarily pass judgement as trials were often suspended for a range of reasons.[71] The discrepancy between the number of denunciations and completed trials is well documented for early modern towns, including for those in Italy.[72] A widespread culture of peacemaking and pardoning accounted for a part of these suspensions, as did the court magistrates' decisions of which cases to pursue based on the onus, the perceived danger of the case or importance to the community, as well as the 'personal qualities' of those involved.[73] Examining the character and content of *both* the denunciations and the investigation dossiers is therefore important. It does not only allow us to shed light on the involvement of men and women in a wider variety of crimes, but also enables the scrutiny of the diverging priorities of plaintiffs and the authorities and, consequently, on gender biases ingrained in the judicial system.

The cases collected from the Bolognese criminal court do not necessarily represent all of criminality among a population. Many scholars have argued that criminal court records above all measured the effectiveness and choices of the judicial apparatus rather than all of society's transgressions.[74] They commonly refer to the 'dark figure of crime' to describe the crimes that were

70 Angelozzi and Casanova, *La giustizia in una città di antico regime*, 433; Blanshei, 'Introduction,' xvi.

71 In late seventeenth Bologna, a verdict was reached in only a little over three per cent of all of the cases that passed through the court. See Angelozzi and Casanova, *La giustizia in una città di antico regime*, 551, 565; Cohen, *Love and death*, 3;

72 A. Pastore, *Crimine e giustizia in tempo di peste nell'Europea moderna* (Rome: Laterza, 1991) 75; Angelozzi and Casanova, *La giustizia in una città di antico regime*, 421; Dean, *Crime and justice in late medieval Italy*, 19.

73 O. Niccoli, 'Rinuncia, pace, perdono. Rituali di pacificazione della prima età moderna,' *Studi storici* 40:1 (1999) 234; C. Nubola, 'Giustizia, perdono, oblio. La grazia in Italia dall'età moderna ad oggi,' in K. Härter and C. Nubola (eds.), *Grazia e giustizia. Figure della clemenza fra tardo medioevo ad età contemporanea* (Bologna: Il Mulino, 2011) 33; Angelozzi and Casanova, *La giustizia in una città di antico regime*, 643; Dean, *Crime and justice in late medieval Italy*, 19.

74 Sbriccoli, 'Fonti giudiziarie e fonti giuridiche,' 494; Casanova, *Crimini nascosti*, 19; Dean and Lowe, 'Writing the history of crime,' 2-3.

neither reported nor recorded by official record keepers.[75] This dark figure is generally believed to have been higher for women than for men.[76] Based on her examinations of criminal court records from seventeenth-century Cheshire, Walker, for example, suggested that "we can surmise that women's place in the household meant that they were especially likely to be excluded from the official court records."[77] For early modern Italy it is similarly contended that women's transgressions were more likely to be dealt with outside the judicial system.[78] While we may never know for sure what proportion of women relative to men committed offences without being formally held accountable, the survival of both the denunciations and the investigation dossiers provide important opportunities to trace discrepancies between the misbehaviours that were reported and those that were subjected to a formal investigation, as well as shedding light on the impact of gender on this process in an early modern northern Italian town.

Court records were by no means neutral and objective sources. In theory, the court notary was bound to record verbatim everything that the plaintiffs, suspects and witnesses said and did. While some scholars would argue that individuals retained very distinct and personal voices in the early modern Italian court papers, these sources were at the same time also clearly a product of the court. Substantial parts of these recordings were very much guided by magistrates' questions, after which replies often followed a recognizably standardised structure and echoed legal terminology and rhetoric.[79] The court officials were not the only key players in this process: the men and women who had their statements of events recorded were equally important. Natalie Zemon Davis and others have convincingly argued that these men and women always, in some measure, strategically constructed their narratives according to rules of both legal and cultural rhetoric.[80] While court records should thus be viewed

75 Schmidt and Pluskota, 'Gevaarlijke vrouwen, gewelddadige mannen?,' 62.

76 Van der Heijden, *Women and crime*, 11.

77 Walker, *Crime, gender and social order*, 12.

78 Sbriccoli, 'Deterior est condicio foeminarum,' 83-84.

79 Cohen, *Love and death*, 4; C. Lansing, 'Concubines, lovers, prostitutes. Infamy and female identity in medieval Bologna,' in P. Findlen, M.M. Fontaine and D.J. Osheim (eds.), *Beyond Florence. The contours of medieval and early modern Italy* (Palo Alto: Stanford University Press, 2003) 90; S. Seidel Mench, 'I processi matrimoniali come fonte storica,' in S. Seidel Menchi and Diego Quaglioni (eds.), *Coniugi nemici. La separazione in Italia dal XII al XVIII secolo* (Bologna: Il Mulino, 2000) 59-68.

80 N. Zemon Davis, *Fiction in the archives. Pardon tales and their tellers in sixteenth-century France* (Stanford: Stanford University Press, 1987); Dean, *Crime and justice in late medieval Italy*, 31; Lansing, 'Concubines, lovers, prostitutes,' 90; J. Hardwick, 'Between state and street: Witnesses and the family politics of litigation in early modern France,' in S. Desan

as 'plausible stories' rather than one-on-one transmissions of the reality of an event, they nevertheless provide one of the best sources for information on the popular culture of early modern Italy, allowing us to glean everyday behaviours of those who left few other documentary traces.[81]

Bologna's early modern criminal court records are therefore examined from two angles in this book. On the one hand they are viewed as being the products of an apparatus of top-down control by the authorities. Not only did the notaries have a hand in shaping the language and rhetoric of the documents but, in a broader sense, prosecuted crime can be viewed as the result of political and institutional choices that dovetail the authorities' attitudes towards various crimes and criminals.[82] However, both in what is and what is not said the sources also distinctly attest to the *Torrone*'s functioning as a forum for bottom-up conflict resolution. References to prior conflicts between plaintiffs and defendants about filing complaints with the court as well as the prevalence of renunciations – suggestive of extrajudicial settlements – speak volumes in this regard. By considering the court records as products of both of these mechanisms, they allow us to probe the extent to which women were able to display considerable, though gendered, agency in both their licit and illicit conduct while navigating what has been referred to as 'a culture of constraint.'[83]

Several previously mentioned analytical concepts require further clarification. What is seen as 'crime' differs over time and space and is generally seen in relation to the interests of the authorities as well as legal prohibitions.[84] Indeed, what behaviours are *prosecuted* as crimes is always the result of political, institutional and socio-cultural choices and definitions.[85] However, this book examines not only prosecuted crimes but also *reported* crime, consequently all of the behaviours brought under the purview of the criminal court by local bailiffs and individuals. The term crime is thus used rather loosely as any action that was deemed injurious and resulted in a complaint or denunciation to the criminal court.

---

and J. Merrick (eds.), *Family, gender and law in early modern France* (University Park: Pennsylvania State University Press, 2009) 101-136.

81 Dean, *Crime and justice in late medieval Italy*, 31; Lansing, 'Concubines, lovers, prostitutes,' 90; Cohen, *Love and death*, 4; Cohen, 'Open city,' 51.

82 Dean and Lowe, 'Writing the history of crime,' 3.

83 Cohen, 'Evolving the history of women,' 343, 354.

84 The Oxford English Dictionary, for example, describes the word 'crime' as "An act or omission constituting an offence (usually a grave one) against an individual or the state and punishable by law." see "crime, n.2." OED *Online* (Oxford: Oxford University Press), accessed 20 June 2018.

85 Dean and Lowe, 'Writing the history of crime,' 3; Dinges, 'The uses of justice,' 166.

A second important concept is that of 'gender.' Rooted in the 1980s, gender differs from the term 'sex' in distinguishing the social and cultural construction of maleness and femaleness as part of an ideological system that can vary across time and space.[86] When this book examines differences and similarities between the male and female offenders before the criminal court, it therefore does not refer to their physiology, but to both the cultural and practical effects of the values and models of comportment that were socially imposed on the sexes. Because of the current state of scholarship, the focus of this book is first and foremost on investigating and weighing the scope of action of women in an early modern Italian town. However, because male and female should be seen as interconnected categories within social hierarchies, power relations and ideology, women are always studied in relation to men.[87]

Another important, related concept is that of 'agency.' Earlier studies have tended to emphasise the constraints that cultural precept and patriarchal ideology imposed on women in early modern Europe. To this day, this idea of subordination looms large in the history of early modern Italian women, who, based on the prescriptive sources alone, could be depicted as propertyless dependents, lacking full legal personhood as well as most institutional authority, and who were furthermore often enclosed either in their homes or religious or civic institutions.[88] However, recent studies have argued that there was a significant difference between the norms that were described in prescriptive literature and the complexities of everyday life.[89] They therefore increasingly explore what early modern women *did* do and say, on their own and in collaboration with men. Agency here is then used not to assume anachronistic gender equality, female liberty or the successful completion of conscious intentions.[90] In line with the definition that Anne Montenach and Deborah

86 C. Casanova, *La famiglia italiana in età moderna. Richerche e modelli* (Carocci: Rome 1997) 148; T. Kuehn, *Family and gender in Renaissance Italy, 1300-1600* (Cambridge: Cambridge University Press, 2017) 3; Cohen, 'Evolving the history of women,' 326.

87 Cohen, 'Open city,' 37.

88 For an overview of important prescriptive sources, see footnote 8 of E.S. Cohen, 'Evolving the history of women,' 327-328; D. Shemek, *Ladies errant. Wayward women and social order in early modern Italy* (Durham: Duke University Press, 1998) 2-3.

89 B. Kane and F. Williamson, 'Introduction,' in B. Kane and F. Williamson (eds.), *Women, agency and the law, 1300-1700* (New York 2013) 1-16; Cohen, 'Open city,' 45; Cohen, 'Evolving the history of women,' 329. An overview of the conceptual evolution of agency is provided by M. Howell, 'The problem of women's agency in late medieval and early modern Europe,' in S.J. Moran and A.C. Pipkin (eds.), *Women and gender in the early modern Low Countries, 1500-1750* (Leiden: Brill, 2019) 21-31.

90 Cohen, 'Evolving the history of women,' 329-331. For a criticism of the notion of agency for early modern women lacking full legal personhood, see T. Kuehn, 'Understanding gender

Simonton recently introduced, this book uses the term agency to designate the spectrum of capacities, choices and behaviours – licit and illicit – of men and women to negotiate their interests within and against the context of societal constraints.[91] This definition takes into account the obstacles that women were confronted with as well as the opportunities nevertheless available to them. It therefore enables us to scrutinise why women committed crime, under what circumstances and how this behaviour came within the criminal court's purview. In their work on England, Bronach Kane and Fiona Williamson argued that the analysis of gender and agency in tandem provides an important avenue to explore not only women's actions, but also the relationship between gender, social practice and the law; which is something this book seeks to do.[92]

4 Composition of This Book

In order to understand the relationship between crime and gender in early modern Bologna, it is necessary to hold various tenacious assumptions about Italian women's lives to the light. Chapter two sets the stage for the rest of the book by introducing the city of Bologna and examining women's social, economic and legal roles and positions in it based on secondary literature. By scrutinising the legal and social restrictions as well as the opportunities for women within the early modern city of Bologna in the spheres of the family and household, labour and urban institutions, this chapter argues that recent scholarship has provided significant evidence that many of the assumptions about women's experiences need to be nuanced. Aside from the more 'restrictive' dowry system and limited legal personhood for women, urban Bologna shared with northwestern Europe many of the socioeconomic characteristics believed to contribute to the relative 'freedom' of women cities: a prevalence of nuclear families, comparable shares of female-headed households and high proportions of women active in the labour market. The existence of an extensive institutional web combining care and control for a variety of vulnerable women emphasises the ambiguous position of women in Italian towns like Bologna.

inequality in Renaissance Florence. Personhood and gifts of maternal inheritance by women,' *Journal of women's history* 8:2 (1996) 58-80, especially 61 and 73.

91 A. Montenach and D. Simonton, 'Introduction: Gender, agency and economy. Shaping the eighteenth-century European town,' in D. Simonton and A. Montenach (eds.), *Female agency in the urban economy. Gender in European towns, 1640-1830* (New York and London: Routledge, 2013) 5.

92 Kane and Williamson, 'Introduction,' 3.

They acted in a culture of constraint, but nevertheless had more room for licit and illicit manoeuvre than is commonly believed.

Chapter three examines the relationship between criminal prosecution patterns and gender in early modern Bologna from the lens of the authorities. It starts out by situating the *Tribunale del Torrone* within Bologna's legal landscape, the organisation of the criminal justice system, which procedures were established, and how criminal justice was administered. Based on the investigation dossiers (*processi*) it is examined what crimes were investigated by the *Torrone* between the mid-seventeenth and mid-eighteenth century, how they were sentenced, and what share women had in these crimes. This chapter distinguishes three important features of women's prosecuted crime in early modern Bologna. First, the types of crimes for which women were investigated bore pivotal similarities to men's and, once more, counter older notions of a dichotomy of masculine and feminine crimes. Second, it highlights the importance of violence in the criminal proceedings for both men and women and, third, it reveals the comparatively low share of women among investigated offenders throughout the century. This chapter furthermore reflects on the ways in which gender could have influenced these prosecution practices and points to the roles of the extensive web of institutions, a reconciliatory legal culture and the judiciary's paternalism in quantitatively obscuring women's involvement in certain deviant behaviours.

While the previous chapter focused more on the top-down control of the *Torrone*, chapter four engages with the latitude that women and men had to use this criminal court as a forum for conflict resolution. It argues that plaintiffs of both genders were well aware of the threat that emanated from a charge, and tried to use it as a coercive measure in conflict resolution. Substantial evidence for this argument is found in the denunciations; sources that were far more plentiful than the *processi* and counted far more women. While these strategized practices of conflict resolution contributed to their lower shares in later stages of the criminal justice process, they highlight urban Bolognese women's legal agency extending far beyond what is commonly assumed.

Individuals' recourse to the criminal court in order to settle personal disputes has been fundamental in shaping the image of violence before the Bolognese criminal court. As the Bolognese authorities had little interest in prosecuting the bulk of the reported (often petty) violent acts, the sources can by and large be viewed from the perspective of the men and women that used litigation as leverage in conducting the small politics of their everyday lives. Chapter five explores the gendered dynamics of these quotidian violent behaviours recounted in the *Torrone*'s *processi* and denunciations. It discusses the particular place of Italy in European comparisons of long-term patterns of violence, and how Italy's 'culture of violence' went hand in hand with that of reconciliation throughout the early modern period. Building on recent scholarship by including pettier forms of violence in its analysis, this chapter examines the differences and similarities between various characteristics of men's and women's violent encounters, the extent to which they reflected socioeconomic realities of their everyday lives, and to what extent they employed gendered tropes of appropriate behaviour as part of a constructed judicial narrative. Most importantly, however, these cases reveal that, despite stringent normative restrictions and cultural discouragement, women's violent behaviour was far too common to be viewed as an anomaly.

Finally, chapter five treats the second most common crime before the *Torrone*: theft. Although the pattern of reported crime was to a large extent moulded by violence, thefts of all shapes and sizes belonged to the 'serious crimes' that the court sought to investigate and prosecute if in any way possible. The interest in prosecuting these kinds of crimes was, for example, apparent in the fact that thefts made up larger shares among the *processi* than among the denunciations, especially for women. This chapter examines the differences and similarities in everyday practices of thieving by male and female offenders in Bologna as well as the inherently gendered legal attitudes that framed female offenders' encounters with the law. It shows how the comparatively low share of female property offenders in Bologna was engendered by a pervasive culture of institutionalisation, peacemaking and judicial paternalism towards women. Rather than interpreting the criminal court records as evidence for early modern Italian women's lack of agency, they allow us to tease out the many factors that concealed their everyday licit and illicit behaviours.

2

Women's Social, Economic and Legal Roles

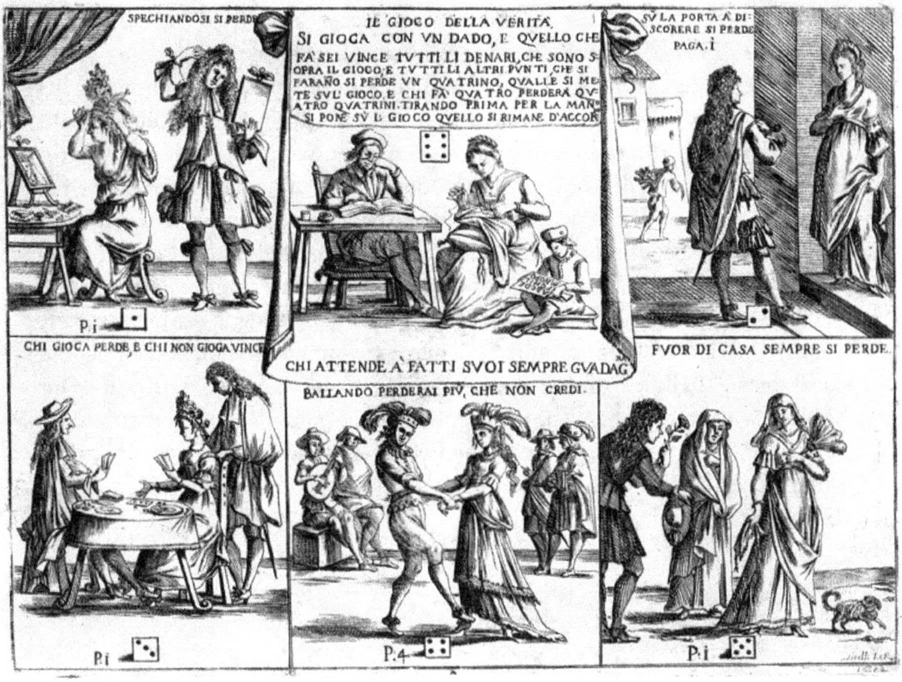

FIGURE 1 Giuseppe Maria Mitelli, Il Gioco della Verità, etching, 1688, British Museum

The figure above is taken from one of the thirty-three didactic games that Bologna-born engraver Giuseppe Maria Mitelli made between 1680 and 1712. Enjoying significant popularity in their time, these dice and board games depicted everyday places and social situations in seventeenth- and eighteenth-century Bologna – often in a humoristic way.[1] Called *Gioco della Verità* (game of truth), this particular game was played with just one die: throwing one to five meant that the player had to pay either one or four coins and a six won the pot. With the six spaces reading captions like 'He who plays loses and he who does not play wins,' 'Dancing you will lose more than you believe' and 'Looking at oneself in the mirror, you lose,' the game provided blatant commentary on how

1 M.S. Riebe, '*Sotto i portici*: Life in seventeenth-century Bologna through the games of Giuseppe Maria Mitelli (1634-1718)' (Unpublished PhD thesis, Bard College, New York, 2010).

men and women should conduct themselves in private and public. The image for a roll of five in the right corner shows two women with a small dog being presented a flower by a man. The accompanying caption ominously reads *Fuor di casa sempre si perde*: outside of the house you always lose.

The notion that an honest woman's proper place was in the home was echoed by a wide range of premodern didactic and prescriptive sources such as conduct books, religious rules and commentaries. Encouraged by ideas of a Mediterranean honour culture, some scholars have taken this literature to understand women as being secluded and enclosed in either convents or strict domestic roles.[2] Seen as a contrast to a freer northern Europe, ideas about 'southern' or 'Mediterranean' family systems, nuptiality, regulations concerning inheritance and dowry as well as labour participation have generally led to a pessimistic view of the position and scope of action of women in premodern Italian cities. Recent scholarship has however suggested that this generalised image misrepresents life for most of these women.[3] This chapter draws on this scholarship to introduce the contours of the city of Bologna during the early modern period and, importantly, to examine women's social, economic and legal roles in it. By scrutinising both the restrictions and the opportunities for women within the spheres of the family and household, labour and urban institutions, it argues that while women acted in a patriarchal culture of constraint they nevertheless had a greater scope of action than was commonly believed.

1 Political and Demographic Developments

During the period under scrutiny in this book, Bologna belonged to the territories under direct sovereign rule of the Pope. In November 1506 Pope Julius II appeared at Bologna's walls accompanied by an imposing army to chase out the ruling Bentivoglio oligarchy, marking the return of papal rule over Bologna which would last until the invasion by the French in 1796. Bologna's character as a 'Republic by contract' – in which the papacy conceded significant local powers and privileges to the city in return for the acknowledgement of the papacy's overarching sovereignty – played a key role in its local political dynamics.[4] From 1513 onwards, Bologna's 'mixed government' (*governo misto*)

2 For a discussion of the literature about cultural precepts relating to women's enclosure, see Cohen, 'To pray, to work, to hear, to speak,' 291-295.

3 Ibidem, 294.

4 The term 'Republic by contract' is coined by Angela De Benedictis, see A. De Benedictis, 'Repubblica per contratto. Una città (Bologna) nello stato (Pontificio),' *Scienza & Politica* 2:4 (1990) 59-72.

was ruled cooperatively by a papal legate with greater abstract authority and a local Senate exercising greater practical power.[5] The members of this Senate were drawn from the major families on either side of the factional divide (pro- and anti-Bentivoglio) who had previously dominated Bologna. Although these noble factions continued to wager for power with each regime change, their incorporation in the urban government established a century of relative social peace in Bologna – one that temporarily unravelled after a series of economic and natural disasters during the 1620s and 1630s and was gradually re-established in the half century that followed.[6] During the eighteenth century a range of foreign wars wreaked havoc throughout the Italian peninsula including in the Bolognese territory, while Bologna's internal politics had sailed into comparatively calmer waters.[7]

Geographically a part of northern Italy (see figure 2), Bologna belonged to one of the most densely populated and urbanised regions of Europe through the medieval and Renaissance period. In around 1300, some 18 per cent of the population in northern and central Italy lived in cities with more than 10,000 inhabitants compared to only 3.5 per cent in England and Wales.[8] However, while urbanisation rates grew significantly in most northern regions of Europe during subsequent centuries, those in central and northern Italy had diminished to around 13 per cent by the eighteenth century. Certain (particularly capital) cities such as Rome and Naples experienced significant growth from the fourteenth century onwards due to political centralisation, but many other towns stagnated as they diminished in importance and migrant attractiveness, due not least to the effects of the Black Death and subsequent epidemics as well as the decline of industrial and commercial activities in these towns.[9]

5 N. Terpstra, "Republics by contract': Civil society in the Papal State,' in N.A. Eckstein and N. Terpstra (eds.), *Sociability and its discontents: Civil society, social capital, and their alternatives in late medieval and early modern Europe* (Turnhout: Brepols, 2009) 298.

6 M. Fanti, 'Bologna nell'età moderna (1506-1796),' in A. Ferri and G. Roversi (ed.), *Storia di Bologna* (Bologna: Bononia University Press, 2005) 212; Terpstra, 'Republics by contract,' 296-302. For an excellent analysis of the social repercussions of the breakdown of social and institutional trust in seventeenth-century Bologna, see C. Rose, *A renaissance of violence. Homicide in early modern Italy* (Cambridge: Cambridge University Press, 2019) 156-180.

7 Fanti, 'Bologna nell'età moderna,' 236-237.

8 And zero per cent in the Low Countries. See page 29 of the appendix to P. Malanima, *L'economia italiana. Dalla crescita medieval alla crescita contemporanea* (Bologna: Il Mulino, 2003).

9 M. Bosker, S. Brakman, H. Garretsen, H. de Jong and M. Schramm, 'The development of cities in Italy 1300-1861,' *CESifo working paper* 1893 <http://www.ehs.org.uk/dotAsset/491c2f80-6f0e-42c2-becb-228b23ef47b7.pdf> 30-31; F. Giusberti and F. Roversi Monaco, 'Economy and demography,' in S.R. Blanshei (ed.), *A companion to medieval and*

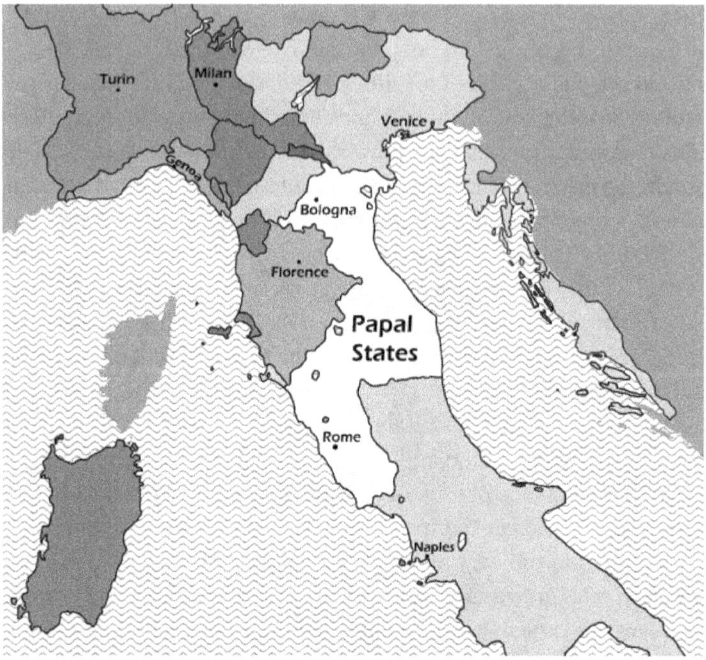

FIGURE 2 Bologna and the Papal States around 1748
MAP BY AUTHOR. BASEMAP DATA PROVIDED BY OPENSTREETMAP

Among these central and northern Italian towns, Bologna developed in a distinctive way: its urban population nearly doubled between the fourteenth and sixteenth century due to the expansion of its industrial base. Unlike other industrial towns such as Genoa, Florence and Milan, Bologna did not endure a sustained decline after the severe sixteenth-century famines, nor after the Great Plague of 1630, but instead continued to enjoy relative economic prosperity throughout the seventeenth century.[10] With between 60,000 and 70,000 inhabitants in the city alone in the early modern period, Bologna was among the 15 biggest cities of early modern Europe.[11] Increasing from 160,000 to 230,000 inhabitants between 1581 and 1799, its rural population grew faster

Renaissance Bologna (Leiden: Brill, 2018) 165; C.F. Black, *Early modern Italy. A social history* (London: Routledge, 2001) 21; P. Malanima, 'Urbanisation and the Italian economy during the last millennium,' *European review of economic history* 9 (2005) 107.

10 Giusberti and Roversi Monaco, 'Economy and demography,' 165.

11 Guenzi, 'L'identità industriale,' 46; A. Bellettini, *La popolazione di Bologna dal secolo XV all'unificazione Italiana* (Bologna: Zanichelli, 1961) 26-27.

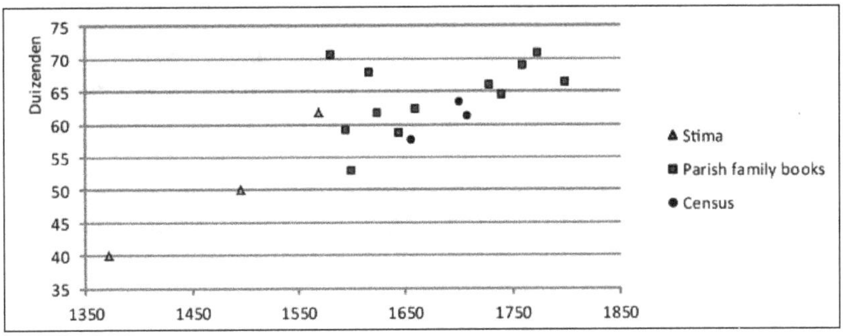

FIGURE 3 Development of the urban population in Bologna between 1371 and 1799
SOURCE: TABLES 1 AND 2 FROM BELLETTINI, *LA POPOLAZIONE DI BOLOGNA*, 25, 48

than its urban centre did, however; a phenomenon that has also been observed elsewhere in eighteenth-century Italy.[12]

Women often outnumbered men in cities across the Italian peninsula. Skewed sex ratios are a well-known feature of western European urban demography in the early modern period, though they varied from place to place.[13] Early modern Holland is, for example, known for its especially high surpluses; a situation that has recently been related to urban women's greater propensity to engage in crime due to their combined independence and vulnerability.[14] Contrary to what some scholars have assumed based on data from Rome, an unusually 'male' city, urban sex ratios in seventeenth- and eighteenth-century Verona, Venice, Florence and Bologna adhered to the 'standard' European pattern and were all skewed towards women.[15] In 1741, for example, 53.8 per cent

12 Calculations based on the urban population as well as the entirety of the Bolognese territory, see table 2 in Bellettini, *La popolazione di Bologna*, 48; D. Carpanetto and G. Ricuperati, *L'Italia del settecento* (Rome: Laterza, 2008) 9-10.

13 K. Lynch, *Individuals, families and communities in Europe 1200-1800: The urban foundations of Western society* (Cambridge University Press 2003) 39.

14 Van der Heijden, *Women and crime*, 18-19, 120, 160; Schmidt and Van der Heijden, 'Women alone,' 22.

15 Between 1600-1800 between 52 and 54 per cent of the Bolognese population consisted of women. For the sex ratios, see table 1.4 in Lynch, *Individuals, families and communities*, 40-41; Bellettini, *La popolazione di Bologna*, 61; E.S. Cohen, 'Open city. An introduction to gender in early modern Rome,' *I Tatti studies in the Italian Renaissance* 17:1 (2014) 41. For the suggestion of divergent sex ratios in northern and southern Europe (based primarily on Rome's anomalous demographic structure), see, for example, T. de Moor and J.L. van Zanden, 'Girl power: The European marriage pattern and labour markets in the North Sea

of Bologna's urban population consisted of women.[16] The persistent stereotypes of southern exceptionalism surrounding women's sheer demographic presence in these urban environments suggest that their involvement and comportment in other areas of the urban life also needs to be reconsidered.

2 Household Structures, Property Rights and Legal Capacity

Ideas regarding legal structures as well as marriage and property regimes have played prominent roles in the conception of premodern Italian society as a place of constraint for women. Much of what would come to represent the 'southern European model' has been based on the studies of the now well-known Tuscan fifteenth-century *catasto* (cadastre).[17] This iconic source revealed a society with large extended families and significant age gaps between marriage partners, and has been remembered as portraying a large patriarchal family and a "bastion of exclusive male authority."[18] Aside from this assumed demographic regime, restrictions in the law provided further grounds for painting a bleak picture of seclusion and lack of autonomy for women.[19] Since a woman's legal capacity was restricted to her own person, she could not hold civic office, were not entitled to a full share of the family patrimony, could not actively possess their dotal assets, and furthermore could not gain full parental authority (*patria potestas*) over their children.[20] Based on these pieces of evidence, it comes to no surprise that Italian women were viewed as nearly always

---

region in the late medieval and early modern period,' *The Economic History Review* 63:1 (2010) 12.

16 See table 7 from Bellettini, *La popolazione di Bologna*, 61.

17 D. Herlihy and C. Klapisch-Zuber, *Les Toscans et leur familles: Une etude du catasto florentin de 1427* (Paris: Éditions de l'École des hautes etudes en sciences sociales, 1978); Klapisch-Zuber, C., 'State and family in a Renaissance society: The Florentine Catasto of 1427-30,' in C. Klapisch-Zuber (ed.), *Women, family and ritual in Renaissance Italy* (Chicago: University of Chicago Press, 1987) 1-22; P.P. Viazzo, 'What's so special about the Mediterranean? Thirty years of research on household and family in Italy,' *Continuity and change* 18:1 (2003) 114-115.

18 Cohen, 'Evolving the history of women,' 333; Viazzo, 'What's so special about the Mediterranean?,' 114-115.

19 This scholarship is reflected upon by T. Kuehn, 'Person and gender in the laws,' in J.C. Brown and R.C. Davis (eds.), *Gender and society in Renaissance Italy* (Longman: London/New York, 1998) 87-88; J. Sperling, 'Dowry or inheritance? Kinship, property, and women's agency in Lisbon, Venice, and Florence (1572),' *Journal of early modern history* 11:3 (2007) 197-204.

20 Kuehn, 'Daughters, mothers, wives and widows,' 99; Groppi, 'A matter of fact rather than principle,' 41.

being subordinate to male authority of some sort, be it that of the father, the husband, or someone substituting for them.[21]

Subsequent research has criticised and nuanced this 'southern European model' in various ways. An important area of historiographical revision pertains to the social and demographic characteristics of early modern Italian towns, which cannot be reduced across the board to the multiple-generation households and a very young marriage age. Critics instead stress complex diversities up and down Italy, between urban and rural areas as well as between socioeconomic groups.[22] Northern and central Italian towns such as Bologna shared important characteristics with towns in northwestern Europe such as late marriage age for both men and women; a feature that is often used to distinguish and explain the relative freedom and independence of northern women.[23] In eighteenth-century Venice the average age to marry was 31.4 for men and 29.3 for women.[24] Similarly, examinations of censuses and parish family books have long shown that early modern households in northern and central Italian urban centres were typically characterised by a nuclear structure.[25] Again for Venice, Daniela Hacke found that the most common household structure between 1589 and 1607 consisted of a married couple heading their own household.[26] This was also the case in the city of Bologna, where a late-eighteenth-century census revealed two-thirds of the urban population living in nuclear households.[27]

The position of women within Italian urban environments was also less distinct than has often been suggested. Some scholars have suggested that women in southern European cities may have had less freedom of movement, not only because it was considered honourable in Italian cities to remain in the home,

21 Palazzi, 'Female solitude and patrilineage. Unmarried women and widows during the eighteenth and nineteenth Centuries,' *Journal of Family History*, 15 (1990) 445

22 For an excellent overview of the many contributions to this debate, see Viazzo, 'What's so special about the Mediterranean?' 111-137; S. Sovič, P. Thane and P.P. Viazzo, 'The history of European families: Old and new directions,' in S. Sovič, P. Thane and P.P. Viazzo (eds.), *The history of families and households. Comparative European dimensions* (Leiden: Brill, 2016) 5-7; Black, *Early modern Italy*, 108.

23 M. Barbagli, 'Three household formation systems in eighteenth and nineteenth-century Italy,' in D.J. Kertzer and R.P Saller (eds.), *The family in Italy from antiquity to the present* (New Haven: Yale University Press, 1991) 254; Black, *Early modern Italy*, 22.

24 Black, *Early modern Italy*, 22.

25 M. Barbagli, *Sotto lo stesso tetto. Mutamenti della famiglia in Italia dal 15. al 20. secolo* (Bologna: Il Mulino, 1984) 219.

26 D. Hacke, *Women, sex and marriage in early modern Venice* (Aldershot 2004) 24.

27 See footnote 8 in M. Palazzi, 'Tessitrici, serve, treccole. Donne, lavoro e famiglia a Bologna nel settecento,' in S. Cavaciocchi (ed.), *La donna nell'economia secc. XIII-XVIII* (Florence: Le Monnier, 1990) 363.

but also because Protestant towns had few if any of the many convents and protective enclosures that may have sequestered as many as 10 to 20 per cent of all urban Italian women.[28] However, the lives of the overwhelming majority of women living outside of these enclosures resembled those of their northern counterpart in important ways. Proportions of female-headed households were comparable to those found elsewhere in Western Europe. Around one-third of late-sixteenth-century Venetian households were headed by women, between 17 and 24 per cent of the households were in early eighteenth-century Rome, an examination of Milan in 1797 recorded 16 per cent of the heads of households as female, and a study of Bologna amounted to 14 per cent.[29] Female household heads were particularly numerous in the lower layers of the urban population. Maura Palazzi found that in Bologna in the poorer areas as many as a quarter of the families was run by a widow or an unmarried woman.[30] For other regions, comparable high levels have been regarded as evidence for women's particular independence and all of the risks that came with it, including a greater likelihood of criminal behaviour.[31]

Scholars have also nuanced ideas about women's legal position. Importantly, they have argued that norms did not necessarily converge with practice and that women found considerable leeway to manoeuvre and mitigate the rigours of their legal subordination.[32] While women did not have full parental authority over their minor children since they did not possess *patria potestas*, a widowed mother could gain guardianship either through the husband's testament or with the magistrates' permission.[33] Another well-known example pertained to the dowry. Despite being the personal property of the bride, the ownership and management of the dowry was put under control of the groom during the marriage. Nevertheless, if women in Florence and Lucca, for

28 N. Terpstra, 'Sex and the sacred. Negotiating spatial and sensory boundaries in Renaissance Florence,' *Radical history review* 121 (2015) 80-82.

29 As summarized by Palazzi, 'Female solitude and patrilineage,' 453; M. D'Amelia, 'Scatole cinesi. Vedove e donne sole in una società d'ancien régime,' *Memoria* 18 (1986) 62-63; E. Armelloni, 'Casa, famiglia e professione nel Milano di fine '700,' *Journal of the Lombard Society of history* 113 (1987) 181-185; M. Chojnacka, 'Singlewomen in early modern Venice. Communities and opportunities,' in J.M. Bennett and A.M. Froide (eds.), *Singlewomen in the European past 1250-1800* (Philadelphia: University of Pennsylvania Press, 1999) 220.

30 Palazzi, 'Female solitude and patrilineage,' 454.

31 Van der Heijden, *Women and crime*, 21-22; Schmidt and Van der Heijden, 'Women alone,' 24-25.

32 D. Lombardi, 'Famiglie di antico regime,' in G. Calvi (ed.), *Innesti. Donne e genere nella storia sociale* (Rome: Viella, 2004) 204; Brown, 'Introduction,' 9; Kirshner, J., *Marriage, dowry, and citizenship in late medieval and Renaissance Italy* (Toronto: University of Toronto Press, 2015) 1-20.

33 Kuehn, 'Daughters, mothers, wives and widows,' 109.

instance, perceived mismanagement of household resources, they could claim their dowries back from their husbands in court.[34] The effects of other legislation are also open to interpretation. The Florentine requirement of a male guardian (*mundualdus*) to draw up a civil notarial act is generally seen as an extremely gendered disability in law. However, because a woman could choose *any* man (related or not) as her guardian, some scholars have argued that this measure may have been less restrictive than is often believed.[35] Importantly, too, many other towns including Bologna, Genoa and Venice did not share these requirements, giving women more options to assume responsibilities in the legal arena.[36]

In general, it is important to emphasise that the roles, expectations and control of women in all of these domains depended on age, marital status and socioeconomic class.[37] As a rule, women's scope of action expanded significantly in the higher age brackets, not only because of widowhood but also because it was no longer necessary for the family to control reproduction. This was also true for women from the lower social strata, where the transmission of property was less of a concern than for the propertied classes.[38] Women's leeway was also highly dependent on local conditions. A French traveller to Bologna in 1691 commented on the freedoms of women with regard to other cities, writing that "the women aren't locked up like in Florence; you encounter them frequently."[39] While Italian women undoubtedly acted in a culture of patriarchal constraint, it is crucial not only to consider the theoretical restrictions of their legal status but also to examine the leeway they had to act in practice.

34 C. Meek, 'Women between the law and social reality in early Renaissance Lucca,' in L. Panizza (ed.), *Women in Italian Renaissance culture and society* (Legenda: Oxford 2000) 187; J. Kirshner, 'Wives' claims against insolvent husbands in late medieval Italy,' in J. Kirshner and S.F. Wemple (eds.), *Women of the medieval world* (Oxford: Blackwell, 1985) 256-303.

35 Kuehn, 'Understanding gender inequality,' 64. For a similar argument about early modern Normandy, see Schneider, 'Women before the bench,' 24.

36 Wray, *Communities in crisis*, 76.

37 Kuehn, 'Daughters, mothers, wives and widows,' 98, 112, 114; Cohen, 'Evolving the history of women,' 326

38 Palazzi, 'Female Solitude and Partilineage,' 456; G. Angelozzi and C. Casanova, *Donne criminali. Il genere nella storia della giustizia* (Bologna: Pàtron Editore, 2014) 47

39 M. Misson, *Voyage d'Italie* (Amsterdam: Clousier, 1743) as cited in G. Ricci, *Bologna: Storia di un'imagine* (Bologna: Arte Grafiche Emiliane, 1976) 178; Riebe, '*Sotto i portici*,' 59.

3 Women within the Urban Economy

Ideas about women's (declining) labour force participation have further contributed to the notion of Italian women's particularly disadvantaged position. Under-registration, underestimation and undervaluing have been common denominators for women's labour force participation all over early modern Europe, and Italy was no exception.[40] More particular to southern European societies is the historiographical association of the dowry-system (i.e. the absence of a conjugal fund) with a negative effect the presence of women on the labour market; a disincentive that was reinforced by the heavy emphasis that was placed on female honour, which caused women to be ideally shielded from the work place.[41]

Similar to the untenability of the 'southern' household structure model, there is a growing body of work that not only criticises the notion of women's absence from the labour force in early modern Italy but instead underpins the importance of women's work in the urban economy.[42] Studies have shown that middle and lower class girls themselves made significant contributions to their dowries through their own earnings and savings, illustrating that the dowry system did not necessarily exclude the development of labour-market-oriented strategies.[43] Moreover, while issues of honour impacted attitudes towards certain lines of work they were outweighed by economic necessity for the largest segment of society, who could not afford to keep half of the population indoors.[44]

Crafts, domestic service and the retail trade were the most diffuse occupations for women in premodern European towns. Economically, the city of Bologna relied heavily on its specialised silk and hemp industry. As mandated by guild regulations, the production of textiles took place within the city walls,

40 J. Humphries and C. Sarasúa, 'Off the record. Reconstructing women's labor force participation in the European past,' *Feminist economics*18:4 (2012) 44-48; B. Zucca Micheletto, 'Reconsidering women's labor force participation,' rates in eighteenth-century Turin,' *Feminist economics* 19:4 (2013) 200-201.

41 De Moor and Van Zanden, 'Girl power,' 8. These statements are reflected upon in Zucca Micheletto, 'Reconsidering the southern Europe model,' 355; S.K. Cohn, 'Women and work in Renaissance Italy,' in J.C. Brown and R.C. Davis (eds.), *Gender and society in Renaissance Italy* (London and New York: Longman, 1998) 114.

42 Zucca Micheletto, 'Reconsidering the southern Europe model,' 367; Bellavitis, *Il lavoro delle donne*, 7-13.

43 Bellavitis, *Il lavoro delle donne*, 88-89.

44 Cohen, 'To pray, to work, to hear, to speak,' 289-311; Bellavitis, *Il lavoro delle donne*, 52; Groppi, 'A matter of fact rather than principle,' 48; O. Niccoli, *Storie di ogni giorno in una città del seicento* (Rome: Laterza 2000) 60

and the silk industry alone employed about a third of the urban population, approximately half of whom were women.[45] Contrary to popular belief, but similar to what is found in other Italian textile manufacturing towns such as Turin and Milan, women had a high share in labour force participation: it is estimated that nearly 64 per cent of Bolognese women aged eleven and over engaged in paid work, more than half of them working in the textile industry.[46] Nicholas Terpstra has argued how 'silk towns,' contrary to even other types of textile industries, created an exceptional concentration of wealth in a handful of immensely wealthy merchants while thousands of poorly paid and part-time workers lived in extreme poverty.[47] The silk industry in Bologna did not only generate a demand for women's relatively cheap labour, but also made their economic contributions indispensable for the survival of the household.[48]

Although Bologna had long stood out among the papal territories for its wealth and relatively high standards of living, the economic crisis hit the city during the eighteenth century – roughly a century later than many other textile industry towns.[49] As a response to the unfolding economic crisis, the textile guilds restructured the mode of production by abandoning the rich, elaborate and expensive textiles to concentrate on the production of the simpler, lighter and cheaper textiles that were predominantly manufactured through women's domestic production.[50] In the light of this restructuring, the incorporation of women into the guild system became increasingly important for the guilds' survival.[51] While women had originally been excluded from the Bolognese textile guilds at their foundation in the sixteenth century, the share of female masters in the silk guild rose from 7.5 per cent in the early seventeenth century

45 Guenzi, 'L'identità industriale,' 464-465. This was the same for Florence, see J.C. Brown and J. Goodman, 'Women and industry in Florence,' *The journal of economic history* 40:1 (1980) 73-80.

46 Palazzi, 'Tessitrici, serve, treccole,' 366-367; S. D'Amico, 'Shameful mother. Poverty and prostitution in seventeenth century Milan,' *Journal of family history* 39:1 (2005) 110; Zucca Micheletto, 'Reconsidering women's labor force participation rates,' 211.

47 N. Terpstra, 'Working the cocoon. Gendered charitable enclosures and the silk industry in early modern Europe,' in K. Kippen and L. Woods (eds.), *Worth and repute. Valuing gender in late medieval and early modern Europe. Essays in honour of Barbara Todd* (Toronto: Center for Reformation and Renaissance studies, 2011) 48-49.

48 Zucca Micheletto, 'Reconsidering the southern Europe model,' 368.

49 D. Dumont, 'Women and guilds in Bologna. The ambiguities of 'marginality,' *Radical History Review* 70 (1998) 6-7.

50 Guenzi, 'L'identità industriale,' 470; A. Guenzi, 'La tessitura femminile tra città e campagna. Bologna, secoli XVII-XVIII,' in S. Cavaciocchi (ed.), *La donna nell'economia secc. XIII-XVIII* (Florence: Le Monnier, 1990) 255, 257.

51 Guenzi, 'L'identità industriale,' 470-472; Dumont, 'Women and guilds in Bologna,' 6, 17, 19.

to a massive 83 per cent in 1796.[52] This guild membership provided women with wage regulations, some forms of assistance and a recognised juridical status, but it also introduced the economic burden of membership fees and an increase in the control over their labour, submitted them to guild jurisdiction and strict regulations regarding production without offering the chance of any real decision-making power.[53] Scholars have therefore questioned whether increased guild membership was a positive development for women in the textile industry.[54]

According to an important Bolognese census from 1796 carried out by the cardinal Legate with the aim of organising charity relief, another 8 per cent of Bolognese women worked in commerce and trade.[55] Throughout early modern Europe the rules of guilds often prevented women from becoming the official proprietors of commercial enterprises. In Bologna, one per cent of the labouring women were recorded as shopkeepers (*bottegara*), although it is assumed that women who operated and managed businesses on a *de facto* basis may have been far more numerous.[56] While the official census data likely underestimated women's economic authority and autonomy, the largest proportion of women probably worked in the lower ends of trade and retail. In the census, the overwhelming majority of Bolognese women listed as performing commercial activities worked as street or market vendors.[57] Among them were many mobile resellers without a fixed place or a stall on the street or market in the city, selling foodstuffs such as fruits, vegetables, grain, bread and sweets and textiles.

An interesting feature of the Bolognese case is that these commercial activities do not appear to have been open to all types of women. Firstly, the late-eighteenth-century census reveals that nearly all women with commercial occupations were born in the city of Bologna.[58] The lack of migrants among those involved in retail and trade is indicative of the difficulty of accessing these occupations as immigrants and the importance of integration into the urban network. A second distinction that specifically applied to women was

52 Guenzi, 'La tessitura femminile,' 252, 255.

53 Dumont, 'Women and guilds in Bologna,' 19; Palazzi, 'Tessitrici, serve, treccole,' 370; A. Groppi, 'Lavoro e proprietà delle donne in età moderna,' in R. Ago and A. Groppi (eds.), *Il lavoro delle donne* (Bari: Laterza 1996) 158.

54 Dumont, 'Women and guilds in Bologna,' 20-21.

55 Palazzi, 'Tessitrici, serve, treccole,' 374.

56 M. Palazzi, 'Economic autonomy and male authority. Female merchants in modern Italy,' *Journal of modern Italian studies* 7:1 (2002) 20; Groppi, 'Lavoro e proprietà delle donne,' 132; Palazzi, 'Tessitrici, serve, treccole,' 374.

57 Palazzi, 'Tessitrici, serve, treccole,' 373.

58 Ibidem, 374.

that commercial activities appear to have been exclusively performed by married women (two-thirds) or widows (one-third). The census data suggest that unmarried women were excluded from commerce and trade, be it in the shops or out on the streets and markets. While it seems unlikely that daughters were never expected to work in their families' shops, this exclusion was probably related to the importance attributed to women's sexual honour and the necessity of protecting it by controlling the movements of unmarried women.[59]

Unmarried women were actively involved in domestic service, which employed about one-fifth of the female workers in Bologna. Scholars have distinguished between a northern European and a southern model of domestic service.[60] In the latter model, servanthood was not a transitory life-cycle stage but a lifelong occupation for female servants as well as their male counterparts, who predominantly served in aristocratic households and made up nearly half of the servant population in early modern Italian towns like Bologna.[61] Contrary to male servants who could marry and establish their own households, however, entering service for women generally entailed living within the master's household while remaining celibate.[62] Another characteristic that fundamentally distinguished this occupation for men and women concerned the issue of social control. Scholars have argued that female servanthood was the object of social condemnation in early modern Italy, since working away from the protection of a male relative was regarded as endangering the girl's honour.[63] Because the female servants' sexual behaviour and honour reflected on the honour of the family that employed them, it has been suggested that a significant degree of control was imposed upon them, more so than on male servants.[64] For seventeenth-century Milan and Florence it has

59 Ibidem.

60 For the discussion of these models, see A. Arru, 'The distinguishing features of domestic service in Italy,' *Journal of family history* 15:4 (1990) 548; Zucca Micheletto, 'Reconsidering women's labor force participation rates,' 215-216; R. Sarti, 'The true servant: Self-definition of male domestics in an Italian city (Bologna, 17th-19th centuries),' *The history of the family* 10 (2005) 421.

61 Italy is known for its comparatively high percentages of male servants compared to other European cities. See R. Sarti, 'Notes on the feminization of domestic service: Bologna as a case study (18th-19th centuries),' *Acta demographica* 13 (1997) 145; Sarti, 'The true servant,' 421; Arru, 'The distinguishing features of domestic service in Italy,' 549.

62 Sarti, 'The true servant,' 420; Palazzi, 'Tessitrici, serve, treccole' 372.

63 Zucca Micheletto, 'Reconsidering women's labor force participation rates,' 216, Viazzo, 'What's so special about the Mediterranean?,' 128; C. Klapisch-Zuber, 'Women servants in Florence during the fourteenth and fifteenth centuries,' in B. Hanawalt (ed.), *Women and work in preindustrial Europe* (Bloomington: Indiana University Press, 1986) 70-75.

64 D. Lombardi and F. Reggiani, 'Da assistita a serva. Circuiti di reclutamento delle serve attraverso le istituzioni assistenziali (Firenze-Milano, XVII-XVIII sec.),' in S. Cavaciocchi

been shown that the social control of female servants could furthermore be exerted by the various charitable institutions that sent some of the women they assisted into service for shorter or longer periods of time.[65] As service in itself was seen as a risk to a woman's sexual honour, these institutions tried to safeguard it through a careful selection of the masters they sent women to, but also by threatening women with the loss of the dowry they could otherwise claim from the charitable institution in case of sexual transgression, and legal action against the deflowerer.

While concerns for women's sexual honour permeated many 'regular' occupations, prostitution was not illegal in Italy. Protestant countries as well as France and Spain had prohibited prostitution by the early seventeenth century, Italian civic governments primarily treated prostitutes as fee- and fine-paying workers in the civic economy.[66] In Bologna, the only consistently enforced legislation was the annual registration with the *Ufficio delle Bollette* (the Office of Receipts) and the regular purchase of licences.[67] The 0.5 to 1.8 per cent of the urban female population that were registered at the *Bollette* most likely represented the more established, long-term prostitutes.[68] Many others are believed to have resisted registration because they did not view themselves as prostitutes, but rather regarded their extramarital sexual activity merely as a step towards marriage, only used their sexuality as a resource occasionally or temporarily, or had only one or few steady partners.[69] While studies on Florence have pointed to an increasing repression and even criminalisation after the middle of the seventeenth century, there is significant evidence that both local authorities and residents were until that time relatively tolerant of prostitutes and prostitution.[70] Recent scholarship has demonstrated that Bolognese and Roman prostitutes were incorporated into local city neighbourhoods and

---

(ed.), *La donna nell'economia secc. XIII-XVIII* (Florence: Le Monnier, 1990) 301-302; Arru, 'The distinguishing features of domestic service in Italy,' 556.

65 Lombardi and Reggiani, 'Circuiti di reclutamento delle serve,' 301-319.

66 D'Amico, 'Shameful mother,' 111; V.G. McCarthy, 'Prostitution, community and civic regulation in early modern Bologna' (PhD thesis, University of Toronto, 2015) 12.

67 McCarthy, 'Prostitution, community and civic regulation,' 12, 212.

68 Compare the total number of registered prostitutes in table 3.2 in McCarthy, 'Prostitution, community and civic regulation,' 149 and the female population according to Bellettini, *La popolazione di* Bologna, 61.

69 McCarthy, 'Prostitution, community and civic regulation,' 238-240; T. Storey, *Carnal commerce in Counter-Reformation Rome* (Cambridge: Cambridge University Press, 2008) 119-122; D'Amico, 'Shameful mother,' 109-120; L. Ferrante, 'La sessualità come risorsa. Donne davanti al foro arcivescovile di Bologna (sec. XVII),' *Mélanges de l'École française de Rome* 99:2 (1987) 989-1016.

70 J.K. Brackett, 'The Florentine Onestà and the control of prostitution, 1403-1680,' *The sixteenth century journal* 24:2 (1993) 298-299.

communities and were 'seen and known' rather than shunned and segregated.[71] They were furthermore integrated into the network of care that unfolded during this period. In addition to special convents for ex-prostitutes, dubbed the *Convertite*, shelters for fallen women were erected in many cities in Italy so that they could be socially cleansed and reinserted into society.[72]

4 Interlocking Systems of Assistance and Control

As the concerns about women in the urban economy already indicated, anxieties regarding women's unrestricted sexuality affected not only those affiliated with prostitution but essentially *all* women in early modern Italy.[73] From the late fifteenth century onwards the poor were increasingly seen as a danger to society, especially the uncontrolled women among them who could use their sexuality as a resource and thereby constituted a liability to the family economy.[74] Centuries before the well-known custodial institutions in Victorian England, integrated networks of semi-public charitable institutions emerged all over Italy from the sixteenth century onwards, seeking to correct, supervise and help 'problematic' women and girls.[75] This system consisted not only of orphanages, workhouses, prisons and conservatories, but also of dowry investment funds, institutions for mutual assistance and, importantly, a variety of enclosed shelters for women at the fringes of society. These institutions, which were also established in other parts of Catholic Europe, essentially aimed to guide women towards matrimony: it helped them save money for their dowry, helped battered women survive their bad marriages, and helped the widowed to remarry.[76]

An important feature of these institutions is that they provided an extensive network linking shorter and long-term care and control throughout women's different life stages. Nicholas Terpstra's sample of women who entered

71 McCarthy, 'Prostitution, community and civic regulation,' 210-211, 270; E.S. Cohen, 'Seen and known. Prostitutes in the cityscape of late-sixteenth-century Rome,' *Renaissance studies* 12:3 (1998) 394

72 Terpstra, *Cultures of charity*, 212, 215.

73 Ibidem, 17.

74 Brackett, 'The Florentine Onestà,' 274; Terpstra, *Cultures of charity*, 59; L. Ferrante, 'Malmaritate tra assistenza e punizione (Bologna secc. XVI-XVII),' in *Forme e soggetti dell'intervento assistenziale in una città di antico regime: Atti del IV colloquio (Bologna, 20-21 gennaio, 1984)* (Bologna: Istituto per la storia di Bologna, 1986) 107; D'Amico, "Shameful mother,' 110.

75 Cohen, *The evolution of women's asylums*, 3, 8.

76 Terpstra, *Cultures of charity*, 17; Ferrante, 'Malmaritate tra assistenza e punizione,' 93.

Bologna's *Casa del Soccorso di S. Paolo* – a sort of halfway house and reformatory for adulterous wives, concubines and prostitutes – is revealing in this regard: at least three of the fourteen women he studied subsequently went to other custodial homes to become servants, and two other women entered a convent.[77] Indeed, in the course of the seventeenth and eighteenth centuries, some Italian cities like Bologna are believed to have developed into an "interlocking and coordinated municipal system, with girls and women moving between institutions according to requirements of protection, instruction, correction or space."[78]

Especially the lay shelters and refuges for women at the fringes of society had an increasingly purgative edge to them that made charity, discipline and enclosure synonymous from the seventeenth century onwards.[79] Although many charitable institutions set out to provide assistance to vulnerable women, they were not necessarily always admitted voluntarily. The *Pia Casa delle Malmaritate*, established in Bologna in 1563 for 'unhappily married women' took in women seeking voluntary refuge from their often violent marriages, but also housed 'difficult women' who could be admitted by their husbands or male kin for years on end.[80] Older institutions such as the *Ospedale degli Esposti*, a foundling home for illegitimate children, also became more punitive towards the mothers that abandoned them. Initially instated as a measure to save the lives of children while allowing women to retain their good reputation, the *Esposti* began charging a 25 *lire* fee to abandon a child, one-sixth of an artisan's average annual wage.[81] If this sum could not be paid, as was the case for many poor working families, the mother had to move into a special dormitory to work as an unpaid wet nurse for a year. It has been argued that the costs of feeding and sheltering these young imprisoned mothers rendered the measure economically counterproductive, suggesting that it was less about

77 Out of the 24 entrants examined, the immediate futures of 14 women were known: 1 was murdered, 8 were expelled 3 were sent to custodial homes and 2 became nuns. See Terpstra, *Cultures of charity*, 214-215.

78 S. Woolf, *The poor in Western Europe in the eighteenth and nineteenth centuries* (London/New York: Methuen, 1986) 25.

79 Terpstra, *Cultures of charity*, 200, 215.

80 Cohen, *The evolution of women's asylums*, 141; M. Cavina, *Nozze di sangue. Storia della violenza coniugale* (Rome: Laterza, 2011) 49-51; Ferrante, 'Malmaritate tra assistenza e punizione,' 84-88.

81 Lombardi, 'Marriage in Italy,' in S. Seidel Menchi (ed.), *Marriage in Europe, 1400-1800* (Toronto: University of Toronto Press, 2016) 111; A. Bianchi, '"L'elemosina di un bambino": Pratica e controllo dell'abbandono all'ospedale dei bastardini (secc. XVI-XVIII),' *Sanità, scienza e storia* 2 (1989) 44.

economic logic than about disincentive and discipline.[82] This dual nature of assistance and control characterised many of the charitable institutions for women in early modern Italy.

Although the constellation of Italian custodial institutions did not principally target women with a criminal inclination, there was a link with deviance and punishment that has not sufficiently been explored in the literature. Alongside the women who entered the convents, workhouses and refuges on their own initiative, an unknown number of them were placed there by family members or magistrates for punitive enclosures.[83] In Victorian England, roughly a quarter of the women who appeared before the court on some criminal charge were sent to a custodial home by a magistrate without ever being convicted.[84] For early modern Italy, we lack such information about the procedures and acts that caused women to be placed in the early modern Italian enclosures. Nevertheless, criminal women *were* sometimes confined in custodial institutions. According to Sharon Cohen, former prostitutes, rape victims, rebellious girls, abused wives, displaced widows and "women who had committed a crime" were all brought together in these 'custodial warehouses' for troublesome, marginalized women.[85]

Lay confraternities, civic rulers and church leaders all cooperated in this system of care and control.[86] The example of illegitimate pregnancies is perhaps most illustrative for the interconnectedness of the various charitable, ecclesiastical and secular criminal institutions of control. In an attempt to prevent infanticide, Bologna's 1613 criminal bylaws added to the local bailiffs' tasks the responsibility for keeping an eye on unmarried pregnant women until they relinquished the new-born to the *Esposti* foundling home.[87] From 1645 onwards, another ordinance furthermore obliged midwives to denounce 'irregular pregnancies' to the *Tribunale del Torrone*. In practice, however, these events were by no means solely a concern for the secular criminal authorities. When pre- or extramarital pregnancies came to light, local officials – contrary to the rules – most likely dealt with them informally.[88] Rather than denouncing them formally to the criminal court, they were first brought to the attention of the

82 Terpstra, *Cultures of charity*, 250-251.

83 Cohen, *The evolution of women's asylums*, 17, 36, 79; Terpstra, *Cultures of charity*, 213; Cavina, *Nozze di sangue*, 48.

84 Zedner, *Women, crime and custody*, 288.

85 Cohen, *The evolution of women's asylums*, 36, 45, 63.

86 Black, *Early modern Italy*, 204; D. Lombardi, 'Famiglie di antico regime,' in G. Calvi (ed.), *Innesti. Donne e genere nella storia sociale* (Rome: Viella, 2004) 206-207.

87 Angelozzi and Casanova, *Donne criminali*, 109-110.

88 Ibidem, 110-111.

religious authorities and the ecclesiastical court in order to assess whether a marriage could be arranged. If this effort proved unsuccessful, the pregnancy was reported to the guardian of the foundling home, where the mother (or her midwife) was expected to leave the child upon birth.[89] Only as a last resort did notices of illegitimate pregnancies reach the criminal court, revealing the many interconnected institutions of control that came before it.

The web of institutional control for early modern Italian women was vast, connecting neighbourhood communities, and civic and charitable institutions as well as the ecclesiastical and secular authorities.[90] This institutional intrusion – seeking above all to preserve and restore the honour of women and their families – not only constituted repression but also offered opportunities to women, in the very least in the sense of a safety net. It was furthermore not uncommon for women or their kin to bring cases before courts themselves. Especially when they were pregnant, women stood fairly good chances before either the ecclesiastical court to appeal to the binding nature of a marriage promise, or before the secular criminal court to file a suit for a non-violent rape, hoping to negotiate either a marriage arrangement or to be dowered.[91] When these types of cases came before the court during the early modern period, women themselves were rarely on the receiving end of punishment.[92] While these legal options for deflowered women deteriorated in the eighteenth century, the system of care and control on the Italian peninsula was still rather extensive compared to other regions in Europe, affecting the lives of a wide range of 'problematic women.'[93]

89 Bianchi, '"L'elemosina di un bambino,"' 42-43; Bianchi, 'Madri e padri davanti al Tribunale arcivescovile,' 42.

90 Lombardi, 'Marriage in Italy,' 111.

91 G. Arrivo, *Seduzioni, promesse, matrimoni. Il processo per stupro nella Toscana del settecento* (Rome: Edizioni di storia e letteratura, 2006) 202; Lombardi, 'Marriage in Italy' 105; N. Terpstra, 'Real and virtual families. Forms and dynamics of fostering and adoption in Bologna's early modern hospitals,' *Mélanges de l'École française de Rome – Italie et Méditerannée modernes et contemporaines* 124-1 (2012), DOI: 10.4000/mefrim.266, 5.

92 Arrivo, 'Sposarsi in tribunale. Sessualità e matrimonio nella Toscana del settecento,' *Storicamente* 6 (2010), DOI: 10.147/stor84 (accessible via <http://dx.doi.org/10.1473/stor 84>) 2; Ferrante, 'La sessualità come risorsa,' 1013; G. Ruggiero, *The boundaries of Eros. Sex crime and sexuality in Renaissance Venice* (New York: Oxford University Press, 1985)42.

93 Ferraro, *Nefarious crimes, contested justice. Illicit sex and infanticide in the Republic of Venice, 1557-1789* (Baltimore: The Johns Hopkins University Press, 2008) 7; Bianchi, 'Madri e padre davanti al Tribunale arcivescovile,' 63; Arrivo, *Seduzioni, promesse, matrimoni*, 20; S. Cavallo and S. Cerutti, 'Female honor and the social control of reproduction in Piedmont between 1600 and 1800,' in E. Muir and G. Ruggiero (eds.), *Sex and gender in historical perspective* (Baltimore: Johns Hopkins University Press, 1990) 100; L. Sandri, 'Matrimoni mancati. "Pericolate" e "gravide occulte" dell'ospizio di Orbatello di Firenze nel XVIII e XIX secolo,' in M. Lanzinger and R. Sarti (eds.), *Nubili e celibi. Tra scelta e costrizione (secoli XVI-XX)* (Florence: Udine, 2006) 73; Lombardi, 'Marriage in Italy,' 107.

5 Conclusion: Agency within a Culture of Constraint

The aim of this chapter was to examine the social, economic and legal position and roles of women in the urban fabric of early modern Bologna. Based on secondary literature, it sought to re-examine older notions regarding a dichotomy between northern and southern European societies in which ideas about supposed southern family systems, nuptiality, regulations concerning inheritance and dowry, and labour participation have led to a pessimistic view of the position of women. These works indicate the potential hazards of extrapolating actual practices from law codes or prescriptive literature alone, and suggest that a simple contrast between a free north and a restrictive southern Europe does not do justice to the social complexities and dynamics of either region.

A persistent scholarly presumption is that a range of structural contours of life on the Italian peninsula was uniquely disadvantageous to women vis-à-vis other European contexts. Italian women were denied active possession of their dotal assets, did not have an equal share in their fathers' patrimonies and furthermore had significantly limited capacity to own and transmit property. Yet the extent to which these legal restrictions effectively curtailed women's agency in these fields has been subject to debate. Not only has the direct link between the dowry system and women's presumed passiveness been dispelled, scholars working on Italy have also located female agency in women's circumvention of their limited legal rights through the manipulation of legal resources. The extensive network of interlinking charitable and civic institutions that enclosed up to one-fifth of the urban female population is also viewed as playing an ambiguous role. Aside from the strategies for lineage preservation strategies of patrician women, these convents, shelters and workhouses functioned as a means for controlling and disciplining women, but simultaneously provided marginal women with a safety net outside of the family structure.

Italian towns possessed many of the characteristics generally attributed to the freer northern Europe. The city had, for example, a prevalence of nuclear families, a comparable share of female-headed households, and proportions of women active in the urban labour markets that were comparable to or even higher than those observed in northern Europe. The historiographical examination of the legal, social and economic structures has thus indicated that stereotypes of radical passivity and seclusion do not capture the complex realities of most Italian women's lives. Since they attest to the discrepancy between norms and practice by their very nature, this book will employ criminal court records to probe women's ability to display agency in their licit and illicit conduct while navigating this culture of constraint.

3

Criminal Prosecution Patterns and Gender

On 6 June 1654 a surgeon from one of Bologna's hospitals reported Carlo Masina's severe and 'suspicious' wounds to the criminal court.[1] Upon interrogation, the dying Carlo pointed to three men (Domenico Pino, and Francesco and Alessandro Lambertini) and one woman (Diamante, Domenico's wife) as the culprits. Earlier, Carlo had seen Domenico talking to 'certain persons' in one of the city's many taverns and had mentioned that his behaviour did not befit a *gentiluomo* (gentleman), but a *becco fotuto* (fucking cuckold). Their quarrel escalated a day later when Domenico was waiting for him with a drawn sword, accompanied by his wife Diamante and the Lambertini brothers. When Carlo tried to duck the stones Diamante and the brothers were throwing at him, Domenico struck him with his sword, causing wounds which would eventually prove fatal for Carlo. Domenico was able to turn the capital punishment he received into a pardon through a peace accord with Carlo's kin and the Lambertini brothers were exiled. Although her role in the homicide was similar to that of the brothers, no sentence is recorded for Diamante.

While the criminal court records do not provide any information as to why Diamante got off so lightly compared to her male co-offenders, perceptions of gender may well have been at play. After all, differences in recorded and prosecuted crime are linked to moral and legal norms, which differed according to offence category as well as the 'quality' of the offender and victim – gender being one of the constituents that magistrates took into consideration when judging a crime. This chapter examines the relationship between criminal prosecution patterns and gender in early modern urban Bologna through the lens of the authorities. By examining both normative writings such as the city's criminal bylaws and a sample of the *Tribunale del Torrone*'s investigation dossiers (*processi*), it sheds light on the legal attitudes and practices of prosecution that played a significant role in shaping women's formal encounters with the law in urban Bologna.

This chapter begins with an overview of the legal landscape and the organisation of the criminal justice system in early modern Bologna. It then discusses how criminal justice was administered, what procedures it followed and what prosecutorial priorities it established in the criminal bylaws. This will reveal that although the procedures and laws in themselves may appear relatively

1 ASBO, Torrone, 6670, fasc. 3.

neutral, they provided the responsible magistrates with ample space for a gender-specific treatment of crime. The next section examines to what extent this legal latitude carried through into practice. Based on the *Torrone*'s formal investigation dossiers (*processi*), it scrutinises women's proportional involvement in prosecuted crime, for what crimes women and men appeared before the criminal court, and the nature of gendered sentencing patterns. By doing so, it distinguishes two distinct features of women's crimes in early modern Bologna (a low share of female offenders among investigated crimes and the significant role of violence), and theorises about its causes.

1 The *Tribunale del Torrone* within Bologna's Legal Landscape

Bologna's early modern lay criminal court, the *Tribunale del Torrone*, was established in around the 1530s and was the result of both local political pursuits and broader, widespread reform efforts. Civic and ecclesiastical authorities across northern Italy reformed their governmental and judicial structures throughout the sixteenth and seventeenth centuries.[2] They did so by specifying the focus of existing courts and civic institutions and by rationalising and bureaucratising their methods, leading to the creation of new bodies and the abolishment or redistribution of others, as well as changes to the cities' judicial systems. The emergence of the *Torrone* can be viewed from the perspective of these reforms aiming to streamline governmental, administrative and judicial systems throughout Italy.

Local interests also played a role in the emergence of the *Torrone*. Established some decades after the conquest of the city of Bologna by Pope Julius II and the expulsion of the Bentivoglio oligarchs, the founding of a new criminal court was also intimately tied to the papal quest to consolidate and expand its power over the territory.[3] Incorporated into the Papal States, the city retained a high degree of autonomy through contracts signed between the city and the pope following each new papal appointment. Within this 'republic by contract,' the papal legate worked in cooperation with the civic Bolognese Senate, made up of local noble families.[4] From this perspective, the establishment of the *Torrone* sprung forth from the wish to firmly insert papal representation

2 McCarthy, 'Prostitution, community and civic regulation,' 119-120.

3 Rose, *A renaissance of violence*, 41-42.; M. Cavina, 'I luoghi della giustizia,' in A. Prosperi (ed.), *Bologna nell'età moderna (secoli XVI-XVIII). Tomo 1. Istituzioni, forme del potere, economia e società* (Bologna: Bononia University Press, 2008) 380.

4 De Benedictis, 'Repubblica per contratto,' 59-72.

into the justice system through the direct operation of the criminal and civil courts.

The 1530s saw not only the establishment of the *Tribunale del Torrone*, which held criminal jurisdiction, but also that of two other courts: the *Tribunale di Rota* and the *Tribunale civile del Legato*. The establishment of the *Torrone* in 1530 and the *Rota* five years later meant that a separation between the administration of civil and criminal justice had been realised.[5] The *Rota* was established as Bologna's main civil court and dealt with cases involving monetary amounts over 100 *lire*, as well as the cases that involved the Bolognese oligarchy.[6] Despite the papal wish to assert its control, it was Bologna's Senate that remained in charge of appointing the judges adjudicating civil matters before this supreme civil court.[7] Soon after the establishment of the *Rota*, a second civil court under the name of the *Tribunale civile del Legato* was set up. This was a court of first instance in which a judge appointed by the papal legate adjudicated in relatively 'simple' civil matters. It was ostensibly designed to render justice more quickly than the *Rota*, but it has been argued that the legate's civil court was also installed to establish its authority over such issues and challenge the oligarchy's claim as the primary authority.[8]

The papal government did succeed in gaining control over Bologna's criminal justice apparatus. Named the 'Tribunal of the Great Tower' after the site of its court and prison in Bologna's main square, the *Tribunale del Torrone* replaced the medieval podestarial court and gradually swallowed the jurisdiction from the medieval *Ufficiali di contado* over ca. 4,000 square kilometres of surrounding countryside villages.[9] Claiming monopoly over criminal justice was paramount to the papal government's aim to undercut the power of the rebellious local elite. Erecting a new centralised criminal court entailed stripping away the nobles' rights to exercise justice, which had in the past occurred in the city by influencing the operations of the podestarial court, and in the rural hinterlands through private courts the elites held.[10] The consolidation of the *Torrone* was a process that lasted almost a century and a half. According to Colin Rose, it took at least to the late 1660s when the leading members of the

5 Angelozzi and Casanova, *La giustizia in una città di antico regime*, 24.

6 McCarthy, 'Prostitution, community and civic regulation,' 121; Cavina, 'I luoghi della giustizia,' 381.

7 Cavina, 'I luoghi della giustizia,' 380; Angelozzi and Casanova, *La giustizia in una città di antico regime*, 21-29.

8 Cavina, 'I luoghi della giustizia,' 382-386.

9 Angelozzi and Casanova, *La giustizia in una città di antico regime*, 111-115.

10 Ibidem, 21; Angelozzi and Casanova, *Donne criminali*, 59; Rose, 'Violence and the centralization of criminal justice,' 102.

rebellious nobility were expelled from Bologna's territory.[11] As will be argued in chapter 4, the provision of a free, efficient and relatively reliable forum for conflict resolution in the shape of the *Torrone* was an important means in this endeavour.

Like elsewhere in the early modern period, Bologna's legal landscape was varied and complex. In general, early modern justice had a patch-work nature and was characterised by a multiplicity of courts. Bologna was no different. The aforementioned three main tribunals existed within a landscape with various other judicial institutions that sometimes held overlapping jurisdictions. Figure 4 shows the various formal institutions that had jurisdiction on criminal, civil and ecclesiastical matters in Bologna during the seventeenth and eighteenth century. While a variety of civil courts dealt with the provisioning of the city, and with trade and weights, others regulated trade disputes related to crafts, trade and bankruptcies. All aspects of prostitution were regulated by the *Ufficio delle Bollette,* and the archbishop's tribunal (*Foro Arcivescovile*) dealt with crimes of the clergy as well as marriage disputes and sexual improprieties of the laity.

Although judicial reforms increasingly defined the competences and jurisdictions of these institutions, the boundaries of jurisdiction between these courts remained blurred and overlapped with each other. This was, for example, the case for the control of prostitution, which had in Bologna been assigned to the *Ufficio delle Bollette* (the Office of Receipts) since the second half of the sixteenth century. The *Bollette*'s tribunal was responsible for fining the women who worked as prostitutes but had failed to register and pay taxes, for dealing with commercial disputes regarding the indebtedness of their clients, and with prostitutes' transgressions of local sumptuary and spatial restrictions. In her study on prostitution in sixteenth- and seventeenth-century Bologna, Vanessa McCarthy suggests that the responsibility for this latter mandate was most likely largely reassigned to the *Torrone* and/or the archbishop's court – even though prostitution itself was not criminalized.[12] Although there is little evidence that this was actively enforced by either one of these tribunals, it demonstrates the blurred boundaries of early modern judicial practice.

Historians have noted that it was not only the courts' competences that determined which cases were brought before which forum, but that the preferences of the plaintiffs were also decisive. Marco Cavina, for example, describes how domestic violence could – at least theoretically – be denounced to either the secular criminal court, for injury, or to the ecclesiastical court as a request

11 Rose, 'Violence and the centralization of criminal justice,' 103.

12 McCarthy, 'Prostitution, community and civic regulation,' 122-124, 125-127.

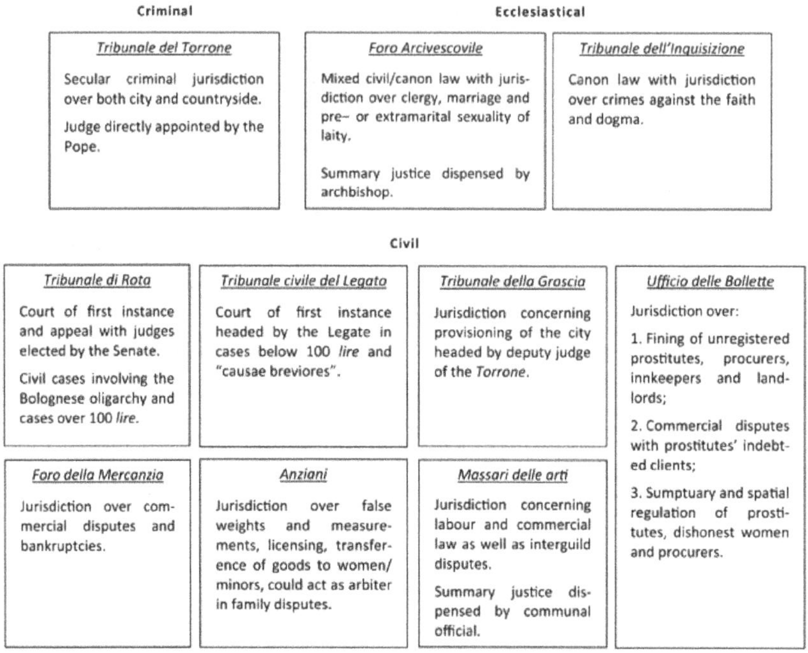

FIGURE 4 Bologna's formal legal landscape, ca. 1530-1796
SOURCES: CAVINA, 'I LUOGHI DELLA GIUSTIZIA'; BELLABARBA, *LA GIUSTIZIA NELL'ITALIA MODERNA*

for separation.[13] Daniela Lombardi has made a similar argument for cases of 'non-violent rape' (*stupro,* in this case meaning broken marriage promises after having had sexual relations), which could be brought before the ecclesiastical or the secular court, depending on the aim of the plaintiff. Before a criminal court a plaintiff could be asked to be dowered, while a marriage fulfilment could only be enforced by the ecclesiastical authorities, as marriage was considered a sacrament.[14]

Despite this legal pluralism and overlapping jurisdictions, scholars have indicated that for many types of cases there was a rough subdivision with regard to which court dealt with what kind of case. Lucia Ferrante noted that while adultery was an offence that could theoretically be adjudicated before both ecclesiastical and secular forums, the latter hardly ever did so in practice in

13 Cavina, *Nozze di sangue*, 111.
14 Ibidem; Lombardi, 'Marriage in Italy,' 107.

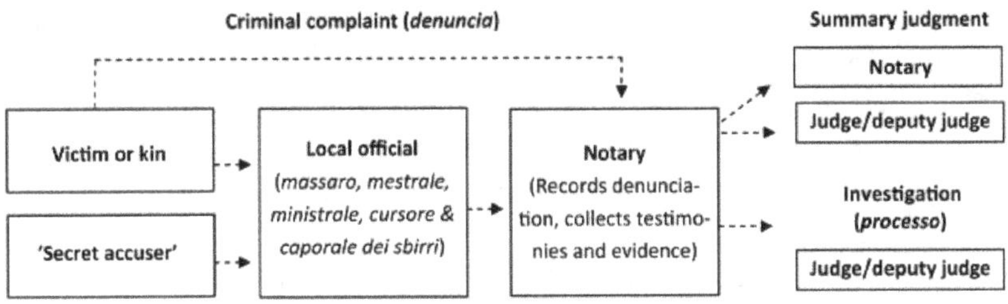

FIGURE 5 Actors in the judicial process in early modern Bologna, ca. 1530-1796

seventeenth-century Bologna.[15] With regard to the control of women's sexuality in early modern Bologna, she therefore argues for the existence of an institutional equilibrium between the *Bollette*'s control of prostitutes, the archbishop's court of other miscellaneous sexual misconduct, and the *Torrone*'s overall non-interference with regard to these matters.[16] Competences, judicial traditions and plaintiffs' preferences thus all played a role in how Bologna's early modern legal landscape was navigated by its inhabitants.

2 The Administration of Criminal Justice

The administration of criminal justice relied on a range of different actors with roles in the various stages. Figure 5 reflects this process. In essence, criminal justice in early modern Bologna was administered by a single judge: the *uditore* or *auditore* of the *Torrone*. These judges were directly appointed by the pope and their activities were only submitted to the control of the cardinal legate who was installed as city governor, or the vice-legates that substituted for him in times of his absence.[17] Nevertheless, the judges are described as serving with full authority, even attracting a reputation for autocracy as their post was only limited by the judge's age and interest. Unlike their medieval Bolognese and contemporary Florentine counterparts, who were foreigners serving in rotating terms of between two and six months in a bid to guarantee impartiality, the judges of the *Torrone* could serve long terms, which gave them a wide knowledge of and deep investment in the daily matters of city and countryside.[18] The judge was aided by two to four deputy judges (*sott'uditori*), who assisted the

15 Ferrante, 'La sessualità come risorsa,' 992.
16 Ibidem, 996.
17 Angelozzi and Casanova, *La giustizia in una città di antico regime*, 43-45.
18 C. Rose, 'Homicide in North Italy: Bologna, 1600-1700' (Unpublished PhD thesis, University of Toronto, 2016) 68.

judge with cases outside of the city. They could dispense judgements, which were reviewed and ratified by the judge.[19]

The brunt of the *Torrone*'s work rested on the shoulders of eight notaries. Formally, their tasks were limited to the documentation relating to the court's investigations, from denunciation and testimonies to the sentencing, supplication and pardons. However, the criminal court's enormous workload resulted in the notaries often also interrogating witnesses and collecting the evidence, particularly in cases of small importance and in those in the countryside, before reporting their findings to the judge, who evaluated the evidence and pronounced sentence.[20] One of the eight notaries was designated the *caponotaio*. This chief notary appointed the other seven notaries, who shared equal competences to hear cases according to a rotating schedule.[21] This meant that all notaries worked on cases from the city and the countryside and that they did not specialise in certain kinds of crimes.

Information about crimes reached the *Torrone* through a 'network of information.' This network consisted of various informants who together – according to some scholars – formed a much more efficient system of social control and surveillance than what is often assumed for the pre-Napoleonic Papal States.[22] Firstly, the criminal court was supported by a staff of rudimentary lawmen known as the *sbirri*, headed by a *baroncello* or *bargello* (a chief constable), tasked with keeping order in the city and arresting delinquents. This premodern police force is estimated to have consisted of 100 lawmen and the cost of its maintenance was subject to continuous protest by Bologna's Senate.[23] The expenses were not the only objection against the *sbirri*. These lawmen were recruited from the poorest classes and were renowned for being violent and corrupt and, being paid for each successful arrest, they had "a greedy zeal that blackened their repute."[24] On the other hand, their contacts within the seedier side of society could also advance cases, providing knowledge about the identity and whereabouts of robbers and killers. The lawmen were responsible for a variety of tasks, such as collecting witnesses and transporting them to the *Torrone*, the delivery of citations and summons, and the protection of notaries and judges.[25] It was through them that public order offences came before the

19 Rose, 'Violence and the centralization of criminal justice,' 106.
20 Angelozzi and Casanova, *La giustizia in una città di antico regime*, 49.
21 Angelozzi and Casanova, *La giustizia criminale a Bologna nel XVIII secolo*, 11.
22 Angelozzi and Casanova, *Donne criminali*, 65.
23 Angelozzi and Casanova, *La giustizia in una città di antico regime*, 51-52.
24 S. Hughes, 'Fear and loathing in Bologna and Rome. The papal police in perspective,' *Journal of social history* 21 (1987) 98; Cohen and Cohen, *Daily life in Renaissance Italy*, 117-118.
25 Rose, 'Violence and the centralization of criminal justice,' 107.

Torrone, since the *sbirri* were also tasked with patrolling the city streets at night to ensure compliance with weapon regulations and public ordinances.

Secondly, in their tasks the lawmen were aided by so-called 'friends of the court,' i.e. informants who provided them with tips and information on crimes that were recently committed or the location of fugitives. These court informants were frequently tarred as 'spies'; an insult that was commonly heard in the Bolognese streets, also used against victims of crime who wanted to take their grievances to court. Examinations of court records indicate that authorities in cities such as Rome, Venice and Bologna often made use of these informants, but that they were less common in rural settings.[26] Some of these informants worked in the open and were known to the court, working as couriers and messengers, or were long-time contacts of the court, such as cursors. Others remained anonymous and were only referred to in the court records as 'secret friends of the court.' They either denounced crimes on their own accord, or provided information through the aforementioned lawmen.

Thirdly, barbers and surgeons of the city's major hospitals also formed an important source of information and intelligence for the *Torrone*. The homicide case of Carlo Masina that this chapter opened with, for example, started with a report from the surgeon who treated his wounds. It was not uncommon for information about instances of serious and less serious violence to reach the court in this way. From the sixteenth century onwards, Bologna's criminal bylaws dictated that physicians were required to denounce 'suspicious injuries' that they treated. There were similar obligations for barbers and other medics in Rome, Lucca, Venice and Verona.[27] Bologna's 1610 summation of the criminal bylaws states that medical practitioners (*medici, cirurgici, barbieri, speciali & simili*) had to report any injury suspected of having been caused feloniously to either the *Torrone*'s chief-notary or to one of the local bailiffs outside of the city within a day of the incident.[28] These reports had to include a description of the wounds, their severity, what weapons may have caused them and, if possible, the name of the assailant. Penalties for failing to denounce consisted of hefty fines of 50 *scudi* per case.[29]

26 Ibidem, 108; Cohen and Cohen, *Daily life in Renaissance Italy*, 118.

27 P. Blastenbrei, 'Violence, Arms and Criminal Justice in Papal Rome, 1560-1600,' *Renaissance Studies* 20 (2006) 70; A. Pastore, *Il medico in tribunale. La perizia medica nella procedura penale d'antico regime (secoli XVI-XVIII)* (Bellinzona: Edizioni Casagrande, 1998) 107-108, 150, 176 and 193; Rose, *A renaissance of violence*, 48-49.

28 *Bando generale dell'illustrissimo, e reverendissimo sig. Benedetto card. Giustiniano legato di Bologna, pubblicato alli 23. di Giugno, & reiterato alli 24. di Luglio 1610* (Bologna 1610) Capitolo XXXI, page 64.

29 A university-trained doctor could earn up to 500 *scudi* a year. By comparison, the average eighteenth-century urban day labourer earned 1 *scudo* a month. A barber-surgeon would

The purpose of the medical practitioners' obligation to denounce injuries was to bring the numerous acts of violence to the attention of the authorities. According to Peter Blastenbrei, who examined physician's reports for sixteenth-century Rome, many of these "hundreds and thousands" of violent acts would otherwise have gone unnoticed by the criminal court, given the "notorious reluctance of the Roman population to give information to the justice."[30] Not only did many victims claim to have been injured as a result of an accident, an unusually high number of unknown or masked aggressors were described. Between 1560 and 1583 only 1.3 per cent of the wounded Roman patients were willing to denounce their aggressors.[31] Such reluctance in denouncing violent offenders was far less apparent among Bolognese subjects by the mid-seventeenth to mid-eighteenth centuries. In urban Bologna, about one-fifth of the cases of physical violence came under the court's purview through these medical practitioners' reports. Only a handful of victims (out of over hundred reports in my samples) described their injuries as accidental and only fifteen described not knowing the aggressor at all. In Bologna, the medical reporting on suspicious wounds therefore served as a significant instrument of criminal prosecution.

Fourthly, and importantly, the *Torrone*'s network of information relied on various officials who acted as local bailiffs. For the countryside, the *Torrone*'s main access point was the *massaro*: a local official appointed from the local ranks on an annual basis who was responsible for relaying crimes that occurred in his jurisdiction (usually one, but sometimes two or three villages) to the *Torrone*.[32] The suburban and urban counterparts of this office were that of the *mestrale* and *ministrale* and were organised at parish level. They served both as the *Torrone*'s contact in the area and also as the source of public knowledge of and participation in justice. Over two-thirds of the crimes occurring outside of the city were brought to the attention of the court by these local bailiffs. In the city their role was trumped by others such as lawmen and medical practitioners, though bailiffs still accounted for one-fifth of the officials responsible for providing first intelligence on criminal misdeeds. While a denunciation by any of these officials proved to be crucial to the court's decision to start an official investigation, Bolognese men and women were also able to make a denunciation to the court's notary in person. This option is rarely discussed in the

earn something in between. See Pastore, *Il medico in tribunale*, 192; Arru, 'The distinguishing features of domestic service in Italy,' 554.

30 Blastenbrei, 'Violence, arms and criminal justice,' 71.

31 Ibidem, 73.

32 Rose, 'Violence and the centralization of criminal justice,' 108; Rose, 'Homicide in North Italy,' 72-73, 76.

historiography on criminal justice, but, as will be argued in the next chapter, was pivotal to urban women's ability to employ the court to their benefit. Despite the frequent occurrence of denunciations by individuals in the urban setting, the existence of this knowledge network of official and semi-official informants spanning from the city to the far reaches of the countryside is important to the understanding of the workings of Bologna's criminal court during the early modern period.

3 Criminal Procedures

The statutes of the *Torrone* were issued in 1541 through a Papal proclamation entitled *Reformationes Turroni Bononiae*.[33] These statutes laid out the procedures and compensation of judges and notaries in criminal cases falling under the *Torrone*. Various phases can be distinguished in the *Torrone*'s criminal procedures. Upon the occurrence of discovery of a crime, the victims or witnesses were obligated to inform their local officials. In this first phase, these officials denounced the crime to a notary of the criminal court. With the denunciation having been made, the notary then decided if the case warranted a summary procedure or a full investigation. For small offences such as a simple complaint about verbal aggression among commoners the notary recorded the complaint in his casebook and generally waited until the parties reached an agreement.[34]

With more serious crimes such as homicide, assault resulting life-threatening wounds, robbery, theft and arson, the notary investigated the crime and gathered information, which he then reported to the judge. An inquisition began with an investigation of the immediate facts of the crime. In the case of homicide, this entailed an inspection of the body by the notary and two locals who knew the victim. For theft this meant an inspection of the damages done to the house or shop from which items were taken.[35]

The third phase, after the denunciation and the *in situ* investigation, was the interrogation of witnesses. The number of testimonies that were collected depended on the type of crime that was committed, the victim's status, the notary's personal preferences and the outcome of the other interrogations. In the case against Alessandro Bernardi, a barber who stabbed goldsmith Giuseppe Gualli on the street when he thought Gualli was reaching for his weapon in 1675, only one eyewitness was interrogated before the case was withdrawn and

33 ASBO, *Bandi e notificazioni*, Serie I, No. 3, fol. 95.
34 Rose, 'Violence and the centralization of criminal justice,' 111.
35 Ibidem, 112.

the offender absolved.[36] On the other hand, no fewer than 23 witnesses testified against reseller Margarita Cesare, who promised to resell jewellery and pieces of clothing for various artisans but never delivered the payments, and was eventually sentenced to public lashing and exile for swindle.[37] The initial list of witnesses was compiled based on the denunciation and the initial investigation, and these witnesses received citations with increasingly severe fines if they did not show up to give their testimonies. After this initial round of interrogations, further citations could be issued by the court officers, also summoning the accused for interrogation on penalty of a heavy fine, corporal punishment, or the risk of being killed with impunity.[38]

Defendants were questioned in a closed room, were generally without counsel, and were unaware of the charges, accuser and evidence.[39] When the aforementioned Margarita Cesare was brought in for questioning for swindle (*truffa*), she was not told why she had been arrested.[40] This was business as usual; in general, the interrogator first circled around the issue, collecting clues and looking for inconsistencies, and when stories did not match up they would confront defendants with other testimonies at their discretion. Margarita's portrayal of her actions as an honest, one-time mistake, for example, became increasingly unconvincing when confronted with a range of testimonies that revealed a chain of deceit of many different victims. As a legal proof, a conviction required strong evidence in the form of a confession or two credible witnesses. Lacking good witnesses, it remained within the *Torrone*'s competency for the magistrates to decide to apply torture. However, like elsewhere in early modern Europe, its use declined significantly in Bologna during the seventeenth century.[41]

After the interrogations, the evidence compiled by the notary was passed on to the judge, who reviewed the case and pronounced sentence. How judges came to their sentencing has largely remained elusive to historians, as sentences lacked any explanation in the court records. Judges also had great *arbitrium* with which they could determine punishments according to the 'qualities' of the crime, the victim and the criminal. Fragmented as the Italian peninsula was politically, it was not until the Zanardelli Code of 1889 that

36 ASBO, Torrone, 7028, fasc. 6.

37 ASBO, Torrone, 7072, fasc.o 1.

38 Rose, 'Violence and the centralization of criminal justice,' 113.

39 Cohen and Cohen, *Daily life in Renaissance Italy*, 119.

40 ASBO, Torrone, 7072, fasc. 1, fol. 6: "[...] e la causa per la quale sono stata presa priggione e che hora mi vuole essaminare io non lo so se non mi si dice."

41 Rose, 'Violence and the centralization of criminal justice,' 114; Angelozzi and Casanova, *Donne criminali*, 230.

penal legislation was unified for Italy. Following the demise of Napoleon after 1814, various territories had started penning their own civil, criminal and commercial codes. Alongside Tuscany, Naples and Piedmont-Sardinia, the Papal States too promulgated a penal code in 1832.[42] Before the introduction of these nineteenth-century penal codes, the legal system in the Italian territories was shaped by two different legal traditions. The first was the *ius commune* based on the Justinianic texts of Roman civil law and texts of canon law, and the second the *ius proprium*, i.e. various local, municipal or regional corpuses of legislation.[43] From the early thirteenth century onwards, the community of Bologna had started issuing civil and criminal statutes, laying down the city's basic legislation and customs in Latin.[44]

During the early modern period, best sources to gauge Bologna's norms regarding prosecution and sentencing were not the civic statutes but the criminal bylaws. Throughout the papal rule over Bologna, the ruling legates provided general regulations for penal justice in the form of proclamations (*bandi*) that according to Paolo Prodi made the civic statutes redundant without formally abolishing them.[45] At the beginning of his legateship over Bologna, each papal legate issued or renewed a *Bando Generale*; a summation of proclamations specifying the definitions and sanctions of crimes for the territory of Bologna. For the seventeenth and eighteenth centuries two of these summations were of major importance: that of 1610 and that of 1756. Legate Benedetto Giustiniani's *Bando Generale* was issued on 23 June 1610 and remained largely unaltered until the middle of the eighteenth century. In 1756 Legate Fabrizio Serbelloni revised the criminal bylaws significantly following Pope Benedict XIV's constitutional reforms of criminal justice a decade earlier.[46] These reforms sought to regulate the criminal procedures within its territory, increase its transparency and curb some of its abuses.[47] It is generally assumed that this

42 *I Regolamenti penali di Papa Gregorio XVI per lo Stato Pontificio* (1832).

43 M. Bellomo, *The common legal past of Europe, 1000-1800* (Washington: The Catholic University of America Press, 1995) 1-2; T. Kuehn, 'Gender and law in Milan,' 408.

44 F. Berlan, *Statuti Italiani. Saggio bibliografico* (Venice: Tipografia del commercio, 1858) xxvi, 12-13.

45 P. Prodi, *The papal prince. One body and two souls. The papal monarchy in early modern Europe* (Cambridge: Cambridge University Press, 1982) 74.

46 Angelozzi and Casanova, *Donne criminali*, 60; Angelozzi and Casanova, *La giustizia criminale a Bologna nel XVIII secolo*, 156.

47 Angelozzi and Casanova mention 8 ways in which Benedetto XIV's reforms sought to end the abuses of the criminal justice system: 1) the regulation of payments of the court's officials, 2) defining who can act as a legal expert, 3) obligation to first emit three citations in the presence of a bailiff before emitting a mandate for capture, 4) increasing the transparency of the process, 5) making witnesses sign their testimonies, 6) improving the

new summation of the criminal bylaws reflected changes in the attitude towards penal justice going back to the turn of the century.

Although the much more elaborate treatment of crimes and their sentences in the 1756 *Bando Generale* clarified many of the obscurities from the past century, it above all provided a normative guideline rather than a reflection of contemporary penal practice. Both the 1610 and the 1756 summations of the city's bylaws predominantly prescribed capital punishments for crime. Among others, a death sentence could be prescribed for various forms of theft, armed robbery, homicide, assault of officials, counterfeiting, rebellion and banditry. Punitive incarceration was rarely prescribed, as it was not only expensive but also considered to be cruel. More commonly prescribed by the bylaws were convictions to the papal galleys in the Mediterranean and corporal punishment and fines for simple infractions.

While the criminal bylaws prescribed capital punishment for a multitude of offences, the actual enforcement of the death sentence declined significantly throughout the early modern period.[48] In Bologna 917 men and women were executed between 1540 and 1600. This number dropped to 556 from 1600 to 1700, and, averaging less than two per year in the 1690s, continued to go down.[49] By the end of the seventeenth century the death penalty was not a generic, common sentence, but was instead issued only to those who represented a threat to the state and the court's hold over that state. A similar discrepancy between penal norm and practice pertained to *esilio* (banishment): while banishment was not mentioned as a punishment for any crime in either of the two criminal bylaws, it was one of the most common penal outcomes for many serious crimes throughout the seventeenth and eighteenth centuries. In Italy as elsewhere in early modern Europe, banishment was used as an instrument to moderate strict laws and often replaced capital punishments or a sentence to the galleys.[50] The convicted suffered exile from the entire legal territory of Bologna for lengthy, often indeterminate periods of time, unless he or she was able to make peace with the victim or the victim's family. The *bandi* therefore once more reveal that the regulations were by no means followed to the letter.

---

rights of the criminals (for example no longer using dogs to capture fugitives), 7) no longer allowing undercover testimonies of prison infiltrators and 8) no longer pronouncing exile while the defendant was *in absentia*. See Angelozzi and Casanova, *La giustizia criminale a Bologna nel XVIII secolo*, 164-182.

48 N. Terpstra, 'Theory into practice: Executions, comforting, and comforters in Renaissance Italy,' in N. Terpstra (ed.), *The art of executing well. Rituals of execution in Renaissance Italy* (Kirksville: Truman State University Press, 2008) 123.

49 Rose, *A renaissance of violence*, 52.

50 Nubola, 'Giustizia, perdono, oblio,' 14.

The example of banishment also illustrates how sentences did not constitute the final stage of the criminal procedure. Convicted Bolognese men and women could request grace from the state authorities (in the case of the Papal States the Papal Prince) via criminal petitions, i.e. supplications (*suppliche*).[51] These supplications were written by notaries working within the judicial structures who received a set fee for their services from the culprit. Each successful supplication was furthermore taxed a proportion of the potential judicial fine for the pardoned crime.[52] When granted, a pardon often stipulated a period of separation between the parties, which meant that killers could, for example, not return to the city or village where the homicide was committed for three years.[53] Other than that, the offender was free to move about the *legato* and was essentially re-integrated into the societal fabric. Whether a pardon would be granted hinged upon certain conditions; peace having been made with the victim or his/her family was often the most important requirement.[54]

According to a growing body of scholarly work, composition and peacemaking had a central function in early modern criminal justice all over Europe.[55] This brokering of reconciliation was a remnant of the older forms of community justice and a continuity of medieval practices. The persistence of peacemaking practices is particularly relevant for the early modern Italian case because of its role in preserving older social systems centred on violent confrontations.[56] Italian governments considered peacemaking the most efficient and rational instrument to ensure social peace and order. Rather than making penal repression the focal point of their endeavours, public authorities from the sixteenth and seventeenth centuries onwards increasingly inserted themselves into the private disputes of their citizens, eventually in the roles of formal arbiters.[57] This meant that peacemaking practices were increasingly

51 Niccoli, 'Rinuncia, pace, perdono,' 221; Nubola, 'Giustizia, perdono, oblio,' 35; C.S. Rose, '"To be remedied of any vendetta": Petitions and the avoidance of violence in early modern Parma,' *Crime, history & societies* 16:2 (2012) 5-6.

52 Rose, 'To be remedied of any vendetta,' 17.

53 Rose, 'Violence and the centralization of criminal justice,' 117.

54 Rose, 'To be remedied of any vendetta,' 17.

55 S. Cummins, 'Forgiving crimes in early modern Naples,' in S. Cummins and L. Kounine (eds.), *Cultures of conflict resolution in early modern Europe* (Surrey: Ashgate, 2016) 255; Cummins and Kounine, 'Confronting conflict in early modern Europe,' 9; Niccoli, *Perdonare*, 38-39.

56 Cavarzere, 'At the crossroads of feud and law,' 55, 69; D. Boschi, 'Knife fighting in Rome,' 150-153, especially 152; Broggio and Caroll, 'Violence and peacemaking in early modern Europe,' 5; Rose, 'Homicide in North Italy,' 20.

57 Cavarzere demonstrates how the evolution of this codification in the sixiteenth-century Pistoiese statutes, and suggests that similar developments took place in other parts of

institutionalised in early modern Italy: to make peace was now a jurisdictional action administered by the public authorities.[58]

A prime example of this institutionalisation in Bologna is to be found in a range of non-continuous government bodies established between the 1540s and 1694 to facilitate peacemaking between high-raking nobles.[59] By the 1650s, this government council was called the *Assunteria de Liti e Paci* and it has been argued to have played an important part in the government's efforts to curtail the nobility's violence during those volatile years of heightened violence.[60] But the institutionalisation of peacemaking was also visible outside of these specific councils. Vicars, local officials (*massari, ministrali*) and even senators are known to have acted as mediators between the victim of violence and/or his kin and the imputed criminal in the pacification of conflicts.[61] According to Rose and others, the court records suggest that the *Torrone*'s magistrates applied a great deal of pressure on the victims and their kin to accept their enemies' peacemaking attempts.[62]

The Bolognese criminal court records clearly demonstrate that arbitration was favoured over formal judicial intervention in the case of petty offences. Drawing on Bologna's civic statutes, the statutes of the *Torrone* affirmed the plaintiff's right to withdraw a complaint.[63] Ottavia Niccoli argued that the *rinuncia* usually followed a financial composition between the plaintiff and defendant, even though this often remains implicit in the sources.[64] The norms dictated that in the case of *levioribus criminibus* (literally lighter crimes, used here for crimes against the person without the spilling of blood) the withdrawal of a complaint brought about the immediate suspension of any legal action. However, the Bolognese criminal court records demonstrate that the withdrawal could halt prosecutions for a broader range of crimes than the norms

Italy between the sixteenth and seventeenth centuries, see Cavarzere, 'At the crossroads,' 64-65, 69.

58 Cavarzere, 'At the crossroads,' 65; M. Bellabarba, 'Pace pubblica e pace privata. Linguaggi e istituzioni processuali nell'Italia moderna,' in M. Bellabarba, A. Zorzi and G. Schwerhoff (eds.), *Criminalità e giustizia in Germania e in Italia. Pratiche giudiziarie e linguaggi giuridici tra tardo medioevo e prima età moderna* (Bologna: Il Mulino, 2001) 189-213.

59 Niccoli, *Perdonare*, 115.

60 Rose, 'Violence and the centralization of criminal justice,' 117; G. Angelozzi and C. Casanova, *La nobiltà disciplinata. Violenza nobiliare, procedure di giustizia e scienza cavalleresca a Bologna nel XVII secolo* (Bologna: Patròn Editore, 2003) 57.

61 Niccoli, 'Rinuncia, pace, perdono,' 228-232; Rose, 'Homicide in North Italy,' 64-65.

62 Rose, *A renaissance of violence*, 54; Cavarzere, 'At the crossroads,' 65-67.

63 R. Mariani, 'Criminalità e controllo sociale nella Crevalcore del seicento' (Unpublished Master thesis, Università degli studi di Bologna, 1991) 74.

64 Niccoli, 'Rinuncia, pace, perdono,' 226.

dictated – from verbal insults to aggressions with serious physical consequences and, more rarely, theft. The next chapter will explore this mechanism in more detail for the denunciations.

Another judicial peacemaking instrument that was particularly used for the graver types of offences was the peace accord. This was an official, notarised document that brought settlement to a dispute between two quarrelling parties. With its historical roots in the medieval accusatorial procedure, it aimed to reintegrate the offender into society and was quite common in most parts of early modern Europe.[65] Theoretically, it carried greater weight than the simple juridical withdrawal of the complaint because it functioned as a social accord and was supposed to bring an end to a conflict between individuals and families once and for all.[66] Like the withdrawals of complaints, peace accords generally involved a financial settlement between the plaintiff and defendant, even though these details were rarely recorded.[67] Before the criminal court, presenting a peace accord could commute a sentence to a lesser one or could halt the prosecution altogether through a pardon by the legate.[68]

The peace accords and other types of reconciliation were common and are generally assumed to have been used by men and women of all social stripes.[69] The importance and frequency of its use in Italy is quantified by various studies. Rose, for example, observed that nearly a third of seventeenth-century homicide trials in Bologna were settled with a notarised peace accord granted by the victim's kin.[70] It is generally assumed that the use of these pacification instruments in the criminal justice system was increasingly restricted during the early modern period, although it has also been noted that even in the nineteenth-century Papal States it was still possible to withdraw a complaint from the judicial process.[71] This highlights the formal incorporation and continued importance of peacemaking in early modern Italy's criminal justice system.

65 K.L. Jansen, '"Pro bono pacis": Crime, conflict, and dispute resolution. The evidence of notarial peace contracts in late medieval Florence,' *Speculum* 88:2 (2013) 446.

66 Niccoli, *Perdonare*, 113.

67 Niccoli, 'Rinuncia, pace, perdono,' 226.

68 Nubola, 'Giustizia, perdono, oblio,' 33.

69 Jansen, 'Pro bono pacis,' 427-456; T. Kuehn, 'Law and arbitration in Renaissance Florence,' in T. Kuehn (ed.), *Law, family and women. Toward a legal anthropology of Renaissance Italy* (Chicago: University of Chicago Press, 1991) 36; A. Zorzi, 'Legitimation and legal sanction of vendetta in Italian cities from the twelfth to the fourteenth centuries,' in S.K. Cohn jr. and F. Ricciardelli (eds.), *The culture of violence in Renaissance Italy* (Florence: Le Lettere, 2012) 34.

70 Rose, *A renaissance of violence*, 55.

71 D. Edigati, 'La pace nel processo criminale. Il caso toscano in età moderna,' in P. Broggio and M.P. Paoli (eds.), *Stringere la pace. Teorie e pratiche della conciliazione nell'Europea moderna (secoli XV-XVIII)* (Rome: Viella, 2011) 408.

4 Italian Women's Involvement in Recorded Crime

While the criminal procedures and bylaws in themselves may at first glance appear relatively gender neutral, there were significant differences in men's and women's experiences of the law. Women's small proportional contribution to recorded crime can be viewed as an expression of these differences, standing testament to the freedoms and restrictions women encountered on the streets and before the courts. It is in this light that studies on the late medieval and Renaissance period paint a rather bleak picture of the centuries thereafter. Samuel Cohn's important study on fourteenth- and fifteenth-century Florence suggests a diminishing participation of women in crime. Before Florence's *Otto di Guardia*, women comprised 22 per cent of the accused a decade before the Black Death (1347-1348) and 17 per cent two decades later (1374-1375).[72] Although the quantitative differences appear modest, Cohn argues that they represent a real decline, reflecting the newly introduced constraints on women's ability to perform public roles and access the court, among others by requiring women to be represented in court by a guardian (*mundualdus*). The notion that Italian women were increasingly worse off has readily captured the imagination, but does require further scrutiny. After all, the Florentine statutory restrictions stemmed from Lombard law and were not universally applied throughout the whole of the Italian peninsula. Other scholarship, such as Elizabeth and Thomas Cohen's work on Rome's sixteenth-century Governor's court, is furthermore suggestive of a wide involvement of both men and women in criminal offences, though they generally lack quantitative assessments to contrast the older data more substantially.[73]

The renowned legal historian Mario Sbriccoli has attributed the (at that point still largely presumed) low level of female involvement in recorded crime in Italy to the workings of the legal system.[74] His premise was that, until the twentieth century, both the law and consequently the criminal justice system were viewed as essentially masculine. This meant that women were kept away from the law and the law was kept away from women, whether as judges, lawyers, plaintiffs or defendants. Not only was the criminal justice system based on male behaviours, it also actively categorised many of women's deviant behaviours (described by Sbriccoli as obscene behaviours, fornication, concubinage, as well as petty crimes) as matters of sin, disorder, irregularity

72 Cohn, 'Women in the streets, women in the courts,' 24, 29.

73 Cohen and Cohen, *Words and deeds*, 14-16.

74 Sbriccoli, 'Deterior est condicio foeminarum,' 81.

or censorable anomalies rather than subject to criminal justice.[75] According to Sbriccoli, women's criminality in Italy was thus largely 'absorbed' into the mesh of extrajudicial control systems, ranging from the domestic sphere to the neighbourhood and the church.[76] Similar arguments have also been made for women's misdeeds elsewhere in Europe. Rather than appearing before a high criminal court, women's crimes were likely more commonly solved through other informal or extrajudicial spheres of social control, such as the family or the neighbourhood.[77]

While it may well be true that women's crimes were more likely to be handled by less formal methods of conflict resolution in the early modern period, by no means all of women's transgressions were dealt with outside the judicial system.[78] Table 1 brings together data from various Italian studies regarding the proportion of women among formally investigated criminal offenders. It also includes figures for urban Bologna, which were collected from the *Torrone*'s investigation dossiers (*processi*) for the sample years of 1655, 1675, 1705, 1725 and 1755. Among the 911 collected *processi*, there were 1,357 identified defendants; 1,287 men and 70 women.[79] This meant that in Bologna women comprised only about five per cent of those individuals subjected to a formal criminal investigation.[80] The other available studies on Italian towns reveal equally low figures, suggesting that women represented a clear minority among indicted criminals.

The early modern period is often viewed as marking a peak for women's involvement in crime. Records from cities in France, England, Scotland, Germany and the Netherlands reveal significantly higher shares of female criminal offenders during the seventeenth and eighteenth century than in the centuries thereafter.[81] During the early modern period women in Western Europe could

75 Ibidem, 83-84.

76 An example of household control in criminal cases is provided by M. Gambier, 'La donna e la giustizia penale Veneziana nel XVIII secolo,' in G. Cozzi (ed.), *Stato, società e giustizia nella Repubblica Veneta (sec. XV-XVIII)* (Rome: Jouvenence, 1980) 566.

77 Dinges, 'The uses of justice,' 167-168.

78 Dinges, 'The uses of justice,' 159-175; R. Shoemaker, *Prosecution and punishment. Petty crime and the law in London and rural Middlesex, c.1660-1725* (Cambridge: Cambridge University Press, 1991) 292; Schwerhoff, *Köln im Kreuzverhör*.

79 The total number of 'offenders' amounts to 1,419 if we include the 62 offenders whose identity and sex are unknown.

80 The share of female defendants among urban *processi* was 2% in 1655, 5% in 1675, 2% in 1705 and 8% in 1725 and 1755.

81 G. Geltner, 'No woman's land? On female crime and incarceration, past, present and future,' *Justice policy journal* 7:2 (2010) 6; Feeley and Little, 'The vanishing female,' 719-757; Jütte, 'Geslechtsspezifische Kriminalität,' 86-116; Van der Heijden, 'Criminaliteit en sexe,' 1-36.

TABLE 1 Female crimes shares in various Italian cities, averages per century

	Urban population in thousands, c.1700	14th c	15th c	16th c	17th c	18th c	19th c
Florence	72	20.9	14.1	–	6.4	–	–
Lucca	24	14	–	–	–	–	–
Viterbo	12	–	7.9	–	–	–	–
Rome	140	–	–	11.5	–	–	–
Bologna	63	–	3.3	–	4.0	5.7	11.5
Siena	16	–	–	–	–	8.8	–
Prato	6	–	–	–	–	4	–

Sources: **Florence:** 14th and 15th century data: S.K. Cohn, 'Women in the streets, women in the courts, in early Renaissance Florence', in S.K. Cohn (ed.), *Women in the streets. Essays on sex and power in Renaissance Italy* (Baltimore: Johns Hopkins University Press, 1998) 16-38; 17th century share based on own calculations from Archivio di Stato di Firenze, Ruota Criminale, Gionale della Ruota, 37 (July-October 1695), **Lucca:** G. Geltner, 'A cell of their own: The incarceration of women in late medieval Italy', *Signs* 38:1 (2013) 31; **Viterbo:** V. Rizzo, 'Giustizia e società a Viterbo nel XV secolo (da una ricerca sui registri dei malefici)', *Biblioteca e società* 3-4 (1999) 49, **Bologna:** 15th century data: S.R. Blanshei and S. Cucini, 'Criminal justice and conflict resolution', in S.R. Blanshei (ed.), *A companion to medieval and Renaissance Bologna* 72; 17th and 18th century data: my own calculations based on the sampled processi for the years 1655, 1675, 1705, 1725 and 1755; the 19th century data: M. Pluskota, 'Petty criminality, gender bias, and judicial practice in 19th-century Europe', *Journal of Social History* 51:4 (2018) 723, **Rome:** C. Vasta, 'Criminal women. Women's violence in sixteenth- and seventeenth-century Rome' (Unpublished conference paper 61th Annual Meeting of the RSA, Berlin, 26-28 March 2015) 6, **Siena:** L.C. Sardi, 'Analisi statistica sulla criminalità nel 1700 (reati e pene) con riguardo allo Stato senese', in L. Berlinguer and F. Colao (eds.), *Criminalità e società in età moderna* (Milan: Giuffrè, 1991) 396, 439, **Prato:** D. Zuliani, 'Reati e pene nel vicariato di Prato prima e dopo la «Leopoldina» (1781-1790)', in L. Berlinguer and F. Colao (eds.), *Criminalità e società in età moderna* (Milan: Giuffrè, 1991) 312. **Urban population data:** P. Malanima, 'Italian urban population 1300-1861 (The database)'.

make up to 50 per cent of all property offenders, while they were only responsible for about 16 per cent of these crimes in the twenty-first century.[82] Based on data on cities in England and the Netherlands, criminologist Malcolm Feeley

82 *European sourcebook of crime and criminal justice statistics 2014* (Helsinki: Hakapaino Oy, 2014) 89.

argued that female involvement in crime dropped after the middle of the nineteenth century as a result of increasing patriarchal structures pushing women out of the public sphere.[83] This notion of the 'vanishing female' has been criticised by various scholars, who did not only question why such a decline occurred but also when and where. Women's relatively high shares among early modern offenders, however, appear largely uncontested.

There is little evidence so far that the early modern period was also the heyday of women's criminality in Italy. Although the aggregated data is too sparse and disparate to draw definite conclusions, there are no known examples of Italian women's crime shares (based on formal criminal investigations or indictments) remotely as high as those found in most other northern European towns. Women accounted for around 30 per cent of the criminal offenders in various towns in Holland during the seventeenth and eighteenth century, and made up 22 and 21 per cent of all suspects investigated in Frankfurt and Surrey.[84] While longer-term studies for these European towns have demonstrated that these crime shares were in constant flux, they were consistently higher than those found for the Italian Peninsula, including Bologna. The early modern period did not constitute a peak for women's criminality everywhere in Europe.

The possibly different long-term development of women's involvement in crime in early modern Italian cities provokes broader questions regarding the explanations for its historical variation over time and space. As has been argued in the previous chapter, many of the structural characteristics of women's lives in early modern Bologna such as the level of labour participation, the shares of female-heading households, and the prevalence of nuclear families were remarkably similar to those found in northern European cities. To understand Italian women's recorded involvement in crime, we should therefore also consider the effects of other societal determinants, such as cultures of honour and violence, specificities of its legal culture, and the care and control exerted by civic institutions.

83 Feeley and Little, 'The vanishing female,' 750.

84 Between 1680 and 1811 Amsterdam, on average 35.2 per cent of defendants consisted of women. Slightly lower, but still comparatively high counts have been found for towns such as Haarlem and Dordrecht. For a summary of these works on Holland, see Van der Heijden, *Women and crime*, 4-9. For an overview of the shares in Germany and some English localties, see Kamp, 'Female crime and household control,' 536, 540; Jütte, 'Geslechtsspezifische Kriminalität,' 93; Beattie, 'The criminality of women,' 81.

5 The Character of Indicted Crime in Bologna

Which crimes were investigated and prosecuted by the criminal courts differed significantly across time and space. Definitions of what is regarded a crime are therefore imperative. Table 2 shows the various types of offences that can be found in the early modern Bolognese criminal court records, which are largely based on the contemporary descriptions found in the records themselves. The front cover of Bologna's *processi* – collected as bundles of dedicated dossiers – nearly always included a Latin or Italian indication of the crime the defendant had been accused of committing. These include *omicidio* for homicide, *vulnere* for wounding, *furto* for theft in related activities, *rapina* for armed robbery and *stupro* for rape or sex out of wedlock. The classification of these offences into the categories of violence, property, public order and sexual misconduct is a modern one, which is based on a reading of the criminal bylaws as well as classifications by other scholars. With these categorisations in mind, we will examine the similarities and differences between prosecuted crimes of male and female offenders as well as between Bologna and other cities in early modern Europe.

The importance of violent crimes among Bologna's criminal investigation dossiers catches the eye. As is shown in table 3, the dockets of the *Torrone* brimmed with violent acts ranging from insults and blows to stabbings, shootings and murder. Making up 43 per cent of the cases investigated by the criminal court, these violent and aggressive offences were the most common reason for an encounter with the law, followed by offences against public order and property. Formal investigations for sexual misconduct were far scarcer. Even when taking into consideration the unidentified offenders who were predominantly responsible for property crimes, violent encounters still constituted the clear majority of cases that the *Torrone* dealt with.

With the preponderance of violent offences among its *processi*, Bologna's 'crime pattern' resembled that of other towns in much of premodern Italy. Both for fourteenth- and fifteenth-century Florence and sixteenth-century Rome, scholars have found violent offences to be the most important crime before criminal courts.[85] By contrast, criminal courts in Holland, England and Germany were as a rule far more prone to prosecuting theft and other property offences.[86] Together with data from Spain, Portugal and South West France,

85 Cohn, 'Women in the streets, women in the courts,' 26; Blastenbrei, *Kriminalität in Rom*, 284.

86 Noordam, 'Strafrechtspleging en criminaliteit,' 228; *Old Bailey Proceedings Online* (<https://www.oldbaileyonline.org/>, version 7.2, March 2015), Tabulating offence

TABLE 2 Categorisation of crimes

Violence	Property	Public order	Sexual misconduct
Homicide	Theft & fencing	Bearing/firing arms	Rape
Infanticide	Burglary & breaking and entering	Suspicious behaviour	Sexual battery
Fighting resulting in serious injury	Pickpocketing	Begging & vagabonding	'Deviation' & adultery
Fighting without serious injury	Robbery	Disorderly behaviour	Sodomy
Threat	Arson & damage to property or animals	Resisting/insulting the authorities	
Insult, defamation & libel	Violation of seizure of goods	Perversion of justice	
		Violation of banishment	
		Fraud & forgery	

TABLE 3 Reported crimes among Bologna's *processi*, ca. 1655-1755

	Male defendants		Female defendants		Total identified defendants*		Unidentified offenders	
	#	%	#	%	#	%	#	%
Violence	565	44	23	33	588	43	11	18
Property	323	25	27	39	350	26	50	81
Public order	350	27	17	24	367	27	1	2
Sex	42	3	3	4	45	3	–	–
Misc.	7	1	–	–	7	1	–	–
	1287	100	70	100	1357	100	62	100

SOURCE: SAMPLE 1 (SEE APPENDIX).
* Calculated from the total of defendants whose sex is known, counted by defendant

the Bolognese case study thus provides tentative evidence for the existence of a distinct southern European prosecution pattern in which violent offences figured much more prominently than in the northern regions of Europe.[87]

Violent altercations continued to make up a significant portion of the Bolognese criminal court cases all throughout the mid-seventeenth to mid-eighteenth century. Both in 1655 and 1755, violent offenders constituted the largest category of criminals investigated by the *Torrone*, although their share among the total body of recorded crime dropped from nearly 60 to just under 40 per cent during the century (figure 6). But this seemingly significant drop in violence is deceiving: foremost because the particular caseload from 1655 and 1675 are by-products of exceptional social disorder following the plague years, and the subsequent increase of policing of arms-bearing in the city to curb the reinvigorated endemic violence. On the whole absolute numbers of violent offenders investigated by the *Torrone* furthermore increased rather than declined throughout the century. The distribution of crimes filling court dockets after the turn of the century seems relatively stable, but they do reveal a small proportional increase of property offenders scrutinised by the court which could potentially be indicative of a longer-term shift. Siena's criminal court handled violence and property crimes in roughly equal proportions in the 1730s and 1750s, but saw the proportional importance of property offenders rise between 1778 and 1786.[88] Records from Prato's vicariate court between 1781 and 1790 also suggest that by this time property crimes constituted the lion's share of judicial consideration.[89]

In spite of the enduring importance of violence before the *Torrone*, women mostly faced formal charges for property crimes. No less than 39 per cent of the female offenders were accused of thieving and other larcenous activities, compared to only one-in-four of their male counterparts (table 3). This distinction cannot be reduced to biological and physical predispositions, in which women's lesser physical strength is equated to their more limited violent transgressions, but instead reflects the profound influence of gendered

---

category, between 1674 and 1800. Counting by defendant; Schwerhoff, *Historische Kriminalitätsforschung*, 116.

87 T.A. Mantecón, 'The patterns of violence in early modern Spain,' *The journal of the historical society* 7:2 (2007) 254; D. Abreu-Ferreira, *Women, crime and forgiveness in early modern Portugal* (Surrey-Burlington: Ashgate, 2015) 17; J.R. Ruff, *Crime, justice and public order in old regime France* (London: Croom Helm, 1984), see figure 1.01 in the introduction, n.p.

88 Sardi, 'Analisi statistica sulla criminalità,' 351, 355-368, 376-377, 402, 412.

89 Zuliani, 'Reati e pene nel vicariato di Prato,' 310.

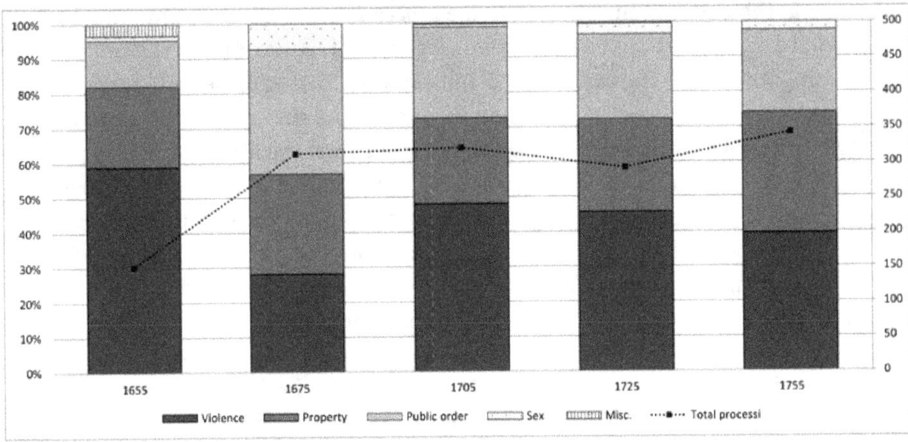

FIGURE 6 Types of *processi* across time, ca. 1655-1755
SOURCE: SAMPLE 1 (SEE APPENDIX)

norms and prosecution policies.[90] Magistrates had significant discretionary powers and did not deem all offences by all offenders equally worthy of prosecutions. Women's violence in particular may have been of little interest to early modern authorities, as it was believed to have posed little threat to public order, which could easily translate into fewer indictments.[91] Bologna's criminal court records indicate that women's violence was indeed disproportionally dismissed by the *Torrone*'s judges.[92] This manifested itself in the clause of *non proceditur stante qualitate facti et personae*: the decision to not proceed with the prosecution due to the qualities of the facts and the persons involved. According to Angelozzi and Casanova, invoking this clause can be viewed as an act of clemency by the judge as well as an assessment of the irrelevancy of the case, in which their sex was a contributing factor.

90 For an overview of the literature discussing these different perspectives, see Crouzet-Pavan, 'Crimine e giustizia,' 56-57; Angelozzi and Casanova, *Donne criminali*, 12; Van der Heijden, *Women and crime*, 9-10.

91 J.R. Ruff, *Violence in early modern Europe, 1500-1800* (Cambridge: Cambridge University Press, 2001) 117-159; K. Callahan, 'Women who kill: An analysis of cases in late eighteenth- and early nineteenth-century London,' *Journal of social history* 46-4 (2013) 1015; D.D. Gray, 'The regulation of violence in the metropolis: The prosecution of assault in the summary courts, c.1780-1820,' *The London journal* 32:1 (2007) 79.

92 Angelozzi and Casanova, *Donne criminali*, 55, 259.

That the patterns emerging from the *processi* do not allow for any straightforward generalisations about women's less violent nature is also evident from a comparison with the early-stage denunciations. Among these far more plentiful formal complaints no less than 82 per cent of the accused women and two-thirds of the accused men were denounced for physical and verbal aggression, which was reduced in the *processi* to 44 per cent of men's crimes and 33 per cent of women's.[93] At the level of the investigations violence thus played a less important role for both men and women, but the discrepancy is particularly striking for the female defendants. Women furthermore made up only four per cent of violent transgressors among the *processi*, whilst their share had roughly been five times that among the denunciations. The opposite can be said for property crimes, where only 11 per cent of the female offenders had been accused of these types of crimes at the level of the denunciations, compared to 39 per cent among the *processi*. This discrepancy can also be observed for men – with property crimes making up 18 per cent in the denunciations and 26 per cent among the *processi* – although the difference is definitely more marked for female offenders. Women were also responsible for 8 per cent of all investigated thefts – twice the share of women among offenders of violence. For a more accurate understanding of women's involvement in everyday crime, it is therefore imperative to look beyond only those offences that the authorities deemed worth prosecuting.

Roughly as important among the offences investigated were myriad acts against public order. About a quarter of men and women were indicted for behaviours that disturbed the public peace, such as gambling, illegal dances and the throwing of stones, often in groups. Another prevalent public order offences typically committed by men was that of bearing arms within the city walls. As in other early modern Italian cities such as Rome, the prevalence of arms was viewed as a cause of the endemic violence in Bologna's streets and villages. From the sixteenth century onwards, weapons therefore became the pillars of public order legislation.[94] This ambition was reflected in the 1610 *Bando Generale*, which prohibited the carrying of a wide range of arms, such as swords, long-bladed weapons and firearms, in Bologna without a licence.[95] Both the city's gatekeepers and its lawmen, the *sbirri*, were given detailed

93 For a closer examination and further discussion of the differences between the outcomes of the *processi* and the denunciations, also see chapter 4 in this book, particularly table 6.

94 Rose, *A renaissance of violence*, 186; Blastenbrei, 'Violence, arms and criminal justice,' 75; *Bando generale della legazione di Bologna e suo contado, fatto pubblicare li 12. ottobre 1756 dall'eminentiss., e reverendiss. sig. cardinale Fabrizio Serbelloni, legato a latere di detta città* (Bologna 1756) Chapter XLVI, No. 7, page 75.

95 *Bando generale Giustiniano 1610*, chapter XXIV, page 43-51.

instructions on how to manage the transgression of these bans and they indeed confiscated weapons on a daily basis. The repeated issuing of weapon bans throughout the early modern period illustrates the authorities' enduring concern with this public order offence as well as its ineffectiveness. Large numbers of summonses were given out on a daily basis for unlicensed weapons, meaning that these arms were constantly to be found among the male Bolognese populace.[96]

A highly gendered offence was that of *vagare la notte*, i.e. wandering about at night. Concerns about public order underpinned an official curfew that restricted women's mobility after sunset's *Ave Maria* bell in many early modern Italian towns.[97] The roots of this criminalisation of women's mobility lay in the sumptuary and spatial regulations of prostitutes, seeking to regulate where they lived, how they dressed, which places they could visit and finally, when they could or could not do all of these things on penalty of public lashings, ridicule or banishment.[98] While these regulations were poorly enforced, it is imperative to stress the implications of these restrictions for the public perception of women present in the urban space.[99] According to the bylaws, respectable women could travel the streets after dark, but only when they were accompanied by their husbands or male kin.[100] When women ventured into the night streets alone or in the company of unrelated men, they were automatically viewed and treated with suspicion. During the night of 3 May 1652, for example, the *sbirri* arrested Anna Maria Campana, a single local woman.[101] She denied being in the wrong because she was merely on her way to a tavern nearby her home to drink some wine. The case against her was suspended three days later for unknown reasons. By the seventeenth and eighteenth centuries, there was no such enforcement of restrictions on men's mobility in the city.[102]

Another crime category that is assumed to have received a decidedly gendered treatment is the one of sexual or moral transgressions. Many early modern European courts considered behaviours such as prostitution, adultery, fornication, concubinage, and illegitimacy as punishable criminal offences;

96 Rose, *A renaissance of violence*, 187-188.
97 Cohen, 'To pray, to work, to hear, to speak, 303.
98 *Bando generale Giustiniano 1610*, 60.
99 McCarthy, 'Prostitution, community and civic regulation,' 125, 127.
100 Cohen, 'To pray, to work, to hear, to speak,' 303.
101 ASBO, Torrone, 6609, fol. 166.
102 Gregory Roberts did still find an active policing and curfew charges against men in thirteenth century Bologna, see 'Vendetta, violence, and police power in thirteenth-century Bologna,' in S.R. Blanshei (ed.), *Violence and justice in Bologna: 1250-1700* (Lanham: Lexington Books, 2018) 6-7, 10, 21.

offences for which women were prosecuted disproportionally.[103] Bologna's criminal court saw relatively few of these kinds of cases: only 3 per cent of the defendants (45 men and 3 women among a total of 1419 offenders) were accused of these kinds of crimes of a sexual nature. That prostitution was taxed rather than criminalised in early modern Italy may be part of the explanation for the low numbers of women among those accused of moral crimes. The *Torrone* did furthermore not have complete control over cases relating to marriage and sexuality, as it was the archbishop's court that exercised jurisdiction over matrimonial disputes and crimes against the sacraments such as pre- and extramarital sexuality.[104] The few 'crimes of the flesh' that were brought within the purview of the *Torrone* predominantly concerned incidences of *stupro* – literally meaning 'rape,' but often used to designate not forced intercourse but rather consensual premarital sex followed by a broken marriage promise. Through the criminal court, the victim or her kin could try to negotiate a substitute dowry, as the official penalties for the violation of women ranged from public torture with the *strappado* to being sentenced to the galleys for ten years and even the death sentence.[105] Overall, the defendants accused of crimes of the flesh were rarely sentenced because of the importance of these infrajudicial negotiations.

Although there were important gender-specific characteristics of indicted crimes, the crimes of men and women in early modern Bologna were in many ways more similar than distinct. The Bolognese court records do not allow for a clear-cut differentiation between 'male' and 'female crimes.' Albeit a minority in statistical terms, women engaged in a wide range of deviant behaviours, from simple thefts to acts of aggression and violence, much like men did. Other scholars have argued in a similar vein. In an examination of theft in late medieval Bologna, Trevor Dean follows Garthine Walker in pointing out that the tendency of historians to emphasise the differences between men and women negates the many similarities that existed among them.[106] He proposes instead that gender should be regarded as a "multi-dimensional spectrum rather than a binary divide, in which masculine and feminine forms of behaviour are present [...] but alongside a broad band of shared, similar behaviours."[107] Distinct

103 Schwerhoff, 'Geslechtsspezifische Kriminalität,' 91; Van der Heijden, 'Criminaliteit en sexe,' 16.

104 Lombardi, 'Marriage in Italy,' 120, footnote 46; Angelozzi and Casanova, *Donne criminali*, 60; Ferrante, 'La sessualità come risorsa,' 995; *Bando generale Serbelloni 1756*, 92.

105 *Bando generale Serbelloni 1756*, 91.

106 Dean, 'Theft and gender,' 400.

107 Ibidem, 412.

about these criminal behaviours was above all how they were perceived and treated.

6 Gender Dynamics in the Sentencing of Crimes

How and to what extent men and women were prosecuted and sentenced for their crimes was decidedly influenced by gender norms and prosecution policies. The question of whether women benefitted from a milder or harsher treatment has been at the forefront of discussions about historical patterns of prosecution in relation to gender. According to the prevalent 'chivalry theory' legal professionals were inclined to treat women with leniency on the assumption of their weakness and need for protection.[108] This weakness was codified in Roman law through the notion of the *fragilitas* or *infirmitas sexus*, a status that in the interpretation of Renaissance jurists likened a woman's legal capacity to that of a child or handicapped person.[109] In the role of plaintiffs, women could be excluded from making criminal accusations and, as witnesses, their testimonies were theoretically regarded as less reliable than men's.[110]The chivalry theory furthermore assumes that legal professionals were generally paternalistically inclined to protect these 'weak women' by treating them with leniency.[111] This could mean that women's culpability was called into question, that they were not prosecuted for the same kinds of crimes, and that their sentences may have differed. Arguments like these have been made not only for Italy, but also for France, the French territories, Spain and England, despite ostensibly gender-neutral criminal codes.[112] Peter King and others have emphasised a possible leniency on the part of magistrates during the punishment process in England too: for a similar crime, women were treated less harshly.[113]

108 Angelozzi and Casanova, *Donne criminali*, 18-19; M. Graziosi, Women and criminal law. The notion of diminished responsibility in Prospero Farinaccio (1544-1618) and other Renaissance jurists,' in L. Panizza (ed.), *Women in Italian Renaissance culture and society* (Oxford: University of Oxford European Humanities Research Centre, 2000) 173.

109 Kuehn, 'Daughters, mothers, wives and widows,' 99 and Graziosi, 'Fragilitas sexus,' 20.

110 M. Graziosi, '"Fragilitas sexus." Alle origine della costruzione giuridica dell'inferiorità delle donne,' in N.M. Filippini, T. Plebani and A. Scattigno (eds), *Corpi e storia. Donne e uomini dal mondo antico all'età contemporanea* (Rome: Viella, 2002) 28; Graziosi, 'Women and criminal law,' 172; Kuehn, 'Daughters, mothers, wives and widows,' 99.

111 Angelozzi and Casanova, *Donne criminali*, 227-54; M. Graziosi, 'Women and criminal law,' 173.

112 Angelozzi and Casanova, *Donne criminali*, 47, 227-254; Graziosi, 'Women and criminal Law,' 173; Buttex, 'L'indulgence des juges?,' 41-65.

113 P. King, 'Gender, crime and justice in late eighteenth and early nineteenth-century England,' in M. Arnot and C. Usborne (eds.), *Gender and crime in modern Europe* (London:

The judicial leniency towards women was by no means a constant. Various scholars have argued that the treatment of men and women differed significantly per crime category.[114] While leniency may have been applied to women's violent misdeeds, crimes such as infanticide and witchcraft were excluded from such a milder treatment.[115] The judicial treatment of women also differed from one legal system to another and from place to place.[116] Contrary to King's assessment of various English towns, Walker, for example, argued that women were generally worse off than men in seventeenth-century Cheshire: women were disproportionally put on trial for homicide, were found guilty relatively more often than men, and were almost twice as likely to receive a death sentence.[117] Because the law embodied inherently male standards, homicides committed by men and women were not only perceived as intrinsically different, but, in addition to this, women had fewer chances of mitigating the death sentence as they could not appeal to the same exceptions as men. The Cheshire example underlines a close contextual examination of the law and penal practice is pivotal to the understanding of the relation between sentencing patterns and gender.

An important aspect about early modern criminal justice is that a significant proportion of the cases brought before criminal courts were never concluded with a formal sentence. This was also the case in early modern Bologna, where only one in five *processi* resulted in what Angelozzi and Casanova called 'real sentences,' such as the death penalty, incarceration, banishment, a sentence to the galleys, corporal punishment or fines (table 4).[118] Even including pardons this still only amounted to about one-third of the total caseload, regardless of gender. Just under half of the outcomes of *processi* were injunctions to compel parties to peace or to re-appear in court, sureties, and the halting of investigations for a variety of reasons such as insufficient evidence or the plaintiff's withdrawal of the complaint.

In the past these unconcluded cases were primarily viewed as the products of a highly flawed and inefficient judicial system, but scholars now emphasise the importance of other mechanisms. Drawing on other studies on criminal justice procedures in early modern Europe, Martin Dinges argued that the

UCL Press, 1999) 66-67; Palk, *Gender, crime, and judicial discretion*, 161, 176.

114 Buttex, 'L'indulgence des juges?,' 61; Angelozzi and Casanova, *Donne criminali*, 227-254; Sbriccoli, 'Deterior est condicio foeminarum,' 85-86.

115 Angelozzi and Casanova, *Donne criminali*, 230.

116 R.N. Tsakiri, 'Deviance and morals. A study of sixteenth-century Crete under Venetian rule. An initial exploration,' *Crimes and misdemeanor* 1:2 (2007) 166.

117 Walker, *Crime, gender and social order*, 113, 158, 197-201.

118 Angelozzi and Casanova, *Donne criminali*, 228, 230.

TABLE 4 Outcomes of Bolognese *processi* for identified defendants, ca. 1655-1755

	Female defendants		Male defendants		Total	
Real sentences[a]	15	21%	242	19%	257	19%
Pardoned (*gratia*)	6	9%	172	13%	178	13%
Secondary sentences[b]	12	17%	128	10%	140	10%
Cancelled[c]	22	31%	455	35%	477	35%
Unknown	15	21%	290	22%	305	22%
	70	100%	1287	100%	1357	100%

SOURCE: SAMPLE 1 (SEE APPENDIX), COUNTED BY IDENTIFIED DEFENDANT
a Include death sentence, galleys, exile, incarceration, corporal punishment, fine
b Include *precetto criminale*, surety
c Includes a small proportion of those found not guilty, as well as cases cancelled due to insufficient evidence and peacemaking.

number of cases without a formal conclusion were also the outcome of the strategic use of juridical procedures by ordinary men and women.[119] He argued that people often did not litigate solely to achieve a conviction from the court, but to try and negotiate other kinds of out-of-court settlements.[120] In this light, recourse to the court should be seen as part of a wider set of formal and informal means of social control. The authorities were also not that interested in punishing each crime that came before the criminal court. While normative writings like Bologna's summations of criminal bylaws prescribed harsh sentences for many crimes, criminal courts regularly mitigated the rigour of the law in practice.[121] They did so because, ultimately, their goal was to maintain peace and order, if possible by mending the inflicted societal wounds through peacemaking, giving pardons and reintegrating the culprit into the community.[122]

The importance of the objective of peacemaking and reintegration can be gleaned from the outcomes of Bologna's *processi*. Overall, about 13 per cent of

119 Dinges, 'The uses of justice,' 159-175; Dean, *Crime and justice in late medieval Italy*, 19-20; Niccoli, 'Rinuncia, pace, perdono,' 234.
120 Dinges, 'The uses of justice,' 161.
121 M. Bellabarba, *La giustizia nell'Italia moderna* (Bari: Editori Laterza, 2008) 84.
122 Rose, *A renaissance of violence*, 54.

the defendants were pardoned for their crimes and had their original sentences overturned. This is comparable to what we know about eighteenth-century Porto, where approximately 16 per cent of prisoners in the local gaol received a pardon.[123] Defendants could particularly expect to receive a pardon for acts of violence, where peacemaking between the offender and the victim or his/her family was believed to have restored the social equilibrium. In Bologna in 1600, nearly 40 per cent of convicted killers received a pardon.[124] The granting of pardons and exemptions in response to a petition was not just an Italian phenomenon, but was widespread and "fundamental to the manner of governing in early modern Europe."[125] Another one-third of the defendants saw the cases against them cancelled, either because they were truly deemed not guilty, because there was insufficient evidence or, not infrequently, because the complaint had been withdrawn by the plaintiff and a peace agreement was signed. Together, the pardon and the cancellation constituted nearly half of the *processi*'s outcomes.

Another 10 per cent of all defendants were discharged with a surety or a criminal injunction (*precetto criminale*). Angelozzi and Casanova distinguished these outcomes from 'real sentences' because the surety and the criminal injunction were ultimately conditional sanctions.[126] The surety entailed that the accused would be released by means of suretyship that he or she would represent themselves to the court at the request of the *Torrone*. This meant that the trial would be suspended until further notice, and could be reopened if new evidence was found.[127] The *precetto criminale* was an injunction that could be imposed for a wide variety of crimes that in one way or the other disturbed public order, and consisted of a conditional fine or sentence that would not be forfeited if the defendant upheld the requirements defined in the injunction.

Overall the outcomes were roughly comparable for female defendants and their male counterparts. Once a case was investigated by the *Torrone*, men and women had roughly the same chances of receiving 'real punishments' and of having the cases against them cancelled. Yet pardoning may have been a somewhat more prevalent outcome for male defendants. Addressing the question of sex ratios in pardoning in premodern France, Natalie Zemon-Davis argued that such a discrepancy was explained by the fact that the crimes traditionally

123 Abreu-Ferreira, *Women, crime and forgiveness*, 3.

124 Rose, *A renaissance of violence*, 91.

125 G. Hanlon, 'Violence and its control in the late Renaissance: An Italian model,' in G. Ruggiero (ed.), *A companion to the worlds of the Renaissance* (Oxford: Blackwell, 2002) 147.

126 Angelozzi and Casanova, *Donne criminali*, 230

127 Ibidem, 229.

associated with women, such as infanticide and witchcraft, were not pardonable.[128] While these were not the types of crimes for which women were investigated in seventeenth- and eighteenth-century Bologna, it does seem likely that the discrepancy was related to the types of crimes for which men and women were investigated. In proportional terms women's *processi* more often concerned property offences, while pardons were predominantly requested and granted for acts of violence and aggression.

Another interesting difference lies in the category of the 'secondary punishment' of the *precetto criminale*, or the criminal injunction. These were formal orders that held those who received them to the injunction on penalty of a hefty fine, corporal punishment or a sentence such as exile, the galleys or a death sentence. Women appear to have been nearly twice as likely to receive such an injunction as men. This discrepancy could be interpreted as an outcome of the perception of the less serious nature of women's crimes, ideas regarding gender-appropriate sentences, and/or as female defendants being treated with indulgence by a judge.[129]

The criminal injunctions that male and female defendants received also differed in their form. Among the denunciations, 'peace orders' (*precetto de non offendendo*) were most prominent, requiring offending parties to keep the peace. Among the *processi*, however, these peace orders made up only about one-third of the *precetti* received. Another one-third of the men receiving a criminal injunction were ordered to remain available to the court for any future interrogations (*precetto de se presentando*) when deemed necessary. The last third of the male recipients of a criminal injunction was instructed to better their lives and 'apply themselves' work-wise, i.e. get a job (*precetto de se applicando*). Occasionally, men received specific instructions, for example to treat their mother-in-law better, or not to visit the tavern at night.[130] For female defendants, the requirement to remain available for future questioning also made up a third of the criminal injunctions. Injunctions to keep the peace were far less prominent outcomes for female defendants in the *processi*, as only one out of 12 female defendants received a *precetto de non offendendo*. Orders for women to improve their lives (*precetto de bene vivendo*) were more prominent, but did not concern their working lives as they did for men. In five cases these injunctions came with specific instructions not to wander outside at night-time (*precetto de bene vivendo e de non vagando di notte*). This was not

128 Zemon Davis, *Fiction in the archives*, 85.

129 The same can be deduced from the data provided by Angelozzi and Casanova, although they themselves have not argued this. See Angelozziand Casanova, *Donne criminali*, 228-229.

130 For example see ASBo, Torrone, 7598-2, fasc. 41; 8171-2, fasc. 30.

TABLE 5 'Real sentences' among urban *processi* by seks, ca. 1655-1755

	Female defendants		Male defendants		Total	
Death penalty	0	0%	7	1%	7	1%
Banishment	11	16%	134	10%	145	11%
Galleys	0	0%	74	6%	74	5%
Incarceration	4	6%	19	1%	23	2%
Corporal punishment	0	0%	2	0%	2	0%
Fine[a]	0	0%	6	0%	6	0%
Other outcomes	55	78%	1052	83%	1107	82%
Total	70	100%	1287	100%	1357	100%

SOURCE: SAMPLE 1 (SEE APPENDIX), COUNTED BY DEFENDANT

a Includes both fines and the restitution of goods or a financial substitution as a sole outcome.

only true for the three cases that revolved around women who had wandered about at night, but also in one case of serious assault and one of attempted rape (either in a contemporary sense or as premarital sexual relations). Norms for appropriate sentences thus clearly bore gender distinctions.

Gender differences can also be discerned from the so-called 'real sentences.' While it was neither a requirement nor common practice to substantiate pronounced sentences in the criminal records, the judges' significant discretionary space resulted in some evidently gender-specific punishments. Both the prescriptions of sentences in the criminal bylaws and penal practice attest to this. The most pronounced example was the sentence to man the oars of the papal galleys in the Mediterranean Sea: a common punishment replacing death sentences from the seventeenth century onwards, never imposed on women.[131] Corporal punishments were also administered differently to men and women. For men the so-called *strappado* (better known in Italy as the *corda*, i.e. the rope) was the most common type of corporal punishment. It entailed a suspect being stripped down to the waist, having his hands tied behind his back and then being hoisted on a pole in the market or at the town

131 Terpstra, 'Theory into practice,' 123; Rose, *A renaissance of violence*, 52.

gate, followed by a predetermined number of jerks to the cord.[132] Women instead received a public whipping through the streets, without being undressed. As a sentence on its own, corporal punishment was very rare: it was more commonly used as an additional punishment before being banished or sent to the galleys, or as a conditional penalty for a breach of criminal injunctions (*precetto criminale*).

Other sentences were less gender-specific in their form. To be sentenced to death was very uncommon for both men and women in early modern Bologna. Executions were hardly a daily event, and furthermore declined significantly throughout the seventeenth century.[133] Out of the seven male defendants who received a death sentence, as many as five were convicted in the sample year of 1655, mostly for homicides. While my samples for Bologna do not contain any women sentenced to death, it was not necessarily a male preserve. Giancarlo Angelozzi and Cesarina Casanova have observed that two out of the 100 female defendants on trial for murder in their sample received a capital punishment, one in 1587 and the other in 1728.[134]

A much more common penalty than capital punishment was banishment. Like elsewhere in early modern Italy, *esilio* (often combined with the confiscation of goods) was the punishment most frequently imposed on defendants in Bologna.[135] Being convicted of theft was the most prevalent reason for banishment, followed by various often undefined acts of 'suspicious behaviour' associated with a mobile, unrooted lifestyle (about a quarter of those convicted). Incarceration was less common during the early modern period than it is today as it was regarded as unnecessarily cruel, unproductive and expensive. In the five years sampled for Bologna, 23 defendants were either sent to perform forced labour at *Forte Urbano* (only men), a military fort at the border of Bologna and Modena built between 1628 and 1634, at Bologna's poor house established in 1563 (mainly but not exclusively women), or were (more rarely) sentenced to a private incarceration.[136]

To what extent can these gender differences in sentencing be understood as a milder treatment stemming from the magistrates' chivalric attitude? According to Angelozzi and Casanova these sentencing patterns do reveal a certain indulgence towards female offenders. First, they argue that women's overall

132 Cohen and Cohen, *Daily life in Renaissance Italy*, 120 and Angelozzi and Casanova, *Donne criminali*, 231.

133 Ibidem, 120, 122; Terpstra, 'Theory into practice,' 123.

134 Angelozzi and Casanova, *Donne criminali*, 228-229.

135 Cohen and Cohen, *Daily life in Renaissance Italy*, 122.

136 *Le chiese parrocchiali della diocesi di Bologna, ritratte e descritte* (Bologna 1849), n.p., section 47 on 'Castelfranco'; Terpstra, *Cultures of charity*, 23, 40.

chances of receiving real sentences for their crimes were considerably slimmer than for men. They do not base this conclusion on the *processi* alone, but on the whole legal process: while about five per cent of all of denunciations against men resulted in a criminal sentence, this was only the case for a little over one per cent of female offenders.[137] Women were more often issued secondary sentences instead; a mechanism possibly related to the notion that certain crimes were perceived as less dangerous or threatening when committed by women. Petty violence especially, as we will also see in the next chapter examining the denunciations, was a much larger part of reported than of prosecuted crime. Although there was a general hesitancy to prosecute these kinds of offences in a full inquisitorial trial, scholars have argued that cases against women were much more likely to be recipients of the judge's clemency due to their assumed irrelevancy.[138]

Second, ideas about women's criminal responsibility and culpability were contingent on the context of the crime. Female offenders were in general taken less seriously by the *Torrone*'s judge if they had one or more male co-offenders. Regardless of whether women were accused of complicity or instigating the crime, the notion of a woman's weakness worked in her favour as she was then punished less severely than her male co-offenders, or not at all.[139] While a woman was certainly regarded as an actor capable of criminal behaviours, ideas regarding the 'qualities' of her person resulted in a gender-specific pattern of sentencing.

7 Conclusion: Distinguishing Features of Women's Prosecution

Indications that the criminal justice system's treatment of women was decidedly gendered are plentiful. As elsewhere in early modern Europe, the Bolognese authorities had a large *arbitrium* in deciding an appropriate penalty for a crime, in which one's sex was an important determinant. It is commonly believed that premodern women were able to benefit from judges' indulgence when they committed crimes not traditionally viewed as 'typically female.'[140] The early modern Bolognese *processi* support this idea, depending on the understanding of this leniency. For example, when subject to a formal investigation, there is little evidence that cases against female offenders were as a whole

137 Angelozzi and Casanova, *Donne criminali*, 230, 259.

138 Gray, 'The regulation of violence in the metropolis,' 79-81; Angelozzi and Casanova, *Donne criminali*, 259.

139 Angelozzi and Casanova, *Donne criminali*, 239, 242.

140 Buttex, 'L'indulgence des juges?,' 61; Angelozzi and Casanova, *Donne criminali*, 230.

annulled more often, but women did receive relatively more secondary sentences than their male counterparts – arguably as a result of their crimes being viewed as less serious or dangerous The observation that women who had offended alongside men were more likely to receive a lesser sentence, such as Diamante in the opening example, strengthens this argument.

While the differentiated treatment of men and women by criminal courts was no unique feature of the Bolognese case, other features were more salient. The examination of the *Torrone*'s investigation dossiers bring to the fore two important features: the first being the very large role that violence played in Bologna's criminal proceedings. *Antico regime* Italy has indeed commonly been described as a particularly violent society, distinguishable from northern European models of delinquency by its sustained and much higher share of violence.[141] As the chapter on violence will show, throughout the early modern period even the lower estimates of homicide rates for Italian towns were higher than the mean rates for other parts of Europe. Seventeenth- and eighteenth-century Bologna is no exception.

The second distinguishing feature of the Bolognese pattern of crime prosecution is the very low share of women among the offenders investigated, especially compared to northern European towns. This raises the question of the extent to which this low share of female offenders can be attributed to the dominant cultures of honour and violence, which are often described as distinctly masculine and prescribed passivity for women.[142] However, a careful reading of the court documents reveals distinctly that the *processi* were also the results of societal filters and biases.

One of the mechanisms that may have affected women's involvement in recorded crime was the existence of an extensive institutional web of care and control in early modern Italy. In discussing limitations to women's freedoms, it is often the household that is discussed as the unit of control, since the *pater familias* had considerable means of exerting informal control over his wife, children and servants.[143] As discussed in the previous chapter, what sets early modern Italy apart is the important role played by a host of semi-public

141 Calzolari, 'Delitti e castighi,' 55; Niccoli, 'Rinuncia, pace, perdono.' 223; Black, *Early modern Italy*, 188; Blastenbrei, *Kriminalität in Rom*, 284; M. Eisner, 'From swords to words. Does macro-level change in self-control predict long-term variation in levels of homicide?,' *Crime and justice* 43 (2014) 68, 80-81, 84.

142 Ruff, *Violence in early modern Europe*, 75; Brackett, *Criminal justice and crime*, 133-134.

143 Palazzi, 'Female solitude and patrilineage,' 445; Kuehn, 'Daughters, mothers, wives and widows,' 98; Cohen, 'Evolving the history of women,' 326; E. Canepari, 'Civic identity, "juvenile" status and gender in sixteenth and seventeenth-century Italian towns,' in D. Simonton, *The Routledge history handbook of gender and the urban experience* (London/New York: Routledge, 2017) 183-184.

charitable institutions in connecting spheres of control for women at the fringes of society.[144] Social control of women was accomplished through 'custody' by respectable relatives, marriage, convents and asylums where women could be sheltered and, if needed, reformed, and then reinstated in society with new or old husbands, in the care of relatives or other shelters. The care that these early modern institutions provided did not only reduce the need for women to engage in crime as a survival strategy, but likely also obscured deviant practices elsewhere brought within the purview of criminal court magistrates.

Early modern Italy's judicial culture also played an important role in the relative scarcity of criminal women among the formal investigation dossiers. Bologna's *processi* represent the cases for which the criminal court was willing and able to start an inquisition, demonstrating the authorities' concern in repressing lethal and life-endangering forms of violence as well as in crimes against property. Yet the *processi* only represented a fraction of the cases brought to the *Torrone*'s attention: after all, there were about nine denunciations for each formal inquisitorial trial.[145] The overwhelming majority of these far more plentiful denunciations concerned so-called 'minor crimes,' such as petty acts of violence, for which peacemaking and extrajudicial conflict resolution was encouraged. The shares of female offenders were much higher among these types of crimes, possibly because women's crimes were more readily regarded as 'petty' to begin with. The combination of the authorities' prosecutorial filter and a reconciliatory legal culture could therefore play a significant role in obscuring the prevalence of women's involvement in certain deviant behaviours. For this reason, a broader perspective that includes recorded (rather than indicted) crime will be employed in the next chapters.

144 Woolf, *The poor in Western Europe*, 24.

145 Angelozzi and Casanova, *La giustizia in una città di antico regime*, 565, 643.

4

Criminal Court and Conflict Resolution: Gender and Legal Agency

On 6 March 1755 Lucia Tessoni, a married spinner of stockings, was treated for a head wound at the Ospedale di Santa Maria della Morte, nearby what is known today as Bologna's Piazza Maggiore.[1] Notified by the surgeon who treated her 'suspicious wounds,' a notary from Bologna's criminal court visited Lucia at her bedside to ask what had put her in this precarious position.[2] The situation she described was that of a quarrel that escalated between her and her neighbour Gertrude Carolini. It started out with simple verbal insults, which Lucia decided to denounce to the criminal court. A month later, the two women encountered each other each other again in the loggia of their apartment building and Gertrude started insulting her once more. Lucia warned her that it would be wise to leave her alone; otherwise she would lodge a further complaint against her. As Gertrude replied that she feared nobody, the heated exchange escalated into a fight in which Lucia received blows to her head with a hammer; an attack from which Lucia died later that month.

While Lucia's recourse to the court ended up being in vain for her personally, this example stands as a testament to the agency of ordinary women as litigants – latitude that has had only little attention in earlier scholarship. The previous chapter discussed the offences that came before Bologna's early modern criminal court primarily from the perspective of the prosecution policies of the authorities. Like other early modern criminal courts, however, the *Torrone* was more than an instrument for the authorities to impose top-down control on its inhabitants. Examining in detail the separately stored denunciations will demonstrate the importance of Bologna's early modern criminal court as a forum for conflict resolution, employed instrumentally and strategically by men and women to pursue their grievances. It will also bring to the fore a richer tableau of women's crimes more representative of their everyday lives than the formal investigations could depict.

This chapter begins with the historiography on women's use of justice in early modern Europe. Together with prescriptive literature, the relatively weak legal position women had in Roman law has provided fuel for notions of a North-South divergence related to the access to and uses of justice. The first section will discuss recent works that call for caution and indicate that the

1 ASBO, Torrone, 8179-2, fasc. 2.

2 Blastenbrei, 'Violence, arms and criminal justice,' 70.

differences may have been less extreme than such a dichotomy suggests. The next section analyses the denunciations and explains that the types of cases brought before the criminal court diverge significantly from the prosecution pattern because of the court's role as a forum for conflict resolution. While this mechanism has been observed in most early modern European legal systems, it will shed light on some of the ways in which Italy's culture of peacemaking stands out. It then looks at who was able to access and use justice, and stresses the importance of unmediated access to the court for women. Lastly, it examines people's objectives in employing justice, ranging from a real call for intervention by the authorities to a threat and an improvement in the litigant's extrajudicial negotiation power.

1 Women and the Uses of Justice

Lucia's case against Gertrude is a good example of the way in which ordinary men and women employed the criminal court in their attempts to resolve their everyday conflicts. The notion that judicial institutions should not only be viewed as instruments of top-down control has been conceptualised by Dinges' 'uses of justice.' Drawing on other studies on early modern criminal justice procedures, he argued that the role of the courts in society was equally determined by the people who made instrumental and strategic use of justice as part of a wider set of formal and informal mechanisms.[3] These men and women did not employ justice solely to obtain a formal conviction from the court, but also – as Lucia's case demonstrates – to try and negotiate other kinds of out-of-court settlements.

It has been suggested that the ways in which people made use of the courts was gendered. Dinges suggests that the judicial records mention fewer women because women were more inclined to solve conflicts through other informal or extrajudicial forms of social control, such as the family or neighbourhood. Women's economically dependent position and legally subordinate status prevented them from making optimal use of generally expensive formal legal procedures.[4] Furthermore, there may in general have been different gender regimes that created more favourable conditions for women to access and make use of justice. Building on similar (though debated) hypotheses regarding labour force participation, residential arrangements and marriage patterns, the prevailing idea is that in Europe a North-South divide may have

3 Dinges, 'The uses of justice,' 161.
4 Ibidem, 167-168.

existed in relation to the opportunities that the different juridical and normative systems gave to women and men to perform public roles in society.[5] Although such a dichotomy has not in itself remained uncontested, Italian women's relatively weak legal position within the patriarchal criminal justice system has contributed to an overall idea of a culture characterised by subordination and constraint, while opportunities for women to participate in public life in northern Europe appear to have been more plentiful.[6]

In the past two decades, it has increasingly been shown how women were able to achieve considerable agency in the management and negotiation of their everyday lives through the instrumental use of law courts.[7] Much of the research on women's ability to negotiate early modern legal systems has focused on examinations of ecclesiastical courts. Studies on England and Germany have shown that these ecclesiastical courts facilitated the participation of female litigants in a greater number than other courts, and that women employed them to pursue slander and defamation, and above all to strengthen their household authority in marital disputes.[8]

Although ecclesiastical courts have been studied most extensively, they were by no means the only judicial forum employed by early modern women. Various studies have indicated a much larger presence of women as litigants among the lower criminal courts than was previously believed.[9] For seventeenth- and eighteenth-century London, it has been shown that battered wives and women who fell pregnant after rape were able to gain recompense through the relatively cheap system of recognizances, making use of gendered preconceptions concerning their physical vulnerability.[10] In seventeenth-century Cheshire these recognizances were also readily employed by women in cases of petty violence, binding over their assailants to peace and good behaviour

5 For an overview of the development of the notion of a distinct 'Mediterranean model' from the 1960s onwards, see Viazzo, 'What's so special about the Mediterranean?,' 111-137. Also see A. Bellavitis and B. Zucca Micheletto, 'Introduction: North versus South – gender, law and economic well-being in the fifteenth to nineteenth centuries,' in A. Bellavitis and B. Zucca Micheletto (eds.), *Gender, law and economic well-being in Europe from the fifteenth to the nineteenth century: North versus South?* (Abingdon: Routledge, 2019) 1-27.

6 An important scholar criticizing the North-South dichotomy is Zucca Micheletto, 'Reconsidering the southern Europe model,' 354-370; Viazzo, 'What's so special about the Mediterranean?,' 111-137.

7 For a recent historiographical assessment of the legal agency of English women, see Kane and Williamson, 'Introduction,' 1-16.

8 Kane and Williamson, 'Introduction,' 7; L. Gowing, *Domestic dangers. Women, words, and sex in early modern London* (New York: Oxford University Press, 1996); Schmidt, 'Hausväter vor Gericht,' 213-236.

9 For an overview, see Van der Heijden, 'Women, violence and urban justice,' 71-100.

10 Hurl-Eamon, *Gender and petty violence*, 49-64.

to assert their authority both in and outside the household.[11] An examination of London's eighteenth-century inexpensive summary courts has furthermore revealed that while assaults between women were often not taken seriously by prosecutors, 'plebeian' women nevertheless regarded these courts as useful public forums for arbitration that they could strategically utilise in the resolution of their violent conflicts with members of their neighbourhood community.[12]

Despite the strong emphasis on the patriarchal orientation of early modern Italian society, a growing body of scholarship increasingly recognises Italian women from all social groups as pragmatic users of the law and the various types of courts in conducting their daily lives. Notably, several important works on ecclesiastical courts in early modern Venice and Rome by Daniela Hacke, Joanne Ferraro and Daniela Lombardi have convincingly argued that while women were undoubtedly victims of patriarchal privilege and an inferior legal status, they did have legal agency and used the court to their advantage in matrimonial disputes.[13] The majority of matrimonial suits recorded came from women who called on the court to protect their well-being, manipulated neighbourhood opinion in order to forward their cause and drew on a series of tropes like violent marriages and sexual dysfunction to support their claims of separation or annulment.

What legal leeway Italian women had outside marital disputes or extramarital sexuality and before other forums has received less scrutiny. There is a broad conceptual consensus in Italian historiography about early modern justice being utilised rather than merely imposed, but there have been few studies specifically examining the gender dynamics of recourse to the law aside from marital disputes.[14] There is nevertheless evidence that women's use of other legal forums was not as uncommon as the historiographical silence may suggest. Angelozzi and Casanova's recent work on women's crimes in seventeenth- and eighteenth-century Bologna remarked that Italian women displayed a 'remarkable familiarity' with criminal justice. Without expanding the argument further, they asserted that the criminal court records reveal women

11 Ibidem, 65-90, 130-131; Walker, *Crime, gender and social order*, 75-112.

12 Gray, 'The regulation of violence in the metropolis,' 79-81.

13 Hacke, *Women, sex and marriage*; Ferraro, *Marriage wars*; D. Lombardi, 'Giustizia ecclesiastica e composizione dei conflitti matrimoniali (Firenze, secoli XVI-XVIII),' in S. Seidel Menchi and D. Quaglioni (eds.), *I tribunali del matrimonio (secoli XV-XVIII)* (Bologna: Mulino, 2001) 577-608; L. Ferrante, 'Marriage and women's subjectivity in a patrilineal system,' in M.J. Maynes et al (eds.), *Gender, kinship, power. A comparative and interdisciplinary history* (New York & London: Routledge, 1996) 115-130.

14 Cummins and Kounine, 'Confronting conflict in early modern Europe,' 4.

demonstrating their "capability of developing effective strategies of accusation and defence."[15] Elizabeth and Thomas Cohen also mention that the machinery of the law was used by ordinary Romans as an instrument of persuasion or chastisement. A woman's suit for rape, they assert, might have been a plot to either "snag a husband or extort a dowry."[16] Another study of sixteenth-century prostitutes' recourse to Rome's Governor's Court furthermore provides evidence for the extensiveness of the practice of criminal litigation that may have stretched to even the lowest, marginal reaches of society.[17] These works suggest that the opportunities women had to use justice in Italy may not have been as different as a simplified North-South model suggests – an inference that merits further investigation.

2 Denunciations before the *Torrone*

Both in Italian scholarship and elsewhere, a common critique of the quantitative analysis of criminal trials has been that they measure not the levels of actual criminal behaviour, but rather the functioning of the criminal justice apparatus.[18] It is argued that the cases that were tried by criminal courts mainly consisted of a selection of the crimes that occurred based on the state's knowledge of offences as well as its interests and prosecutorial priorities. The notion that the trials only represent a small fraction of actual criminal behaviour has been linked to the so-called 'dark number,' a concept referring to those crimes that occurred but were not reported or tried by the state or did not lead to a conviction, which therefore escape historians' awareness.[19] In this light scholars have argued that examinations of verdicts and sentences only provide a partial view and an underestimation of women's participation in the legal process.[20] Some have therefore begun examining alternative forms of legal

15 Angelozzi and Casanova, *Donne criminali*, 257.

16 Cohen and Cohen, *Words and deeds*, 20.

17 E.S. Cohen, 'Honor and gender in the streets of early modern Rome,' *Journal of interdisciplinary history* 22:4 (1992) 609.

18 E. Grendi, 'Premessa,' *Quaderni Storici* 66:3 (1987) 695-700; M. Sbriccoli, 'Fonti giudiziarie e fonti giuridische. Riflessioni sulla fase attuale degli studi di storia del crimine e delle giustizia criminale,' *Istituzioni giudiziarie, criminalità e storia* 29:2 (1988) 491-501. This is also reflected upon by for example Van der Heijden, *Women and crime*, 11; Kilday, *Women and violent crime*, 2.

19 Van der Heijden, *Women and crime*, 3.

20 Walker, *Crime, gender and social order*, 4.

action, such as prosecution by a recognizance, which featured much greater numbers of women in the roles of both complainants and offenders.[21]

In the case of many Italian cities it is possible to gain a broader view of legal action beyond trials by examining the denunciations, i.e. the criminal complaints. Formal statements about alleged crimes were lodged either by state officials or, much more commonly, by aggrieved parties or their kin. In Bologna these denunciations have been preserved in the casebooks of the *Torrone*'s eight notaries, who stored them separately from the trial dossiers. Because these denunciations represent all documented, reported crime, they were understandably much more plentiful than the *processi* (the investigation dossiers examined in the previous chapter). There were about nine complaints for every initiated formal investigation, amounting to thousands of denunciations each year.[22] Although these denunciations are by no means an unbiased representation of the entirety of offences that took place in the city of Bologna, they do allow us to gauge reported rather than prosecuted crime. They furthermore present an image that comes closer to the everyday reality of perceived criminality because of the absence of the state's filter of prosecutability as well as the sheer quantity of offences recorded.

The types of offences denounced to the court are shown in table 6. It indicates the distribution of offence categories among 1,358 defendants (903 men, 241 women and 214 offenders whose identity is unknown) for 1,054 criminal complaints sampled between the mid-seventeenth and mid-eighteenth centuries. The largest share of the reported offences was concerned with violence: over two-thirds of the defendants were accused of some kind of physical or verbal aggression. Property crime, mainly consisting of theft, burglary and fencing, but also (much more rarely) of pickpocketing and robbery, was the second most common offence reported to the criminal court. It was among these property crimes that complaints were made against unidentified offenders: over half of the thefts and burglaries from shops and houses were discovered hours after they had occurred and were reported to the court without any knowledge of who had committed the offence. About one-tenth of the denunciations centred on a range of public order for offences, such as the bearing of weapons within the city walls without a licence, not having the correct licence to stay in the city, begging and vagabondage, the violation of banishment and resisting the authorities. Sexual offences, as discussed before, were rarely denounced to the criminal court.

21 Ibidem, 5; Shoemaker, *Prosecution and punishment*, 207-216; Hurl-Eamon, *Gender and petty violence*, 129-130.

22 Angelozzi, and Casanova, *La giustizia in una città di antico regime*, 565, 643.

TABLE 6 Reported offences in urban denunciations, ca. 1655-1755

	Female defendant		Male defendant		Total[a]		Unidentified offender		Total in *processi*[b]
Violence	197	82%	602	67%	799	70%	4	2%	43%
Property	27	11%	163	18%	190	17%	209	98%	28%
Public order	11	5%	119	13%	130	11%	0	0%	26%
Sex	2	1%	5	1%	7	1%	0	0%	3%
Misc	4	2%	14	2%	18	1%	1	0%	1%
	241	100%	903	100%	1144	100%	214	100%	100%

SOURCE: SAMPLE 2 (SEE APPENDIX)
a Total excludes unidentified offenders
b Total from *processi* is derived from Chapter 3, table 3

The pattern of crimes denounced resembled that of the investigation dossiers (*processi*) in broad strokes, but there were also important differences, particularly for female defendants. As we have seen in the previous chapter, violence constituted the largest offence category among the *processi*, but featured even more prominently among the denunciations. In the *processi*, about 44 per cent of the male defendants were accused of various violent acts compared to two-thirds in the denunciations. Interestingly, the difference is even larger for women. While a third of the female defendants in the *processi* were charged with violence, women's violent acts made up 82 per cent of their reported crimes in the denunciations. This observation counters popular assumptions regarding women's passivity in violence and highlights the need for a reappraisal of stereotypical categorizations of 'male' and 'female' crimes. In Bologna the supposedly quintessential 'male crime' of violence bore much greater proportional importance to women's palette of recorded deviancy than that of men. Even though this is not reflected in what magistrates decided to take to trial, the records of women's violent encounters constitute an important point of departure to re-evaluate women's deviant behaviour in general, and what this tells us about their use of justice.

Another aspect that stands out from the denunciations compared to the formal investigations concerns the share of women among offenders. Bolognese women made up 21 per cent of the denounced offenders against a mere five per cent among the *processi*. The denunciations' higher female crime share was not dissimilar to those found among lower criminal jurisdictions elsewhere in early modern Europe.[23] A large share of these female protagonists 'vanished' from the casebooks during the judicial process; a mechanism partially attributable to magistrates' paternalistic attitude towards women's crimes. Yet this did not necessarily mean that these denunciations were futile from the perspective of complainants themselves. To understand why this was the case, we must delve deeper into the functioning of the criminal court and the objectives of litigation.

3 The *Torrone* as a Forum for Conflict Resolution

Discrepancies between crimes denounced and investigated stemmed not only from the magistrates' prosecution priorities, but also from the *Torrone*'s functioning as a forum for conflict resolution. Criminal complaints could reflect the authorities' concerns, as local officials denounced and captured people who acted against public order as described in the city's bylaws. But in the city of Bologna this only constituted a small fraction of the complaints recorded in the criminal casebooks: instead, the large majority of cases were brought within the court's purview by those who were wronged themselves. These aggrieved parties brought to the fore a large number of complaints concerning petty brawls with former friends, acquaintances, neighbours and co-workers; minor crimes among the lower classes that the judges were generally disinclined to prosecute in a full inquisitorial trial. The *Torrone*'s statutes specifically instructed magistrates not to pursue these types of crimes, and judges' manuals discussed alternative instruments appropriate for misdeeds such as these.[24] In general, these petty offences were treated very much as civil matters rather than criminal concerns, meaning that they were regarded as conflicts between individuals, warranting arbitration and compensation instead of punishment and reform. Interestingly, the *Torrone*'s magistrates accommodated inhabitants' use of the court as a forum for conflict resolution, and are in fact believed to have played an active role in encouraging and pressuring victims and their kin to accept their enemies' peacemaking attempts.[25]

The extent to which inhabitants were able to utilize criminal courts for the purpose of conflict resolution was intimately tied to the historical development of the legal system. Composition and peacemaking had a central

23 Van der Heijden, 'Women, violence and urban justice,' 71-100.

24 Angelozzi and Casanova, *La giustizia in una città di antico regime*, 391; F. Mirogli, *Istruzzioni teorico-prattiche criminali di Filippo Mirogli Romano fiscal generale dedicate alla santita di nostro signore Clemente PP.XIII. Tomo primo* (Rome 1758) 80.

25 Rose, *A renaissance of violence*, 54.

function in early modern criminal justice. It aimed to re-integrate the assailant into the fabric of society and was a remnant of the older forms of community justice that customarily occurred extra-judicially. As justice became more hegemonic during the early modern period, communities gradually lost the right to settle disputes themselves. Pardoning by the authorities remained an active component of the justice system throughout the early modern period, as did peacemaking procedures in newly established summary and peacemaker courts at the lower end of the criminal justice system across England and the continent.[26] Overall, however, it is believed that the increasing institutionalisation and centralisation of judicial administration entailed for communities an overall decline or even disappearance of power to negotiate.[27]

The mixing of law and reconciliation bears particular relevance for the history of crime and criminal justice in Italy. Some scholars have pointed to the intricate relationship between Italy's pervasive culture of peacemaking and the relative social acceptance, legitimacy, and comparatively higher rates of violence.[28] During the early modern period peacemaking procedures were not repealed but incorporated into the states' developing structures of judicial administration, encouraging arbitration among its plaintiffs and defendants and favouring social harmony over formal judicial intervention.[29] Although early modern Italian states had an inquisitorial legal system, some accusatory procedures related to peacemaking survived.[30] Crime victims and their close kin had the right to lodge an accusation against assailants and also had the right to withdraw this complaint following composition. The exact regulations regarding this right to withdraw differed from city to city, and varied over time, but it is clear that plaintiffs before Italian courts had a legitimate and recognised

26 P. King, 'The summary courts and social relations in eighteenth-century England,' *Past & Present* 183 (2004) 126-127; Gray, 'The regulation of violence in the metropolis,' 76; G. Vermeesch, 'Reflections on the relative accessibility of law courts in early modern Europe,' *Crime, history & societies* 19:2 (2015) 53-76.

27 A. Bettoni, 'Fama, shame punishments and the history of justice in the sixteenth and seventeenth centuries,' in J. Rowbotham, M. Muravyeva and D. Nash (eds.), *Shame, blame and culpability. Crime and violence in the modern state* (London: Routledge, 2013) 35-36; B. Lenman and G. Parker, 'The state, the community and the criminal law in early modern Europe,' in V.A.C. Gatrell, B. Lenman and G. Parker (eds.), *Crime and the law. The social history of crime in Western Europe since 1500* (London: Europa Publications, 1980) 40.

28 Cummins, 'Forgiving crimes in early modern Naples,' 255; Cummins, and Kounine, 'Confronting conflict in early modern Europe,' 9; Broggio and Caroll, 'Violence and peacemaking in early modern Europe,' 5; Rose, 'Homicide in North Italy,' 20; O. Niccoli, *Perdonare*, 38-39.

29 Bellabarba, 'Pace pubblica e pace privata,' 189-213.

30 Cummins, 'Forgiving crimes in early modern Naples,' 260-261.

basis for negotiation outside of formal judicial intervention.[31] The *Torrone* should therefore be seen as a prosecutorial body, a place for summary justice procedures, and as a forum for peacemaking.

The development of an accessible criminal justice system promoting conflict resolution in Bologna was furthermore encouraged by some specific local political developments. According to Rose the establishment of the *Torrone* as a new, professional criminal court with firm representation of papal authority served to undercut the power of the powerful, rebellious local elite by expanding the papal authority's hold on the community.[32] As a free and relatively efficient and reliable forum for conflict resolution, the *Torrone* functioned as an alternative to the capricious and now illegal feudal courts. The inhabitants' use of the criminal justice system was thus considered pivotal to the consolidation of state power and, indeed, men and women increasingly flocked to the court to resolve their conflicts.

In Bologna under papal rule, law and the informal practice of dispute resolution mixed throughout all stages of the criminal justice procedure. The denunciation was not always a request for formal state intervention, but could also function as a stepping stone to settle the conflict out of court. Instruments of infrajudicial conflict settlement included the well-known notarised peace contracts and petitions for pardon.[33] They also encompassed a range of underexamined semi-informal settlement procedures in which the court's magistrates acted as arbiters, or, perhaps even more commonly, where the mere act of lodging a complaint set reconciliation in motion. The denunciations bear witness to manifold strategies in employing the criminal court to settle conflicts, which will be explored in more detail later on in this chapter. Rather than being emblematic of the authorities' prosecution policies, a large proportion of these criminal complaints are indicative of the interests, priorities and strategies of the plaintiffs.

4 The Urban Context of Women's Litigation

While the *Torrone* presented itself as an accessible, reliable and free forum for conflict resolution, there were certain impediments to accessing it. In theory, inhabitants from even the most remote hamlets in the territory could bring

31 Niccoli, 'Rinuncia, pace, perdono,' 234; Cohen and Cohen, *Words and deeds in Renaissance Rome*, 16, 26.

32 Rose, *A renaissance of violence*, 43.

33 Cummins, 'Forgiving crimes in early modern Naples,' 255; Cummins and Kounine, 'Confronting conflict in early modern Europe,' 9.

conflicts to the court through an elaborate intelligence network of local officials. In practice, however, location mattered. Bologna's legal territory of 4,000 square kilometres was vast and mountainous, and the *Torrone* was situated in the city centre of Bologna. Most people from the countryside understandably relied heavily on the official go-betweens to reach the criminal court: over 90 per cent of the cases in the countryside were brought by a *massaro*. In the city of Bologna individuals could also reach out to local officials such as the *ministrale*, the *massaro*'s urban counterpart, but could furthermore decide to make a complaint to a notary of the court in person. In the city the large majority of denunciations were made by the victims themselves. The share of urban female litigants was also considerably higher: compared to the countryside, urban women were more than twice as likely to make a denunciation.

Risks and opportunities specific to the urban environment engendered higher shares of women among urban litigants. Women's litigation was intimately tied to the share of female criminals before the court, since many of the denunciations against female offenders were made by other women. One aspect of the urban environment observed across early modern Europe was that female crime was more prevalent than in rural areas. John Beattie was among the first to explain the urban-rural disparity in female crime shares for early modern England by arguing that women in cities lived more independent and public lives.[34] They had a wider range of economic opportunities and more social contacts, but lacked at the same time the support networks and the communal informal control that could keep women out of the criminal justice system. Evidence from criminal courts in various Dutch, French and English towns has also demonstrated that it was precisely the combination of their independence and vulnerability that contributed to the high crime shares in the urban context.[35] In Bologna women's crime shares were also higher in the city than in the countryside. Angelozzi and Casanova explained this discrepancy by pointing to the freedom of the city, the less extensive social control exerted by the male authority, the neighbourhood and the parish, as well as the greater opportunities for socialisation that led to more occasions for conflict.[36]

34 Beattie, 'The criminality of women,' 80-116.

35 Schmidt and Van der Heijden, 'Women alone,' 21-38; Van der Heijden, 'Women, violence and urban justice,' 71-100; K. Lambert, *Itinéraires féminins de la deviance. Provence 1750-1850* (Aix-en-Provence: Presses Universitaires de Provence, 2012); D.D. Gray, *Crime, prosecution and social relations. The summary courts of the city of London in the late eighteenth century* (Basingstoke: Palgrave Macmillan, 2009); Shoemaker, *Prosecution and punishment*, 208-209.

36 Angelozzi and Casanova, *Donne criminali*, 69.

The Bolognese case furthermore highlights the factor of access to justice. Robert Shoemaker suggested that the high share of female litigants in urban areas was related to the fact that they were less likely to have access to informal mediators such as local landowners or the clergy.[37] The denunciations from Bolognese countryside villages are suggestive of the role of the *massaro* in this process. Ordered to relay crimes that occurred within their assigned territory to the *Torrone*, these local officials likely functioned as mediators and arbiters in local conflicts in Bologna's surrounding villages. While fights between men made it into the *massaro*'s casebooks, records of women's deviant behaviours were far sparser. According to the dominant 'urban freedom and vulnerability'-thesis women's crimes may have been less prevalent in rural areas, making it necessary for fewer women to complain to the *massaro*. Another scenario is that rural women succeeded better than their urban counterparts in resolving their conflicts informally.

A more pessimistic assessment is that rural women simply had fewer opportunities to use judicial instruments. Angelozzi and Casanova have argued that the sheer dependency on the local officials to register and report matters to the criminal court may have particularly restrained women's possibilities in bringing cases within the court's purview. They asserted that women's complaints were more likely to be deemed unworthy of the *massaro*'s time investment necessary to write down complaints and to investigate the offence.[38] Women's disputes and petty crimes were therefore less likely to be relayed to the *Torrone* than men's because of their perceived unimportance. While women's disputes may have also been settled to their satisfaction through these informal means, it is important to note that not only women's preferences determined their involvement of the law. Particularly in the countryside, practical restraints could be decisive.

In the urban environment Bolognese women had better opportunities to formally bring their grievances before the criminal court because they did not have to rely on the assessment, judgment and intervention of a third party. It has been noted that women in the city of Bologna were much more likely to lodge a complaint against their husbands, fathers and brothers for subjecting them to violence, abuse and humiliation than in the countryside, where these matters were either dealt with without resorting to justice or were handled informally by the *massaro*.[39] The examination of the denunciations demonstrates that the same is true for other types of offences, such as physical or

37 Shoemaker, *Prosecution and punishment*, 209.

38 Angelozzi and Casanova, *Donne criminali*, 70, 257.

39 Ibidem, 118.

verbal injury. Urban women's greater access to justice impacted the kinds of offences recorded in the casebooks. The ability to lodge a complaint brought with it a new set of possibilities to negotiate and manipulate the outcomes of their disputes. The urban environment may not have provided only a more precarious context that may have prompted deviant behaviour, but it also offered women who were the victims of crime better opportunities to resolve conflicts through the criminal justice system.

5 The Users of Justice

Who were these women and men appearing before the court to pursue their grievances? In recent years, scholars have called attention to the need to be more specific about which sections of early modern communities made use of justice systems. Importantly, in her historiographical survey of works on both civil and criminal courts, Griet Vermeesch argued for a more socially differentiated analysis of the category of 'ordinary people' who were able to draw on formal legal infrastructures to be able to better assess the developments in the accessibility and functioning of early modern law courts.[40] In a similar vein, Cohen argued that the catch-all term of 'women' needs to be broken up into differentiating aspects that drastically affected the experiences of activities like litigation alongside gender, such as social class and life cycle.[41] Whether and under which circumstances women could bring their grievances before the court themselves, or through a legal guardian, was also of importance.

It is generally assumed that in Italy 'ordinary people' were able to employ judicial instruments and courts and instruments in the resolution of their conflicts, but to what extent these ordinary people included women is often not clear. The most explicit evidence on this topic comes not from criminal or civil courts, but from studies on notarial arbitration during the Renaissance period. Based on the records of one Florentine notary, Thomas Kuehn put forward that arbitration was a rather open system used by 'all sorts of people.'[42] Both Andrea Zorzi's and Katherine Jansen's works on thirteenth- and fourteenth-century notarial peace contracts in Florence confirm this view, stating (without elaborating) that the protagonists of notarial peace settlements were generally not aristocratic magnates, but ordinary people, ranging from "humble

40 Vermeesch, 'Reflections on the relative accessibility of law courts,' 56, 68.

41 Cohen, 'Evolving the history of women,' 326.

42 Kuehn, 'Law and arbitration,' 36.

paupers, servants and shoemakers" to wealthier artisans and merchants.[43] For fourteenth-century Reggio Emilia, Joanna Carraway Vitiello similarly argues that peacemaking was used by people of every social standing, both men and women.[44] That these conclusions about the broad participatory basis of private arbitration are also relevant for criminal litigation seems plausible, since private concords could and frequently did halt prosecution before formal legal tribunals.

Some other scholars have called the broad participation of ordinary men and women in the legal process into question. Shona Kelly Wray was among the most explicit critics of this notion based on her examination of private notarial arbitration in fourteenth-century Bologna. She too included peace agreements in her study, but placed them among other notarial compromises that primarily involved the transfer of property to conclude that, overall, most of the disputants actually belonged to the rather narrow societal stratum of the landed elite.[45] She furthermore noted that even the peace acts, which have been described as daily occurrences among all walks of life, were above all a male endeavour: about nine per cent of the disputants were female, but only about one per cent of the offenders.[46] While she posits a different perspective on the social composition of users of the law, Wray does remark that people were nevertheless probably more familiar with notarial culture than with the courts, which in her estimation remained foreign to especially women, poor and rural residents.[47]

Studies on later periods are more unanimous in their assessment that litigation in Italy was open to men and women from all walks of life. James Shaw's study on civil litigation in sixteenth- and seventeenth-century Venice argues that while women were underrepresented in the civil court, making up six per cent of all plaintiffs and ten per cent of all defendants, civil litigation was common among the lower classes who sought recompense for crimes, resulting in small claims.[48] Before the ecclesiastical court during the same period, women constituted the largest proportion of litigants. In her work on marital litigation in sixteenth- and seventeenth-century Venice, Joanna Ferraro calculated that

43 Jansen, 'Pro bono pacis,' 428; Zorzi, 'Legitimation and legal sanction,' 34.

44 J. Carraway Vitiello, *Public justice and criminal trial in late medieval Italy* (Leiden, Brill: 2016) 186.

45 S.K. Wray, 'Instruments of concord. Making peace and settling disputes through a notary in the city and contado of late medieval Bologna,' *Journal of social history* 42:3 (2009) 735.

46 Ibidem, 745.

47 Ibidem, 751.

48 J.E. Shaw, *The justices of Venice. Authorities and liberties in the urban economy, 1550-1700* (Oxford: Oxford University Press, 2006) 19, 166.

TABLE 7 Information about marital and occupational status in the denunciations, ca. 1655-1755

	Women				Men			
	Defendant (N=241)		Plaintiff (N=331)		Defendant (N=903)		Plaintiff (N=877)	
Only marital status	76	32%	168	51%	37	4%	32	4%
Only occupation	32	13%	23	7%	453	50%	460	52%
Both	24	10%	62	19%	52	6%	16	2%
Neither	109	45%	78	24%	361	40%	369	42%

SOURCE: EXTRACTED FROM SAMPLE 2 (SEE APPENDIX)

women made up 75 per cent of petitioners before the ecclesiastical court.[49] She also mentions that while the petitioners ranged across the social spectrum, patricians were fewer than the people from the 'common orders,' i.e. middle-to-lower classes, such as weavers, bricklayers, textile workers, merchants and fruit vendors. She suggests that this meant that men and women of all classes "in this urban centre thought they had a real chance to change their domestic circumstances."[50]

Less is known about the individuals who appeared before early modern Italy's criminal courts as defendants or plaintiffs. While it is assumed that 'ordinary' men and women also employed criminal justice procedures to pursue their grievances, who these commoners were has remained largely unstudied, especially as far as women are concerned.[51] This is understandable from the perspective of the source material. As others have noted, the characteristics of wealth and status that marked social division during the early modern period were fluid, and the language of social description was imprecise.[52] In the Bolognese casebooks recordings of these markers of identity were inconsistent and incomplete, especially at the earliest stages of judicial processes, and furthermore reveal a gendered skew in the information provided (table 7). Factors such as provenance and age are meaningful and important, but were sparsely

49 Ferraro, *Marriage* wars, 29.
50 Ibidem.
51 Cummins and Kounine, 'Confronting conflict in early modern Europe,' 4; Niccoli, *Perdonare*; Cohen, 'Honor and gender in the streets of early modern Rome,' 597-625.
52 T. Hitchcock and R. Shoemaker, *London lives. Poverty, crime and the making of the modern city, 1690-1800* (Cambridge: Cambridge University Press, 2015) 4.

recorded in the denunciations. What will be treated here are the occupational and marital statuses of plaintiffs and defendants.

Occupation or information on estate was far more commonly recorded for men than for women. The *Torrone*'s casebooks provide information for over half of the men and about a quarter of the women involved in criminal disputes during the mid-seventeenth and mid-eighteenth centuries. The notion that common city dwellers engaged in litigation is reflected in the wide range of occupations recorded in the Bolognese criminal court proceedings. While many nocturnal burglars of houses and workshops remained unidentified, most of those that were identified did not belong to the margins of society, regardless of whether they were men or women. For their livelihood, defendants and plaintiffs of both sexes performed a wide range of professions, from servants, labourers, market vendors, and struggling textile workers, to shopkeepers, skilled master artisans and some public officials such as notaries, and even the occasional beggar found their way to the court to lodge a complaint. Most of the complaints concerned conflicts between those of similar social status. That a broad band of ordinary men and women appeared in the *Torrone*'s records not only as defendants but also as plaintiffs was in part due to the lack of financial barriers. Whereas civil litigation and notarial peace accords were costly, denunciations to Bologna's criminal court could be made at little to no cost.

As opposed to information on occupation or estate, marital status is far more often recorded for women than for men in the criminal court documents. Women were often listed as 'daughter of,' 'wife of' or 'widow of,' whereas men were always referred to as 'son of,' meaning that their marital status must be gleaned from secondary evidence in the denunciations. Such information is provided for the large majority (70 per cent) of the female plaintiffs before Bologna's early modern criminal court, and for 42 per cent of the female defendants, but for less than ten per cent of the male accusers and accused. Nicole Castan also observed this discrepancy in her eighteenth-century French sources, and suggested that the scarcity of this information for men was due to the fact that men's social position was determined far less by marital status than women's was.[53] There was a notable prevalence of married offenders and victims: of the plaintiffs and defendants before the *Torrone* whose marital statuses have been recorded, the married group was largest, followed by the unmarried (as in never-married) group and only lastly those who were widowed (table 8).

Judicial documents elsewhere in early modern Europe also reveal similar patterns, though scholars question to what extent this means that it was

53 Castan, *Les criminels de Languedoc*, 36-37.

TABLE 8 Marital statuses of defendants and plaintiffs in the denunciations, ca. 1655-1755

	Women				Men			
	Defendant (N=241)		Plaintiff (N=331)		Defendant (N=903)		Plaintiff (N=877)	
Unmarried	14	6%	36	11%	17	2%	5	1%
Married	84	35%	176	53%	71	8%	42	5%
Widowed	2	1%	18	5%	1	0%	1	0%
No data	*141*	*59%*	*101*	*31%*	*814*	*90%*	*829*	*94%*

SOURCE: EXTRACTED FROM SAMPLE 2 (SEE APPENDIX)

predominantly married women who sought out and encountered the law. For the recognizances in seventeenth- and eighteenth-century Middlesex, Robert Shoemaker argued that only the marital status of married women was recorded systematically. He therefore assumed that the women whose marital status was not described (71 per cent of all women in his samples) were probably predominantly unmarried.[54] This led him to conclude that urban single women were most likely to enter into disputes and settle their disputes in or through the court. While it is indeed important to consider the implications of this underreporting, I am unconvinced that all plaintiffs and defendants without a recorded marital status in Bologna's criminal court records were unmarried. Another explanation for the large proportion of married women in the casebooks may be found in the *Torrone*'s function as a forum for conflict resolution: before English's courts too, wives constituted significant proportions of plaintiffs and defendants in assault cases.[55]

Married or not, it is important to stress that most of the urban women brought their own complaints to early modern Bologna's criminal court. Only in fewer than five per cent of the cases and almost exclusively for higher-class women did husbands, fathers, sons or employees make a denunciation in their name. While Renaissance Florence women's legal scope of action is thought to have diminished due to the requirement of legal guardians before the court, seventeenth- and eighteenth-century Bolognese women known to make denunciations for their young sons and also sporadically for their husbands.[56]

54 Shoemaker, *Prosecution and punishment*, 209.

55 Walker, *Crime, gender and social order*, 76; Beattie, 'The criminality of women,' 102, 106-107.

56 Cohn, 'Women in the streets, women in the courts,' 38; Angelozzi and Casanova, *Donne criminali*, 463.

While *antico regime* Italy's women were normatively protected first by their fathers, husbands or legal guardians, it is clear that this did not necessarily shield them from engaging in criminal behaviour, nor did it prevent them from seeking redress through a criminal court. The different ways in which litigation could serve ordinary men and women in settling their everyday conflicts will be discussed in the next sections.

6 Objectives of Litigation

Making a denunciation to the criminal court was a means to various possible ends. What did men and women hope to get from going to the criminal court? The court records speak to the existence of at least three possible objectives that will be explored in the following paragraphs: the initiation of a criminal prosecution, the bolstering of one's negotiation power, and a hybrid form combining negotiation alongside judicial interference. The wish to initiate a formal prosecution was not perceived as the sole function of the criminal court, but early moderners did certainly look to the criminal courts to seek justice in the sense of a legal conviction of their adversaries. In the *Torrone*'s records we can find references to the desired outcome of castigation by the authorities. In 1674, for example, Barbara, wife of Sabatino Barache, made a denunciation against her neighbour Francesca, who had not only insulted her with many injurious words, but had also damaged two pots and flowers in her yard by throwing stones.[57] In Barbara's eyes this was clearly retaliation for an earlier incident between their daughters. She concluded her complaint by stating that she was making this denunciation so that Francesca would be castigated.[58]

These kinds of requests were quite common among the seventeenth- and eighteenth-century denunciations. As a matter of fact, the objective of having the antagonist reprimanded occurred often and in a largely standardised form. In addition to the broad request for castigation, plaintiffs would ask for fair punishment. In his denunciation, innkeeper Giacomo Borelli, for example, describes wanting Gio Francesco Rossi punished 'according to what the judicial system prescribed' after realising Rossi had attempted to engage a contract killer as a way to avoid having to pay his debts.[59]

57 ASBO, Torrone, 7028, fol. 20-21.

58 Ibidem: "gle ne dò la querela, per che siano castigati."

59 ASBO, Torrone, 6609, fol. 100: "gli ne do querela, et faccio instantia che il medemo Rossi venghi punito conforme vuole la giustitia."

TABLE 9 Outcomes of denunciations for theft and violence in urban Bologna, ca. 1655-1755

	Unknown outcome		Withdrawn		Cancelled		Surety or *precetto criminale*		Indicted		Total
Theft	84	56%	12	8%	15	10%	14	9%	24	16%	149
Violence[a]	337	42%	184	23%	55	7%	201	25%	22	3%	799

SOURCE: EXTRACTED FROM SAMPLE 2 (SEE APPENDIX), COUNTER PER IDENTIFIED OFFENDER

a The category of violence includes homicide, physical violence resulting in life-endangering wounds, petty physical violence, verbal aggression and the miscellaneous acts of aggression receiving a *precetto criminale*

The appeal to court intervention is perhaps clearest in the case of theft. In more than half of the complaints concerning thefts and burglaries, the plaintiff came to the court despite expressing having no knowledge about who the culprit was. As we will see in chapter six, the authorities nevertheless took these kinds of crimes very seriously by the authorities and if caught perpetrators could face a harsh sentence. Asking for intervention by the authorities did not only mean that the offender would be punished for stealing, but could moreover entail that the retrieved stolen goods would be returned to the injured party. Compared to violent quarrels, mentions of out-of-court settlements were significantly less common for denunciations of theft (table 9). Less than one in ten of accused thieves saw the cases against them withdrawn (*rinuncia*), while complaints against violent offenders were renounced following a settlement in nearly a quarter of the cases.

At the same time, chances of a theft denunciation leading to an indictment and formal investigation also seem to have been higher. Although the administration of subsequent judicial steps was patchy at best, at least 16 per cent of the complaints were followed up by a formal investigation. These were much better odds than for many other offences such as physical violence. Chances of a formal investigation of the case and the possibility of retrieving the stolen goods provided a clear incentive for victims to make an appeal for the prosecution of thieves.

Motives beyond formal intervention often played a role too, regardless of what plaintiffs stated as their reasons for bringing their complaint within the criminal court's purview. The case of the aforementioned Barbara against her neighbour Francesca for insult and property damage, for example, unfolded in a way that so many did: it ended up in a withdrawal of the complaint presumably following an extrajudicial financial settlement.[60] In doing so she followed an established pattern, as by far most of the complaints lodged by litigants of both genders did not result in a 'full trial.' When presented to the court's magistrates, peace agreements – official, notarised documents that brought settlement to a dispute between two quarrelling parties – could and frequently did halt criminal investigations.[61] The simple juridical withdrawal of the complaint (the *rinuncia*) bore less social weight than a peace agreement, but was nevertheless an established part of the legal process used by men and women of all social strata. Rita Mariani's study of criminal justice in Crevalcore, a village in the Bolognese countryside also subject to the authority of the *Torrone*, illustrates how roughly a third of all denunciations between 1633 and 1642 were withdrawn by plaintiffs – highlighting once more the fundamental incorporation of negotiation and conflict resolution into the early modern Italian criminal justice system.[62]

Rather than a straightforward request for court prosecution, litigation must also be viewed as part of a negotiation process.[63] Based on his reading of various European studies on criminal justice, Dinges argued that plaintiffs of both genders were well aware of the threat emanated by a charge, and tried to employ it as a coercive measure in conflict resolution.[64] The act of the denunciation to the criminal court added a formal dimension to the negotiation that was considered at the very least to be troublesome to the defendant, and potentially also threatening and shameful. Cohen, in her examination of criminal court proceedings concerning house-scorning in sixteenth-century Rome, has suggested that the act of litigation gave the victims a way to bring down shame on their attackers.[65] That litigation was considered a part of the negotiation process is confirmed in the Bolognese sources. In 1674, Domenica Galli tried convince fellow market vendor, Antonio di Silvestrone, to stop insulting her on a daily basis, by threatening to lodge a criminal complaint against him.[66] Unfortunately for her, he seemed rather unconcerned with the prospect, and told her to go for it.

60 ASBO, Torrone, 7028, fol. 20-21.

61 Nubola, 'Giustizia, perdono, oblio,' 33.

62 R. Mariani, 'Criminalità e controllo sociale nella Crevalcore,' 71-73.

63 Cummins and Kounine, 'Confronting conflict in early modern Europe,' 6.

64 Dinges, 'The uses of justice,' 163; C. Lansing, 'Conflicts over gender in civic courts,' in J.M. Bennett and R. Mazo Karrass (eds.), *The Oxford handbook for women and gender in medieval Europe* (Oxford: Oxford University Press, 2013) 119.

65 Cohen, 'Honor and gender in the streets of early modern Rome,' 624.

66 ASBO, Torrone, 7028, fasc. 26.

Ambivalence was not a standard response to having been accused of an offence in a court of law. Many plaintiffs in fact found themselves harassed by the defendants after making a denunciation, with demands to retract it and clear their name.[67] In 1705 Andrea Mascagni referred to the complaint made against him three years earlier by his former female employers as a heavy burden, and requested it be retracted.[68] That this could happen even years after the fact, demonstrates that a criminal complaint was not considered a triviality. Defendants did not necessarily limit themselves to merely inquiring about a possible withdrawal either. In March of 1675 Francesca Pochettini found herself chased down the street by a dagger-wielding man called Donnino, against whom she had lodged a complaint some two months earlier for unspecified 'insolences.'[69] Rather than withdrawing the complaint, she reported her assailant again. Another example comes from the complaint against Pavolino Balini, who insulted, hit and threatened to kill his fellow coachman Rafael di Negrini with a sword in his hand after he had refused to withdraw a complaint from four years earlier.[70] After several troublesome encounters, Rafael lodged a new complaint, declaring that he feared for his life after Pavolino had come to his house in the middle of the night. Later that day, an agreement was apparently reached and the complaint was withdrawn. These examples illustrate how litigation was not always a clear-cut request of formal intervention by the authorities per se. Instead, the pressure of an official criminal denunciation was used by ordinary men and women in the negotiation of their interests within the community.

The Bolognese casebooks also reveal hybrid objectives between hoping to achieve concrete action from the authorities and the bolstering of the plaintiff's bargaining power. The appeal to specific legal instruments such as the peace injunction is a good example of this objective, calling into play mechanisms of negotiation, empowerment and shaming alongside judicial interference. This is illustrated by the case of Bolognese biscuit seller Ignazia Odorici, who appeared before one of the *Torrone*'s notaries to file a complaint against Francesca Tacchini, a seller of used goods, on 23 December 1755. Francesca had a way of finding Ignazia wherever she went and always insulted and threatened her. While the underlying causes of the dispute remain undisclosed, Ignazia emphasised that this was a long-lasting conflict that she had been unable to settle herself through other measures. After a particularly vexing day when

67 ASBO, Torrone, 7606-1, fasc. 278; 7606-1, fasc. 81.

68 ASBO, Torrone, 7606-1, fasc. 27-30.

69 ASBO, Torrone, 7028, fasc. 254-255.

70 ASBO, Torrone, 6653, fasc. 296-297.

Francesca had also insulted and threatened her family, Ignazia made her way to the court describing 'being compelled to send for an injunction.'[71] The phrasing here is meaningful: Ignazia did not request just any kind of formal intervention; she assumed she could go to court and get a peace injunction. The court records demonstrate that these legal instruments were not solely top-down measures of control, but that men and women were active and knowledgeable litigators steering the case towards a specific outcome enhancing their negotiating position. In some instances, they were successful.

The *precetto de non offendendo* (literally an 'injunction to not offend') was a peace injunction issued by the criminal court's judge, most often through summary procedure in the phase of the denunciation. In its function it resembled the recognizances issued by London's Justices of the Peace at the Quarter Sessions as well as so-called 'Letters of Lawburrows' in Scotland.[72] All of these judicial procedures bound people to keep the peace through sureties or conditional fines. The Bolognese peace injunctions forbade defendants to 'violate or harass' the plaintiff and were, like the recognizances, the most popular form of dealing with assault in Bologna during the seventeenth and eighteenth centuries.[73] An authoritative eighteenth-century judges' manual described the instrument of the *precetto criminale* as an easy measure suitable for a wide range of frequent but relatively minor offences (*leggiere deliquenze*).[74] These could be violations of the public order such as 'being suspicious' or vagabondage, and could be used to release defendants under the condition that they would present themselves again to the court again if deemed necessary by the authorities. In Bologna between the mid-seventeenth and mid-eighteenth century, the most commonly ordered injunction was the *precetto de non offendendo*, after verbal or physical (yet not life-threatening) fights.

The Bolognese peace injunctions differed from London's recognizances in their form. As the name suggests, the recognizances entailed a sum of money that would not be forfeited in case of good behaviour. Three sureties pledged this monetary amount as a guarantee that the offender would appear in court to answer to a charge and keep the peace.[75] No such sureties seem to have been necessary for the Italian peace injunctions, as the *precetto* functioned more

71 ASBO, Torrone, 8171-1, fasc. 275: "sono stato costretta spederle un precetto da questa tribunal."

72 Hurl-Eamon, *Gender and petty violence*, 130; Kilday, *Women and violent crime*, 94; Shoemaker, *Prosecution and punishment*, 207.

73 Hurl-Eamon, *Gender and petty violence*, 129.

74 Mirogli, *Istruzzioni teorico-prattiche criminali*, 80.

75 Dinges, 'The uses of justice,' 162-163; Hurl-Eamon, *Gender and petty violence*, 129.

like a cautionary and conditional monetary punishment.[76] The penalties for violation of the injunction differed for men and women but were severe for both, ranging from a hefty monetary fine of 25 to 200 *scudi* (a servant's monthly wage consisted of about half a *scudo*) to public flogging for women or a sentencing to the galleys for a certain number of years (five, seven or ten years, or a lifetime) for men.[77] Another specificity was that while the *precetto* had a standardised form that included the order to not violate or harass each other any longer, the exact configuration of the injunction could be tailored to the situation presented to the court, including clauses regarding specific places, times of day, or specific unsanctioned behaviour, such as drinking in public.[78] For the criminal justice system it was therefore a practical tool to achieve public order, since it relied less on active surveillance than on the community's willingness to report violations.[79] The *precetti* became increasingly used throughout the early modern period: in the Bolognese casebooks the share of the peace injunctions increased from around seven per cent of all recorded outcomes of denunciations in 1650 to around 16 per cent in the mid-eighteenth century.

The state and the urban authorities were not the only actors who had a stake in the injunctions; plaintiffs did too. Like London's recognizances and Scotland's Letters of Lawburrows, the seventeenth- and eighteenth-century Bolognese peace orders were especially popular among women.[80] By the end of the seventeenth century the *precetto* had a distinctly urban character and seemed to have been of particular importance to female plaintiffs and defendants: 27 per cent of all denunciations brought before the *Torrone* by a female plaintiff resulted in a *precetto* against their adversary, compared to only 12 per cent of denunciations by male plaintiffs. Out of the 196 peace injunctions issued for violence in my samples, women were relatively over-represented both as plaintiffs (42 per cent of all plaintiffs) and as defendants (42 per cent of all defendants) compared to their proportionally lower share among violent offenders.[81]

---

76 There are references to the surety of the *precetto de non offendendo* in Rome: Fosi, *Papal justice*, 64 as well as in Bologna: Angelozzi and Casanova, *La nobiltà disciplinata*, 164-189.

77 M. Di Sivo, 'Per via giustizia. Sul processo penale a Roma tra XVI e XIX secolo,' *Rivista storica del Lazio. Giustizia e criminalità nello stato pontificio* 9: 4 (2001) 30.

78 M.A. Savelli, *Pratica universale del dottor Marc Antonio Savelli* (Parma 1717) 227.

79 S. Hughes, *Crime, disorder and the Risorgimento. The politics of policing in Bologna* (Cambridge: Cambridge University Press, 2002) 72, 79, 89.

80 Hurl-Eamon, *Gender and petty violence*, 130; Shoemaker, *Prosecution and punishment*, 207; Kilday, *Women and violent crime*, 94.

81 In the 684 cases concerning all kinds of violence collected for this sample of denunciations, with 919 defendants, women made up 22.3% of the defendants and 30.2% of the plaintiffs.

Theoretically there was no legislative distinction between the city and the countryside, but the court proceedings clearly show that *precetti* were mainly issued to city dwellers who had made a denunciation in person.[82] As mentioned before, urban women were not only more likely to become involved in criminal activities compared to their rural counterparts, but also had better access to the criminal justice system to make a denunciation. Without having to rely on local officials as go-betweens, plaintiffs were apparently better able to present their grievances in such a way that they could call upon this legal instrument.

Why were women disproportionally represented among plaintiffs and recipients of peace injunctions? On the one hand, the criminal court may have been more inclined to issue a restraining order for female plaintiffs due to women's perceived weakness and their need for protection. The prevailing chivalry theory assumes that early modern as well as modern legal professionals were generally inclined to protect 'weak women' by treating them with leniency in sentencing.[83] It seems plausible that this motive of protection played a similar role in the disproportional adjudication of the peace injunctions to female plaintiffs and defendants. Even if the woman was the aggressor against a male plaintiff, the idea that women needed to be protected 'against themselves' may be viewed from this perspective. This protection motive is reinforced by the fact that Italy's ecclesiastical courts ordered comparable peace orders to husbands who mistreated their wives.[84] According to the canonical treaties, women had the right to ask for a so-called *cauzione di non offendere*, a similar kind of security deposit intended to ensure that she would not be violated again.

Women themselves may have also preferred appealing to these particular means over seeking more informal community mediation methods or violent confrontation. While the court records certainly attest to women's ability and audacity in violently confronting their male and female adversaries, women, unlike men, had little honour to gain from it as it was considered 'unladylike' comportment frowned upon by contemporaries.[85] Historians of the nineteenth century have also argued that while women employed violence, it did not have specific resonances for their identity as women.[86] Because the

82 My sample counts only 2 countryside *precetti* (0.6% of the cases).

83 Graziosi, 'Women and criminal law,' 166-181; Angelozzi and Casanova, *Donne criminali*, 227-254.

84 Cavina, *Nozze di sangue*, 119.

85 Ibidem, 616; Brackett, *Criminal justice and crime*, 133-134.

86 S. D'Cruze, 'Unguarded passions. Violence, history and the everyday,' in S. D'Cruze (ed.), *Everyday violence in Britain, 1850-1950. Gender and class* (Harlow: Longman, 2000) 14.

practice of asking the authorities for a forced peace had no place within the traditional masculine conventions of honour, men may have more readily opted for other responses, such as peacemaking or even the challenge to a fight, as these entailed higher esteem than court-ordered sanctions.[87]

In the process of conflict resolution, coercive instruments like the *precetto* may have afforded more bargaining power particularly to those who customarily lacked it. Cohen has expressed a similar view in her examination of prostitutes' recourse to the criminal court in sixteenth-century Rome. While she argued that established households might resolve attacks on honour via other routes, prostitutes found in the criminal tribunal a "public and socially sanctioned forum in which to air their grievances and, within the conventions of honour culture, to spread shame on their attackers."[88] Nicoletta Rolla argued along a similar vein for eighteenth-century Turin.[89] Litigation may have been a means for women to find an alternative response to violence. It not only spared them the inconvenience and potential further dishonour of other possible strategies, but also augmented their leverage. For London, it has been argued that the motive behind assault prosecution was to achieve some kind of compensation for the injuries that were inflicted, either financial or in the form of public apologies for attacks on their characters as well as their bodies.[90] What the litigious Bolognese women expected of the law was not just an effective protection from their assailants, but also encompassed the negotiation of authority and power, with offenders whom they would not challenge to a fight.

7 Conclusion: Criminal Litigation, Gender and Agency

Overall, the dominance of the notion of women's inferior legal status derived from Roman law has contributed to the idea that women may have had limited legal agency, yet the examination of the Bolognese criminal court in the seventeenth and eighteenth centuries provides further evidence for a more diverse practice in which women, like men, employed justice strategically to settle their conflicts. Not only does this confirm the notion proposed in other studies that women had certain legal agency within the household, it also shows that this extended to areas outside the home. Various works have already shown

87 Dinges, 'The uses of justice,' 163.

88 Cohen, 'Honor and gender in the streets of early modern Rome,' 624.

89 N. Rolla, 'Per strada e in giustizia. Strategie di difesa dentro e fuori il tribunale (Torino, XVIII secolo),' *Quaderni storici* 141:3 (2012) 654-656.

90 Gray, 'The regulation of violence in the metropolis,' 81, 83.

that women did not have to submit to mistreatment and could (and did) seek redress in ecclesiastical tribunals.[91] The criminal court records shed further light on this relationship between women and their communities. In this formal legal structure of the criminal court, women found a forum through which they could wield and manipulate the power of social control and exert it over their community members.

While the authorities' disinterest in prosecuting petty offences seems non-discriminatory, the experiences of litigation were undeniably gendered. In the Bolognese case, the reliance on male local officials in the countryside to relay cases to criminal court established a very structural impediment to women's formal access to justice. It has been argued that for women more so than for men, direct access to the court was pivotal since the local officials were representatives of a culture that was biased against them. Women's use of criminal justice was therefore largely an urban preserve. The *Torrone*'s function as a forum for conflict resolution opened up the chances for men and women to use the court to pursue relatively petty grievances within their community, especially in cases of non-lethal violence. Whether urban women were more violent, more subjected to formal control or simply more litigious remains an open question, but what is certain is that the urban context did provide better opportunities for women to seek redress before the criminal court.

Compared to men, women could more often (in relative terms) count on the legal instrument of the peace injunction for violent offences. It does not seem unlikely that the importance of this conditional punishment for women was related to a protective motive from the judicial apparatus, but to understand its function it is also crucial to emphasise that women consciously used it as part of their negotiations. The ability to negotiate legal jurisdictions depended on various factors such as socioeconomic status, as well as the expectations of the law.[92] The criminal court records provide evidence that women were well-aware of the existence and threatening function of the peace injunctions, and expected to have a good chance of obtaining them. The very concrete inconvenience of conditional high fines, supplemented with corporal punishment and forced labour (in the case of male defendants) or public whipping (for women), provided useful leverage in the resolution of everyday conflicts. That Italian women made these requests in the face of a patriarchal legal system suggests that they in practice had more legal agency than their legal position

91 Hacke, *Women, sex and marriage*; Ferraro, *Marriage wars*.

92 Kane and Williamson, 'Introduction,' 3.

alone would allow us to assume. An unintentional outcome of the patriarchal system was that women's supposed marginality meant not that they were powerless, but that they were in some cases able to turn their status into bargaining power instead.[93]

93 A similar conclusion is drawn from rural weaver women's petitions to counter guild claims, see Dumont, 'Women and guilds,' 5-25.

5

Gendered Dynamics of Violent Behaviours

On Tuesday 17 March 1705 a notary from Bologna's *Tribunale del Torrone* visited Maddalena Faesini at her sickbed in the *Ospedale di Santa Maria della Vita* to interrogate her about the life-threatening wounds to her face that brought her there.[1] She stated that she had received many blows to the head and jaw with an unidentified blunt object from a woman called Domenica Gombi. They knew each other and lived in the same street, and Maddalena suggested having been beaten up so badly because Domenica believed she had badmouthed her to the merchant they both worked for, presumably as spinners or weavers. The investigation of this injury, which had not only slashed the skin on Maddalena's face but also caused her teeth to fall out, was halted when the two made peace roughly two weeks later.

The casebooks of Bologna's criminal court's notaries are filled with violent altercations similar to this incident. Though discordant with normative expectations of women, these aggressions were an integral part of the day-to-day lives of male and female artisans, peddlers and labourers in Bologna's dense urban fabric. These violent altercations were also considered an unwelcome interaction worth denouncing to the court. This chapter explores the gendered dynamics of these quotidian violent behaviours recounted in the *Tribunale del Torrone*'s denunciations and *processi* between the middle of the seventeenth and eighteenth centuries. Through the examination of these criminal court records, this chapter will draw attention to the distinguishing features of early modern Italy's culture of violence and, importantly, establish women's place in it. It will ultimately argue that women's violent behaviour was far too common to be viewed as an anomaly.

To this end, this chapter will first discuss the particular place of Italy, as a representative of the 'southern pattern,' in European comparisons of long-term patterns of violence. It will deal with how violence was regarded in the eyes of the law and how it was dealt with in practice, as the culture of violence went hand in hand with that of reconciliation throughout the early modern period. The next sections scrutinise women's participation in homicide as well as verbal aggression and, importantly, a wide range of non-fatal physical acts of violence. This chapter builds on recent scholarship that includes the pettier forms of violence in its analysis, which were far more common than their

1 ASBO, Torrone, 7602-2, fasc. 19.

lethal counterparts, and are therefore more telling of men's and women's everyday encounters with violence and the law. The last sections will inquire about the gendered nature of this everyday violence through several important aspects: the use of weapons, the social profiles of and relations between offenders and victims, the spatial contexts in which violence took place as well as some recurring narrative frameworks regarding the violence of men and women in the judicial sources.

1 The Culture of Violence between Prosecution and Reconciliation

At least until the seventeenth century, violence was considered to be a regular feature of everyday life among many Western societies.[2] Robert Muchembled went so far as to state that "like death, like the cemetery which is at the heart of the village, violence is at the heart of life in the fifteenth, sixteenth, and seventeenth centuries."[3] A special place in the discussions about the role of violence in everyday life in the early modern period is held by the South of Europe, with the Italian peninsula as its main representative. Based on his work on sixteenth-century Rome, Peter Blastenbrei explicitly spoke of distinct Northern and southern European models of delinquency, in which the South distinguished itself by exhibiting much higher shares of violence.[4] The equation of Italy with the South has not remained uncriticised. Scholars have, for example, called the cultural homogeneity of the region into question, and furthermore suggest that there are too few comparable quantitative analyses for most parts of this area to substantiate any such claim.[5] Yet, a cautious eye on the available international literature seems pertinent to understand specificities and commonalities in societies' attitudes towards violence across early modern Europe.

Italy has been described as particularly violent compared to other early modern European societies.[6] The special position of Italy in the long-term development of violence is furthermore highlighted in Manuel Eisner's

2 Davies, 'Introduction,' 1.

3 R. Muchembled, 'Anthropologie de la violence dans la France moderne (XVe-XVIIIe siècle),' *Revue de synthèse* 108 (1987) 40, as translated by Davies, 'Introduction,' 1.

4 Blastenbrei, *Kriminalität in Rom*, 283-284.

5 The equation of Italy with the south or the Mediterranean has also been subject to substantial criticism. Not only have scholars called the cultural homogeneity of the region into question, but there are also few comparable quantitative analyses for most parts of this area to substantiate any such claim. See Mantecón, 'The patterns of violence,' 243; Eisner, 'From swords to words,' 84-85.

6 Carroll, 'Revenge and reconciliation,' 101-142 106-107; Calzolari, 'Delitti e castighi,' 55; Niccoli, 'Rinuncia, pace, perdono,' 188.

integrative survey of European homicide rates.[7] In England and Holland a sustained decline of lethal violence set in during the sixteenth century, followed soon after by Scandinavia, Germany and Switzerland during the first decades after 1600, but the homicide rates in Italian cities remained high until well in the nineteenth century, only after this time declining steeply. As we will see in the next section, evidence from seventeenth- and eighteenth-century Bologna nuances this image, but does not contradict the broad outlines of the theory.

Why Italy remained so violent throughout the early modern period has been subject to much contemplation, but answers remain tentative. Scholars have often drawn on Norbert Elias' theory of the civilising process to explain the relatively quick decline in violence, including lethal violence, witnessed in northern Europe.[8] The rise of greater self-control as individuals internalised social constraints was promoted by the expansion of the state, with its monopoly on violence, and the extension of the market economy. In a recent article Stuart Carroll aptly summarises why the case of Italy complicates this image.[9] Already during the Italian Renaissance, social and economic interdependencies had reached levels far in advance of any in the North of Europe. Sophisticated bureaucratic and legal mechanisms had also been developed early on. In spite of these early administrative and judicial developments, the new regimes that emerged in Italy during the first half of the sixteenth century lacked the political legitimacy to effectively suppress the widespread factional violence at least until the middle of the seventeenth century.[10]

Scholars have also drawn on other cultural-institutional factors to explain the prevalence of violence in early modern Italy. Some have pointed to the persistence of an honour culture as a distinguishing feature of the Mediterranean region until well into the twentieth century.[11] In an honour-based culture one's honour was measured and conferred by one's peers. Having a clear social function, violence was considered both legitimate and sometimes obligatory to assert, defend and win masculine honour and escape shame.[12]

7 Eisner, 'Long-term historical trends,' 83-142; M. Eisner, 'Modernization, self-control and lethal violence. The long-term dynamics of European homicide rates in theoretical perspective,' *British journal of criminology* 41 (2001) 618-638.

8 Its most notable supporter w Pieter Spierenburg. See, for example, Spierenburg, *Violence and punishment*; R. McMahon, J. Eibach and R. Roth, 'Making sense of violence? Reflections on the history of interpersonal violence in Europe,' *Crime, history and societies* 17:2 (2013) 7-11.

9 S. Carroll, 'Revenge and reconciliation in early modern Italy,' *Past & present* 233 (2016) 105.

10 Ibidem, 106.

11 Eisner, 'Modernization, self-control and lethal violence,' 632; Carroll, 'Introduction,' 35; Davies, 'Introduction,' 1; Calzolari, 'Delitti e castighi,' 55.

12 Carroll, 'Introduction,' 23, 27; Wood, 'Conceptualizing cultures of violence,' 87.

According to Carroll, a distinctive feature of early modern Italy was the widespread secular literature on the gentlemanly laws of honour and its relation to peacemaking. While the practice of peacemaking between individuals as a legitimate and honourable response to violence came under attack in northern Europe, it continued to be held in high esteem in Italy throughout the early modern period.[13] The long continuity of peacemaking procedures in early modern Italy – notably also in a formal, judicial sense – and its role in preserving a social system based on violent confrontation has been treated more extensively earlier in this book.

Though some scholars have argued that it was comparably ineffective, premodern Italian states had since long attempted to contain violent behaviours.[14] Indeed, medieval and early modern towns are considered to be the birthplace of measures of violence prevention and containment.[15] On a regular basis, statutes, civil oaths and bans defined violent acts as deviant behaviour, a view that was supported by a range of arms bans and night curfews renewed throughout the early modern period. In early modern Bologna important sources that shed light on the authorities' stance towards violence are the *Bando Generale* of 1610 by cardinal legate Benedetto Giustiniani, and the one issued in 1756 by Fabrizio Serbelloni; summations of the criminal bylaws issued on the occasion of the new cardinal legate taking office. Although the prescribed sentences were not rigidly enforced, as we will see, they nevertheless reveal broader trends in the changing attitude towards deviant behaviours.[16]

While also delineating aggravating *and* extenuating factors, the seventeenth- and eighteenth-century criminal bylaws shared a pronounced disapproval of a wide range of violent behaviours and prescribed harsh sentences – even for instances where no blood was drawn (see table 10). According to Serbelloni's 1756 *Bando Generale*, homicide was considered to be one of the gravest crimes humans could commit.[17] It was viewed as both contempt of the Papal Prince and as an offence against God. As a baseline all killers were

---

13 Carroll, 'Revenge and reconciliation,' 132.

14 F. Ricciardelli, 'Violence and repression in late medieval Italy,' in S.K. Cohn jr. and F. Ricciardelli (eds.), *The culture of violence in Renaissance Italy* (Florence: Le Lettere, 2012) 68; M.B. Becker, 'Changing patterns of violence and justice in fourteenth and fifteenth-century Florence,' *Comparative studies in society and history* 18:3 (1976) 282.

15 Dean, *Crime and justice in late medieval Italy,* 169; .G. Schwerhoff, 'Social control of violence, violence as social control: The case of early modern Germany,' in H. Roodenburg and P. Spierenburg (eds.), *Social control in Europe. Volume I, 1500-1800* (Columbus: The Ohio State University Press, 2004) 235.

16 Angelozzi and Casanova, *La giustizia criminale a Bologna nel XVIII secolo,* 219-240.

17 "Fra li delitti, che nell'uman genere soglion commettersi, uno de' più gravi certamente è quello dell'omicidio volontario, che contiene in se una particolare offesa della Maesta

TABLE 10 Sentences for violent acts prescribed by the criminal bylaws of 1610 and 1756

Category	Condition	Punishments 1610	Punishments 1756
Homicide		Death penalty	Death penalty
Wounding (*ferite*), blows (*percosse*) or threat	Scarring to face/injury of genitalia	Fine of 200 *scudi* + 5 years galleys	Life-long galleys
	Injury to other parts of the body	Fine of 200 *scudi* + strappado	–
	Serious danger to life	–	Life–long galleys
	Some danger to life	–	7 years galleys
	No danger to life	–	5 years galleys
	With arms, no bodily harm	Fine of 100 *scudi* + strappado	Min. 5 years galleys
	With sticks, stones, fists, pushes or kicks	Fine of 100 *scudi*	–
Libels	–	Death penalty + confiscation of goods	Death penalty + punishment of 'degradation'
Insult/banter	–	Fine of 50 *scudi* + strappado	Strappado
Spitting in face	–	Fine of 50 *scudi* + strappado/1 month imprisonment	Strappado, in case of noble/respect-able victim galleys
House–scorning	Against citizens, nobles or those of 'honest condition'	Galleys for 5 years	Life-long galleys
	Against *Persone vili o meretrici*	Fine of 200 *scudi* + 'strappado'	Life-long galleys, subject to reduction
Violent kissing/touching of virgins or other honest women	–	Fine of 300 *scudi* + galleys for 5 years	–
Serenading widows, single women or other honest women	–	Fine of 100 *scudi* + imprisonment for 1 month	Strappado

SOURCES: *BANDO GENERALE* (1610) 15-24; BANDO GENERALE (1756) 11-38, 108-110.
– Indicates that the category or criterion was not specifically addressed

therefore prescribed a capital punishment in both bylaws. In Giustiniani's 1610 *Bando Generale* additional post-mortem corporal torture and disfigurements (*supplizio*) were stipulated for aggravating factors such as patricide.

One particularly gruesome capital punishment was imposed on Andrea Malagù on 15 July 1675.[18] Upon imprisonment for murder he had helped some other prisoners escape with a false key, but he had been caught and sent for trial. The printed announcement of his execution, which was intended as an invitation to the public, set out the grim procedure that awaited him: Andrea would be beaten to death, would have his throat slit and then quartered as a punishment for his crimes. Judging from the court records, elaborate spectacles like these were not that common during the seventeenth century and became increasingly rare as time went on. In the 1756 bylaws explicit mention of these additional defaming measures are notably absent, which is in line with the notion that punitive regimes during the early modern period moved away from the publicly visible infliction of pain and suffering as a symbol of the repressive potential of the state.[19] Extenuating circumstances such as killing without malice and premeditation (resulting in five years in the galleys or forced labour) are treated more exhaustively in the eighteenth-century bylaws. Overall, the more elaborate treatment of these topics in the bylaws must be viewed foremost as the intent to clear up past ambiguities and systematise the application of criminal justice, and to diminish the discretion of the judges.[20]

There was a significant discrepancy between written laws and judicial practice. First, the penalty decreed by these bylaws would not necessarily be assumed in sentencing. As Gregory Hanlon has observed for the Renaissance period, statutory penalties were often deemed too harsh to apply.[21] There were many aspects to a crime – such as the age, gender and social status of the offender and victim – that allowed the judge to apply judicial discretion and adjust the sentence. For this they did not only rely on the criminal bylaws, but also consulted the legal opinions by jurists such as Gian Domenico Rainaldi, who wrote several renowned books on legal topics based on his time as a judge in Bologna between 1671 and 1676.[22] Second, many sentences in early modern Bologna were overturned and converted into pardons. This was especially true

divina, ed umana, un'atto di soprasina superbia contro Dio, ed il Principe, ed un'infinità d'altri mali." See *Bando generale Serbelloni 1756,* chapter VI, no. 1, page 11.

18 ASBO, Torrone, 7030, fasc. 9.

19 Eisner, 'From swords to words,' 103.

20 Angelozzi and Casanova, *La giustizia criminale a Bologna nel XVIII secolo*, 223.

21 Hanlon, 'Violence and its control,' 147.

22 See for an examination of his work Angelozzi and Casanova, *La giustizia in una città di antico regime*, 375-448; Casanova, *Crimini nascosti.*

for acts of violence, where peacemaking between the offender and the victim or his/her family could result in a significant reduction of the sentence or a general pardon as the peace had restored the social equilibrium. In the case of homicides committed in seventeenth-century Bologna, nearly 40 per cent of the killers received a pardon.[23] The granting of pardons and exemptions in response to a petition was not just an Italian phenomenon, but was widespread and is viewed as "fundamental to the manner of governing in early modern Europe."[24]

A third way in which penal practice diverged from the norms specifically relates to the treatment of various types of violence. Compared to the daily practice represented by the *Torrone*'s denunciations and indictments, the heavy penalties prescribed for the pettier forms of violence are striking. For the wounding of another person without (in the eyes of the surgeon) any danger to life, the 1756 bylaws prescribe a sentence of five years rowing in the papal fleet. Insults and insulting banter could yield three pulls of the *strappado*. In practice, however, the *Torrone* only prosecuted the more serious forms of violence. As we can see in table 11, the notaries' record books brimmed with complaints about fights and brawls that did not result in life-threatening wounds. The criminal investigation dossiers on the other hand were disproportionally concerned with homicide and serious wounding.

The punishments that the bylaws prescribed also differed significantly from the ones that the criminal court pronounced in practice. As has already been observed by others, criminal court cases in early modern Bologna only rarely ended with 'real sentences,' such as the death penalty, a sentence to the galleys or exile.[25] Homicide garnered a relatively large number of capital punishments, banishment sentences, and sentences of forced labour in the papal galleys compared to other types of violent crimes (table 12). A substantial proportion of killers were eventually pardoned, but they were less likely to be absolved from the get-go than was the case for other violent offenders. Cases against defendants in non-lethal violence cases were by and large cancelled, either due to insufficient evidence or, commonly, because the plaintiff withdrew the complaint due to an unmentioned settlement. Most of the non-lethal violence was concluded through peacemaking, despite the harsh sentences prescribed by the law.

The judicial treatment of women's violence differed from men's in some respects. From a theoretical viewpoint it is often believed that legal professionals

23 Rose, *A renaissance of violence*, 91.
24 Hanlon, 'Violence and its control,' 147.
25 Angelozzi and Casanova, *Donne criminali*, 228.

TABLE 11 Violent crimes among denunciations and *processi*, ca. 1655-1755

	Homicide	Wounding with danger to life	Wounding without danger to life	Verbal aggression	Undefined violence[a]	Total
Denunciations (N=1043)	1%	7%	56%	22%	14%	100%
Processi (N=825)	20%	45%	20%	15%	1%	100%

SOURCE: PROCESSI EXTRACTED FROM SAMPLE 1 AND 2B, DENUNCIATIONS FROM SAMPLE 2A (SEE APPENDIX), COUNTED BY IDENTIFIED DEFENDANT

a As measured by the issuing or breach of a *precetto de non offendendo*

TABLE 12 Sentences for violent crimes committed by men, ca. 1655-1755

	Capital punishment	Exile	Galleys	Incarceration	*Precetto*[a]	Surety	Cancelled[b]	Pardon
Homicide (N=107)	6%	7%	21%	1%	–	2%	24%	39%
Wounding with danger to life (N=205)	–	2%	3%	–	9%	1%	75%	10%
Wounding without danger to life (N=204)	–	2%	1%	–	7%	4%	77%	8%
Verbal aggression (N=66)	–	2%	–	–	14%	9%	71%	5%
Undefined violence (N=86)	–	–	–	–	100%	–	–	–

SOURCE: EXTRACTED FROM SAMPLE 1 AND SAMPLE 2 (SEE APPENDIX)

a *Precetto de non offendendo*

b Includes both cases that were absolved due to presumed innocence or lack of evidence as well as cancellations due to the complaint being withdrawn

treated female offenders with a particular leniency due to the assumption of their weakness and their need for protection (also called 'the chivalry theory').[26] Based on their extensive study of criminal justice in early modern Bologna, Angelozzi and Casanova concluded that the few women indicted for homicide

26 Ibidem, 18-19; Graziosi, 'Women and criminal law,' 173.

TABLE 13 Sentences for violent crimes committed by women, ca. 1655-1755

	Capital punishment	Exile	Galleys	Incarceration	*Precetto*[a]	Surety	Cancelled[b]	Pardon	Total known
Homicide (N=2)	–	–	–	50%	50%	–	–	–	100%
Wounding with danger to life (N=10)	–	–	–	–	30%	–	70%	–	100%
Wounding without danger to life (N=54)	–	–	–	–	24%	4%	67%	5%	100%
Verbal aggression (N=28)	–	–	–	–	29%	7%	64%		100%
Undefined violence (N=62)	–	–	–	–	100%	–	–		100%

SOURCE: EXTRACTED FROM DENUNCIATIONS AND *PROCESSI* FROM SAMPLE 1 AND SAMPLE 2 (SEE APPENDIX)

a *Precetto de non offendendo*

b Includes both cases that were absolved due to presumed innocence or lack of evidence as well as cancellations due to the complaint being withdrawn

disproportionally received clemency, particularly when they had male co-offenders. In this case they were punished less severely or not at all.[27] Rose similarly contended that the few women that came before the *Torrone* for homicide during the seventeenth century were treated as accomplices rather than as killers with agency.[28]

Acts of non-lethal violence were more common and allow for better examination of gendered sentencing patterns. What stands out is the importance of the *precetto criminale*, a conditional fine demanding the discontinuance of offending and molestations (see table 13). In proportional terms female offenders were on average at least twice as likely to receive such peace injunctions as their male counterparts, for all types of recorded violent transgressions. It is not unlikely that the women's legal minority played into the scale to which these measures were imposed on them. Not only did these injunctions serve to protect the victims (often other women) from further aggression, but they were likely also imposed to protect female offenders against themselves. Whether this meant that women's violence was largely irrelevant in the eyes

27 Angelozzi and Casanova, *Donne criminali*, 239, 242, 259. My own sample only includes four female offenders indicted for lethal violence. Two of them were sentenced: one was incarcerated and the other female offender received a *precetto criminale*.

28 Rose, *A renaissance of violence*, 150.

of the court, or that they were actually subjected to close institutional scrutiny due to an intolerance of women's public violence, is still to be unravelled.

The criminal court records also reveal a decisive similarity in the judicial treatment of violence, regardless of gender. After all, the majority of cases against female fighters were also cancelled and absolved following the withdrawal of the complaint, just like men's. Cultural and judicial norms neither prevented women from employing violence, nor excluded them from employing the peacemaking practices that are believed to have been so intrinsic to the Italian culture of violence.

Although violence was viewed as undesirable, it also enjoyed a certain degree of tolerance. This was not only the case in Bologna and other Italian towns, but has also been observed for other regions during the early modern period. In Germany, for example, only notorious violent offenders faced severe sanctions like imprisonment or banishment, while non-lethal violent acts were commonly only punished with fines.[29] Rather than punishment, the goal was to reconcile the two parties, to reintegrate the culprit into society and to re-establish social peace. Even though the Bolognese criminal bylaws officially prescribed harsh sentences, its court officials themselves are believed to have played active roles in pressuring the victims and their kin to accept their enemies' peacemaking.[30]

Expectations of peacemaking extended to all reaches of society, something which is illustrated by the case of Giacoma Ferranina against Pellegrina Gentili in 1655.[31] As Giacoma, a prostitute, was walking home with her mother and sister after mass, Pellegrina beat her with a stick and scarred her face. This was a serious offence, punishable by a hefty fine and a five-year sentence to the galleys. Offender Pellegrina understandably tried multiple times to have Giacoma renounce her complaint, which she refused. Pellegrina then turned to the court with a petition. She explained that she had previously been insulted and provoked by the plaintiff, which had led to the attack. She furthermore declared only having wounded Giacoma slightly, had many times (unsuccessfully) asked for a renunciation and was therefore now pleading for the case to be annulled by the judge without the renunciation.[32] The petition was granted

29 Schwerhoff, 'Social control of violence,' 223, 235.

30 Rose, *A renaissance of violence*, 54.

31 ASBO, Torrone, 6670, fasc. 9.

32 Ibidem, n.p, fol. 7: "Pellegrina Gentili humilmente espone all'curia esser stata querelata nel Torrone da donna Margherita Ferranina, et sua figliola meretrice perche essendo stata ingiuriata, et provocata dalle sud: le dasse con un bastone alcune percosse dalle quali restò pochissimo offesa, et havendogli l'querelatrice più volte fatto addimandargli la

and the case was annulled against Giacoma's wishes. Clearly, reintegration was valued over punishment in cases such as these.

While the practice of peacemaking as a socially acceptable answer to acts of violence was shared within much of Europe, scholars have argued that it nevertheless may have been at the root of Italy's especially violent society. A scholar of the nineteenth century himself, Daniele Boschi stressed the decisive relationship between the persistent high rates of violence and the late modernisation of the criminal justice system in Italy.[33] In particular, he points to the long-standing tradition of judicial indulgence towards interpersonal violence. Throughout the early modern period, he asserts, people accused of non-lethal violent crimes easily managed to avoid at least the most severe forms of punishments thanks to the complex system of judicial pardons and private reconciliations. And although criminal courts all over Italy received several thousand reports each year concerning a wide range of crimes, they effectively only dealt with a very small proportion of these offences. Therefore, until well into the nineteenth century the judicial system only exerted a very moderate deterrent power over violent aggressors. The question whether the practice of peacemaking and pardoning was more commonplace in Italy than elsewhere or whether it is more visible in the extant sources merits further investigation. However, what is certain is that peacemaking was of continued importance to the way interpersonal violence was dealt with all throughout the early modern period.

2 Lethal Violence in the Seventeenth and Eighteenth Centuries

In the scholarly debates on the decline of violence over time, homicide rates have formed the most important evidence to argue for the existence of regional differences. Eisner has been a main driver of the conceptualisation of these large-scale and long-term geographical variations.[34] He argued for a largely synchronised decline in violent crime across the Western world, where lethal encounters dropped from anywhere between 20 and 50 per 100,000 inhabitants in late medieval cities, to rates below one by the mid-twentieth century.[35] England and the Netherlands led the way in this development during the sixteenth century, followed soon after by Scandinavia, Germany, Belgium,

---

renoncia sempre ha ricusato di fargliela, che perciò supp.ca l'curia a farle grazie d'ordinare che le sia cassata detta querella senza detta renoncia."

33 Boschi, 'Knife fighting in Rome,' 150-153, especially 152.

34 For his most recent account, see Eisner, 'From swords to words,' 65-134.

35 Ibidem, 67.

Switzerland and France. Italy (representing the 'southern' pattern) pursued a different trajectory, with consistently higher rates than those in northern Europe followed by a gradual decline from the early nineteenth century onward.[36] A simplified version of Eisner's data – which illustrates Italy's divergent trajectory – is presented in table 14.

Despite the clear overall trend of higher mean homicide rates in Italy, a closer look at the data reveals significant variations between cities and time periods.[37] For the premodern, pre-statistical era Eisner had to rely on discontinuous local estimates from various towns such as Rome, Florence, Venice, Siena, Mantua and Bologna. At least until the middle of the seventeenth century, high and low rates alternated without a distinguishable pattern. In fourteenth-century Florence, for example, the rate of 25.6 homicides per 100,000 inhabitants in 1344-1345 surged to a massive 152 five years later (1350-1352), to drop to 16.4 again a quarter of a decade later (1374-1375).[38] Similarly, local estimates for sixteenth-century Rome diverged from 73 in 1560-1562 to 40 in 1571-1573.[39] Between cities, too, significant variations arise. In the city of Mantua between 1601 and 1605, the mean homicide rate was 31. In Lecce during roughly the same time period (1601 to 1610), the rate was a lower 19.3.[40] However, despite these variations even many of these lower estimates for Italian towns were higher than the mean rates for other parts of Europe throughout the early modern period.

The capriciousness of early modern homicide rates can also be observed in Bologna. Figure 7 displays these rates for the period between 1600 and 1755 collected from the criminal court's indictments. With an average of 27 homicides per 100,000 inhabitants throughout the century, it shows that – as a whole – the Bolognese saw many killings.[41] Compared to the average rates of the

36 Ibidem, 68, 80-81, 84.

37 I would like to express my gratitude to Manuel Eisner for kindly sending me his database (sent on 9 January 2014), in which he has collected and calculated the homicide rates for individual towns.

38 Based on Eisner's database, who gathered this data from A. Zorzi, 'La pena di morte in Italia nel Tardo Medioevo,' *Clio & Crimen* 4 (2007) 47-62; A. Zorzi, 'Aspetti e problemi dell'amministrazione della giustizia penale nella repubblica fiorentina I. La transizione dal XIV al XV secolo,' *Archivio storico italiano* 145 (1987) 391-453.

39 Based on Eisner's database, who gathered this data from Blastenbrei, *Kriminalität in Rom*.

40 Based on Eisner's database, who gathered this data from M.A. Romani, 'Criminalità e giustizia nel Ducato di Mantova alla fine del cinquecento,' *Rivista storica Italiana* 92 (1980) 679-706; N. Perego, *Homini de mala vita. Criminalità e giustizia a Lecco e in terra di Brianza tra cinque e seicento* (Lecco: Oggiono, 2001) 196.

41 For fourteenth- and fifteenth-century Bologna, homicide rates ranged from 30 to 80 per 100,000 inhabitants. See T. Dean, 'Eight varieties of homicide. Bologna in the 1340s and 1440s,' in T. Dean and K. Lowe (eds.), *Murder in Renaissance Italy* (Cambridge: Cambridge

TABLE 14 Mean homicide rates in European regions, 1350-1925

	1350-1399	1400-1449	1450-1499	1500-1549	1550-1599	1600-1649	1650-1699	1700-1749	1750-1799	1800-1849	1850-1874	1875-1899	1900-1925
England and Wales	13.0	...	...	...	5.2	5.8	3.5	2.0	1.4	1.6	1.6	1.3	0.8
Netherlands	20.7	59.1	...	35.9	8.9	7.6	3.1	3.4	1.9	...	0.8	0.9	0.6
Germany	30.1	6.6	18.6	...	9.0	10.1	3.1	5.0	4.6	2.4	1.5	1.6	2.1
Italy	71.7	62.0	...	...	38.7	39.1	10.2	16.9	7.1	8.0	7.0	5.7	3.9

SOURCE: EISNER, 'FROM SWORDS TO WORDS', 80-81

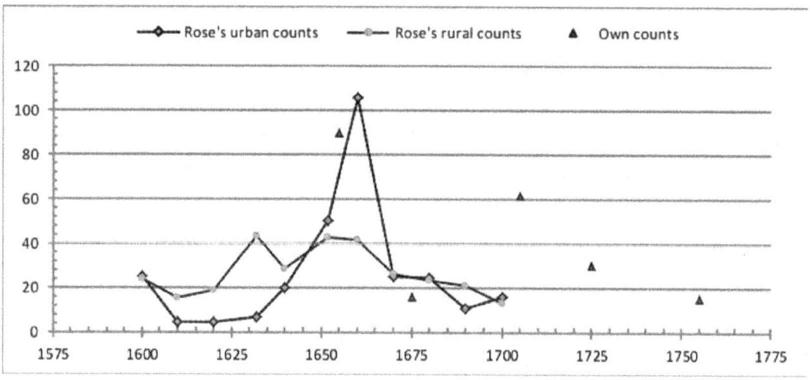

FIGURE 7 Bologna's urban homicide rates based on the processi, 1600-1755
SOURCES: SAMPLE 1 (SEE APPENDIX); C. ROSE, A RENAISSANCE OF VIOLENCE, 79-140. COUNTED AS HOMICIDES PER 100,000 INHABITANTS

Netherlands and England, Bologna's homicide rate of 25 at the beginning of the century was already quite high, but this was nothing compared to what was yet to come. In the decades after the outbreak of the bubonic plague in 1630, accompanied by a general dissolution of social order, the rates would surge to 50 in 1652 and to a staggering 106 homicides per 100,000 inhabitants in the city

University Press, 2017) 85; S. Rubin Blanshei, 'Homicide in a culture of hatred: Bologna 1352-1420,' in T. Dean and K. Lowe (eds.), *Murder in Renaissance Italy* (Cambridge: Cambridge University Press, 2017) 113.

of Bologna in 1660.[42] A decade later, however, the rates reached near parity again with those from the beginning of the century. With the high 1705 data point as an outlier, the post-1770 rates apparently continued the early modern routine, without a sensational deviation from the high rates associated with the 'southern pattern.'

Aside from the period of crisis between the 1630s and 1660s, lethal violence in Bologna shared many of the same characteristics throughout the seventeenth and eighteenth centuries and resembled what is known about lethal violence in other early modern towns. They social realm of violent offenders will be treated more extensively in a later paragraph, but it is interesting to briefly point out its most important features. According to Rose, who provides an in-depth study of lethal violence in seventeenth-century Bologna, the Bolognese rarely killed strangers during times of peace.[43] Instead, homicides took place within the orbit of family and sociability. Artisans, labourers and merchants killed each other, their families, their lovers, friends and neighbours. Their motivations were generally rather 'prosaic' or 'trivial,' revolving around revenge for an insult, romance and escalated robbery as much in the 1600s as it did one and a half centuries later. In about a quarter of the cases killers fought alongside their family members, their co-workers or faction members, but much of the violence was a solitary affair. The violent encounters that led to the deaths recorded by the *Torrone* generally occurred in the course of daily conflict, a reality that early modern Italians were accustomed to and, indeed, embraced to a certain extent.[44]

As is known for lethal violence all over early modern Europe, the demographics of fatal violence in seventeenth- and eighteenth-century Bologna included few women. Men overwhelmingly accounted for the killers and their victims, which has led to the characterisation of homicide as "masculine bravado" revolving around "maintaining face, demonstrating character, not wanting to be pushed around, in short the requirement to defend one's (masculine) honour and reputation."[45] Congruent with this dominant image of public male-on-male violence, women were much less frequently prosecuted for homicide and were also relatively uncommon among the reported victims of fatal interpersonal violence. Shares of female offenders in this category of violence range from 30 per cent in Surrey between 1660 and 1800 to about

42 Rose, *A renaissance of violence*, 137-138, 159.

43 Rose, *A renaissance of violence*, 91, 98, 103.

44 Ibidem, 91.

45 Carroll, 'Introduction,' 20.

8 per cent in Amsterdam during the same time period.[46] A similar, though amplified, image emerges for early modern Bologna. Rose calculated that women made up about 9 per cent of the victims of homicide and a mere 2.5 per cent of killers in seventeenth-century Bologna.[47] For the period from 1583 to 1779, Angelozzi and Casanova similarly allege that women made up less than five per cent of the indicted killers.[48] My samples of urban Bologna between the mid-seventeenth and mid-eighteenth centuries concur with these assertions, and suggest that only three per cent of killers identified by the criminal court consisted of women.[49]

That women were only held accountable for a rather small proportion of homicides should not lead us to conclude that women were rarely violent at all. Recent studies have demonstrated that the examination of women's violence requires a different approach and a different set of sources than commonly employed. Rather than being dealt with by the higher courts, women's crimes were more likely to be handled by less formal methods of conflict resolution as well as in lower criminal courts.[50] In recent decades, scholars have contended that focusing on petty violence – like petty criminality in general – helps significantly in arriving at a clearer image of daily tensions in early modern communities as well as early modern men's and women's perceptions and experiences of violence."[51] In Bologna too, the examination of a broader spectrum of violence beyond homicide bring a much more significant group of deviant female protagonists into view.

---

46 As offenders in lethal violence, women made up almost 30% in Surrey (1660-1800) when including infanticide, and 13% of offenders of homicide and manslaughter alone. Women furthermore consisted of about 25% in Denbighshire (1660-1730), about one-fifth in seventeenth-century Cheshire, 21% in eighteenth-century Scotland and 8% in Amsterdam between 1650 and 1810. See J.M. Beattie, *Crime and the courts in England, 1660-1800* (Princeton: Princeton University Press, 1986) 83, 115; Beattie, 'The criminality of women,' 85; S. Howard, 'Crime, communities and authority in early modern Wales: Denbighshire, 1660-1730' (Unpublished PhD thesis, University of Wales, 2003) 83; Walker, *Crime, gender and social order*, 109; Kilday, *Women and violent crime*, 43; P. Spierenburg, 'How violent were women? Court cases in Amsterdam, 1650-1810,' *Crime, history & societies* 1 (1997) 17.

47 Rose, *A renaissance of violence*, 148.

48 Angelozzi and Casanova, *Donne criminali*, 84.

49 My sample of the urban *processi* from 1655, 1675, 1705, 1725 and 1755 includes a total of 74 homicides resulting in 126 accused offenders. Four of these perpetrators were women.

50 Schwerhoff, *Köln im Kreuzverhör*; Shoemaker, *Prosecution and punishment*, 292; King, *Crime and law in England*, 202-210; Gray, *Crime, prosecutions and social relations*, 9, 170-171; Dinges, 'The uses of justice,' 159-175.

51 Hurl-Eamon, *Gender and petty violence*, 11; Jones, *Gender and petty crime*, 8; Walker, *Crime, gender and social order*, 270; Kilday, *Women and violent crime*; Ruitenbeek, 'Niet zonder kleerscheuren,' 62-85; Van der Heijden, 'Women, violence and urban justice,' 90.

3 Insults and the Politics of Daily Life

Compared to compelling accounts of murder, complaints about verbal affront may at first glance appear rather inconsequential. Yet early modern magistracies heard numerous insult cases on a daily basis, revealing in the very least a contemporary sensitivity to vilification that rendered it worthy of legal recourse. The desire to discipline interpersonal violence, whether physical or verbal, was intrinsically tied up with ideas about honour. Both words and physical actions were believed to have the power to wound the victim physically or through the loss of reputation, could provoke further violence, damaged wider family networks, and required reparation.[52] The statutes that many Italian communities published from the Middle Ages onwards therefore treated hostile words and physical assaults in a similar manner.[53] In Bologna the criminal bylaws discussed these types of 'injuries' in the same paragraphs and prescribed the same harsh punishments, while the judiciary in practice actively pushed for reconciliation.[54]

Italian women's roles in these acts of violence are still largely uncharted. As a result of the relatively strict gender norms and the ethics of honour it is assumed that women would not have partaken in the physical violence so very omnipresent in early modern Italy. Retributive violence was a culturally accepted and sometimes even demanded means to maintain one's honour – for men, but not for women. In his work on criminal justice in late Renaissance Florence, John Brackett has argued that for women it was neither 'expected nor desirable' to engage in violence for any reason.[55] The ethics of honour prescribed passivity to women, submitting her to the control of men and relying on them to defend her honour and reputation.

Scholars have long assumed that women instead relied on insults and defamatory slurs as the primary means of conducting the small politics of their daily lives.[56] Women, it is commonly argued, primarily assisted in violent

52 Carroll, 'Introduction,' 23, 27.

53 References to statutes are mentioned in E. Horodowich, *Language and statecraft in early modern Venice* (Cambridge: Cambridge University Press, 2008) 93-96.

54 Chapter XLVII 'On injuries and insults': *Bando generale della legazione di Bologna e suo contado, fatto pubblicare li 12. ottobre 1756 dall'eminentiss., e reverendiss. sig. cardinale Fabrizio Serbelloni, legato a latere di detta città,* Bologna, 1756, 86-87.

55 Brackett, *Criminal justice and crime in late Renaissance Florence*, 133-134. Also see L. Martines, 'A way of looking at women in Renaissance Florence,' *Journal of medieval and renaissance studies* 1 (1974) 15-28.

56 S.T. Strocchia, 'Gender and the rites of honour in Italian Renaissance cities,' in J.C. Brown and R.C. Davis (eds.), *Gender and society in Renaissance Italy* (London: Longman, 1998) 52-54.

scenes with their voices and gestures.[57] Scholars like Daniel Lesnick and Sharon Strocchia have argued that the ritualized vocabulary of vilification – aimed at influencing friends, neighbours or relatives in the community – was in fact a distinctly female form of crime that gave women of all social classes an informal but major means of influencing and shaping public opinion in a highly patriarchal society.[58] "The language of slander," Laura Gowing asserts based on her research into seventeenth-century London, "offered particular linguistic powers to women through which they asserted their verbal, physical, and legal agency to judge and condemn other women."[59] As such, court records reveal the important roles of women in policing the social and sexual morality of their communities through gossip and insults.[60]

It would nevertheless be erroneous to characterize verbal affront as a 'typically female crime.' There is an increasing body of evidence that early modern European women did not limit themselves to verbal aggression. In seventeenth- and eighteenth-century Bologna, over four-fifths of the complaints made to the *Torrone* against female offenders concerned violence in its broadest sense of the word, but only one-fifth of these complaints spoke of verbal violence alone.[61] The court dockets suggest that women physically fought their neighbours, acquaintances, economic competitors, their customers and their employers – and played considerably larger roles as defendants before the criminal court than normative prescriptions would ever suggest. Of course, the verbal assaults that were litigated in court only represent a small fraction of the conflicts arising at the most basic levels of everyday life. Many physical assaults also mention the exchange of injurious words, often setting in motion a chain of physical aggression around which the case would then centre. Clearly, however, early modern women did not solely rely on the sharpness of their tongues to settle their conflicts; an observation that is also confirmed by other recent studies on towns in Italy and elsewhere in Europe.[62]

57 Crouzet-Pavan, 'Crimine e giustizia' 57.

58 D.R. Lesnick, 'Insults and threats in medieval Todi,' *Journal of medieval history* 17 (1991) 76; Strocchia, 'Gender and the rites of honour,' 54;

59 Gowing, *Domestic dangers*, 109.

60 Ibidem, 101; Rublack, *The crimes of women in early modern Germany*, 220; S. Lipscomb, 'Crossing boundaries: Women's gossip, insults and violence in sixteenth-century France,' *French history* 25:4 (2011) 411.

61 Counted in the denunciations, where the judicial filter was arguably the smallest. Among the 241 female offenders in the denunciations collected, 46 were accused of insults, threats or other forms of verbal aggression.

62 Vasta, 'Per una topografia della violenza femminile,' 59-81; Angelozzi and Casanova, *Donne criminali*; Cohen, 'Honor and gender in the streets of early modern Rome,' 616, 623; S.K. Taylor, 'Women, honor, and violence in a Castilian town, 1600-1650,' *The sixteenth*

Moreover, defamatory speech was by no means a female preserve. A study of Venice's *Avogaria di comun* in the sixteenth and early seventeenth century revealed that the brunt of the state lawyers' rigour fell on the verbal aggression by and against men up the social ladder: on male members of the underclasses hurling insults at nobles or state officials, disrupting civic peace.[63] Records from other councils such as Venice's *Signori di notte*, which primarily shouldered the responsibility to control verbal injuries in early modern Venice, could have perhaps balanced the scale, had these records survived the passing of time.[64] The dissonant images of the social landscape of aggression that different court records paint, emphasize that a characterization of verbal injury as 'typically female' is too simplistic. In early modern Bologna, women constituted around one-fifth of the *bolognesi* accused of insults and threats between the mid-seventeenth and mid-eighteenth century.[65] This does not deny that defamatory speech was a powerful tool for women to negotiate power in their everyday lives, but instead suggests that these mechanisms were not exclusive to them. In an honour-based culture, the power of insults to mar reputations rendered them useful currency for both men and women.

Verbal injury is often viewed in relation to morality. While the court records attest to women's ability and audacity in violently confronting their male and female adversaries for a wide range of motives, court testimonies reveal that it was nonetheless considered 'unladylike' comportment that was explicitly frowned upon by contemporaries.[66] By acting aggressively, women disrupted order in a practical sense, as well as normatively by defying their prescribed gender roles. Morality was also important because of the lexicon of verbal affront, which for women often made allusions to her indecency. Peter Burke convincingly argued that insults can be viewed as breaches of social and cultural codes of conduct, but that they did follow cultural rules and conventions 'as closely as a sonnet.'[67] Indeed, in early modern Italy the vocabulary of affront drew from a 'stereotyped, gender-loaded stockpile of invectives which both

---

century journal, 35:4 (2004), 1080; Lipscomb, 'Crossing boundaries,' 411; D. Roussel, 'La description des violences féminines dans les archives criminelles au XVIe siècle,' *Tracés. Revue de Sciences humaines* 19 (2010) 71; Hurl-Eamon, *Gender and petty violence*, 2005; Kilday, *Women and violent crime in Enlightenment Scotland*; Van der Heijden, *Women and crime in early modern Holland.*

63 Horodowich, *Language and statecraft*, 101.

64 Ibidem, 98.

65 In my sample, 53 out of 260 defendants accused of insults, defamation and threats were women.

66 Cohen, 'Honor and gender,' 133-134.

67 P. Burke, *The historical anthropology of early modern Italy* (Cambridge: Cambridge University Press, 1987) 96.

women and men adapted according to the needs of the situation.'[68] Defamatory speech therefore followed gendered conventions and value systems.

Research on towns all over medieval and early modern Europe has distinguished a basic division between the insults directed at women and those directed at men.[69] Evidence both from secular and ecclesiastical courts suggests that the term of insult against women were often sexual in form.[70] Research on medieval Todi and late-medieval Bologna suggest that insults to women were indeed overwhelmingly sexual, impugning her as some variant of a whore, adulteress or procuress.[71] Slurs for women in early modern Bologna also regularly referred to their sexual honour and, as Angelozzi and Casanova remarked, often concerned a substantial subordination to the dominant masculine cultural model: *puttana* (whore), *buzzerona* (a woman dedicated to sodomite practices), *sfondata* (worn out), *porca* (sow), *vacca* (cow) and *ruffiana* (pimp) were the most common abuses used for women.[72]

A traditional understanding of these slanderous words is that they directly called into question the sexual reputation of their victim. Since a woman's moral value was bound up in her sexual status and role as a producer of legitimate heirs, defamers would consciously draw upon the specific, gendered meanings of words such as 'whore' or 'cuckold' to make their insults as effective as possible, exposing the private acts of their victims.[73] More recently, however, scholars working on early modern England, Germany and Spain have argued that sexualized insult was only obliquely related to women's actual sexual behaviours. Sexualized insults actually represented concerns about a wide range of economic and social resources, such as financial extravagance or economic independence.[74]

Occasionally the slurs recorded in the Bolognese court records referred to the (surmised or imputed) sexual behaviours of the female recipients. In 1725

---

68 Strocchia, 'Gender and the rites of honour,' cit., p. 54.

69 D. Garrioch, 'Verbal insults in eighteenth-century Paris,' in P. Burke and R. Porter (eds.), *The social history of language* (Cambridge: Cambridge University Press, 1987) 104-119; J.A. Sharpe, *Defamation and sexual slander in early modern England: The church courts at York* (York: University of York, 1972) 15; Horodowich, *Language and statecraft*, 99.

70 Gowing, *Domestic dangers*, 59-138; Lipscomb, 'Crossing boundaries,' 417; Taylor, 'Women, honor and violence,' 1083.

71 Dean, 'Gender and insult,' 219, 231; Lesnick, 'Insults and threats,' 71.

72 Angelozzi and Casanova, *Donne criminali*74.

73 As for example argued by M.R. Greenshields, *An economy of violence in early modern France. Crime and justice in the Haute Auvergne, 1587-1664* (Oxford: British Library, 1986) 233.

74 Gowing, *Domestic dangers*, 115, 118; Taylor, 'Women, honor and violence,' 1084-1085; Rublack, *The crimes of women*, 26.

some of her neighbours shouted "injurious words, treating me like a women with little honour" at Rosa, an unmarried daughter of Domenico Mazzoni.[75] She had been standing in the doorway of her apartment building talking to a young man she describes as her friend and her neighbours had disapproved of the conversation and, implicitly, what it could lead to. Conversely, sexual probity garnered the same result in a case from 1675. Anna Maria, wife of Angelo Michele Capelli, refused to have sexual intercourse with barber Giovanni Battista Bordani, explaining she was an honourable woman. Anna Maria declared that after this rejection, Giovanni Battista started calling her a *puttana* (whore), a *buzzerona* (female sodomite) and similar words, threatening to beat her up because she did not want to submit to his wishes.[76]

More often than not, however, these insults pertained to a wide range of social and economic behaviours outside of the sphere of sexual behaviours. In 1653, Maria, wife of Giovanni Battista Chiarini, was called a *buzzarona infame puttana* (infamous sodomite whore), alongside other similar words, by the son of a man who had an outstanding debt with her husband.[77] Similarly, a year earlier the carpenter Horatio Foglia called his direct neighbour Domenica, wife of Battista Secchandi, not only a *ladra* (thief) but also a *puttana* after accusing her of stealing wine from their shared cellar.[78] Aside from disputes over debts and possessions, another example from 1674 demonstrates how sexualised slurs were also used in the context of mundane neighbourhood enmities. The mother and sister of Anna Maria Caballi were coming over to visit her apartment and knocked loudly on the door and windows. These loud noises vexed her neighbours Georgio, Giovanna and Elena Bonetti to such an extent that they started shouting insults at Anna Maria, her mother and sister, saying that they were all whores and scoundrels, even though her "sister was a young honourable single girl."[79] Rather than implying knowledge about actual sexual impurity, this case demonstrates how the sexualised rhetoric of honour and dishonour could be employed as a tool in the pursuit of a broader range of social and economic interests.

As a rule, insults against men were more varied. Men were also called *bastardo* (bastard), *becco* (cuckold) or *becco fottuto* (fucking cuckold) in Bologna, but it is clear that these sexual insults were essentially female-centred, aiming

75 ASBO, Torrone, 7869-1, fol. 201: "parole ingiuriose trattandomi da donna poco da bene."

76 ASBO, Torrone, 7028, fol. 178-179: "puttana buzzarona e simile, e minaccio di darmi de pugni, perche non volevo acconsentire alle sue voglie."

77 ASBO, Torrone, 6653, fol. 41.

78 ASBO, Torrone, 6609, fol. 254.

79 ASBO, Torrone, 7028, fol. 80-81: "con dirci che siamo tutte puttane, e barone nonostante che detta mia sorella sia putta zitella honorata, e da bene."

to ridicule men's affiliation with women who did not adhere to the sexual mores.[80] Similar to what has been argued for insulted women, these verbal affronts did generally not infer actual sexual transgressions. Again, they consisted of stock insults suitable for a wide spectrum of circumstances, ranging from theft and outstanding debts to noise complaints. For example, in 1652 Sabattino Alterino caught sight of Anna and her son Pellegrino on the lawn behind his house. Commenting that they would crush his grass, they started calling Sabattino bad words, such as seed of a cuckold thief, and said that his daughters were whores, which offended him because he considered himself an honourable man.[81]

Men often also received non-sexual insults, referring to their honesty or ability to carry out a profession. Men in medieval Todi were often called 'liar,' 'thief' and 'crook,' accusations that undermined their economic credibility and called into question their success and stature as a merchant, tradesman, artisan or labourer.[82] In seventeenth- and eighteenth-century Bologna men were also commonly insulted with these economic aspects of their good or bad reputation: *ladro* (thief), *barone* (scoundrel), *birichino* (rascal), *poltrone* (good-for-nothing), *guidone* (scumbag) and *furbo* (crook). For example, Vincenzo Tura was called a scumbag, failure and a traitor (*guidone, un fallito, et un traditore*) by Nicolo Mini in 1705. He had failed to pay off the still outstanding amount of 30 lire for a house his father had purchased from him, making the references to his economic failure befitting.[83] In other cases, the connection between the direct meaning of the slur and the behaviour was less clear, suggesting that these verbal affronts could be used at random, and in a range of different combinations.

Injurious words such as *ladra* (thief), *poltrona* (good-for-nothing) or *barona* (scoundrel) were also hurled at women. However, both the late-medieval and early modern Bolognese court records suggest that this non-sexual form of slur was used less commonly for women than for men and, furthermore, that the vocabulary of affront was less varied and more repetitive when directed at women than the insults directed at men.[84] Alongside gendered differences in the repertoire of verbal affront, part of the reason for the 'semantic poverty' of insults towards women may be found in the magistrates' prosecutorial indifference.

80 Strocchia, 'Gender and the rites of honour,' 54; Dean, 'Gender and insult,' 221.

81 ASBO, Torrone, 6609, fol. 209: "'villanie, cioe razza di becco ladro, et simile, et che ho da figliole che sono puttane," which offended him 'per essere un huomo honorato."

82 Lesnick, 'Insults and threats,' 71.

83 ASBO, Torrone, 7608-1, fol. 197-198.

84 Dean, 'Gender and insult,' 226; Angelozzi and Casanova, *Donne criminali*, 75.

The criminal court records support the idea that the petty violent acts among the lower classes were generally not a priority to the authorities. Many of the court records merely mention the exchange of 'injurious words' (*parole ingiuriose*), 'dishonest words,' 'impoliteness's' (*villanie*) or 'insolent remarks' (*insolenze*), without specifying what words had been used exactly. When specific slurs were jotted down by the notaries, it was rather imprecise and summarily, with some examples of slurs followed by 'and other similar ones' (*ed alter simile*). As discussed, the potential harm of verbal injuries to the honour and reputation of individuals and their families was widely recognized. The harsh sentences that the criminal bylaws prescribed bore witness to the fear of violent retaliation and vendetta that insults could bring forth as easily as physical affront could. But while the defamation of a social superior was generally taken very seriously by the authorities, verbal aggressions among commoners of roughly equal status was not.[85] It was exactly this group that made up the bulk of those appearing before the criminal court. How notaries documented details about their affronts must be viewed within this context.

These mechanisms of judicial disregard were likely exacerbated for women. Women's assumed 'weaker nature' and judicial minority derived from Roman law may well have caused their violent behaviours to have been taken less seriously than men's.[86] In the Bolognese countryside, the village's local bailiffs (*massari*) were reluctant ant to relay women's complaints to the criminal court, as their concerns were more likely to be perceived as trivial.[87] Similarly, the lack of female offenders prosecuted for verbal injury by Venice's *Avogaria di comun* probably also had less to do with a hypothetical confinement of women to the domestic arena than with a judicial disregard.[88] It is not difficult to reconcile the notion of a magistracy seeking to protect civic order and the stability of the state with a judicial paternalism towards women probably widely shared among court magistrates.[89] At times this judicial paternalism resulted in less harsh sentencing, and other times in women not being prosecuted at all.

Most litigants themselves did not seek out the criminal court to pursue their complaints about insults to a full criminal trial either. Some scholars have

85 Burke, *The historical anthropology of early modern Italy*, 99. For the insults against nobles and state officials that were taken seriously and prosecuted by the state authorities, see Horodowich, *Language and statecraft*, 105-112.

86 For more on women's legal position according to Renaissance jurists, see Graziosi, 'Fragilitas sexus,' 19-38.

87 Angelozzi and Casanova, *Donne criminali*, 70, 257.

88 The cautious suggestion regarding women's confinement to the domestic arena was put forward in Horodowich, *Language and statecraft*, 101.

89 For the notion of judicial paternalism, see Casanova, 'Crimini di donne, giudici benevoli,' 3.

argued that taking conflicts to the judicial authorities may have been particularly appealing to those with a marginal position in society. In her examination of sixteenth-century Rome, Elizabeth Cohen asserts that while established householders might resolve attacks to honour through other routes, prostitutes found in the criminal tribunal a 'public and socially sanctioned forum in which to air their grievances and, within the conventions of honour culture, to spread shame on their attackers.'[90] For early modern Bologna there is little evidence that those appealing to the criminal court belonged to a particularly disreputable segment of the urban lower classes. Yet the mechanism that Cohen identifies may be comparable. By bringing their grievances to the criminal court, Bologna's common labourers and small-time artisans hoped to gain additional leverage in often long-term conflicts with their social peers. What they expected from the law was not an intervention by the authorities per se, but an advancement of their extrajudicial settlement options.

While recourse to the criminal court may have been a common strategy to enhance one's social bargaining power, it was also frowned upon on a broader social scale. Such sentiments were not only reflected in disgruntled responses by those incriminated in denunciations, but the political dimension was also in a tangible way incorporated into the vocabulary of verbal affront. There is evidence for early modern Bologna, Rome and Venice that the corpus of insults was complemented with invectives of 'traitor' and, above all, 'spy' (*spia*).[91] Spy was a serious insult because it conjured up associations with the inquisition and oppressive social control.[92] Locally, within the Papal States, the insult furthermore specifically alleged deceitful collusion with the foreign 'operators of justice'; represented in Bologna by the *Torrone* and its *sbirri*. Local officials or others working directly for the authorities formed the most obvious target of these slurs. The denunciation by Stefano a Porta, a local bailiff of the Via Nuova in Bologna's inner-mural parish of San Giorgio, from the early 1650s is illustrative in this regard. While investigating a brawl that had taken place in his district, he encountered the day-labourer Giovanni Monti, who upon questioning started calling him so much as a 'fucking cuckold spy' and a 'thief who was a spy by profession.'[93] People who performed duties for the court, such its messengers delivering court citations, were understandably similarly targeted with these kinds of slurs.

---

90 Cohen, 'Honor and gender,'. 624.

91 Cohen and Cohen, *Words and deeds*, 159-187; Angelozzi and Casanova, *Donne criminali*, 76.

92 Rose, *A renaissance of violence*, 173; Horodowich, *Language and statecraft*, 100.

93 ASBO, Torrone, 6609, fasc. 142: "[...] et esso subito mi ha ingiuriato di parole dicendome spia becca fotuta, ladro, dicendome inoltre ch'io vada a fare la spia, ch'è mio mestiere."

This particular kind of slander extended beyond these actual officials to the wide range of ordinary labourers (textile workers, cobblers, tanners and so on) who merely took recourse to the law. Although this specific form of verbal aggression was most prevalent among male recipients, there is ample evidence that the contempt for cooperating with the criminal court was shared equally by men and women of all social classes.[94] The example from the beginning of this chapter, in which Angela accused her neighbour Maria of having acted as a spy (*fare la spia*) after having her incarcerated for her previous misbehaviour, is a good example of this.[95]

The contempt for taking recourse to the law can be attributed to a combination of cultural and political factors. Traditional understandings of honourable behaviour precluded the use of criminal courts. According to the *scienza cavalleresca* (i.e. the laws of honour which governed gentlemanly conduct first codified in the 1550s but is still widely discussed in eighteenth-century Italy) a man of honour was required to punish offences without recourse to the law because a true gentleman demanded satisfaction for himself rather than punishment by a third party.[96] Even though these codes formally only pertained to the honour of gentlemen, there were broader social and political tensions that made both conceptions of honour and using the law a contested affair for men and women of all social standings. The use of the *Torrone* furthermore led to indignation due to its intimate ties to the papal government. Being ruled by priests was widely resented, with the Pope (and consequently Bologna's papal government) being viewed by parts of the population as a foreign despot.[97] Involving this 'foreign' institution rather than resolving a conflict informally was therefore regarded a deplorable 'collaboration.' Recourse to the law was thus both very efficient particularly because of this external leverage, but also, ultimately, morally reprehensible. However, the deep-seated contempt revealed by the continued use of *spia* and *fare la spia* throughout the eighteenth century did not curtail the use of law courts by those seeking to resolve disputes, whether it concerned verbal or physical forms of aggression.

94 Angelozzi and Casanova, *Donne criminali*, 76.

95 ASBO, Torrone, 7869-1, fasc. 163.

96 Carroll, 'Revenge and reconciliation,' 102, 113.

97 G. Angelozzi and C. Casanova, 'Il tribunale criminale di Bologna,' in M. Cavina (ed.), *La giustizia criminale nell'Italia moderna* (*XVI-XVIII sec.*) (Bologna: Pàtron Editore, 2012) 252-253.

4 The Importance of Petty Physical Violence

Aside from verbal aggression, petty physical violence is increasingly recognised as a regular feature of women's everyday life in the early modern period. Just how regular this violence was, and what this represents in comparison to the figures of other regions, is difficult to ascertain due to differences in source material as well as contemporary classifications. Much of the recent research on women's violence in towns in northern Europe has emphasised women's relatively high shares among offenders of petty violence.[98] Examining physical violence prosecuted by Rotterdam's (lower) court of correction during the first half of the eighteenth century, Manon van der Heijden argued that women's share among 'fighting' (the least serious category of physical violence she distinguishes) was 42 per cent.[99] This was significantly higher than the share before the regular criminal courts in Rotterdam and Amsterdam, which amounted to around 6 per cent. Studies on sixteenth- and eighteenth-century Paris suggest that women's proportional share as offenders of petty violence ranged between five and 17 per cent.[100] A broader definition of petty violence is used in the scholarship on 'assault' on England, which includes threatening gestures and words alongside physical violence.[101] In his examination of the prosecution of assault before two summary courts in London between 1784 and 1796, Drew Gray found that 31 per cent of those accused of assault were female.[102]

In Bologna women were also more prominent among offenders of petty violence. While only between 2.5 and 5 per cent of homicide defendants consisted of women, they made up about 21 per cent of all offenders of petty violence among the denunciations. A categorisation closer to that of 'assault' results in an average of 26 per cent between the mid-seventeenth and the mid-eighteenth

98 Hurl-Eamon, *Gender and petty violence*; Kilday, *Women and violent crime*; Van der Heijden, *Women and crime,*; Walker, *Crime, gender and social order*, 25.

99 The average share of women accused of the broad category of violence (including fighting with another person and the destruction of property and belongings) prosecuted by Rotterdam's correctional court was 24%. See Van der Heijden, 'Women, violence and urban justice,' 84.

100 A. Farge and A. Zysberg, 'Les théâtres de la violence à Paris au XVIIIe siècle,' *Annales. Économies, sociétés, civilisations* 34:5 (1979) 986; Roussel, 'La description des violences féminines,' 71.

101 Gray, 'The regulation of violence in the metropolis,' 78.

102 Deduced from table 5.4 based on the minute books of the Guildhall and Mansion House justice rooms in Gray, *Crime, prosecution and social relations*, 108.

century.[103] In 1675, no less than 39 per cent of the offenders of petty violence consisted of women.

The involvement of early modern European women in petty acts of aggression has also been quantified based on particular judicial procedures that bound people to keep the peace. These measures were used for a wide range of acts of physical and verbal aggression similar to the English category of assault. Studying London's recognizances between 1680 and 1720, Jennine Hurl-Eamon found that female assailants made up one-third of the total.[104] For Scotland between 1750 and 1815, Anne-Marie Kilday has calculated that no less than 41 per cent of the so-called 'Letters of Lawburrows' were brought and granted against women.[105] Both for England and Scotland it has been argued that these measures were particularly preferred by those seeking redress for assault when the assailant had been a woman.[106] The accessibility, efficiency and effectiveness, as well as the low costs associated with this form of prosecution may well have contributed to the popularity of this judicial procedure among early modern women. As I have argued earlier, the seventeenth- and eighteenth-century Bolognese peace injunctions functioned in a similar way to these English and Scottish measures and produce strikingly similar figures. In Bologna, 44 per cent of the offenders who were made to promise not to injure or harm the other person again consisted of women accused of petty physical or verbal aggression.

The proportional share of petty violence among the total of reported crimes also speak to the importance of these forms of aggression in the everyday lives of Italian women. Studies on Italian towns during the Renaissance and early modern period have demonstrated the continuous high share of primarily petty violence among the recorded crimes of women and men. This stood in marked contrast to most northern European towns, where property crimes often ranked highest on the criminal courts' dockets.[107] In fourteenth- and fifteenth-century Florence between a quarter and half of all urban female offenders were brought before the court for assault and battery.[108] Non-lethal

---

103 In the Bolognese case this would include the categories of physical violence not resulting in life-endangering wounds, threats and other forms of verbal aggression as well as the recordings of *precetti* issued for a range of undefined physical or verbal acts of violence.

104 Hurl-Eamon, *Gender and petty violence*, 67.

105 Kilday, *Women and violent crime*, 94.

106 Hurl-Eamon, *Gender and petty violence*, 130; Kilday, *Women and violent crime*, 94; Shoemaker, *Prosecution and punishment*, 207.

107 See for example J. Kamp, *Crime, gender and social control in early modern Frankfurt am Main* (Leiden: Brill, 2019) 68; I.A. Cameron, *Crime and repression in the Auvergne and the Guyenne, 1720-1790* (Cambridge: Cambridge University Press, 2011) 179.

108 Cohn, 'Women in the streets, women in the courts,' 26.

TABLE 15 Relative importance of violence among denunciations and *processi*, ca. 1655-1755

	Female defendants		Male defendants	
	Denunciations (N=241)	*Processi* (N=70)	Denunciations (N=903)	*Processi* (N=1287)
Lethal violence	–	6%	1%	9%
Physical violence with danger to life	2%	13%	7%	19%
Physical violence without danger to life[a]	34%	10%	34%	9%
Verbal aggression[b]	19%	4%	15%	7%
Undefined violence (*precetto*)[b]	26%	4%	10%	1%
Other crime categories	18%	63%	33%	55%
Total	100%	100%	100%	100%

SOURCE: SAMPLE 1 AND 2 COMBINED (SEE APPENDIX), COUNTED BY DEFENDANT

a 'Petty physical violence'

b 'Petty violence' in its broadest sense includes the categories of petty physical violence, verbal aggression and the undefined violence

violence was also the most common crime that brought men and women before Viterbo's fifteenth-century podestarial court.[109] This observation is echoed by the few examinations of later periods. In sixteenth- and seventeenth-century Rome, the largest proportion of deviant behaviour by women who appeared before the Governor's criminal court concerned brawls and other forms of petty violence.[110]

Bologna's criminal casebooks also brimmed with denunciations concerning violent altercations such as scuffles. As in other Italian towns, petty violence constituted a significant share of the crimes reported to Bologna's criminal court: among the denunciations, nearly 80 per cent of all female and over 58 per cent of all male offenders had been accused of non-fatal, physical violence without life-endangering wounds (see table 15). Significantly more so than

109 Rizzo, 'Donne e criminalità,' 13.

110 C. Vasta, 'Per una topografia della violenza femminile (Roma, secoli XVI-XVII),' *Genesis* 14:2 (2015) 67.

verbal affronts or homicide, petty physical altercations formed the largest cause for *bolognesi*'s encounters with the law.

Like verbal injuries, these scuffles, brawls and assaults were only prosecuted to a small degree. This is clearly visible in the diverging shares of the different crime categories during the criminal court process as demonstrated in table 15. While hundreds of *bolognesi* flocked to a court's notary each year to denounce these types of violent altercations, these non-fatal attacks among the lower classes very rarely led to the start of an inquisitorial trial as they were largely considered too insignificant to prosecute.[111] That the *Torrone*'s statutes specifically instructed its judges not to pursue so-called 'minor crimes' such as insults, threats and non-life-endangering fights among the lower classes, is a telling example of this attitude.[112]

Violence was not condoned or ignored, however, even if it was 'petty' in character. Communities in early modern Europe did their best to maintain law and order through a range of formal and informal sanctions.[113] Both the Bolognese authorities' active encouragement of peacemaking among its plaintiffs and defendants as well as the stream of bylaws issued concerning weapon regulations underscore this point. For those men and women who came to the court, too, the insistence on pressing charges reveals a popular concern over petty violence, as did the frequent appeal to and issuing of the aforementioned peace injunctions for petty violence.[114] If the denunciations are evidence of popular perceptions of misbehaviour, women's violence was clearly considered an unwelcome aggression deemed worth denouncing to the court.

5 Severity and Weapons

Recognising that women were considered capable of a significant degree of violence, scholarship from the past decade has commenced re-evaluating the relationship between gender and violence. Recently various scholars have argued that petty violent offences were, in many ways, 'not sex-specific' or even 'ungendered.'[115] Factors that contributed to this assessment were the ways in

111 This also happened in England, see Hurl-Eamon, *Gender and petty violence*, 3;

112 Angelozzi and Casanova, *La giustizia criminale a Bologna nel XVIII secolo*, 391.

113 Dinges, 'The uses of justice,' 159-175; Kilday, *Women and violent crime*, 93.

114 Hurl-Eamon, *Gender and petty violence*, 4; J.M. Beattie, 'Violence and Society in Early Modern England,' in A.N. Doob and E.L. Greenspan (eds.), *Perspectives in criminal Law: Essays in honour of John L.J. Edwards* (Aurora: Canada Law Book, 1984) 42.

115 Hurl-Eamon, *Gender and petty violence*, 3, 66, 70, 88; J. Turner, 'Summary justice for women. Stafford Borough, 1880-1905,' *Crime, history & societies* 16:2 (2012) 55.

which violence was described in criminal court records, as well as the form and seriousness of this violence. As elsewhere in early modern and modern Europe, Bolognese casebooks reveal that men assaulted in greater numbers than women, but that when women did commit an assault there were many similarities to be found.

Although both men and women were capable of inflicting serious damage, the relative 'pettiness' that can be considered the most typical aspect of the reported violence of men and women. The pettiness related both to the causes of the altercation as well as the physical repercussions. The denunciation by Gio Batta Spinelli against barber Antonio Leli on 19 August 1705 is typical in this regard.[116] When the two men passed one another on the street, Antonio bumped into Gio Batta, which caused Gio Batta to fall on the ground. He disgruntledly showed his now dirty hand to Antonio and asked if he wanted to be soiled as well, after which Antonio gave him two blows with his barber scissors. According to Gio Batta this wounded him in his right shoulder and left arm, wounds that the court officials would have been able to see at the time of the denunciation a day later if he "had not had himself medicated." The records indeed note *vulneribus minime*; minor wounding.

A similar situation is found some twenty-odd years later, when Anna Vandoni's tenants were yelling at each other all night and she asked them if they were not ashamed of all the obscene words that came out of their mouths.[117] Anna Marchesini, one of these tenants, had responded by throwing a foot stove in her face, hurting her – even though the wounds could not be seen anymore when the denunciation was made one day later. While the *Torrone*'s prosecutorial effort concentrated on the more severe forms of violence, by far the largest share of violent behaviours reported to the court had led only to minimal or no visible physical wounds at all.

How men and women fought, and how this may have differed between the sexes, has been subjected to important scrutiny the past decades. In her work on crime and gender in seventeenth-century Cheshire, Walker explicitly dismisses both the stereotypical notion of women's violence as a modern 'catfight' involving "a few scratches, a slap in the face, or pulling hair" and the

116 ASBO, Torrone, 7608-1, fol. 76.

117 ASBO, Torrone, 7869-1, fol. 19. "Hieri sera all'ave maria senti che le sopradette gridavano con Lucia Giordani pigionante nella loro casa a causa che tutta notte andava delle gente su per le scale della medema, il che sentita da me, dissi, che vera non era vergogna per le gran parole oscene [... e] che pertanto le medeme tutte uscite mi cominciorono a strappazzare con parole ingiuriose e la sopradetto Anna mi tiro lo scaldino, che haveva in mano, e mi feri nella fronte, la qual ferita VS non puol vedere, atteso i medicamenti."

association of weapons with distinctly masculine combat as somewhat anachronistic.[118] She instead argued that male and female defendants, as proportions of the total number of defendants of their own sex, were equally likely (just over 40 per cent of the total) to be prosecuted for armed assault. Percentages for other regions and time periods diverge. In eighteenth-century Rotterdam, only a quarter of the male defendants are reported to have used a weapon compared to ten per cent of the women.[119] Moreover, percentages as low as four per cent (for female defendants) to seven per cent (for male defendants) have been found for seventeenth- and eighteenth-century London.[120] In seventeenth- and eighteenth-century Portsmouth, 16 per cent of the male offenders of physical assault and 15 per cent of the women used weapons.[121]

Bologna's early modern criminal court records suggest that weapons were commonly used in physical altercations. Over one-third of the women reported to have engaged in physical violence and 57 per cent of the male defendants were described as having used a weapon in their affront. Even among petty physical violence cases, just under half of the total defendants had used a weapon.

High rates of weaponry use in physical violence have also been found in examinations of violence in Rome and southwestern France: 42.5 per cent of the cases in Rome were committed with arms between 1561 and 1584, and Julius Ruff found that a staggering 63.3 per cent of homicide and physical assault trials in the Sénechausséés of Libourne and Bazas between 1696 and 1789.[122]The relationship between the high rates of weapon use in southern Europe and the prevailing culture of violence is not clear-cut. Some scholars noted early modern Italians' particular "comfort with violence and a familiarity with weaponry that pervaded all levels of society."[123] At the same time, it has been argued that the proactive enforcement of weapon-possession laws in Italian towns like Bologna is commonly overlooked in discussions such as these. Gregory Roberts recently contended that the strict regulation of the right to bear arms through police patrols and a government licensing regime from the mid-thirteenth cen-

118 Walker, *Crime, gender and social order*, 77-78. Walker here quotes Spierenburg, 'How violent were women?,' 10. Also insisting that women were usually unarmed is S. Amussen, '"Being stirred to much unquietness": Violence and domestic violence in early modern England,' *Journal of women's history* 6:2 (1994) 75.

119 Van der Heijden, 'Women, violence and urban justice in Holland,' 88.

120 Hurl-Eamon, *Gender and petty violence*, 73.

121 See table 1 in J. Warner, J. Riviere and K. Graham, 'Women behaving badly. Gender and aggression in a military town, 1653-1781,' *Sex roles* 52 (2005) 294.

122 Blastenbrei, 'Violence, arms and criminal justice,' 75; Ruff, *Crime, justice and public order*, 79.

123 Rose, *A renaissance of violence*, 90.

tury onwards "resulted in the arrest, trial, and conviction of scores of men, including political elites, each year."[124] Attempt by Bologna's legislators to suppress interpersonal violence through the active policing of arms-bearing, and the keen interest in recording factors such as weapon use, may thus also have played an important role in explaining the high degree to which weapons were mentioned in the criminal court records.

Women did not solely rely on the sharpness of their tongues, nor did they refrain from using weapons as much as stereotypes would suggest. Nevertheless, many scholars have observed clear gender differences in the types of weapons that male and female protagonists used. Among weaponry types, swords and firearms are the most notable and distinctly gendered, as they were nearly exclusively used by men.[125] This was also the case in Bologna. Swords and other long-bladed weapons were not just the particular preserve of men, but of nobles and their retainers. As elsewhere in early modern Europe, the right to bear these kinds of arms was reserved for the nobility of the senatorial class and their licensed servants.[126] In the eyes of papal justice, the possession of arms constituted a crucial cause of the endemic violence. In a bid to improve public order and mitigate violence in Bologna's streets and villages during the seventeenth century, weapons became the pillars of the public order legislation from the sixteenth-century onwards.[127] The ambition to curb violence was reflected in the 1610 *Bando Generale*, which prohibited the carrying of a wide range of arms in the city and countryside.[128] The carrying of swords without a licence was also forbidden on pain of the loss of the arm, a fine of 25 gold *scudi* and three pulls of the cord (*tratti di corda*).[129] The right to carry swords was outlawed on broad social levels, but a massive number of civic officials and notables were exempted from its provisions, beginning with the *Anziani* and the *Tribunale delle Plebe* and including the counts, senators, judges, soldiers, notaries, captain gatekeepers, artisans, and citizens and inhabitants who returned from outside the city.[130] The special status of these officials and notables was largely upheld in later edicts throughout the seventeenth century, although further restrictions and conditions were imposed upon them

124 Roberts, 'Vendetta, violence, and police power,' 5

125 Hurl-Eamon, *Gender and petty violence*, 74; Walker, *Crime, gender and social order*, 79.

126 Rose, *A renaissance of violence*, 187.

127 Ibidem, 230; Blastenbrei, 'Violence, arms and criminal justice,' 75; *Bando generale Serbelloni 1756*, chapter XLVI, No. 7, page 75.

128 *Bando generale Giustiniano 1610*, chapter XXIV, page 43-51.

129 Ibidem, 47.

130 Ibidem, 47-49.

regarding the bearing of other blades such as daggers, the length and blunting of blades, and the licensing of servants.[131]

Firearms, another male preserve, were also heavily regulated. In Bologna throughout the seventeenth and eighteenth centuries, archebuses were often subject to an absolute ban. Under the section of prohibited arms in the 1610 criminal bylaws, the arms mentioned first were the *archibugietti* – longer than three palms and suitable to wound from far away – which were absolutely forbidden.[132] The punishments for the bearing of these rudimentary firearms ranged from death by hanging for the *archibugietti corti da ruota*, and a fine of 200 *scudi* for the *archibugio longo a ruota* and pistols, to three pulls of the cord for the *arcobugio da fuoco*.[133]

Despite these harsh prescribed punishments, it has been argued that firearms were nevertheless readily available either through the widespread licensing system if not through the black market.[134] In their campaign against bandits, the *Torrone* decreed in 1614 the obligation of all *contadini* in Bologna's rural surroundings to keep in their house "at least one, and preferably two, loaded wheel-lock archebuses, and to carry one with them at all times when out in their fields and around their villages."[135] Due to the many disorders and homicides that accompanied the rise of firearms ownership, the decree was reversed within two and a half years. However, the ubiquity of the firearms continued to haunt the *Torrone*, as men continued to use them in their fights and murders throughout the seventeenth and eighteenth centuries.[136] The high number of citations issued on a daily basis by the criminal court's lawmen for unlicensed weapons demonstrated a continuous ubiquity of these arms among the male Bolognese populace.[137]

While the use of swords and firearms was thus distinctly reserved to men, both men and women used a broad range of items in their violent altercations (see table 16). Together, swords and firearms only made up a quarter of the weapons used by men in Bologna. With their specific connotations of noble (the swords) and pre-meditated violence (the archebuses), these arms were not necessarily the most representative for men's quotidian violence, neither

131 Rose, *A renaissance of violence*, 187-188.

132 *Bando generale Giustiniano 1610*, chapter XXIV, no.2, page 43.

133 Ibidem, 43-45.

134 Rose, *A renaissance of violence*, 117..

135 ASBO, *Legato Bandi*, 1600-1700, bando of 7 June 1614, as cited in Rose, *A renaissance of violence*, 53-54.

136 For a detailed examination of the predominance of archebuses as weapons in the prosecution of long-standing conflicts resulting in death, see Rose, *A renaissance of violence*, 79-140.

137 Ibidem, 187.

TABLE 16 Weapons used in reported physical violence, ca. 1655-1755

	Firearm		Edged[a]		Work tool[b]		Houseware[c]		Stick		Stone		Misc.	
Female defendants (N=54)	0	0%	11	20%	8	15%	21	39%	5	9%	7	13%	2	4%
Male defendants (N=317)	19	6%	141	44%	38	12%	20	6%	41	13%	53	17%	5	2%

SOURCE: SAMPLE 2 AND 3 (SEE APPENDIX)
Included are the categories of lethal physical violence, serious physical violence and petty physical violence. Not included in this table are the allegedly unarmed assailants: 133 women, 214 men. The distribution is roughly the same for petty physical violence alone.

a Includes swords, daggers and knives. Out of the 141 male defendants recorded to have used edged weapons, 49 used swords (35%)

b Included are tools carried outside of the household setting, often referred to as tools for certain professions such as 'cobbler's knife' or 'instruments', hammers, scissors, sickles and shovels

c This category includes a range of items found around the house such as foot stoves, rolling pins, pots and pans and pieces of furniture

quantitatively nor contextually. For the spontaneous rises to violence that characterised much of the quotidian altercations filling the *Torrone*'s court records, aggressors reached for their knives, their tools or other handy implements they had on them or could find in their nearby surroundings.[138]

Various work tools were among the items weaponised in the event of escalated disputes. In proportional terms these tools were used equally often by men and women, making up 15 per cent of women's weapons and 12 per cent of men's. They broadly reflected their occupations and work environments, as they were either picked up during the fight or, in case of the smaller items, were carried around as part of the offender's profession. For men the tools they used in their violent altercations reflected their work in stables (shovels, pitchforks, horse bridles and leather whips), agriculture (sickles), textile (textile rods, spools and scissors) and as artisans (hammers), among which the tools of cobblers were most prominent (cobbler knives, leather punchers and moulds). Women's tools also refer to their textile work (textile rods, spindles) and furthermore included sickles and shovels.

A broad range of knives were utilised as weapons in violence. Various kinds of knives and daggers (though rarely the elite stiletto) made up 29 per cent of the weapons mentioned in men's violence when excluding swords, and 20 per cent of women's. Knives were ubiquitous in the urban space, as they were far

138 This was also the case for male-on-male killings, see Rose, 'Homicide in North Italy,' 180.

less regulated than for example firearms and swords and furthermore had many functions. Men and women of all social stripes were accustomed to carrying a blade, ostensibly for cutting bread or eating and only occasionally, when quarrels escalated, for fighting.

Literature commonly associates certain weapons with particular kinds of social segments. While swords were at least in normative terms reserved for gentlemen and their aides, knife fighting was affiliated with the population's lower social strata.[139] In Bologna, too, those fighting with swords clearly belonged to a higher social segment and included a variety of those exempted from the ban on weapons, such as a marquis, chevaliers, a notary's son and seven nobles' servants.[140] Those fighting with daggers resemble the group of the sword fighters, including one gentleman (jailed nine times previously, however), a knight and three servants, as well as various artisans.[141] The knife fighters on the other hand clearly belonged to the broad band of urban artisans and labourers, such as cobblers and various types of textile workers. Based on his research on knife-fighting in seventeenth- and eighteenth-century Amsterdam, Pieter Spierenburg asserted that knife fighters may have occupied a social position along the border of the 'respectable and disreputable segment' of the urban lower classes.[142] How to determine whether this was true for Bologna is difficult to say. What the court records do reveal is that only two of the knife fighters were known to have been jailed before. One of them was Francesco Antonio Angeloni, an arms keeper, who had wounded an innkeeper, and the other was tanner Girolamo Romagnoli, having spent 17 days in the bishop's jail for an unspecified offence.[143] Some knife fighters were also described as having the reputation of a scoundrel (*barone di piazza*), but the large majority of them did not.

The social profile of knife fighters resembled that of those wielding sticks. Sticks as well as stones were among the more 'circumstantial' weapons, as they

139 Boschi, 'Knife fighting in Rome, 138; P. Spierenburg, 'Knife fighting and popular codes of honor in early modern Amsterdam,' in P. Spierenburg (ed.), *Men and violence. Gender, honor and rituals in modern Europe and America.* (Columbus: Ohio State University Press, 1998) 109-110.

140 The category of 'swords' includes 2 sables. Among the 31 known professions of the sword fighters (out of 43), there were also various merchants (5), (master) artisans (9) as well as various seemingly lower-class professions such as cleaners (2), gong farmers (2) and even a vagabond that fought with swords that they had either stolen, acquired through the licensing system or through the black market. For 14 sword fighters, the occupation was unknown.

141 The 19 'dagger fighters' record 10 professions: 1 gentleman, 1 chevalier, 3 servants, 2 barbers, 2 coopers and 1 painter.

142 Spierenburg, 'Knife fighting and popular codes of honor,' 109-110.

143 ASBO, Torrone, 7869-2, fasc. 10; 7869-1, fol. 149.

were often picked up during a fight rather than carried about the person. They made up significant proportions of weapons used by both men and women: nine per cent of the women and 13 per cent of the male fighters employed sticks in their fights. According to Spierenburg's theory, sticks were predominantly used by the more respectable people who refused to become involved in knife fights and instead, when threatened or challenged, tried to ward off the danger by other means such as a stick.[144] Not many of the stick-wielding *bolognesi* appeared to have had a criminal past: only one of them has been reported as having just been released from prison for an unspecified crime.[145] But while some of the stick fighters indeed attained respectable social positions (for example as church guardians and gilders), the majority appeared to have belonged to the same, ambiguous group of artisans (primarily coopers, bricklayers and various apprentices), complemented by porters and an unemployed beggar. What does stand out among the stick fighters is the number of apprentices and porters among them, a peculiarity shared by those that hurled stones.

Stones formed opportune weapons for men and women alike, making up 13 per cent of women's weapons and 17 per cent of men's. The streets were littered with stones, roof tiles and pottery shards and it therefore comes as little surprise that people in early modern Italy were often reported to have carried them and used them in their fights. In seventeenth-century Rome, police "were forever stopping" people with rocks on them; in their pockets, under their cloaks, up their sleeves, in their work aprons or even in the lining of their hats.[146] Much of the appeal of stones as weapons lay in their ubiquity, as they could easily be picked up during a brawl. In Bologna on 9 February 1706, the angered barber's apprentice Gio Battista Rampone, for example, spontaneously threw a stone at the back of Giovanni Alberti, a matrass maker's apprentice, after he had played a prank on him.[147] Similarly, Domenico and Marta Pongetti, two textile cutters, took offence at their co-worker Giuseppe Fiorentini's jokes on 6 August 1755.[148] Marta hurled a stone at him, hitting Giuseppe in the eye.

A relatively small but culturally significant proportion of the fights with stones concerned the so-called *sassaiole* or *sassate*. A continued series of edicts issued against these rock-throwing battles in many Italian towns throughout the centuries attest to the failure to push rock-throwing out of the civic

144 Spierenburg, 'Knife fighting and popular codes of honor,' 109-110.

145 ASBO, Torrone, 6653, fasc. 2.

146 R. Davis, 'Say it with stones. The language of rock-throwing in early modern Italy,' *Ludica* 10 (2004) 113.

147 ASBO, Torrone, 7608-1, fol. 176.

148 ASBO, Torrone, 8171-1, fol. 157.

mainstream. The unsuccessful outlawing of this practice in Perugia (also part of the Papal States) reconstructed by Davis mirrors the situation in Bologna, where both the criminal bylaw of 1610 and that of 1756 reiterated the hefty fines and public corporal punishment prescribed to those that participated in, or went to see, the rock-throwing battles.[149] Yet, as in Perugia, the early modern Bolognese court records contain many references to these forbidden practices, particularly because the treating doctors were required to denounce their patients – nearly always claiming to be an innocent bystander – to the *Torrone*. The denunciation by Gaetano Ordelassi is no exception and is indeed in many ways emblematic of these rock-throwing battles.[150] On 6 August 1674 this eight-year-old boy found himself before one of the court's notaries with a barber's report describing the grave head wound he had sustained the previous Saturday. He described how many boys were battling each other near the burial grounds for those that were hanged. One of their stones hit Gaetano in the middle of the head, wounding him 'with some danger to life.' He denied having participated, however, claiming that he just happened to be there, coincidentally sitting somewhere nearby.

While stones were used as weapons by men and women alike, the *fare a sassate* is considered to be a crime typically committed by groups of young men and boys.[151] Rather than merely functioning as weapons that caused physical injury, Davis argued that the fights with stones must also be viewed as a 'complex means of discourse' that involved moral hurt, personal vilification and had an anti-authoritarian, anti-papal connotation.[152] Being hit by stones in these battles was considered shameful as it likened the victim to an uncivilised beast.[153]Although women certainly did use stones as weapons in their violent one-on-one altercations, there is little evidence that they partook in the local legacies of the *sassate*. Bolognese court records as well as Perugia's police accounts seem to support the notion that the offenders were young men. Although systematic inquiries into the age of offenders were lacking in the Bolognese court dossiers, the groups of stone-throwers were invariably referred to as *ragazzi*, i.e. boys. Often, though not always, victims were also boys themselves. The denunciation by Girolamo Blasio is illustrative in this regard.[154]

149 *Bando generale Giustiniano 1610*, chapter XXV, no. 5-7, page 52-53; *Bando generale Serbelloni 1756*, chapter LXII, no. 8-9, page 112; Davis, 'Say it with stones,' 119.
150 ASBO, Torrone, 7028, fol. 50.
151 Angelozzi and Casanova, *Donne criminali*, 83.
152 Davis, 'Say it with stones,' 118, 127.
153 Ibidem, 114-115.
154 ASBO, Torrone, 6620, fol. 273.

After being treated for a dangerous head wound, he identified the principal perpetrator as a boy – "big like me" – of around twelve years old.[155]

Scholarly literature commonly contrasts knives, swords and firearms to the pottery, dishes, pots and pans that women are believed to have employed frequently.[156] In Bologna various types of housewares were indeed common among the arms that women wielded amidst their violent confrontations. Pots and pans, rolling pins, bottles, water buckets, chairs and food items made up no less than 39 per cent of their weapons (see table 16). The importance of these kinds of items is striking when compared to men's use of housewares, which was limited to a comparatively meagre six per cent of their weapons.

Despite the false sense of domesticity that the category of housewares may instil on the violent affairs of women, these altercations were not necessarily as harmless as they may seem. Pieces of furniture (like a chair) were used to beat one another, which could cause significant bodily harm. A very significant number of women – constituting nearly half of the items within the category of housewares – also flung foot stoves at their adversaries. The trial against Ursula Bagliardi on 5 February 1755 is a telling example of the damaging potential of this kind of weapon.[157] Her neighbour, the married spinner Barbara Lambertini, had to be treated in the hospital for a serious head wound after getting into a fight with Ursula. Barbara had seen her sixteen-month-old toddler being hit with a stone by Ursula's young daughter and smacked the girl in the face to discipline her. After finding out about these events, Ursula sought out Barbara and threw a foot warmer still full with fire (*pieno di fuoco*) in her face. According to the surgeon who treated Barbara, this resulted in life-endangering wounds. Other victims of still lit foot stoves describe similar unnerving effects. In 1725, for example, Maria Corellini threw one at her neighbour Antonia Vignecchi, angered by having to pay more rent, causing Antonia to end up with wounds all the way from her mouth to her stomach.[158] Moreover, it should not be forgotten that in over half of the reported cases women had assaulted others with knives, work tools as well as sticks and stones they found on the ground. As Walker argued for seventeenth-century Cheshire, both women and men armed themselves with whatever they had at hand.[159]

---

155 Ibidem: "[...] non conosco detto ragazzo, ne si chiama, ma è grande come sono, et puole havere dodici anni in circa [...]."

156 Van der Heijden, 'Women, violence and urban justice,' 88; Hurl-Eamon, *Gender and petty violence*, 72-73.

157 ASBO, Torrone, 8166-2, fasc. 50.

158 ASBO, Torrone, 7869-1, fol. 30.

159 Walker, *Crime, gender and social order*, 79.

Despite the normative prescriptions that continue to colour historians' perceptions of women's violence, there is little evidence that women's behaviour was characterised by a particular weakness or passivity. At the same time, it is important to emphasise that men's violence as a whole was by no means always deadly, nor did the type of weapons they used diverge inherently from those employed by women. To understand the meaning and purpose of women's violence in early modern Italian society, the next sections will explore the social profiles of offenders and victims, which are believed to have been highly gendered, as well as where and when violence occurred.

6 Violence and Social Relations

Who were the men and women involved in violence? Much of our understanding of the social composition of violent offenders is based on studies on lethal violence. These studies emphasise that the majority of murderers were (and are still) young men between the age of twenty and twenty-nine, whose victims were often of the same age and sex.[160] While no scholar disputes the predominance of men among killers, the focus on homicide has led to very particular, arguably inaccurate characterisation of quotidian violence in early modern Europe. Due to its function as a forum for conflict resolution, the *Torrone*'s casebooks allow us to also gauge large numbers of non-fatal violent altercations. The examination of the social characteristics of those involved in physical and verbal aggression will demonstrate the prevalence of violence among broad sections of the population.

Ascertaining the social positions of offenders and victims of violence is no easy feat. As others have noted, the characteristics of wealth and status that marked social division during the early modern period were fluid, and the language of social description was imprecise.[161] Even though the 'quality' of a person could be a decisive factor in sentencing, most early modern criminal court records did not systematically record socioeconomic characteristics of defendants and plaintiffs. For this reason, markers of identity such as provenance and age, while meaningful and interesting, are beyond the scope of this section. What will be treated here are the occupational and marital status of the plaintiffs and defendants, who they fought and what relationships existed among them.

160 R. Muchembled, *A history of violence: From the end of the Middle Ages to the present* (Cambridge: Polity, 2012) 9.

161 Hitchcock and Shoemaker, *London lives*, 4.

The occupations of fighters recorded in the Bolognese casebooks represent a broad section of society. For their livelihood, defendants of both sexes pursued a wide range of professions, from servants, labourers, hawkers, and struggling textile workers, to shopkeepers, skilled master artisans and even some public officials, as well as nobles. In this regard the Bolognese situation mirrors that of other late medieval and early modern towns, in which violence originated not from fringe groups as much as from the centre of communities.[162] Far from being marginalised to the social periphery, violence belonged to the cultural repertoire of most classes and groups in premodern Europe. Craftsmen, especially apprentices but also masters, have been identified as the core group among urban perpetrators.

Criminologists, sociologists and historians generally agree that the men who were predominantly responsible for violent offences were young and unmarried.[163] This has been contended for towns all over early modern Europe, as well as for earlier and later time periods. With less than ten per cent of men's marital statuses defined, the Bolognese casebooks exclude any real proof to the contrary. Women's marital ties were recorded regularly, since their social standing is believed to have been much more contingent on their relationship to other men.[164] Married women constituted by far the largest proportion of those involved in violence (over two-thirds of the assailants whose civil status was recorded), followed by unmarried (one-eighths) and lastly widowed women.

Other scholars also observed that the women coming before criminal courts for violent offences were often married.[165] Walker noted that married women constituted over half of all female defendants in assault cases in seventeenth-century Cheshire.[166] Similarly, Beattie found that in the urban parishes of eighteenth-century Surrey over 60 per cent of women accused of crimes against the person were married.[167] He furthermore argued that many of these married, violent women belonged to the more settled and established positions in the

162 Schwerhoff, 'Social control of violence,' 227, 241.

163 Ruff, *Violence in early modern Europe*, 125; Eisner, 'Long-term historical trends,' 113-115; P. Spierenburg, *A history of murder. Personal violence in Europe from the middle ages to the present* (Cambridge: Polity, 2008) 90-91; Mantecón, 'The patterns of violence in early modern Spain,' 245, 248; Schwerhoff, 'Social control of violence,' 227; Blastenbrei, *Kriminalität in Rom*, 95.

164 Castan, *Les criminels de Languedoc*, 36-37.

165 Beattie, 'The criminality of women,' 101-102, 115; Kilday, *Women and violent crime*, 94; Walker, *Crime, gender and social order*, 76.

166 Wives constituted 54.2 per cent, spinsters 35.6 per cent and widows 10.2 per cent of defendants according to Walker, *Crime, gender and social order*, 76.

167 Beattie, 'The criminality of women,' 101-102, 115.

community, with a good proportion being married to 'men of some substance,' rather than being part of the "dispossessed and rootless sections of society."[168] In Bologna too, the embeddedness of these women in the community may have been an important part of the reason why it was that *their* violence specifically came to the notice of the courts. Given the *Torrone*'s functioning as a forum for conflict resolution, charges generally served the purpose of extracting reparations for the damage done, monetary or other. Litigation of this kind bore most meaning when it occurred within the context of community.

An interesting feature of the Bolognese case – and arguably more broadly of the premodern Italian one – was the violence perpetrated by members of the nobility. Although labourers and artisans had invariably constituted the largest group of perpetrators of quotidian violence, recent historical works have revealed how early modern states saw noble violence as a threat to the maintenance and expansion of their authority.[169] Looking back on the past centuries of private vendettas, Legate Serbelloni's 1756 summation of the criminal bylaws describes factional violence as "destroying human society."[170] This perceived threat was also reflected in the criminal court records. For towns all over medieval Europe, scholars have observed an overrepresentation of the upper classes in violent behaviours compared to their demographic proportions.[171] Although long-term comparisons on the social status of offenders are lacking, it has been suggested that the involvement of the upper classes in criminal violence declined sooner in northern than in southern Europe.[172] While noble violence in England, for example, is assumed to have declined after 1550, upper-class violence remained prevalent in Italy well into the early modern period.

Criminal court records indeed reveal a significant concern with the violence of notables. According to a study on seventeenth-century Bologna, nearly half of the homicide victims in the urban and rural territory had consisted of members of the nobility and their servants.[173] In Siena, in 1600, nobles committed around 30 per cent of the homicides prosecuted, but this share declined

168 Ibidem, 102.

169 Cummins, 'Forgiving crimes in early modern Naples,' 255.

170 *Bando generale Serbelloni 1756*, chapter VI, no. 3, page 12

171 Eisner, 'Long-term historical trends,' 116-117; G. Ruggiero, *Violence in early Renaissance Venice* (New Brunswick: Rutgers University Press, 1980); S.R. Blanshei, 'Crime and law enforcement in medieval Bologna,' *Journal of social history* 16:1 (1982) 123; B. Hanawalt, *Crime and conflict in English communities: 1300-1348* (Cambridge: Harvard University Press, 1979) 131.

172 See for a summary of this evidence Eisner, 'Long-term historical trends,' 117.

173 Rose, *A renaissance of violence*, 93.

afterwards: to 16 per cent by the mid-century and to eight per cent by 1700.[174] Nobles also figured less and less prominently in the violence recorded in the urban Bolognese casebooks. Defendants with noble statuses were explicitly labelled as such on the cover pages of investigation dossiers. For offenders of all types of violence, over half of these mentions were found in the 1655 sample year.[175] In that year, nearly one-seventh of the violent offenders consisted of nobles or their servants; *bravi, socci* and *servitorii*. The share of nobles among violent offenders in Bologna dropped to a mere two to three per cent in the following century.[176] While the premeditative violence of the nobility had put its definite mark on the seventeenth century, scholars have argued that love rivalries, futile arguments and escalated drunken brawls typified violence the century afterwards.[177]

The upper-class violence, as well as the papal government's campaign against it, was deeply entrenched in Northern Italy's political history. The re-establishment of papal authority in northern Italy from the fifteenth century onwards has been called 'a violent project' as it was confronted with continued resistance by local oligarchies that wished to retain their power.[178] This resistance and particularly the refusal of Bologna's leading Bentivoglio clan to adapt to papal rule led to the conquering of the city 1506 as well as to the expulsion and hanging of dozens of leading, rebellious oligarchs throughout the sixteenth and seventeenth century. But the nobility's violence was not only directed against the nascent papal rule: they also fought each other. Under papal rule factional identities (Republican and Oligarchic) that had dominated the late-communal period continued to divide Bologna's nobility.[179] Many of the edicts issued throughout the seventeenth century therefore aimed to curb the

174 O. Di Simplicio, *Peccato, penitenza, perdono: Siena 1575-1800. La formazione della coscienza dell'Italia moderna* (Milan: Franco Angeli Storia, 1994) 103, 130 as quoted in Hanlon, 'Violence and its control,' 148.

175 In a representative sample of all urban *processi* collected for the years 1655, 1675, 1705, 1725 and 1755, 13 out of 588 identified offenders indicted for physical or verbal aggression were explicitly named as *D.* (*don*, notable) on the cover page of the trial dossier. Seven of these offenders had offended in the sample year 1655, 2 in 1675, 1 in 1705, 2 in 1725 and 1 in 1755.

176 In the 1655 sample, 20 out of 144 offenders with an indication of profession or estate belonged to the nobility or their retainers. For 1675 the sample includes only 2 references (out of 100 offenders), and in the periods after that only 7 (out of 267) offenders are categorised as such.

177 Angelozzi and Casanova, *La giustizia criminale a Bologna nel XVIII secolo*, 183.

178 Rose, 'Homicide in North Italy,' 35-37.

179 Ibidem, 31, 38.

nobility's independence, power and violence in the city of Bologna and its rural hinterlands.[180]

There is important evidence that Bologna's factitious local nobility had indeed been pacified by the turn of the eighteenth century. Angelozzi and Casanova attributed this 'disciplining' of the nobility to a programme of re-education in enlightenment values and a new chivalric code that emphasised courtly civility over violent revenge as the defining trait of the nobleman.[181] Others, however, contended that the Bolognese nobility were not so much civilised or re-educated, as that the more violent ones were prosecuted and banished to beyond the borders of the Papal States.[182] This culminated in the expulsion of a large swathe of the local nobility in 1664. The 'retreat of the nobility' from violence – much later than in much of northern Europe – should be seen in this light.[183]

As elsewhere in early modern Europe, violence did not commonly challenge presiding hierarchies and structures of social and political authority.[184] This meant that the victims of violence by and large belonged to similar social groups as their offenders. Public officials or other figures of authority who endured violence as a kind of occupational hazard are largely responsible for the middle and wealthier classes being very slightly better represented among victims of violence. The efforts of local bailiffs in conducting criminal investigations were not always appreciated, after all.[185] Court messengers, delivering the *Torrone*'s citations summoning suspects or witnesses of a crime to report to the court, were also ill-received. After receiving such a citation in 1706, Giovanni Gambalunga, a seller of chestnut cookies, did not want to accept the citation and was even more disinclined to pay the courier the twenty-six *quattrini* demanded for his services.[186] When the courier tried to seize a towel as collateral, Giovanni was angered further, raised his arm to punch him and shouted at him to let go of his possessions, leading the *cursore* to scurry away and lodge a complaint. Acts of aggression against 'social superiors' nevertheless only represent a minority of the cases recorded by the criminal court. Overall, most perpetrators of violence belonged to the lower reaches of society and offended

180 G. Hanlon, 'The decline of violence in the West: From cultural to post-cultural history,' *English historical review* 128:531 (2013) 390; Hanlon, 'Violence and its control,' 144.

181 Angelozzi and Casanova, *La nobiltà disciplinata*, 243-288.

182 Rose, 'Homicide in North Italy,' 2, 228.

183 Eisner, 'Long-term historical trends,' 117.

184 Schwerhoff, 'Social control of violence,' 227-228; Rose, *A renaissance of violence*, 36.

185 ASBO, Torrone, 6609, fasc. 142. "[...] et esso subito mi ha ingiuriato di parole dicendome spia becca fotuta, ladro, dicendome inoltre ch'io vada a fare la spia, ch'è mio mestiere."

186 ASBO, Torrone, 7608-1, fol. 235.

those of roughly equal status.[187] More typical of everyday violence were the brawls that erupted among artisans, peddlers and porters during their daily affairs, such as social discourtesies, money issues, drunkenness and competition for work. In 1706, for example, Domenico Maria Giacometti lost out on an employment opportunity to his fellow wine porter Giuseppe Tomasi because he had a nosebleed.[188] Not long after, he spitefully drew his knife and stabbed Giuseppe with it. Cases against female aggressors reveal similar patterns. In a denunciation from 1724, vegetable seller Fiorina was fed up with labourer Giacomo Ruspulini's lingering around her stall and insinuated he should get on with it and purchase something before he died.[189] Giacomo sneered he would erect the gallows for her husband then, if she had one, after which Fiorina hit him in the face with her stool. With a bloodied face he hurried away, first to the market chief and then to the hospital to have his wounds treated. While women's violence did also generally adhere to hierarchies of class and social status, this did not necessarily prevent them from offending against men. The diminishing share of the nobility and their retainers is nevertheless important to the understanding of the changing face of violence during the seventeenth and eighteenth centuries.

This brings us to the question of who fought whom in early modern Bologna. Scholars have observed that in early modern European towns in the majority of cases the patterns of interaction in quarrels reveal 'gender homogeneity.'[190] This meant that men generally faced men and women opposed other women. The idea that women's violence should be categorised as 'same-sex' violence has nevertheless been questioned. Seventeenth-century Cheshire, for example, revealed an entirely different image of violence: here nearly three-quarters of the victims in female-perpetrated assaults were men.[191] Among the recognizances too, men comprised nearly half of those who sought the security of peace against women. The costs of prosecuting by indictment in the English system – for which men are assumed to have possessed greater means – may partially explain why women assaulted men to this degree, it has been argued that but the patterns of women's violence were also informed by

187 Dean, *Crime and justice in late medieval Italy*, 171; Ruff, *Violence in early modern Europe*, 125; Rose, *A renaissance of violence*, 36, 90; Becker, 'Changing patterns of violence and justice,' 283; G. Ruggiero, *Violence in early Renaissance Venice* (New Brunswick: Rutgers University Press, 1980) 120.

188 ASBO, Torrone, 7608-2, fasc. 30.

189 ASBO, Torrone, 7869-1, fol. 2.

190 Schwerhoff, 'Social control of violence,' 227; Spierenburg, 'How violent were women?,' 21; Van der Heijden, 'Criminaliteit en sexe,' 29-30; Vasta, 'Per una topografia della violenza femminile,' 60.

191 Walker, *Crime, gender and social order*, 79-80.

household structures and obligations.[192] Walker argued that wives exercised *de facto* control of the domestic space and defended household boundaries against men, who were "numerically more likely than women to be aggressors in such situations."[193] It was thus in the role of the mistress of the household that women most often became involved in disputes that the criminal courts heard about; when household concerns were at stake.

For early modern Bologna, the truth lies somewhere in the middle between the 'gender homogeneity' proposed by most scholars and Cheshire's high share of female-on-male assaults. The majority of violent protagonists offended against adversaries of their own sex, but women's aggression was slightly less gender-specific than men's. Men – alone or in groups – constituted nearly one-third of the victims of women's verbal and physical aggression recorded in the criminal court documents, while women were only assaulted by men in one-fifth of the cases. If women had a male accomplice, they were more likely to assault a man than vice versa, but this did not mean that women merely had an 'assisting role,' as some scholars have suggested.[194] In 1654 cobbler Vincento di Stantini declared that he had been assaulted by bread seller Leonora and her assistant Lorenzo after complaining he did not like the bread and wanted his money back.[195] Lorenzo had stones in his hand, but it was Leonora who had hit Vincento with a stick, making her the clear protagonist in this violent altercation. Men, however, were more likely to co-offend with male accomplices, fought in proportionally larger groups, and under all circumstances predominantly offended other men. In proportional terms, men's violence in Bologna was more 'same-sex' than women's was.

The relatively lower levels of male-on-female violence reflect contemporary cultures of violence in which men frequently fought each other, as well as gendered methods of conflict resolution and prosecution. Rates of men victimising women would have definitely been higher had spousal violence been brought to the attention of the Bolognese criminal court more often and consistently. In Italy men had the right to chastise their wives and the law did little to correct men who abused this right. Several studies on the subject suggest that the right to chastise was enacted in legislation, respected by the law courts, and assumed by husbands in everyday marital life.[196] In its most extreme form, the husband's right to discipline his wife functioned as an extenuating factor or

192 Ibidem, 80.

193 Ibidem, 52, 76, 80.

194 Angelozzi. and Casanova, *Donne criminali*, 113-117.

195 ASBO, Torrone, 6653, fol. 131.

196 T. Dean, 'Domestic violence in late-medieval Bologna,' *Renaissance studies* 18:4 (2004) 527; Cavina, *Nozze di sangue*, 30; Lombardi, 'Marriage in Italy,' 112-113.

even an acquittal in trials involving wife-killing. In non-lethal forms of domestic violence, too, Italian men brought before the court often appealed to their natural right of correction.[197] While 'moderate correction' largely went uncontested, uncontrolled wife-beating was condemned by family members and neighbours alike.[198] Domestic violence nevertheless rarely came to the notice of the *Torrone*, and when it did these complaints were generally either rejected due to insufficient evidence, or they were settled semi-voluntarily in the form of reconciliation.[199]

Since 'matters of the family' were not considered to be the business of the criminal court, domestic violence by women was also underrepresented in the court dossiers.[200] Aside from the habit of dealing with these situations informally, underreporting of women's misdeeds was furthermore heightened by perceptions of the unimportance of women's violence as well as humiliation.[201] The case of apprentice Francesco Vitali – one of the few domestic cases recorded among the *Torrone*'s case files – supports this view. When Vitali claimed to have acquired his head wound through an unlucky fall, the surgeon responsible for medicating him deemed his explanation implausible and reported him to the criminal court.[202] Only days later, after hearing that his wife had taken various items from their house during his hospital stay, he admitted to lying about the cause in his earlier declaration and that it actually had been his wife who had beaten him on the head with a hammer. The general reluctance to involve the secular criminal court in these potentially embarrassing matters of the family – experienced by both the authorities and the victims themselves – provides a contextual explanation for the public character of the violence recorded in Bologna's criminal court files.

The overwhelming majority of cases documented by the *Torrone* concerned what Kilday has called 'communal' violence; disturbances that occurred not between members of the same household or family, but between neighbours,

197 Cavina, *Nozze di sangue*, 111.

198 Hacke, *Women, sex and marriage*, 141.

199 Cavina, *Nozze di sangue*, 111, 115; Casanova, *Crimini nascosti*, 81.

200 There is not a lot of evidence that ecclesiastical courts actively sought to interfere in these matters either. Cavina, *Nozze di sangue*, 111, 115; Casanova, *Crimini nascosti*, 81. For a more elaborate discussion of the Italian criminal justice system's treatment of domestic violence in a comparative perspective, see M. van der Heijden and S. Muurling, 'Violence and gender in 18th-century Bologna and Rotterdam,' *Journal of social history* 51:4 (2018) 695-716.

201 Angelozzi and Casanova, *Donne criminali*, 120; Eibach, 'Böse Weiber und grobe Kerle,' 680; Beattie, 'The criminality of women,' 87.

202 ASBO, Torrone, 8171-1, fi97.

co-workers, with customers, and so on.[203] Even though the likelihood of violence among strangers was probably higher on urban streets and in town alehouses than in close-knit rural surroundings, studies suggest that most people involved in quarrels in early modern towns generally knew each other.[204] For seventeenth-century Bologna, Rose has demonstrated that most homicides occurred within known relationships, where the victim and offender were at the very least acquainted with each other.[205] In early modern Bologna, too, the court records suggest that the vast majority of violent altercations in the city of Bologna occurred between people who knew each other at least by name and acquaintance, rather than between strangers. Only about one-tenth of the urban Bolognese offenders were entirely unknown to the victim.[206]

Rather than complete strangers, offenders and victims of violence were commonly relatives, fellow professionals, acquaintances and neighbours. These relationships, broken down in table 17, could be gathered for nearly half of the sampled denunciations and *processi* for physical and verbal aggression between the mid-seventeenth and mid-eighteenth century. This data testifies to the similarities between the everyday violence committed by men and women, demonstrating that the overwhelming majority of reported violence in Bologna had taken place outside of household or family relations. Although studies on lethal violence suggest that women probably committed violence against 'intimate victims' such as children, husbands and servants, the same cannot be assumed for violence in general.[207] Instead, women, like men, had many other opportunities for socialisation and conflict outside of the 'domestic realm' in the city.

In proportional terms, the relationships forged by women's activities in the urban economy were at least equally important as violent conflicts within the sphere of the family. Similar to other textile manufacturing towns such as Turin and Milan, women's labour force participation was high in Bologna: according to estimations nearly 64 per cent of Bolognese women aged eleven and

203 Kilday, *Women and violent crime*, 52, 92.
204 Schwerhoff, 'Social control of violence,' 227; Eisner, 'Long-term historical trends,' 119.
205 Rose, *A renaissance of violence*, 91, 98, 103.
206 From the 451 offenders whose relationship to the victim was known, 45 declare not knowing the offender at all, not even from sight.
207 Howard, 'Crime, communities and authority,' 85-86; Kilday, *Women and violent crime*, 52-53; O. Hufton, 'Women and violence in early modern Europe,' in F. Dieteren and E. Kloek (eds.), *Writing women into history* (Amsterdam: Historisch Seminarium van de Universiteit van Amsterdam, 1991) 82-84; Beattie, 'The criminality of women,' 83-84; Spierenburg, *A history of murder*, 16.

TABLE 17 Social and economic relationships between offenders and their victims, ca. 1655-1755

		Women		Men	
		#	%	#	%
Family		8	10%	40	12%
Neighbourhood	Neighbours	58	57%	38	11%
	Landlord-tenants	8	8%	5	1%
Work and the urban economy	Employer-employee	1	1%	19	5%
	Colleagues-competitors	3	3%	37	11%
	Vendors-clients	3	3%	24	7%
	Creditor-debtor	2	2%	23	7%
Undefined friends & acquaintances		17	17%	117	34%
Unacquainted		1	1%	44	13%
Total		102	100%	347	100%

SOURCE: SAMPLE 2A AND 2B (APPENDIX), COUNTED BY DEFENDANT
Calculations based on denunciations and *processi* of physical violence, verbal aggression and issuances and breaches of the *precetto criminale* (*de non offendendo*), where sufficient information was provided on relationships between offender and victim

over had paid employment.[208] More than half of them worked in the textile industry. Most women thus had an economic life of their own, be it in their husband's business or outside of it. Orsola, who made and sold headdresses out of her home, for example, mistreated Paolo Salani, a citizen of Bologna, and his female acquaintance who wanted to return one of the three headdresses bought the week before. When setting a price, they had done so based on a total purchase of three, and Orsola did not agree with the restitution of one third of the price. With "bad words, and little respect" she mistreated Paolo and his acquaintance and started pushing both of them aggressively.[209]

Female fighters also came in the shape of market vendors competing in the market place and defending their economic interests with words and deeds.

208 Palazzi, 'Tessitrici, serve, treccole,' 366-367; D'Amico, 'Shameful mother,' 110; Zucca Micheletto, 'Reconsidering women's labor force participation rates,' 211.

209 ASBO, Torrone, 8171-1, fol. 80.

A good example of the fierce competition over preferred places on the market comes from Elisabetta Spadoni and her husband Melchiore, a goldsmith, who together threatened to strike another goldsmith by the name of Gasparo Cavalli with a cane if he would not give up the market stall she had set her eyes on.[210] Similarly, Barbara Romare was pulled by the hair, dragged across the piazza and scratched in the face by another vendor who was upset with her for selling similar wares near to her stall at too cheap a price.[211] Examples such as these echo women's broader socioeconomic roles in the fabric of early modern towns.

Aside from the similarities, various gender differences in the perpetrator-victim relationships can be distilled from the court records. First, the group of undefined friends and acquaintances was much larger for male than for female offenders (34 compared to 17 per cent). Many of the conflicts in this category occurred in the context of sociability, for example in and around inns as well as on the street. Conflicts revolved around losing and cheating at gambling as well as jokes and drunken banter taken the wrong way. Although women certainly visited taverns too – the Bolognese criminal court records feature several of these visits – the world of sociability is assumed to have differed for men and women.[212] More so than for men, the presence of women in public spaces in early modern Italian towns was shrouded by normative restrictions, which when violated could not only impact her perceived respectability but also made her liable for criminal prosecution. When women fought with present and former friends and acquaintances, they instead appear to have primarily done so in and around the home. In the criminal records women are often reported to have hung out around houses, for example leaning out of the window or standing in the doorway. This will be examined in more detail in the next section that discusses the importance of houses as spaces for women's violence. The prevalence of neighbours and the neighbourhood may therefore help to explain the relatively lower share of undefined friends and acquaintances for female offenders.

Second, while it is important to recognise that women's violent altercations also emerged from their activities in the urban economy, it is noteworthy that

210 ASBO, Torrone, 8171-1, fol. 128.

211 ASBO, Torrone, 8171-2, fasc. 31. "[...] quale venuta meco a contesa a motive della nostra uniforme professione, pretendo essa dassi le mie a troppo vile prezzo [...]."

212 S.K. Taylor, 'Women, honor, and violence in a Castilian town, 1600-1650,' *The sixteenth century journal* 35:4 (2004) 141; Howard, 'Crime, communities and authority,' 76-77; M. Prior, 'Private spheres and public records. Reconstructing women's history for the early modern period,' in F. Dieteren and E. Kloek (eds.), *Writing women into history* (Amsterdam: Historisch seminarium van de Universiteit van Amsterdam, 1990) 61.

these kinds of relations were recorded more frequently for male than for female fighters (30 compared to 9 per cent). It does not seem unlikely that this difference was related to the gendered division of labour. As mentioned before, a significant proportion of men and (even more so) women in early modern Bologna found employment in the urban textile industry, as spinners, weavers, hosiery manufacturers and seamstresses.[213] But while male artisans worked on heavier silks of greater value on shops, factories and mills, lighter and simpler textiles were left to women's 'domestic' production.[214] The largest majority of the female textile labourers therefore worked from home through a sort of putting-out system organised by merchant contractors. Although the testimonies in the criminal records reveal that women did not necessarily always ply their trades on their own, this gendered labour division likely affected the extent to which socialisation and consequently conflicts occurred between co-workers or between employers and employees. It furthermore reminds us that to understand the social dynamics of violence, the spatial environment needs to be taken into consideration.

7 The Gendered Geography of Violence

Another important issue in the debate on the gendered nature of crime relates to the places in which violence took place. The early historiography on the relationship between gender and early modern urban geography was characterised by a strong emphasis on a gendered divide between the public and private spheres. Based on didactic and prescriptive literature as well as travel descriptions, the idea was put forward that women, because they were secluded and enclosed by moral norms, were typically absent from the public spaces. Dennis Romano's work has been particularly influential for early modern Italy.[215] As sites of business and politics, he described Renaissance Italy's piazzas, bridges, canals and streets as male spaces, whereas female spaces were thought to have been more confined to the 'home.' Other studies have on the other hand indicated that, especially for non-elite men and women, such a binary divide between public and private spaces was an anachronistic projection of ideals that

213 For 1726 it has been calculated that women made up 62 per cent of the urban weavers in Bologna, see Guenzi, 'L'identità industriale,' 464.

214 Palazzi, 'Tessitrici, serve, treccole,' 368-369; Guenzi, 'La tessitura femminile,' 251-253; Dumont, 'Women and guilds,' 7, 9; Terpstra, 'Working the cocoon,' 48-49.

215 D. Romano, 'Gender and the urban geography of Renaissance Venice,' *Journal of social history* 23 (1989) 339-350.

did not reflect the complex realities of past everyday lives.[216] As Cohen suggested, women, like men, regularly used many if not most of the urban spaces, and for various reasons: to attend religious or civic events, to go to church, to work, for recreation and for transgressive behaviour.

In spite of this criticism, the 'domestic space' has continued to be equated with the 'typical female arena,' also in relation to violence. Men are usually seen as being able to navigate between public and private places, committing violence in both realms, while for women it is often the setting of the household that is emphasised.[217] Various studies on women's lethal violence in the early modern period, have stressed the 'domestic nature' of this violence, stressing that women's conflicts were based on the tensions and conflicts of 'household life and relationships' and that they primarily made 'intimate victims' such as family members and servants, whereas for men this was much more varied.[218] Explanations as to why this was the case have revolved around early modern women's more restricted social and economic roles.[219]

It would be erroneous to extrapolate this 'domestic character' of lethal female violence to violence as a whole. Indeed, while it is uncontested that women's killings generally took place within the household setting, there is abundant evidence that the much more common acts of non-fatal violence did not. In early modern Bologna, the vast majority (59 per cent) of female defendants were accused of offending outside the house. Furthermore, both accused male and female fighters victimised non-family or household members, even within the house. The acts of violence that were brought to the

216 Cohen, 'To pray, to work, to hear, to speak,' 294; A. Jacobsen Schutte, 'Society and the sexes in the Venetian Republic,' in E.R. Dursteler (ed.), *A Companion to Venetian History, 1400-1797* (Leiden: Brill, 2013) 363; A. Vickery, 'Golden Age to separate spheres? A review of the categories and chronology of English women's history,' *The historical journal* 36 (1993) 383-414.

217 P. Spierenburg, 'Masculinity, violence, and honor: An introduction,' in P. Spierenburg (ed.), *Men and violence. Gender, honor and rituals in modern Europe and America.* (Columbus: Ohio State University Press, 1998) 17; M. Wiener, 'The Victorian criminalization of men,' in P. Spierenburg (ed.), *Men and Violence: Gender, Honor, and Rituals in Modern Europe and America* (Columbus: Ohio State University Press, 1998) 207; Boschi, 'Knife fighting in Rome,' 144; Walker, *Crime, gender and social order*, 33, 37, 76; C.R. Corley, 'On the threshold. Youth as arbiters of urban space in early modern France,' *Journal of social history* 43:1 (2009) 144; Howard, 'Crime, communities and authority,' 85-86.

218 Howard, 'Crime, communities and authority,' 85-86; Kilday, *Women and violent crime*, 53; Spierenburg, 'Masculinity, violence, and honor,' 16; Walker, *Crime, gender and social order*, 135; Hufton, 'Women and violence in early modern Europe,' 82-84; Beattie, 'The criminality of women,' 83-84; J.S. Cockburn, 'Patterns of violence in English society: homicide in Kent, 1560-1985,' *Past & Present* 130 (1991) 95.

219 Kilday, *Women and violent crime*, 57.

TABLE 18 Locations of violence before the *Torrone*, ca. 1655-1755

	Female defendants (N=120)		Male defendants (N=484)	
	#	%	#	%
House	49	41%	79	16%
Street (incl. markets, squares and outside public buildings)	65	54%	228	47%
Inn/tavern	4	3%	70	14%
Shop/workshop	2	2%	76	16%
Church	–	–	29	6%
Misc.	–	–	2	0%

SOURCE: SAMPLE 2A AND 2B (APPENDIX)
Calculations based on denunciations and *processi* for (predominantly) all degrees of physical violence as well as verbal aggression and issuances and breaches of the *precetto criminale* (*de non offendendo*)

criminal court's notice were largely communal events in which women sought violent redress for their disputes under the gaze of others.

Examinations of towns elsewhere in early modern Europe also note this publicness of most of women's reported violence. For eighteenth-century Scotland, Kilday found that while homicides by women were largely confined to mariticides (the killing of husbands), the overwhelming majority of common assault cases perpetrated by women were in fact committed outside of the domestic sphere, stressing its communal character.[220] In Rotterdam's eighteenth-century so-called fight books almost all (95 per cent) of the female aggressors acted outside of the home.[221] Finally, in sixteenth- and seventeenth-century Rome, nearly two-thirds of women's violence that came before the Governor's court was committed on the city streets and squares that also formed the stage of men's violence.[222] Since petty violence was much more common than homicide, for women as well as for men, it can be argued that the communal context was much more typical for female violence as a whole than its' supposed 'domestic nature.'

220 Kilday, *Women and violent crime*, 52, 92.
221 Van der Heijden, 'Women, violence and urban justice,' 19.
222 Vasta, 'Per una topografia della violenza femminile,' 69.

Although the violence of men and women largely took place outside of houses, they nevertheless constituted important sites of conflict. With 41 per cent of women's violence occurring in a house (as opposed to male defendants' 13 per cent), this was particularly true for female fighters. But most of the violence that took place in these houses should not be categorised as private, domestic disputes. As is known, the early modern house was not a private domain in a modern sense of the word, as there was no strict spatial divide between working and living.[223] Aside from the artisan's workshops and inns in which families often both worked and resided, the organisation of Bologna's textile industry furthermore ensured that many of women's economic contributions were made from houses. As a site where violence erupted, the court records reflect this connection between women's work and the house: the aforementioned denunciation by Paolo Salani against Orsola concerning the headdresses she made and sold out of her apartment is a notable example.[224]

Houses furthermore had social functions, which formed important contexts in the eruption of violence. The fights reported to the criminal court above all concerned acquaintances and community-members and the 'after-party' of weaver Anna Grilli and her husband is a rather exceptional yet telling example of in-house sociability.[225] On Saturday 6 September 1755, Anna, her unnamed husband, her sister Margarita and some other unnamed women had frequented a tavern nearby their home and around its closing hours, on the fourth hour of the night, her husband decided to invite some of the tavern-goers over to their house for some more drinks. One of the guests who came along was Guido Gennasi. He had already had an altercation with the women before, commenting on their drunken, unladylike behaviour which he believed to be below their level. Being invited over to the house, he took aside Anna's young sister, Margarita, and confronted her again while armed with a knife. This enraged the already drunk Anna, who – nicknamed *La diavoletta* (the little she-devil) for good reason – responded by saying she did not tolerate such behaviour from him, after which she threw a pair of scissors (candle snuffer) across the

223 For an elaborate discussion of public and private spheres in the early modern period, see J. Eibach, 'Das offene Haus. Kommunikative Praxis im sozialen Nahraum der europäischen Frühen Neuzeit,' *History & Archaeology* 38:4 (2011) 621-664; S. Muurling and M. Pluskota, 'The gendered geography of violence in Bologna, 17-19th centuries," in D. Simonton (ed.), *Routledge history handbook of gender and the urban experience* (Abington: Routledge, 2017) 153-163; E.S. Cohen, and T.V. Cohen, 'Open and shut: The social meanings of the cinquecento Roman house,' *Studies in the decorative arts* 9 (2001-2002) 61-84; A. Cowan, 'Gossip and street culture in early modern Venice,' *Journal of early modern history* 12 (2008) 314-315.

224 ASBO, Torrone, 8171-1, fol. 80.

225 ASBO, Torrone, 8175-2, fasc. 7.

room, unfortunately missing its target (Guido), into the face of another male guest (Pietro Berti) who was standing in the doorway. While exceptional in her ferocity, this case clearly demonstrates how houses could function as contested sites of sociability.

While the social functions of the house remain understudied, the importance of the more 'public' sites of sociability in engendering particularly men's violence has been widely acknowledged.[226] Together, taverns, shops and workshops, and (most commonly the exterior of) churches were the sites of roughly one-third of the recorded violent disputes by male assailants compared to one-tenth of the female fighters. Though not overly important in quantitative terms, ale-houses have been understood as particularly significant for men and, allegedly, their violent 'performance' of masculinity.[227] With taverns came joking, drinking, smoking, dancing and gambling with peers, and it was these rituals that according to scholars produced masculinity.[228] In his research on the socio-cultural meanings of spaces in eighteenth-century Frankfurt, Joachim Eibach has argued that it was this symbolic meaning of the tavern that made them highly contested spaces. Seemingly trivial conflicts concerning payment of the bill, rude jokes and accusations of cheating in games were therefore always – in some way or another – about honour. A Bolognese example serves to illustrate this point. Whilst playing the hand game of the Morra, a very fast game infamous for raising tempers, Bartolomeo Boscardini accused fellow player Antonio Marco Pallati of cheating, and after a back and forth of insults Bartolomeo was stabbed with a knife.[229] A crucial aspect of most of these brawls was that they were instigated by insults and challenges made in a public place. Recognising that reliability and trustworthiness were regarded as important features of a man's honour and reputation, violence could be an appropriately masculine response to avoid the loss of face in the presence of others.[230]

---

226 J. Eibach, 'Violence and masculinity,' in P. Knepper and A. Johansen (eds.), *The Oxford handbook of the history of crime and criminal justice* (Oxford: Oxford University Press, 2016) 240; Eisner, 'Long-term historical trends,' 119-121.

227 Howard, 'Crime, communities and authority,' 76; S. Rau, 'Public order in public space: Tavern conflict in early modern Lyon,' *Urban history* 34:1 (2007) 102-103; Eibach, 'Böse Weiber und grobe Kerle,' 678; Schwerhoff, 'Social control of violence,' 229; Rose, *A renaissance of violence*, 115-116; S. Amussen, 'Punishment, discipline and power. The social meaning of violence in early modern England,' *Journal of British studies* 34:1 (1995) 24-26.

228 Eibach, 'Böse Weiber und grobe Kerle,' 678; F. Nevola, 'Street life in early modern Europe,' *Renaissance Quarterly* 66:4 (2013) 1337; ASBO, Torrone, 8171-1, fol. 49, 157.

229 ASBO, Torrone, 8171-2, fol. 6.

230 Walker, *Crime, gender and social order*, 37.

Despite the historiographical tendency to describe taverns in relation to violence as quintessential 'male spaces,' the court records do contain examples of women acting aggressively there. The denunciation against Margarita Borsi, a married spinner, made to the *Torrone* on 30 September 1754 demonstrates this.[231] According to the plaintiff, the Bolognese lumberjack Alessio Corsini, he was sharing a drink with Margarita – whom he assumed to be a prostitute (*donna di mala vita*) – in the *Osteria della Pellegrina* when another man tried to join the two. According to his account, he told the other man to leave them alone, after which Margarita suddenly took out her knife and stabbed him in the face three times. Margarita herself admitted to stabbing Alessio "a few times," but insisted it was because she overheard him telling his three friends that he wanted to take her up to his room. Trying to escape the situation, she walked away, but Alessio grabbed her headdress, slapped, pushed and started choking her, and she declared only stabbed him to liberate herself.

Criminal court records like these show that women were indeed present in taverns: sometimes as perpetrators of violence and, arguably more often, as victims (commonly as personnel) and witnesses (as guests). Scholars like Eibach generally assume that their presence was both quantitatively modest as well as normatively frowned upon.[232] As has also been argued for German and English towns, unaccompanied Italian women who visited taverns were looked upon with suspicion, particularly regarding their moral status.[233] The case of Margarita and Alessio echoes these normative ties, as Alessio automatically assumed she was a prostitute because she was there by herself. The normative restrictions were backed up by many of the Italian cities' criminal bylaws: respectable women should be accompanied in public spaces by male kin, or were otherwise considered to be *donne di mala vita* (supposedly bad women, prostitutes) and could be subjected to punishments ranging from public whipping to exile.[234] Although these bylaws were not actively enforced, they essentially criminalised women's unescorted mobility in certain places and at certain times. It is therefore no surprise that scholars have argued that women's social lives revolved more around houses – their own and those of others – while men gravitated more towards taverns, piazzas and other open spaces.[235]

231 ASBO, Torrone, 8171-1, f23.

232 Joachim Eibach also found women primarily as victims and witnesses to violence in taverns. See Eibach, 'Böse Weiber und grobe Kerle,' 678.

233 Ibidem; Prior, 'Private spheres and public records,' 61; Angelozzi and Casanova, *Donne criminali*, 104.

234 Angelozzi and Casanova, *Donne criminali*, 104.

235 Taylor, *Honor and violence*, 141, 176; Howard, 'Crime, communities and authority,' 76-77; Prior, 'Private spheres and public records,' 61.

Streets, fairs and markets have been recognised as notable contexts for contests about masculine honour and authority.[236] Like elsewhere in early modern Europe, violence in Bologna was above all a 'spectacle of the streets.'[237] Comprising streets, alleyways, squares, street markets and the exterior of public buildings, this space was by no means less important to women than to men. In proportional terms it was even slightly more prominent among women's reported violent offences (54 per cent) than among men's (47 per cent). The reasons that caused blood to boil on the streets were manifold and ranged from disputes over such issues as property and debts or presumed thieving, the mishandling of shared resources (such as the neighbourhood well), spontaneous social altercations and work-related arguments.

The case against a female market vendor nicknamed *La sbirazza* demonstrates that the defence of economic interests was not reserved for men. On 6 August 1755 married market vendor Barbara Romare had herself medicated by a surgeon at Bologna's *Ospedale di Santa Maria della Morte* located near to the city's *Piazza Maggiore*, for a forehead contusion and various facial abrasions.[238] They were caused by another vendor – *La sbirazza* – who had pulled her by the hair and dragged her across the piazza while scratching her face with her nails for selling similar wares nearby her stall for too cheap a price. Although these market fights do not carry much quantitative weight among the criminal court records, this kind of violence typifies women's socioeconomic interwovenness in and importance to the urban economy. As economic actors, whether working in the public market place or at home, women did not shy away from defending their economic interests.

Both male and female fighters thus above all settled their violent quarrels in public, but they did not always choose the same location within the urban space. A closer reading of the descriptions of street locations hints at a significant difference between men's and women's use of 'liminal spaces.' Bologna's criminal court proceedings suggest that a lot of women's conflicts occurred not just anywhere in the street, but rather on the doorsteps of their homes, on the threshold, as has also been noted by Christopher Corley for early modern Dijon.[239] Indeed, it is noteworthy that in 41 per cent of the cases (i.e. a notable two-thirds of the 'street' category) women declared being just outside their

---

236 Howard, 'Crime, communities and authority,' 76.

237 J. Eibach, *Frankfurter Verhöre: Städtische Lebenswelten und Kriminalität im 18. Jahrhundert* (Paderborn: Ferdinand Schöningh, 2003) 222; Vasta, 'Per una topografia della violenza femminile,' 69; Farge, 'Les théâtres de la violence,' 989-992.

238 ASBO, Torrone, 8171-2, fasc. 31: "[...] quale venuta meco a contesa a motive della nostra uniforme professione, pretendo essa dassi le mie a troppo vile prezzo [...]."

239 Corley, 'On the threshold,' 149.

homes when the violence erupted: when entering or leaving their house, when using the shared spaces in the apartment complexes, while standing in the doorway, leaning against the window and sitting on the doorsteps under the city's *portico*. The role of these types of locations as descriptive markers in male plaintiff's reports was more limited: 12 per cent in total and 27 per cent of the street category.[240]

The following case of two quarrelling neighbours in 1706 is therefore in many ways typical of women's everyday violence committed in early modern Bologna. On 30 March Anna Cattarina Gaspari made her way to one of the criminal court's notaries to denounce her neighbour Teresa following a long-standing conflict between the two. Up until then, Anna Cattarina had been insulted daily by Teresa, who on numerous instances called her an adulterous whore even though she, as she asserts, was in fact a *donna da bene* – a respectable woman.[241] On this day, matters escalated into physical violence after Teresa had become vexed by Anna Cattarina's dog walking through her vegetable garden. Upon their encounter just outside their houses, Teresa pelted Anna Cattarina with stones, which did not cause her significant harm because she evaded them and fled the scene.

Violence erupted in places where men and women interacted on a daily basis and the criminal court records suggest that the immediate neighbourhood bore great importance for women – greater than for men. Indeed, it is known that the microcosm of neighbourhood relations functioned as a dense social fabric of interdependencies and reciprocal social control. Most middle or lower class inhabitants of Bologna could not afford to rent or buy their own house and instead lived in apartment complexes with shared courtyards, passageways and entrances to the street. Avoiding those neighbours one was at odds with may have been difficult in these shared spaces, but even the houses themselves offered little privacy since many people merely rented a room within a house. As in other early modern towns, the close proximity to one another and sharing of resources formed an understandable source of conflict and animosity in Bologna. This contextualised the vast array of neighbourly conflicts that made up the bulk of women's violence before the *Torrone*, motivated by anything from accusations of theft[242] and taking offence to a another woman presumed flirting with one's husband,[243] to smaller lingering annoyances[244],

240 The meaning of this difference in the description of spaces in relationship to violence will be treated in the next paragraph.

241 ASBO, Torrone, 7608-1, fol. 210-211.

242 ASBO, Torrone, 8171-1, fol. 117, 147, 177.

243 ASBO, Torrone, 8171-1, fol. 64.

244 ASBO, Torrone, 8179-2, fasicolo 2.

gossip[245] as well as competition over shared resources and space. The aforementioned wrecking of Teresa's vegetable garden is but one of the many examples of neighbourly petty violence captured in the *Torrone*'s court records in which women acted as protagonists.

The significance of the neighbourhood for women's violence is also distinguished for many other early modern towns in Italy, France, Germany, Holland, and England.[246] While different source types and administrative traditions render direct comparisons difficult, some 30 per cent of the violent women that came before Rotterdam's lower court had taken place in the neighbourhood, on the sidewalks and streets near their houses.[247] Similarities in the gendered geography of violence in various early modern towns are suggestive of the existence of a broader, shared pattern relating to women's use of the urban space. While dominant gender norms did not in practice enclose most women inside religious or domestic walls, be it in Catholic or in Protestant regions, they may have meant that that the lives of women, more so than those of men, unfolded mainly in the their neighbourhood streets. The everyday quarrels, brawls and scuffles that found their way into the criminal court records reflect these characteristics.

A comparison of violent offences before the *Torrone* and Rotterdam's lower criminal court during the first half of the eighteenth century reveals both important overarching similarities and indications of differences.[248] Similarities between regions and genders were above all found in the profile of the offenders: women were by no means passive accomplices but, like men, mostly acted alone and on their own behalf in their violence against other city dwellers in the public urban space. Importantly, however, Rotterdam's female fighters made up a larger proportion of offenders than in Bologna, and it is hypothesised that the locations of women's fights may help explain this discrepancy. While the geographies of violence were very similar for men and women in Rotterdam, the Bolognese records reveal more distinctly gendered patterns. For male Bolognese fighters, the locations very much resembled those of Rotterdam: 84 per cent of the men accused of committing physical violence before the Bolognese criminal court had fought their quarrels out in the street, on markets and squares, near public buildings, in taverns, and at work-related

---

245 ASBO, Torrone, 8171-1, fol. 36

246 L. Nussdorfer, 'The politics of space in early modern Rome,' *Memoirs of the American Academy in Rome* 42 (1997) 162; Roussel, 'La description des violences féminines,' 78; Eibach, 'Böse Weiber und grobe Kerle,' 679; Van der Heijden, *Women and crime*, 87; Beattie, 'The criminality of women,' 83, 87, 102.

247 Van der Heijden, *Women and crime*, 87, 92.

248 Van der Heijden and Muurling, 'Violence and gender,' 695-716.

locations – just like their violent male and female counterparts in Rotterdam. The prevalence of houses and their immediate vicinities for Bologna's female fighters set them apart. They furthermore much more rarely operated in taverns, near public buildings or workshops.

Several factors that may have caused these gender differences in Bologna's geography of violence in Bologna have already been discussed, such as practices related to labour and sociability. Another factor was the built urban environment, in which apartment complexes and their communal facilities, passageways, courtyards and gardens were separated from the street by a large door, and imposed a notoriously intrusive cohabitation that lay at the basis of many quarrels.[249] This especially affected women, since both their work and social lives were centred in these spaces more so than men's. Lastly, Italian cities' legislation functioned as the normative framework for the gendered geography of violence. Bologna's municipal decree against unescorted mobility targeted presumed prostitutes, but ensured that all women not shepherded by their husbands or male kin after dad were liable to be treated as courtesans by the men in town as well as by the police. The existence of this type of legislation likely meant that authorities did actually expect women to be in the streets, and there is furthermore little evidence of a strict enforcement of these regulations.[250] Nevertheless, the court records do illustrate that the gendered expectations presented limitations to women: as it stigmatised if not restricted their presence, movement and behaviour in the urban space.

8 Framing Men's and Women's Violence

Normative perceptions of how men and women should behave also influenced criminality in a different way. The judicial records reflect both real and fictional differences in how, where and why men's and women's violence was committed. Zemon Davis described how supplicants appealing for mercy in sixteenth-century France constructed tendentious versions of their lives and crimes to persuade the king and courts to issue a pardon for their crimes. Through the example of these so-called 'pardon tales,' she scrutinised the fictional qualities of judicial records, i.e. the "forming, shaping and moulding elements: the crafting of a narrative."[251] As well as a historical account of past

249 Ibidem, 127-128; Muurling and Pluskota, 'The gendered geography of violence in Bologna,' 159.

250 Ibidem, 304.

251 Zemon Davis, *Fiction in the archives*, 3.

actions or observations, texts of crime should therefore also be viewed as a series of narratives that are packaged in a certain way to augment their probative power, directed at pleasing a certain audience.[252] An examination of the fictional dimensions of these narratives is particularly relevant for the study of violence since its punishment was decidedly negotiable.

Fictionalisation does not equate to falsity per se, nor does acknowledging that judicial records were subject to moulding and shaping mean that these sources cannot be used to gain an image of actual fights. In his examination of knife fighting in seventeenth- and eighteenth-century Amsterdam, Spierenburg contended that there was no "fiction in the archives here" because of the magistrates' careful inquiries, the interrogation of several witnesses, and the fact that the interrogation protocols regularly contained different versions of the defendants' confessions.[253] As such, he contrasts the fiction of the archives with "the real story," although he also admitted that the defendants' "strategies certainly played a part."[254] There is little need to oppose these aspects, as they were, according to Zemon Davis and others, two sides of the same coin. Scrutinising prevalent narrative tropes helps both in discerning ideas about appropriate and inappropriate behaviour, as well as in determining the strategies used by plaintiffs and defendants in employing them to their advantage.

The forming, shaping and moulding of details occurred at all levels of the criminal process. Zemon Davis' account of the pardon tales describes the defendants' attempts to convince the judge that they should receive a pardon for their crimes. But not only defendants moulded their narratives. Already in the late 1980s Thomas Kuehn cautioned against a naïve reading of court cases without reference to the formative role of the court in the witness testimony.[255] He argued instead that legal procedure shaped the testimony of witnesses and, consequently, that the filter of legal rules and terms subtly restructured social realities.[256] In a similar vein Edward Muir and Guido Ruggiero have emphasised that both accusations and investigations tried to force the details of an event in the mould of what was required or perceived to be required to designate a specific action as a crime.[257]

252 For a recent treatment of the narratives in crime texts, see P. Arnade and E. Colwill, 'Crime and testimony: Life narratives, pardon letters and microhistory,' *Journal of medieval and early modern studies* 47:1 (2017) 147-166.

253 Spierenburg, 'Knife fighting and popular codes of honor,' 106-107.

254 Ibidem.

255 T. Kuehn, 'Reading microhistory: The example of Giovanni and Lusanna,' *The journal of modern history* 61 (1989) 518.

256 Ibidem, 515, 519.

257 E. Muir and G. Ruggiero, 'Afterword. Crime and the writing of history,' in E. Muir and G. Ruggiero (eds.), *History from crime* (Baltimore: Johns Hopkins University Press, 1994) 235.

A judicial narrative's mould was not only shaped by perceptions of criminality, but was furthermore constructed along lines of gender and class. Notably, Zemon Davis' argues that early moderners, especially the men, could draw upon distinctive understandings intrinsic to their estate.[258] From the pardon tales she discerned various different 'anger plots,' i.e. the contexts and procedural unfolding of violent escalations, which clustered around the social types of gentleman, artisan and peasant.[259] While 'peasant tales' often involved either the rivalry of suitors or inheritance, the 'gentleman's tale' revolved around defending his rights as a seigneur and his honour as a gentlemen, while the tales of artisans and tradesmen concern disputes in the realm of work, payment, theft and debt. Although further examination is necessary, it is not difficult to imagine that this typology would also hold for the rest of the criminal court proceedings.

Aside from class, themes and assumptions also clustered distinctly around gender. Ideas about appropriate masculinity and femininity take up an implicit yet fundamentally formative role in the representation of behaviour in the judicial records. For men, court records hint at notions of culturally demanded retributive violence. One good and almost stereotypical illustration of this is the homicide trial against Nicolo Sgariglia, a *cavaliere* nicknamed *Il Sergente*, who was prosecuted for the murder of another soldier called Marsilio Tomassini in June 1652.[260] The death of Marsilio, who had wounds on the left side of his hand and arm and was found deceased just outside a tavern, was brought to the attention of the *Torrone* through a 'secret friend of the court,' who informed the *bargello* (chief of police). Figuring out who had committed this murder did not prove to be too difficult, as there had been several witnesses to the act – though perpetrator Nicolo was nowhere to be found. The witness testimonies speak volumes regarding the motivation behind the fight. Tavern keeper Antonio Santi vividly described how the offender came into his *osteria* to eat and drink and had an argument with victim Marsilio over a previous altercation with his friend. Marsilio had asked Nicolo why he had bothered his friend, which Nicolo denied doing. Nicolo then asked to speak to Marsilio outside the tavern, saying he would not stand for such accusations, that he was an honourable soldier and demanded 'satisfaction.' Marsilio cursed at Nicolo, calling him a *gridone et un ladro* (bawler and a thief), to which Nicolo responded by saying he was in fact a *galanthuomo* (gentleman) and that he was willing to defend this reputation with his sword. He urged Marsilio to retrieve his own sword

258 Zemon Davis, *Fiction in the archives*, 43.

259 Ibidem, 38.

260 ASBO, Torrone, 6620, fasc. 3.

from inside, saying that he was a pig if he would not fight him, and waited for him. Once outside, the two men drew their swords and started battling. Marsilio received a deadly blow to the head and Nicolo – in absentia – was convicted and sentenced to the galleys for ten years.

The murder case of Marsilio and Nicolo speaks to the ritualised nature of violence in early modern societies. Although the court records make no explicit mention of it, the circumstances that led to Marsilio's untimely death very much resembled the duels treated extensively in historical literature. It also contains many of the classic ingredients of Zemon Davis' honour-driven 'gentleman's tales.' The dispute started in a tavern, took place between gentlemen who fought each other one-on-one with equal weapons after an encroachment upon the honour of one of them and a challenge to fight outdoors to settle the dispute once and for all. Although concepts of honour in relation to violence are usually discussed at the level of the nobility, it has been argued that they were crucial to individuals of all social levels.[261] According to Spierenburg much of the knife fighting in Amsterdam until the eighteenth century followed distinct rules and norms and represented a plebeian manifestation of male codes of honour.[262] He therefore called this kind of violence 'popular duels.'

In the Bolognese court records both the 'equal' and 'unequal' fights among the lower social strata relate to masculine honour in one way or another. The denunciation against Giovanni Cancella, a tavern boy from Medicina in Bologna's countryside, underlines that violence was considered an accepted and sometimes even demanded response to an encroachment of their honour for men of all social stripes. On 10 December 1652, the Bolognese stable master Piero Rovani denounced Giovanni Cancella for having hit him on the head with a pitchfork in the stable where Piero worked.[263] Piero asserted that Giovanni had probably hit him because he had previously intervened in a quarrel between Giovanni and another worker. When interrogated some ten days later, however, Giovanni himself provided quite a different explanation. After asking Piero for a key to one of the stables, Piero had mocked Giovanni and had called him a blind man and a fucking cuckold (*huomo orbo, becco fotuto*) in the presence of another colleague. Angered by this belittlement, Giovanni hit Piero on

261 T.V. Cohen, 'The lay liturgy of affront in sixteenth-century Italy,' *Journal of social history* 25:4 (1992) 610.

262 P. Spierenburg, 'Faces of violence. Homicide trends and cultural meanings: Amsterdam, 1431-1816,' *Journal of social history* 27:4 (1994) 709-711; N. Worden, 'Public brawling, masculinity and honour,' in N. Worden (ed.), *Cape town. Between East and West* (Hilversum: Verloren, 2012) 197; Spierenburg, 'Knife fighting and popular codes of honor,' 103-127.

263 ASBO, Torrone, 6620, fol. 171-172, 221-225.

the head with the pitchfork. When asked by the court whether he perceived his actions as a criminal offence, he answered that he did not think so: if Piero had not insulted him, he would not have hurt him either. He had only wounded Piero, he stressed, "for his necessary defence."[264] In this regard, even these supposed unfair fighters appealed to cultural notions of honour and retributive violence to defend their actions. Giovanni portrayed responding violently as inevitable, "because he felt there was no other possibility; he just had to do it."[265]

Appeals to the interlinked culture of honour and violence were by no means constant over time, nor were they shared among the entire population. That the Bolognese examples were derived from the very first sample period does not seem to have been a coincidence. Amsterdam's deadly, 'honourable' knife fights are believed to have disappeared after around the 1720s in favour of the violence emanating from conflicts in intimate relationships.[266] Some scholars have suggested that conceptions of honour changed during the eighteenth century, lessening the need to act in a certain way because of it.[267] In the Bolognese judicial narratives female fighters, furthermore, never alluded to the necessity to respond violently to an encroachment of their honour. Even though the circumstances and contexts from which violence erupted often comparable to men's, women would or could not invoke the same tropes suitable for and useful to men's judicial narratives.

That the testimonies of women regarding violence did not employ the same topoi or tropes as men's is likely to have had a cultural explanation. The first part of this rationale related – again – to the honour code. Various scholars have remarked that early modern Italian women's engagement in aggressive behaviour was neither expected nor desirable from a cultural perspective.[268] In a very practical sense there were no customary rules for fighting women, and they could not be formally challenged in honourable fights. In terms of defence, women's anger therefore seemed to have few acceptable uses. According to Zemon Davis' account of sixteenth-century France, for a woman,

264 Ibidem, fol. 223v: "[...] et vedendome cosi strapazzate, me sapito per li mani quell forcale de ferro et per mia diffesa da una sola bastonata al medemo Piero che lo colpi nella testa [...]" and fol. 224r: "[...] non penso d'essere incorso in pena alcuna per havere ferito il sudetto Pier Rovani per mia necessaria diffesa, che se lui et Battistino non mi ingiurivano io non l'haverei tocco, ne dato fastido [...]."

265 As cited for popular duels by Spierenburg, 'Knife fighting and popular codes of honor,' 105.

266 Ibidem, 107, 121.

267 Spierenburg, 'Masculinity, violence, and honor,' 5-7; McMahon, Eibach, and Roth, 'Making sense of violence,' 15-21; E. Hofman, 'Dikwijls bespied. Sociale controle onder buren in het achttiende-eeuwse Kortrijk,' *De Leiegouw* 55 (2013) 38;

268 Brackett, *Criminal justice and crime*, 133-134; Spierenburg, 'Knife fighting and popular codes of honor,' 118.

only the exceptional scenarios of genuine self-defence, the defence of her children, property, inheritance or religion could be used to justify her anger erupting into violence.[269]

A second part of the explanation lies in literary conventions. It has been remarked that women lacked a dependable set of narrative techniques, as "the general storytelling, Biblical and folktale tradition was ill-supplied with accounts of how women fought."[270] This made it difficult for women to appeal to these modes to explain their behaviour. The language of masculine violence permitted the framing of their conflicts in terms of manhood and honour, while women had significantly fewer conventions to draw on.[271]

In their denunciations and testimonies, women therefore employed different narrative strategies from men. There is abundant literature linking women's legal status in Roman law (as the *imbecillitas* or *fragilitas sexus*) to leniency in the prosecution and sentencing of women, but there is no consensus on whether or not women actively appealed to their supposed weakness in their defence. Summarising the works of others on various German early modern towns, Eibach suggested that women appearing before the criminal court presented themselves as weak women, whose disposition was disinclined towards violence.[272] Zemon Davis on the other hand found few of these kinds of references. In her examination of the French sixteenth-century pardon tales, female offenders neither pleaded their *imbécillité*, nor did they claim irresponsibility due to their husband's presence or directions.[273] While female offenders in early modern Bologna certainly encountered discretionary gendered paternalism, the court records lack references to their active appeal to notions of weakness or minority.

One of the most noticeable gender-specific narratives for women instead related to their use of space; a narrative formed by plaintiffs rather than defendants. In their denunciations female victims of violence invariably portrayed the street as a thoroughfare rather than a space of sociability. They reported walking to and from certain places during the day and evening, particularly to and from mass, but did not declare congregating with their friends as men often did. Lined with its distinct porticos, court testimonies depict Bolognese streets as places where men gathered socially. Male plaintiffs reported having become the victims of violence while sitting on benches under the

269 Zemon Davis, *Fiction in the archives*, 81, 94-96.

270 Ibidem, 101-102.

271 Walker, *Crime, gender and social order*, 97; Zemon Davis, *Fiction in the archives*, 104; Howard, 'Crime, communities and authority,' 85.

272 Eibach, 'Böse Weiber und grobe Kerle,' 672.

273 Zemon Davis, *Fiction in the archives*, 84.

porticos, while playing cards, watching puppet plays on the piazza, playing games, or drinking in and around the taverns or the city gates throughout the day and evening. With the notable exception of the plaintiffs who were working in the market or in the city's many *osterie* when they became the subject of violence, the majority of female plaintiffs invariably stated that they were walking to or from home or church. Otherwise, these women declared that they were standing in doorways, leaning on window sills, sitting on the steps and so forth when they were mistreated.

Both the descriptions of being nearby the house as well as justifiable mobility should be viewed from the perspective of gendered tropes of appropriate behaviour. Court testimonies were moulded by a combination of the conventions of law and judicial practice as well as by popular discourse and the personal, micro-political interests of the speakers.[274] While it is highly unlikely that the women who reported being assaulted strictly used the streets as thoroughfares from and to home, it is nevertheless telling that they chose to frame their use of this space as such. Although it is known that lower- and middle- and arguably even upper-class women used the public urban space for a wide range of purposes, women's uncontrolled presence in it was regarded as threatening.[275] That many Italian cities' criminal bylaws implicitly link women's unrestricted movement through the city to prostitution is illustrative. Women who were violated on the streets appealed – as a litigation strategy – to tropes of women's acceptable presence in the urban space, which did not extend beyond what was necessary, regardless of their actual behaviour. While male defendants referred in their testimonies to violence as a necessary means to defend one's honour, the statements of women remained rather matter-of-fact, commonplace and devoid of such clear appeals. A certain mundaneness of the descriptions of women's violence in court records has also been observed by scholars working on other regions in early modern Europe.[276] Ideas about appropriate feminine behaviour do rise to the surface through the denunciations, in which female plaintiffs framed their presence and mobility in the urban space in terms that they probably believed strengthened their positions.

---

274 E.S. Cohen, '"Courtesans" and "whores." Words and behavior in Roman streets,' *Women's studies* 19 (1991) 204.

275 Brackett, 'The Florentine Onestà,' 274.

276 Walker, *Crime, gender and social order*, 97; Zemon Davis, *Fiction in the archives*, 101-104.

9 Conclusion: Everyday Violence and the Uses of Justice

The violent tenor of everyday life in early modern Italy is undisputed, yet its special position within Europe has gone largely undiscussed. The Italian criminal court records attest to a pervasive culture of violence that in some ways stands in stark contrast to developments elsewhere in Europe. Not only do these records expose homicide rates much elevated from those found in more northerly parts of Europe, but they also show a clear preoccupation with a broad spectrum of non-fatal violent behaviours. Overall, in Bologna, violence of all sorts made up over three-quarters of the criminal complaints for which an offender was named. These are significantly higher levels than those recorded in northern European cities, even those brought before the lower summary courts.[277] Scholars have commonly linked the prevalence of violence in premodern Italy to the enduring cultural importance of a distinctly masculine honour culture, in which men frequently clashed over slights to reputation and status. Combined with presumed restrictive gender roles, the ethics of honour meant that it was neither expected nor desirable for women to engage in aggressive acts.

Despite these stringent normative restrictions, violent behaviour was in practice by no means the preserve of men. This chapter demonstrates that this was as much the case in Italy as it was elsewhere in early modern European societies. Although women arguably did not play a substantial role in the lethal violence committed in the city of Bologna, the criminal court records attest to women's ability and audacity in violently confronting their female and male adversaries. When including the more prevalent pettier forms of violence, urban Bolognese women made up about one-fifth of the violent offenders between the mid-seventeenth and mid-eighteenth centuries – a figure not unlike the ones found in other parts of Europe. Rather than relying solely on men for the defence of their reputation and interests – as prescribed by the ethics of honour – many Italian women took matters into their own hands. While women's violent behaviour may not have found much cultural encouragement, it was too common to be viewed as an anomaly.

Women's violence in early modern urban Bologna was distinct from men's in some ways, but also shared many of its characteristics. Importantly, the overwhelming majority of the non-fatal violence that the *Torrone* dealt with was 'public,' and concerned brawls between members of their own sex during their daily affairs, arming themselves with whatever items came to hand. Rather than pointing to women's 'enclosed' lives, the reported violent interactions of

277 Gray, 'The regulation of violence in the metropolis,' 83.

Bolognese women testify to the full range of women's engagement in social and economic relations in the early modern town. In some ways their experiences were nevertheless undeniably gendered. The criminal court records reveal that women's violence, more so than men's, often erupted in their immediate neighbourhood and involved their direct neighbours, reflecting some gendered socioeconomic realities of everyday life concerning women's labour activities and sociability, legal constraints limiting women's mobility in the urban space, as well as gendered tropes of appropriate behaviours and spaces in the framing of these violent events.

Individuals' recourse to the criminal court has been fundamental in shaping the image of historical violence. After all, the Bolognese authorities had only little interest in prosecuting the bulk of the reported violent acts and instead accommodated and generally favoured peacemaking practices – which were also preferred by many of the plaintiffs. As such, the verbal and physical aggression recorded in the court records must be viewed from the perspective of conflict resolution, in which men and women used the criminal court as leverage in the small politics of their everyday lives. In seventeenth-and eighteenth-century Bologna, its inhabitants had been exposed to at least hundred years of institutional intrusion. In addition to the widespread culture of violence, both men and women turned to litigation to mediate and settle their personal disputes, to establish personal boundaries and to make individual statements. Italy's early development of judicial and administrative structures had not thwarted its culture of violence and instead, until the judicial reforms of the nineteenth century, saw it go hand in hand with a culture of peacemaking. As we have seen in this chapter, women were active in both.

6

Legal Attitudes Towards Thieving

On Monday 9 February 1756 dyer Giuseppe degli Agostini made his way to one of the criminal court's notaries to denounce a theft that had occurred the day before.[1] He described having had a pig slaughtered two months prior and keeping six salted pieces in his apartment near Porta Sant'Isaia. After his wife left the apartment door open when they went out, they found upon their return that some of their cured ham was missing. A trail of salt grains led them to the apartment of one of their fellow tenants, Catarina Benserati. This evidence was presented to Bologna's *Tribunale del Torrone*, and Catarina was brought in for questioning soon after. Catarina, a widowed Bolognese spinner, excused her actions by saying she had walked past the apartment, had seen the meat through the open door and had hidden it in her room – but only as a joke. She claimed she had intended to return it later, but was unable to do so since she was incarcerated in the meantime. The case was concluded when, a week later, the ham was returned to Giuseppe, and Catarina was released from custody that same day without a criminal sentence.

While in many ways atypical, this case serves well to illustrate some of the general characteristics and circumstances of the many quotidian thefts in early modern Bologna. For both male and female offenders, opportunistic thefts from houses by neighbours featured prominently among the cases passing through the criminal court. The example furthermore speaks to the specific position that female offenders held before the early modern Italian justice system. While thefts and other property offences formed an important focus of law enforcement, there is significant evidence that female property offenders like Catarina were disproportionally dismissed of criminal culpability. This chapter, which examines the gendered dynamics of theft in early modern Bologna, therefore aims to shed light on both of these aspects: on the differences and similarities in everyday practices of male and female offenders as well as on the legal attitudes that framed their encounters with the law in early modern Italy. It argues that the comparatively low share of female property offenders among the higher echelons of Bologna's criminal justice system was engendered by a pervasive culture of institutionalisation, peacemaking and judicial paternalism towards women.

1 ASBO, Torrone, 8179-2, fasc. 16.

To this end, this chapter will start with a discussion of the legal attitudes towards thieving by the Bolognese authorities. Bologna's local criminal bylaws provide evidence for a continuing hardening of the attitudes towards property offending. They furthermore demonstrate that ideas about the prosecution and punishment of property crime were inherently gendered. The next part discusses various aspects of everyday practices of thieving based on the representative samples of denunciations and *processi* collected from the *Torrone* between the mid-seventeenth and mid-eighteenth centuries. Because of the small number of women in these representative samples, an additional set of theft *processi* involving female offenders has been collected to be able to scrutinise women's involvement in more detail. Based on these sources, this section examines the importance of theft among offenders denounced and prosecuted in early modern Bologna, the role of women in these cases, and the judicial treatment in practice, to point out two peculiarities of early modern Italy's legal culture: the pervasive peacemaking practices and the significant judicial indulgence towards women's involvement. Following this, the social characteristics of these property offenders will be discussed, suggesting that Bolognese thieves belonged to the working poor that incorporated occasional theft as part of their makeshift economies. The subsequent sections discuss what types of goods were stolen and where they were stolen from, and furthermore attempt to trace the journeys of these stolen goods through the urban environment. They suggest that the differences in practices and treatment of male and female thieves must be understood as existing alongside a wide range of shared behaviours, demonstrating the complexity of the relationship between thieving and dynamics of gender.

1 Legal Attitudes towards Theft

Property crimes in early modern Italy have received little scholarly attention, especially compared to elsewhere in Europe. Examinations of Italy's administration of criminal justice reveal the new political regimes' preoccupation with curbing the endemic violence as well as rural banditry rather than theft and other property offences.[2] From a legal perspective Italy shared a similar preoccupation regarding theft with the rest of Europe. Based on legal treatises and

2 See, for example, Tedoldi, *La spade e la bilancia*, 119-135; C. Povolo, 'Aspetti e problem dell'amministrazione della giustizia penale nella repubblica di Venezia, secoli XVI-XVII,' in G. Cozzi (ed.), *Stato, società e giustizia nella Repubblica Veneta (sec. XV-XVIII)* (Rome: Jouvenence, 1980) 220-236.

theological-ethical debates, Paolo Prodi argued that theft, from the twelfth century onwards, was increasingly conceptualised not only as a sin but also as an infraction of the concrete societal rules about the possession and use of goods.[3] Combined with a fundamental change in Christian solidarity regarding poverty, this reconceptualization led to an expansion of repressive penal legislation concerning crimes against property and the prescription of increasingly heavy punishments for thieves, in Italy and elsewhere in early modern Europe.

In a normative sense, the Bolognese authorities indeed regarded property offences as grave violations of public and private order during the seventeenth and eighteenth centuries. Scholars have contended that criminal courts prosecuted these kinds of offences with great determination, even if the value of the stolen goods was quite low.[4] In the Bolognese criminal bylaws, the prescribed penalties for property offences (or "theft and other similar offences" (*furto, & altri simili delitti*)) were severe. The *Bando Generale* of 1610, promulgated by Legate Benedetto Giustiniani, prescribes a place in the pillory or whipping combined with banishment for a first-time thief without extenuating or aggravating circumstances. Thefts of great value as well as second-time offenders could, however, be punished with a 10-year sentence to the galleys and a third offence to death by hanging. With aggravating factors, death sentences were readily prescribed.[5]

It is generally assumed that the authorities' attitudes towards crimes against property offences continued to harden during the eighteenth century.[6] According to some scholars, a growing social concern about the increased unemployment and impoverishment of the urban population due to the textile industry crisis formed the backdrop to this development in Bologna.[7] The criminal bylaws are sources in which such an increasing concern with property offences was most visible. Legate Fabrizio Serbelloni's 1756 *Bando Generale* is the first heavily revised summation of criminal bylaws since the beginning of the seventeenth century and is viewed as a reflection of the changing penal attitudes in Bologna.[8] This summation of the criminal bylaws for the first time

3 P. Prodi, *Settimo non rubare. Furto e mercato nella storia dell'Occidente* (Bologna: Il Mulino, 2009) 108, 208-209, 244.

4 Angelozzi and Casanova, *Donne criminali*, 243.

5 *Bando generale Giustiniano 1610*, 26-29.

6 For the situation in England, see Gray, *Crime, prosecution and social relations*, 68; J. McEwan, 'Negotiating support. Crime and women's networks in London and Middlesex, c.1730-1820' (Unpublished PhD thesis, University of Western Australia, 2008) 147.

7 Angelozzi and Casanova, *Donne criminali*, 243; Angelozzi and Casanova, *La giustizia criminale a Bologna nel XVIII secolo*, 142-147.

8 Angelozzi and Casanova, *La giustizia criminale a Bologna nel XVIII secolo*,219-220.

explicitly discusses the social dangers of theft. The opening paragraphs on theft state that this crime was in some ways considered to be more dangerous than homicide. The reasoning for this was as follows: while homicide was a great evil, it was essentially not repeatable. Theft on the other hand could be repeated endlessly, which made it most pernicious to both public and private order.[9] Although the rigorous punishment of theft may seem cruel and unjust, the document continues, the growing human malice and proclivity for this offence required such sentencing, because without it, it would be impossible to cope with the "impetuous torrent of thieves."[10]

Moreover, compared to the older bylaws, the 1756 *Bando Generale* defines in much more detail what is understood as theft, which categories of indictable property offences are distinguished and what the corresponding sentences were to be. In these new criminal bylaws the value of the stolen goods, recidivism and aggravating circumstances were key determinants for the severity of the punishment (see table 19). 'Normal' theft was called *furto semplice* and consisted of a range of larcenous activities. Aside from the act of stealing itself, it also covered the receiving of stolen goods. In line with juridical opinions elsewhere in early modern Europe, the Bolognese authorities considered receiving stolen goods to be just as bad as stealing itself.[11] According to Serbelloni's *Bando Generale* of 1756, these two acts should be treated and punished in the same way, since one could not operate without the other.[12] Three types of receiving actors are distinguished. First, those who had acted in good faith, buying from acquaintances, were not subject to punishment aside from having to return stolen goods without reimbursement of money spent. Those who had acted in 'bad faith,' for example by buying goods from strangers or at night not only had to return the goods or pay a monetary substitute, but if they sold the goods on they were furthermore liable for prosecution by the criminal court. A third category describes the true accomplices, who faced the same sentences as thieves. For pickpockets (*borsaiolo*) and purse cutters (*tagliaborse*) the same punishment guidelines were prescribed as for thieves.

9 "L'Omicidio seguito, che sia eg'è certamente un grandissimo male, mà non è di sua natura reiterabile; all'icontro il Furto ha in se questa pessima essenza, e da questa reiterazione seguendono la frequenza diviene perniciosissimo alla pubblica, e privata quiete, e di pessimo esempio." See *Bando generale Serbelloni 1756*, 39.

10 Ibidem: "Sembrerà a tal'uni queste pena crudele, ed ingiusta [... ma] vedendosi l'umana malizia sempre più accrescersi, ed esser facile, a proclive a questo Delitto, è stato più che necessario esacerbar le pene control il medesimo, senza le quali si renderebbe impossibile di far argine ad un Torronte così impetuoso di Ladri."

11 K. Callahan, 'On the receiving end. Women and stolen goods in London 1783-1815,' *The London journal* 37:2 (2012) 106, 108.

12 Angelozzi and Casanova, *Donne criminali*, 96; *Bando generale Serbelloni 1756*, 53-55.

The category of *furto qualificato* considered aggravating factors that, according to the norms of the 1756 *Bando Generale*, included the use of fake keys, lock picking, climbing walls with ladders or forcing windows or doors open. Even if the value of the stolen goods was relatively low, these kinds of thefts were punishable by death. The criminal bylaws state that this was due to people having no other options to protect their belongings than through

these locks and walls. Their violation was thus interpreted as a public offence against the papal prince who was responsible for the protection of the city and its houses.[13] Another aggravating factor that is mentioned separately was connected to labour relations. Responding to a perceived need to sanction this particular behaviour, Serbelloni's *Bando Generale* pays specific attention to domestic thefts, i.e. thefts committed by domestic servants or employees. As they were considered deceitful and difficult to defend oneself against, these kinds of thefts were subject to harsher punishments.[14] Compared to the *furto semplice*, the prescribed sentences were always a tier more severe. For example, while a first-time theft of an item worth 50 to 100 lire was prescribed a sentence of 5 years to the galleys in case of a simple theft, a theft of the same value by domestic servants would lead to a 7-year sentence.

Although quite specific in the punishments it prescribed per crime category, the criminal bylaws left ample room for the judge's discretion. In the introduction of Cardinal Benedetto Giustiniani's *Bando Generale* of 1610, it is declared that the inviolable laws must be observed by "each person of any sex, status, level, quality or condition."[15] However, early modern justice was tailor-made and in Bologna the judge was also explicitly given the discretion to take into account the causes, persons, places, time, the 'quality' and quantity, and other mitigating or aggravating circumstances when passing judgement.[16] That factors like age and gender were considered among the 'personal qualities' that could lead to a reconsideration of the prescribed punishments can be observed in the core text of Giustiniani's *Bando Generale*. Being younger than fourteen years of age, for example, exempted offenders from the death penalty for theft, and women were not to be sentenced to three pulls of the cord (*strappado*) for the taking away of possessions from fields or gardens as men were, but rather to three months of incarceration.[17] Similar distinctions can also be observed for other kinds of offences.

13 *Bando generale Serbelloni 1756*, 42-43.
14 Ibidem, 44-46; Angelozzi and Casanova, *Donne criminali*, 93.
15 *Bando generale Giustiniano 1610*, 4.
16 Ibidem, 72.
17 Ibidem, 26, 28.

TABLE 19 Sentences for common property offences in the criminal bylaws of 1756

Category	Condition	Value*	Punishment
'Furto semplice'	First time	<10	Pillory or Strappado
	"	Oct-50	Lashing
	"	50-100	5 years galleys
	"	100-300	7 years galleys
	"	300-500	10 years galleys
	"	500-1000	Life-long galleys
	"	>1000	Death by hanging
	Second time	Any	10 years galleys
	Third time	<20	Life-long galleys
	"	>20	Death by hanging
	Fourth time	15-20	Death by hanging
'Furto qualificato'	Aggravating circumstances	>10	Death
Swindle	First time	<25, 25-500, >500	Strappado, Lashing, Galleys
	Second/third	Any	5 years galleys
	More times	Any	10 years to life-long galleys
Robbery	Type of good/ time of theft		Life-long galleys to death by hanging
Property damage	Location/ what is damaged		Life-long galleys to death by hanging

SOURCE: *BANDO GENERALE* (1756) 40-62
* Counted in Roman *scudi* (1 Roman *scudo* = 5 Bolognese *lire*)

Serbelloni's 1756 *Bando Generale* for the first time explicitly mentions sex as a factor of systematic sentence differentiation. By then, these criminal bylaws no longer distinguished appropriate punishments for men and women in the text about the specific crimes themselves. Instead, they stress in the introductory remarks that the judge is free to impose judgement on women proportional to their sex, commuting punishments like the galleys and public *strappado* to the more suitable options of confinement, exile or lashing.[18] Understanding

18 *Bando generale Serbelloni 1756*, 3-4: "Dichiara, che in tutte, e single disposizione del presente Bando sono comprese le Donne, benchè di esse non se ne veda fatta alcuna espressa

how and to what extent the penal norms transcended the theoretical realm and were put into practice thus requires further scrutiny of the criminal court records.

2 Prosecution and Sentencing

The widespread culture of violence and the use of the criminal court as a forum for conflict resolution meant that acts of aggression rather than property crimes constituted the main reason for an encounter with the law in early modern Bologna. The several hundreds of complaints about property crimes each year made up about one-sixth of the denunciations to the *Torrone*. Similarly, the average of 80 criminal investigations constituted just over a quarter of the *processi* (see table 20).[19] These shares seem rather modest compared to those found in towns in northern Europe, where criminal courts were as a rule far more prone to prosecute theft and other property offences.[20] However, as has already been discussed, the preponderance of crimes against the person rather than against property before criminal courts seems to have been shared among towns in early modern southern Europe.[21]

Despite constituting a modest portion of the *Torrone*'s judicial dealings, theft and other property offences were considered serious threats to public

menzione, e loggiaceranno alle pene cominate, come se inciascun Capitolo fossero particolarmente nominate, nelli Delitti però a loro convenienti, e possibili a commettersi, e nelle pene altresi proporzionate al lor sesso, mentre rispetto alle pene non convenevoli, come di Galera, Corda in pubblico, e simili, si commuteranno nella Rilegazione, Esiglio, Carcere, Frusta, ed altre ad arbitrio secondo la qualità delle Persone, e circostanze de'fatti."

19 During the period under investigation, the *Tribunale del Torrone* employed 8 notaries who recorded the denunciations. One of them was the chief-notary who oversaw the others. My samples of the notebooks of one notary per focus year have led me to estimate that the number of denunciations for property crimes must have ranged between 200 and 450 each year. For an average 45% of the thefts reported to the Torrone no suspects were identified, for example because the thefts had transpired at night-time or for other reasons had no witnesses. The indicated number of *processi* here is based on an exhaustive survey of (extant) criminal court investigation dossiers for the five sample years.

20 Noordam, 'Strafrechtspleging en criminaliteit in Delft,' 228; *Old Bailey Proceedings Online* (www.oldbaileyonline.org, version 7.2, March 2015), Tabulating offence category, between 1674 and 1800. Counting by defendant; G. Morgan and P. Rushton, *Rogues, thieves and the rule of law. The problem of law enforcement in north-east England, 1718-1800* (London: UCL Press, 1998) 60; Schwerhoff, *Historische Kriminalitätsforschung*, 116.

21 Cohn, 'Women in the streets, women in the courts,' 26; Blastenbrei, *Kriminalität in Rom*, 284; Mantecón, 'The patterns of violence in early modern Spain,' 254, Abreu-Ferreira, *Women, crime and forgiveness*, 17; Ruff, *Crime, justice and public order*, see figure 1.01 in the introduction, n.p.

TABLE 20 The share of property offences among denunciations and *processi*, ca. 1655-1755

	Among total known offenders	Among female offenders	Among male offenders
Denunciations	17%	11%	18%
Processi	26%	39%	25%

SOURCES: SAMPLE 1 AND 2A (SEE APPENDIX), COUNTED BY DEFENDANTS

order. The interest in prosecuting property crimes was visible in the harsh sentences prescribed by the criminal bylaws. It was also reflected in the increased importance of property offences among the *processi* between the mid-seventeenth and mid-eighteenth century. Among the *processi* 26 per cent of the offenders were accused of property crimes compared to only 17 per cent of the offenders at the level of the denunciations. Some other crimes, such as the petty acts of violence so prevalent among the denunciations, were almost never turned into a formal investigation. This was different for property crimes: the authorities were keen to try to locate and prosecute the offenders even for small-value thefts.[22] It was not uncommon for a criminal investigation concerning petty theft to be more elaborate and complex than a homicide trial, in some cases involving dozens of testimonies and hundreds of folios.[23]

Property offences made up a significant part of the crimes for which women were subjected to a formal investigation by the judicial magistrates. The importance of this type of offence rose throughout the criminal justice process, which is witnessed by the discrepancy between the proportional share of property crimes among the denunciations and the *processi* for both men and women. This disparity was nevertheless particularly stark for female defendants. At the level of the denunciations, only 11 per cent of the female offenders were accused of having committed a property crime; far outweighed by complaints about all sorts of violence. Among the *processi,* however, the share of property offences rose to 39 per cent, making it the most important crime category for women at this level. This was most likely not only due to the perceived seriousness of property crimes. After all, the fact that property offences ranked so highly on the types of crimes for which women were investigated was also contingent on the fact that other offences brought before the *Torrone,*

22 Angelozzi and Casanova, *Donne criminali*, 243.

23 Angelozzi and Casanova, *La giustizia criminale a Bologna nel XVIII secolo*, 143.

TABLE 21 Types of urban property crimes before the *Torrone*, ca. 1655-1755

	Theft (*furto*)	Swindle (*truffa*)	Cutpursing (*crumenari*)	Robbery (*rapina*)	Property damage (*danno dato*)	Violation of seizure (*violatione di sequestro*)	Misc.	Total
Female offenders (N=91)	86%	6%	1%	1%	3%	3%	–	100%
Male offenders (N=583)	76%	5%	1%	11%	3%	1%	3%	100%

SOURCES: CALCULATIONS BASED ON ALL DENUNCIATIONS AND PROCESSI CONCERNING PROPERTY CRIMES FROM SAMPLES 1, 2A, 2B AND 3 COMBINED (SEE APPENDIX), COUNTED BY DEFENDANTS

such as their violent encounters, were not. The judicial ambiguity that female property offenders faced will be treated more extensively later in this section.

Theft figured prominently among the different property offences committed by men and women. The property crimes that were reported to the *Torrone* ranged from violation of the terms of seizure, property damage to animals, trees, shops or houses, to robbery, cutpursing or pickpocketing, swindle and theft (table 21). Contemporary classifications of these crimes can be deduced from the criminal court records, and can, amongst others, be gleaned from thc top right corner of dossiers' front cover. Following these contemporary categorizations, theft (*furto*) consists of the successful or attempted theft of goods or animals of values big or small, with or without breaking in, during the day or at night.[24] This category furthermore includes the receiving of stolen goods, since neither the criminal bylaws nor the *processi* classifications differentiated between the acts of stealing and receiving.[25] Theft as such constituted over three-quarters of the male and female property offenders that came before the *Torrone*.

The prosecution of property offences was not solely a matter of top-down control. Victims and other private individuals played key roles in the identification of suspects in the preliminary stages of the criminal process in early modern Europe.[26] In Bologna the overwhelming majority of theft cases were brought to the court's attention by victims who had noticed missing items

24 *Bando generale Giustiniano 1610*, 26-28; *Bando generale Serbelloni 1756*, 39-62.

25 Angelozzi and Casanova, *Donne criminali*, 96; *Bando generale Serbelloni 1756*, 53-55.

26 C. Herrup, 'New shoes and mutton pies: Investigative responses to theft in seventeenth-century East Sussex,' *The historical journal* 27:4 (1984) 817; Rublack, *The crimes of women*, 28.

from their domiciles, shops or purses, rather than by public officials or patrolling lawmen. When reporting a theft to one of the criminal court's notaries, a little over half of the victims revealed already having vague or more concrete suspicions about the offender's identity. Court records reveal that accusations were often based on rumours heard in the neighbourhood, and sometimes on a personal investigation. In a case from 1705, for example, the widow Orsola Borzaghi initially had no knowledge about who had stolen her two dresses, estimated to be worth about 25 *lire*. After visiting a prison to ask around if anyone there had any information, one of the women incarcerated there pointed her towards the eighteen year-old, unmarried silk weaver Anna Bellisia, whom she ended up denouncing to the *Torrone*.[27] Orsola's statement reveals the strategic purpose of her statement: in her denunciation she explains: "*Però son comparsa as esporre querela contro chi sarà stato il ladro* [...] *ad effetto, che sia castigiato et io rifatto del danno*" – she had lodged this criminal complaint to have the thief reprimanded and, furthermore, to be reimbursed for the damages.[28]

Despite the clear interest in finding and prosecuting thieves, the casebooks reveal that both authorities and plaintiffs were only able to do so for a limited number of them. Many of the reported thefts did not indicate a possible culprit because break-ins often transpired at night or because thieving for other reasons had no witnesses. This occurred quite frequently: for about 45 per cent of the thefts among the denunciations no suspects were identified. Even following a formal investigation, one-fifth of the theft cases still had no recorded suspect.[29] The inability to locate such a proportion of the culprits is not likely to have been a specificity of the Bolognese or Italian criminal justice system. More than anything they reveal the range and richness of the judicial administration on the Italian peninsula. Even cases that had little chance of being solved were carefully recorded and archived.

Among the property offenders that were identified and indicted as part of a formal investigation, a little less than half were found guilty. Chances of being banished (*esilio*) were particularly high (table 22). Even though this type of sentence was undiscussed in the city's criminal bylaws, nearly a quarter of the 393 defendants who were formally investigated for property crimes was sentenced to be banished from the Bolognese territory for an undetermined amount of time. The prevalence of banishment sheds light on its function: as it was commonly used as an instrument to moderate strict laws and often

27 ASBO, Torrone, 7602-2, fasc. 26.

28 Ibidem, fol. 1v.

29 This was calculated based on the exhaustive sample of *processi* for the years 1655, 1675, 1705, 1725 and 1755, which include 39 investigations for theft in which no suspect is identified (out of 209 theft cases).

TABLE 22 Registered sentences for property crimes among *processi*, ca. 1655-1755

	Female defendants		Male defendants	
Capital punishment	–	–	–	–
Banishment	10	24%	78	31%
Galleys	–	–	21	8%
Incarceration	4	10%	11	4%
Corporal punishment	–	–	1	0%
Fine	–	–	4	2%
Pardon	5	12%	17	7%
Surety/*precetto*	6	14%	48	19%
Cancelled/absolved	17	40%	72	29%
Total outcome known	42	100%	252	100%
Outcome unknown	16		83	

SOURCE: COMBINATION OF THE *PROCESSI* FROM SAMPLE 1 AND ADDITIONAL *PROCESSI* INVOLVING FEMALE OFFENDERS FROM SAMPLE 3 (SEE APPENDIX)

replaced capital punishments or a sentence to the galleys.[30] Some scholars have argued that capital punishments were most commonly prescribed for property offences. Based on the registers of people that were sentenced to death in early modern Bologna, it has been shown that more defendants were sentenced to death for property offences than for any other type of crime.[31] The Bolognese casebooks reveal that capital punishments for thefts and other property offences were nevertheless fairly uncommon between the mid-seventeenth and mid-eighteenth centuries. Other punitive and reconciliatory measures were preferred.

In early modern Italy there was a strong connection between banishment, reconciliation and pardon. Elsewhere in Europe it was common to make a distinction between lifelong banishments – which entailed the loss of all civil rights and the confiscation of possessions – and temporary banishments from the town, region, province or country for periods of 1 to 50 years.[32] In Bologna the convicted generally suffered exile from the entire legal territory for

30 Nubola, 'Giustizia, perdono, oblio,' 14; Tedoldi, *La spade e la bilancia*, 144, 152.

31 Angelozzi and Casanova, *Donne criminali*, 244.

32 A. Schmidt and J.M. Kamp, 'Excluding the unwanted? Banishment in early modern cities: Frankfurt am Main and Leiden in the 17th and 18th centuries' (Unpublished conference paper, Urban History Conference 2016).

indeterminate periods of time, until he or she was able to make peace with the victim or the victim's family. After a peace accord had been achieved, offenders could request a pardon for their crimes. Although not systematically recorded by the extant criminal court records, most of the pardoned Bolognese property offenders had initially received a banishment sentence. The pardon rates for property crimes were significantly lower than for crimes such as homicide: while nearly 40 per cent of the recorded killers were pardoned, less than 10 per cent of the property offenders could count on one. Nevertheless, the culture of reconciliation played a significant role in how inhabitants and magistrates dealt with property offences in early modern Bologna.

The importance of peacemaking procedures is also apparent in the cancellations of *processi*. Over one-fifth of the formal investigations for property offences by the *Torrone* were halted. Reasons for halting an investigation could be the lack of evidence, because the defendant was considered innocent, or because a settlement had been reached between the plaintiff and the defendant. At least half of the cancellations stemmed from a withdrawal of the complaint by the plaintiff (*rinuncia*), which generally meant that a peace accord or another kind of agreement had been achieved, often involving some form of compensation.[33] In this respect too, the proportion of cases that were cancelled is lower than for acts of violence, but is nevertheless indicative of the pervasiveness of the culture of peacemaking in the criminal justice system.[34]

While reconciliation played an important part in the judicial dealings of both male and female offenders, some salient gender differences in sentencing can be discerned. A few 'typical' differences apparent from the Bolognese sources have also been observed for other early modern towns.[35] A sentence to man the oars of the papal galleys, for example, was reserved for male offenders. Female property offenders, on the other hand, appear to have been somewhat more likely to be incarcerated than their male counterparts. Ideas about the gendered suitability of certain punishments, also reflected in the criminal bylaws, arguably played a role in shaping these patterns. The tendency towards locking away women should also be viewed within the context of the early proliferation of institutions for 'problematic' women and girls in Italy following the Counter-Reformation.[36] Fearing their potential poverty-driven immorality,

---

33 Niccoli, 'Rinuncia, pace, perdono,' 224.

34 Sara Cucini also observed that theft cases were less frequently halted than those for violence, see S. Cucini, 'Législation statutaire et gouvernement pontifical en Italie centrale. Le cas de l'administration de la justice criminelle à Bologna, deuxième moitié du Xve siècle' (Unpublished PhD thesis, Université Paul-Valéry, 2014) 359.

35 King, *Crime and law in England*, 170.

36 Cohen, *The evolution of women's asylums since 1500*, 3, 8; Terpstra, *Cultures of charity*, 17.

a continuum of correctional and charitable institutions – unprecedented in number and scope – sought to help, supervise and correct women in various stages of their lives. The case against the single domestic servant Maria Cantelli illustrates a cycle of care and control from which she could not escape.[37] She was sent out from the workhouse (the *Mendicanti*) where she was residing to work as a domestic servant in a noble house. When her employer wanted her to return to the work house after eight days, Maria fled with some of her employer's clothing and pearls worth 15 *filippi*. Upon her capture she stated she had resorted to the theft because she had dreaded returning to the workhouse, "where the circumstances and people were so bad." Despite her plea, she was transported back to the *Mendicanti* not long after.

Although the sentences that male and female offenders received were not drastically different, there are important signs that women's involvement in property crimes was not always taken as seriously as men's. Overall, women made up 14 per cent of the accused property offenders among the denunciations, but only a little over half that (7.7 per cent) at the level of the *processi*. Female offenders' 'vanishing' from the criminal justice process can at least in part be attributed to the considerable degree of indulgence in the treatment of female property offenders observable in the criminal court dossiers. Female offenders were often absolved before even being formally interrogated if they had one or more male co-offenders in other types of crimes – especially in the case of theft.[38] Angelozzi and Casanova justly remarked that this indulgent 'chivalry' should not be viewed as a display of favour, but rather as paternalism rooted in ideas of women's minority and subordination in every social sphere.[39] Women's involvement was thus often considered irrelevant, regardless of their role in the crime.

That women with male co-offenders might receive little scrutiny from the criminal court for their roles in property crimes becomes apparent from a case that deals with the theft from Elena Leni.[40] She complained to the criminal court that clothing and jewellery worth around 300 *scudi* (or 1500 *lire*) had been stolen from her house, accusing her husband Pietro Maria Gentili as well as her two tenants: the married couple Marco Antonio and Camilla Alberti. Both the husband and the male tenant were arrested by the criminal court's lawmen, were held in prison for twelve days and were tortured for a confession through the *corda*. Despite the contradictions in their stories, they insisted on

---

37 ASBO, Torrone, 7859-2, fasc. 51, especially fol. 13r and 16r.

38 Angelozzi and Casanova, *Donne criminali*, 239, 242.

39 Ibidem; Casanova, 'Crimini di donne, giudici benevoli,' 1.

40 ASBO, Torrone, 5674, fol. 301r-352v, 570r-589v, as discussed in Angelozzi and Casanova, *Donne criminali*, 244-246.

their innocence and the two men were liberated into exile until they were able to receive a pardon several months later. Camilla, however, did not only escape torture but was furthermore released after only a short initial interrogation, despite the fact that all of the evidence seemed to point as much as to her as to the two men. That the role of Camilla in this theft – as a young woman in the presence of men – was so readily dismissed is certainly telling of the attitude of the magistrates in the criminal process.

Although property offences were considered grave crimes in early modern Bologna, judicial practice diverged significantly from the letter of the law. The specific functioning of the legal system across the Italian peninsula played an important role in bringing about this disparity. The legal culture that accepted and stimulated peacemaking efforts so prevalent among cases of violence was also apparent among the judicial dealings of property offences, in spite of the importance attached to prosecuting these types of crimes. The prosecution of property offences was furthermore contingent on gender expectations and gendered notions of responsibility, culpability and judicial relevance. As we have seen, this affected not only how property offences were punished but also the extent to which the authorities considered women to be criminal actors in the first place.

Property offences nevertheless constituted the most important crime category for which women were investigated by the criminal court. If and to what extent the circumstances and characteristics of their crimes were gendered therefore deserves further scrutiny. Because of its importance among property offences dealt with by the *Torrone* during the mid-seventeenth and mid-eighteenth centuries, it will be thefts and the related activities of receiving and reselling stolen goods that take centre stage in this examination.

3 The Social Profile of Thieves and Economies of Makeshift

Economic conditions and experiences of poverty have played important roles in the scholarly thinking about the contexts of property crimes. The increasing economic deterioration has figured prominently in the scholarship about *antico regime* Italy. A prevailing idea since the 1950s has been that Italy became increasingly poor throughout the sixteenth and seventeenth centuries as economic leadership shifted from the Mediterranean to the northwest Atlantic.[41] In his work from the late 1980s, Stuart Woolf surmised that this pauperism in

41 For an overview, see A. Cavaterra, 'Economia, povertà e consumi in età moderna,' in B. Coccia (ed.), *La quarta settimana: Storia dei bisogni e dei consumi degli italiani che oggi*

Italy was reflected in the decline of urban employment, falling levels of consumption, the organisation of institutional charity and the growing exploitation of female and child labour.[42] However, more recent works have argued for regional differentiation and have furthermore shifted this caesura to the eighteenth century. Large cities like Venice lost out in sea transport during the seventeenth century, though towns like Bologna endured only relatively mild decline – at least until the mid-eighteenth century, when living standards worsened drastically in Italy due to the decline of real wages and a significant increase of price levels.[43] While the real economic crisis was still to come, Bologna's stagnating textile industry undoubtedly impacted the lives of many underemployed and underpaid inhabitants relying on textile work to make ends meet throughout the seventeenth and eighteenth centuries.

As far as the Bolognese criminal court was concerned, the problem of pauperism was predominantly one of men. Particularly after 1750 pickpocketing and small-value thefts as well as cases against male beggars and vagabonds deprived of any credible means of subsistence surged among the *Torrone*'s casebooks; a result both of deteriorating economic conditions and of biased policing.[44] For female offenders there is no evidence for such an increase in property crimes, vagabonding or begging. Concerning property crimes, Angelozzi and Casanova found 30 female offenders in their sample of *processi* and denunciations from 1671 compared to only 16 in 1775-1779 (constituting 8.6 per cent of all recorded female offenders versus 13.6 per cent in 1671).[45] In the face of hardship the *Torrone* increasingly dealt with certain criminalized deeds of men, but largely neglected to do so for women. The tendency in Italy since the Renaissance to institutionalise rather than criminalize women as an answer to the threat of their poverty-driven sexual immorality, may provide a partial explanation for this difference.

The relationship between poverty and theft prosecutions is not only inconclusive for women in Bologna, but has been debated in early modern European historiography more broadly. Most historians tend to accept that theft was a key survival strategy employed by the poor in times of need, and that

---

non arrivano alla fine del mese (Rome: Editrice APES, 2009) 15-25; Malanima, 'Urbanisation and the Italian economy,' 97-98; Black, *Early modern Italy*, 32-35.

42 Woolf, *The poor in Western Europe*, 51-53.

43 Black, *Early modern Italy*, 35; Guenzi, 'L'identità industriale,' 449; P. Malanima, 'An age of decline. Product and income in eighteenth-nineteenth century Italy,' *Rivista di storia economica* 12:1 (2006) 111; P. Malanima, 'I consumi in età moderna. Crescita o decline?,' in E. Sori and R. Giulianelli (eds.), *Consumi e dinamiche economiche in età moderna e contemporanea* (Napels: ESI, 2011) 44.

44 Angelozzi and Casanova, *Donne criminali*, 71.

45 See table 2 in Angelozzi and Casanova, *Donne criminali*, 73.

fluctuations in property crimes were tied to economic conditions in one way or another.[46] Three factors are deemed particularly important: the prices of necessities, especially food, and the availability and remuneration of work. The results from statistical analyses linking indictments for property offences to price indexes in early modern Europe nevertheless provide unclear results. Beattie found "a general relationship" between these variables for the late eighteenth-century rural parishes of Surrey and Sussex, but found that the situation for London was more complex.[47] Neither the massive peaks in indictments for property crimes, nor the long-term trends in the city of London seem to have been related to the development of prices. Similarly, German historians have also found no or only marginal evidence for a correlation between rye or bread prices and property offences in sixteenth-century Cologne and eighteenth-century Frankfurt.[48]

The difficulty of finding quantitative evidence for the link between economic hardship and theft has recently been confirmed by Kilday. In her statistical analysis of eighteenth-century rural Oxfordshire she set off the variables of wages, prices and weather conditions against the indictment levels for theft to demonstrate that the correlations were rather weak. This suggests that while temporary poverty may have been a motivating factor for some to steal, "motives for theft may well have been more closely related to opportunism and acquisitiveness."[49] Similar conclusions have recently been drawn for towns in early modern Holland, which also endured crisis in various economic segments during the second half of the eighteenth century.[50] While the share of property offences rose in some towns, in others such as Leiden (which, like Bologna, endured a significant textile crisis) it did not.

The influence of economic fluctuations on criminal activity was thus noticeable but not straightforward. Bologna's seventeenth-century criminal records also attest to this. In the period from 1625 to 1629 a temporary increase in thefts committed by women can be observed, which could be explained by the grain shortage and the rise in bread prices in the city at that time.[51] In these crisis years, thefts constituted far higher shares of reported crimes than in the

46 Beattie, 'The criminality of women,' 103; A.M. Kilday, '"Criminally poor?" Investigating the link between crime and poverty in eighteenth century England,' *Cultural and social history: The journal of the Social History Society* 11:4 (2015) 507.

47 J.M. Beattie, 'The pattern of crime in England 1660-1800,' *Past & present* 62 (1974) 91

48 Schwerhoff, *Köln im Kreuzverhör*, 358-361; Eibach, *Frankfurter Verhöre*, 93-99.

49 Kilday, '"Criminally poor?,"' 521.

50 Van der Heijden, *Women and crime*, 74-75.

51 Angelozzi and Casanova, *Donne criminali*, 96.

sampled years before and afterwards.[52] However, for other periods with similar crises this connection is less apparent. When another increase in bread prices in 1671 provoked riots and attacks on bakeries in the city of Bologna, the *Torrone*'s records provide no evidence for any proportional or absolute increase in the reported thefts by women.[53]

When the effects of economic fluctuations on property crime are discussed, scholars generally agree that the context of theft in the early modern period was one of large parts of the population living a hand-to-mouth existence. For this they commonly draw on Olwen Hufton's concept of the 'economy of makeshifts.'[54] Originally devised to summarise the eighteenth-century French experience of marginality, this concept refers to the wide range of disparate activities and survival strategies that poor commoners employed to support themselves in the face of economic hardship. Initially these makeshifts only included economic activities such as subsistence migration, begging and gleaning, which complemented often temporary and poorly paid jobs. As the concept was adopted by others, 'making shift' came to include the numerous and often combined short-term strategies and local resources that ensured the survival of individuals and families, including formal and informal relief as well as various types of marginal criminality such as prostitution and petty theft.[55]

The overarching notion of makeshift economies is also useful to contextualise the situation in early modern Bologna. Here, as elsewhere in Europe, a combination of need, greed and opportunity occasionally drove its inhabitants to steal in their attempts to make shift.[56] While the criminal bylaws expressed worry about the repeatability of theft and its effects on public order, only few professional thieves seem to have passed through the Italian criminal courts

52 In their samples of denunciations and *processi* taken together, thefts constituted 6.6% of women's crimes in 1583-1587 and 13.6 per cent in 1671. See Angelozzi and Casanova, *Donne criminali*, 73.

53 L. Ferrante, '"Tumulto di più persone per causa del calo del pane..." Saccheggi e repressione a Bologna (1671, 1677),' *Rivista storica italiana* 90 (1978) 770-809.

54 O. Hufton, *The poor in eighteenth-century France, 1750-1789* (New York: Oxford University Press 1974) 259.

55 For an overview of the evolution of Olwen Hufton's concept of the economy of makeshift, see A. Tomkins and S. King, 'Introduction,' in S. King and A. Tomkins (eds.), *The poor in England 1700-1850. An economy of makeshifts* (Manchester: Manchester University Press, 2003) 12-13.

56 Brackett, *Criminal justice and crime*, 118; P. Wettmann-Jungblut, '"Stelen inn rechter hungersnodtt." Diebstahl, Eigentumsschutz und strafrechtliche Kontrolle im vorindustriellen Baden 1600-1850,' in R. van Dülmen (ed.), *Verbrechen, Strafen und soziale Kontrolle. Studien zur historischen Kulturforschung* (Frankfurt am Main: Fischer Taschenbuch Verlag, 1990) 154-155.

before the nineteenth century.[57] The Bolognese criminal court records only make occasional references to defendants being repeat offenders or *ladri famosi* (famous thieves). Among over more than one hundred identified offenders of theft in the formal investigation dossiers, only 14 were recorded as having a criminal history.[58] Since recidivism was an aggravating factor in sentencing, it does not seem very likely that the people whose criminal past was unrecorded in the criminal court dossiers were known to be repeat offenders.

The Bolognese sources furthermore provide little evidence for the incorporation of thieves into larger criminal associations. When stolen wares were sold on, the criminal court actively tried to establish who was involved in the distribution of the stolen goods and whether intermediaries were accomplices in the crime or had acted in good faith.[59] Nevertheless, while the small percentage of armed robbers commonly offended in small groups, the *Torrone*'s criminal court records suggest that the large majority of thieves operated independently. In three-quarters of the recorded thefts only one offender was accused.[60] This was the same for male as for female defendants and has also been observed for sixteenth-century Rome.[61] In the quarter of the cases where the *Torrone* did identify co-offenders, women were more likely to commit thefts in mixed-sex groups (mostly with their husbands or other male family members) than in groups with only other women. The opposite is true for men, who more commonly offended in all-male groups. The Bolognese pattern in which women and men largely committed thefts on their own corresponds with what has been observed for other towns in early modern Europe.[62] A lack of an expansive apparatus of criminal justice and policing undoubtedly contributed to shaping this pattern. Nevertheless, the criminal court records attest to the role

57 J.K. Brackett, 'The Florentine criminal underworld. The underside of the Renaissance,' in W.J. Connell (ed.), *Society and individual in Renaissance Florence* (Berkeley: University of California Press, 2002) 301, 308; L. Lacché, *Latrocinium. Giustizia, scienza penale e repressione del banditismo in antico regime* (Milan: Giuffrè Editore, 1988); Angelozzi and Casanova, *Donne criminali*, 94, 96; Dean, *Crime and justice in late medieval Italy*, 186.

58 In the entire extended sample of all crimes in Bologna (samples 2 and 3, see appendix 1) only 16 men and 4 women were described as having previously been in contact with the law for a criminal offence. However, the written court records do not provide systematic information on all offenders, even for those officially indicted by the criminal court and/or incarcerated for questioning. Among the 108 offenders of theft in the *processi* alone, 28 were investigated regarding their previous criminal activities; 14 of them were recidivists.

59 Angelozzi and Casanova, *Donne criminali*, 96; *Bando generale Serbelloni 1756*, 53-55.

60 The thefts for which no offender was identified are excluded in this calculation.

61 Blastenbrei, *Kriminalität in Rom*, 193.

62 Van der Heijden, *Women and crime*, 75-76.

of predominantly unorganised and occasional theft as one of the many short-term strategies used by commoners to get by.

The most important characteristic of property offenders throughout the mid-seventeenth and mid-eighteenth centuries is that they had some sort of occupation, however menial. Although unemployment appears to have been more common among defendants accused of thieving than for other crimes, the role of the truly destitute beggars was limited: out of over a hundred property offenders whose occupational status was recorded, only four were described as poor beggars going around the city asking for money and food. Scholars have referred to this kind of group as the structural poor, i.e. those incapable of earning a living for reasons of age, mortal illness or physical handicap and hence fully dependent on assistance or begging.[63] There are contemporary estimations of Bologna's urban poor for the year 1639, which suggest that a little over two per cent of the Bolognese inhabitants belonged to the category of beggars (*mendicanti, poveri che cercano per la città*).[64] In 1726, they constituted just under three per cent of the urban population.[65] This means that the share of beggars before the criminal court was roughly equal to their share among the urban population.

A large share of thieves brought before the *Torrone* probably belonged to the large group of the conjunctural poor: inhabitants that were dependent on low wages or casual employment, but could also include artisans, small retailers and petty officials.[66] They all found themselves in a fragile equilibrium, could fall easily and repeatedly beneath subsistence level and experienced cyclical poverty. Italian and French case studies have shown that the proportion of the urban poor could include as many as 50 to 70 per cent of all households.[67] Contemporary estimations of Bologna's urban poor for the year 1639 surmised that the group receiving charitable assistance during Easter and Christmas consisted of over half of the urban population.[68] As the repercussions of the shrinking

63 Black, *Early modern Italy*, 105, Woolf, *The poor in Western Europe*, 6.

64 L. Ciammitti, 'Fanciulle, monache, madre. Povertà femminile e previdenza a Bologna nei secoli XVI-XVIII,' in *Arte e Pietà: I patrimoni culturali delle Opere Pie* (Bologna: CLUEB, 1980) 448.

65 F. Giusberti, 'La città assistenziale. Riflessioni su un sistema piramidale,' in M. Fanti (ed.), *Forme e soggetti dell'intervento assistenziale in una città di antico regime. Atti del IV colloquio, Volume II* (Bologna: Istituto per la storia di Bologna, 1984) 23.

66 Black, *Early modern Italy*, 105; Woolf, *The poor in Western Europe*, 6.

67 Woolf, *The poor in Western Europe*, 6.

68 For this calculation I have used Ciammitti et al's data for 1693 and compared them to the 1,701 estimates of the total urban population provided by Bellettini, which was the nearest in time. Compare Ciammitti, 'Fanciulle, monache, madre,' 448; Bellettini, *La popolazione di Bologna*, 48.

textile sector and consequent reforms of the production process were felt increasingly by the many textile workers in Bologna, it is unlikely that this share of the working poor diminished during the subsequent period.[69]

The occupations of those accused of theft in the Bolognese criminal records represent a broad dissection of predominantly lower-class society. Defendants of both sexes indicate performing a wide range of professions for their livelihoods, albeit on-and-off or underemployed. Some of the accused held esteemed occupations such as civil notaries or worked as skilled master artisans and shopkeepers, but most of those involved in theft belonged to the city's large group of textile workers, cobblers, bricklayers, porters, servants, and market vendors. The court records shed some light on the precarious nature of their employment and the role of theft in easing economic burdens. In August 1674 Giovanni Biaccati had stolen two rings and gold earrings worth 21 *lire* from his neighbour's unlocked trunk when he was in her house listening to a violinist playing on the street opposite to her apartment.[70] Giovanni, who had fled the city together with his wife after the theft, was described as a woodworker, yet the testimony by the culprit's former boss underlines how the irregularity of work drove artisans like Giovanni to other forms of employment. When times were tough and there was no work to be found in his profession as a woodworker, Giovanni had to compete for unstable and ill-paid porter jobs to try and make ends meet. Examples such as these clearly illustrate the role of underemployment and cyclical hardship in the lives of early modern *bolognesi* and the lure of the temporary alleviation theft could provide.

The women featured in the Bolognese criminal court records for their misdeeds were no better off socioeconomically. Female offenders worked as market vendors, domestic servants, or performed odd jobs. A significant share of these women were active in the textile industry in the less prestigious and poorly paid functions of spinners, weavers, hosiers, and seamstresses who relied on the uncertainties of piecework and the capricious supply of work through a kind of putting-out system headed by merchant contractors.[71] Catarina Benserati, the aforementioned widow who stole salted pork from her neighbours, for example, described herself as a woman "living how god wanted her to through spinning and some charity bestowed upon her by her neighbours."[72] She was only one example of the broad category of the working

69 Guenzi, 'L'identità industriale,' 449, 470-472, 507.

70 ASBO, Torrone, 7028-2, fasc. 7.

71 Terpstra, 'Working the cocoon,' 48-49; Dumont, 'Women and guilds in Bologna,' 7, 9; Guenzi, 'La tessitura femminile,' 250

72 "Io sono una povera donne vecchia che vivo come iddio vuole con filare e con qualche carità che mi viene fatta dalli vicini," ASBO, Torrone, 8179-2, fasc. 16. Also see 6620, fol. 285.

poor who lived just above or on subsistence level and attempted to maintain a livelihood through the household's combined labour efforts, occasional charity and, for some, opportunistic theft.

There are some indications that married locals were prominent among Bologna's thieves. The criminal court records suggest that where marital status was registered, over two-thirds of the property offenders were married. Furthermore, fewer than one in seven of the accused property offenders were recorded as being from outside of the Bolognese *legato* and thus as foreigners. These findings go against the dominant historiographical grain that stresses an important link between high mobility, economic vulnerability and theft. In his well-known contribution on women's criminality in eighteenth-century Surrey, John Beattie contrasted the socioeconomic profile of thieving women to those who came before the court for violence. While most of the women accused of crimes against the person were married, prosecutions for theft revolved around single and widowed women.[73] Similarly, in his examination of the social background of female property offenders in late eighteenth-century London, Peter King found that over two-thirds of them were single or widowed and over half of them were born outside the metropolis.[74] Scholarship on early modern towns in Holland and in Frankfurt am Main has painted a similar picture of young female migrant thieves.[75]

The social profile emerging from the Bolognese criminal court records may in part be due to the character of the source material. During the early modern period, the recording of biographical data such as marital status and birth place in the judicial sources increased and was progressively standardised, but was still patchy at best by the mid-eighteenth century.[76] Especially incomplete was the information on the marital status for men, as it was only recorded for about one-fifth of the male property offenders. Furthermore, although over half of the court records shed light on the birth place of the defendants, the interpretation is ambiguous. While the majority of property offenders were recorded as being 'Bolognese' (*Bononien*), it is not entirely clear whether this only referred to Bologna's urban centre or to the entire legal territory of the *legato*, which included a vast terrain of 4,000 square kilometres of its suburban

73 Beattie, 'The criminality of women,' 101-102, 106-107.

74 P. King, 'Female offenders, work and life-cycle change in late-eighteenth-century London,' *Continuity and change* 11:1 (1996) 69, 72, 75.

75 Van der Heijden, *Women and crime*, 74; Kamp, 'Female crime and household control,' 538.

76 For female defendants, 57% of the cases include her marital status and 50% a birth place. For male defendants, this was 22% (for marital status) and 58% (for birth place).

and rural counterparts.[77] According to Matteo Troila, Bologna's endemic urban population deficit was mainly replenished by the inhabitants from its suburbs, an agricultural zone of between five and twelve kilometres adjacent to the city walls.[78] More research is necessary to demonstrate whether or not these men and women who were born outside the city were also legally considered migrants by the *Torrone*, as they would have been in many other European towns.

While caution must be exercised in interpreting the imperfect source material, the demographic, social and economic context of Bologna can serve to at least in part account for the social profile of thieves. First, pertaining to the suggested 'localness' of Bolognese property offenders in particular, various studies have asserted that in communities characterised by low migration theft was naturally more commonly committed by non-migrants.[79] For rural Tuscany, Brackett contended that theft was linked to a "common misery of a peasantry that always lived on the edge of survival."[80] The same has been argued for the eighteenth-century Sénéchaussée of Libourne in France, where three quarters of reported thefts involved "the more stable members of local society."[81] In the small textile town of Prato, the large majority of criminal defendants in the eighteenth century also consisted of locals who were by and large born in the city.[82] Bologa was an important centre of trade and transit, and had large numbers of itinerant travellers spending limited time in the city.[83] Still, as a middle to large city that did not belong to the important pull areas for temporary migration or agricultural mobility on the Italian peninsula, it does not seem incongruous that Bologna's thieves largely came from the local population.[84]

---

77 For fifteenth-century Bologna, Sara Cucini observed a relatively fair split between citizens (32%) and those being born in the *contado* (37%) among criminal offenders. 'Only' 21% of the offenders were foreigners (and the provenance of 10% was unknown). See Cucini, 'Législation statutaire et gouvernement pontifical,' 369.

78 M. Troilo, 'Popolazione e proprietà attraverso le fonti fiscali bolognesi nell'età moderna,' *Popolazione e storia* 12:1 (2011) 25.

79 Kilday, 'Criminally poor?,' 513

80 Brackett, '"Criminally poor?,"' 100.

81 Ruff, *Crime, justice and public order*, 122.

82 Zuliani, 'Reati e pene nel vicariato di Prato,' 312.

83 Rose, *A renaissance of violence*, 9.

84 According to Alberto Guenzi, immigration to Bologna, especially to the city, was very modest in the fifteenth century, rarely exceeding 1,000 per year. See A. Guenzi, 'L'immigrazione urbana e rurale a Bologna in una fonte del secolo XV,' *Rassegna degli Archivi di Stato* 44 (1984) 149-163; M. Sanfilippo, 'Il fenomeno migratorio italiano: storia e storiografia,' in A. Miranda and A. Signorelli (eds.), *Pensare e ripensare le migrazioni* (Palermo: Sellerio, 2011) 245-272; J. Lucassen, *Migrant labour in Europe 1600-1900* (London: Croom Helm, 1987) 259.

Economic characteristics of towns also contributed to a particular social composition of the men and women who appeared before the criminal court. Reflecting on the discrepancy between London's higher and Newcastle's lower shares of single female property offenders, Gwenda Morgan and Peter Rushton hypothesised that the difference may have been related to the distinctive economic life of Newcastle.[85] They suggest that the slow growth of the town and the character of (largely seasonal) employment possibly drove more impoverished married women towards crime. However, that criminal courts in various early modern European towns with similar economic structures and circumstances were preoccupied by an apparently different population of thieves, suggests that other factors than purely economic ones were probably more decisive.

One of these other relevant factors was the extrajudicial or informal control exerted by households. It is widely accepted that women's crimes all over early modern Europe were more likely to be handled by less formal methods of conflict resolution than men's.[86] Certain categories of women, such as the generally single domestic servants, are believed to have been extra prone to underreporting as their crimes were probably dealt with within the sphere of the household.[87] Italy was probably no different, particularly because the *paterfamilias* had considerable legal room to manoeuvre in exercising control over his wife, children and servants.[88] When thirteen year old ribbonmaker Flaminia Ruggi had stolen a golden ring from Lucia de Zannoni's house, Lucia first approached Flaminia's parents, who promised to find out the truth.[89] After a few days they knocked on Lucia's door to confirm that Flaminia had meanwhile confessed to the theft, and begged her for patience so that they could try to retrieve the ring without interference of the court, and punish Flaminia themselves. While Lucia still denounced Flaminia, this example nevertheless is suggestive of the commonness of extrajudicial negotiations to shield errant family members out of the hands of criminal justice. Unmarried women may have been prime candidates for a special treatment. The importance attached to women's sexual honour in early modern Italy was above all channelled into households' and institutions' attempts to scrutinise and control

85 Morgan and Rushton, *Rogues, thieves and the rule of law*, 101-102.

86 Schwerhoff, *Köln im Kreuzverhör*; Shoemaker, *Prosecution and punishment*, 292; King, *Crime and the law*, 202-10; Gray, *Crime, Prosecutions and social relations*, 9, 170-1; Dinges, 'The uses of justice,' 159-75.

87 Beattie, 'The criminality of women,' 94; Kamp, 'Female crime and household control,' 543.

88 Cavina, *Nozze di sangue*, 25; Arru, 'The distinguishing features of domestic service in Italy,' 556; Sbriccoli, 'Deterior est condicio foeminarum,' 83-84.

89 ASBO, Torrone, 7028, fol. 54.

the movements of single women.[90] The ability of married women to move somewhat more freely through Italian cities than their single counterparts may have exposed them to more opportunities for theft.

Although the socioeconomic characterisations leave much room for further thought, most of Bologna's thieves appear to have belonged to the large group of the city's working poor. Their often ill-paid and irregular labour activities were merely complemented by theft, if the opportunity presented itself, as part of their economy of makeshifts.[91] In this sense, the situation in Bologna reminds us of accounts of other early modern towns. It was furthermore largely comparable for male and female property offenders. The next paragraphs will explore the relationship between thieving, the physical and social urban landscape and dynamics of gender in more detail.

4 Stolen Goods

In the early modern period as much as nowadays, what goods were stolen depended on which goods were at hand. Historians have wondered whether the growing market for consumer goods during the early modern period affected patterns of theft. Scholars such as Beverly Lemire have explicitly stressed the link between the criminal targeting of certain goods, particularly clothing, and the burgeoning popular yearning for new luxury goods and fashionable items.[92] In Italy, already from eleventh century onwards, the globalisation of trade networks brought in new material goods such as gems, ceramics, cottons, brocades and Turkish carpets.[93] The indulgence in these material objects by Italy's elite led Richard Goldtwaithe to famously argue that the consumer society was therefore born not in northern Europe in the seventeenth and eighteenth centuries, but in Renaissance Italy.[94] Other scholars have questioned the extent to

90 Palazzi, 'Tessitrici, serve, treccole,' 374.

91 For a recap of criminological theories about the role of employment as either facilitating or halting property crimes, see B. Gallée and J. Ligthart, 'De remmende werking van huwelijk en arbeid op vermogensdelicten. Rotterdam, 1812-1820,' *Tijdschrift voor criminologie* 57:4 (2015) 353-367.

92 B. Lemire, 'The theft of clothes and popular consumerism in early modern England,' *Journal of social history* 24:2 (1990) 255

93 J.M. Ferraro, 'The manufacture and movement of goods,' in J. Jeffries Martin (ed.), *The Renaissance world* (New York: Routledge, 2007) 88; A. Clemente, 'Storiografie di confine? Consumo di beni durevoli e cultura del consumo nel XVIII secolo,' *Società e storia* 109 (2005) 591

94 R. Goldtwaithe, *Wealth and demand for art in Italy, 1300-1600* (Baltimore: Johns Hopkins University Press, 1993) 16.

which this consumer culture of Renaissance Italy was able to spread to non-elite segments of the population, if it was sustained throughout the early modern period and furthermore whether this prefigured the developments in eighteenth-century London or Paris.[95] After all, most forms of retailing remained remarkably stable in Italy and the growth of a mass market remained absent. Combined with declining wages and increasing price levels, Italy's early modern period is generally discussed not as the seed-bed of 'modern consumer culture' but from the perspective of economic decline.[96]

Nevertheless, scholars have convincingly demonstrated that the structure of consumption in Italy did change significantly throughout the early modern period. The available data suggest that a considerable drop in the consumption of foodstuffs coincided with a significant rise in that of durable goods.[97] Alongside economic indicators, important evidence for a widening demand for consumer goods is derived from probate inventories. Research on these sources reveals an expansion in the number and types of objects held by households across the social spectrum, both in cities in Italy and in the countryside.[98] Furthermore, the rise of a 'fashion system' increased the demand for certain types of clothing and new accessories such as neckerchiefs.[99] Despite the economic decline, the mercer trade in Venice, for example, underwent spectacular growth during the seventeenth century.[100] Moreover, the second-hand clothing

95 E. Welch, *Shopping in the Renaissance. Consumer cultures in Italy 1400-1600* (New Haven: Yale University Press, 2005) 4-5, 14; Ferraro, 'The manufacture and movement of goods,' 96; Clemente, 'Storiografie di confine,' 590-592.

96 For an overview, see Cavaterra, 'Economia, povertà e consumi in età moderna,' 15-25; Malanima, 'Urbanisation and the Italian economy,' 97-98; Black, *Early modern Italy*, 32-35.

97 P. Malanima and V. Pinchera, 'A puzzling relationship. Consumptions and incomes in early modern Europe,' *Histoire & mesure* 27:2 (2012) 198; Malanima, 'I consumi in età moderna,' 67.

98 P. Hohti, "Conspicuous' consumption and popular consumers: Material culture and social status in sixteenth-century Siena,' *Renaissance studies* 24:5 (2010) 660; Malanima and Pinchera, 'A puzzling relationship,' 214; R. Ago, *Gusto for things. A history of objects in seventeenth-century Rome* (Chicago: University of Chicago Press, 2013) 7, 127.

99 C.M. Belfanti and F. Giusberti, 'Clothing and social inequality in early modern Europe: introductory remarks,' *Continuity and change* 15:3 (2000) 361-362.

100 P. Allerston, 'Meeting demand: Retailing strategies in early modern Venice,' in B. Blondé, E. Briot. N. Coquery and L. van Aert (eds.), *Retailers and consumer changes in early modern Europe. England, France, Italy and the Low Countries* (Tours: Presses Universitaires François-Rabelais, 2005) 170, 182; Belfanti and Giusberti, 'Clothing and social inequality in early modern Europe,' 361, R.T. Rapp, *Industry and economic decline in seventeenth century Venice* (Cambridge: Harvard University Press, 1976) 103; R. Mackkenney, *Tradesmen and traders. The world of guilds in Venice and Europe, c.1250-c.1650* (London: Croom Helm) 90-97, 102-111.

market boomed in all main towns, bringing a great range of attire within easier reach and responding quickly to consumers' changing tastes.

The increasing demand for a wide range of consumer goods and a growing fashion sensitivity affected strategies of theft. Research on eighteenth-century Antwerp and Rotterdam suggests that thieves' loot included all sorts of popular clothing and luxury items, such as neckerchiefs, lace caps, stockings and aprons made of silk or cotton.[101] Although unprocessed fabrics such as linen and cotton were also frequently stolen in Antwerp, relatively new goods, intended for resale, were especially popular. Apparel stolen in England was also described as in many instances epitomizing "elements of style and the lure of elite fashions."[102] Court depositions in Bologna also allude to the demand for popular goods such as aprons and other garments. Some of these clothes were in used conditions, others brand new. Some were dyed into more fashionable colours to increase their resale value,[103] while the immediate appeal of other garments can readily be understood, such as the white and grey damask skirt and the silk iridescent gown with pink details and silver embroidering that Maria Cantelli was accused of stealing in 1725.[104]

Patterns of theft did not only reflect consumption patterns, but were also contingent on dynamics of gender. In the historiography it is commonly assumed that the thefts of men and women differed regarding types of stolen goods, value, venue, mode and motivation.[105] Various studies have stressed the distinctiveness of women's larcenous activities, tying their thefts to their traditional association with providing food for the family and direct household consumption.[106] A notable example of this is Barbara Hanawalt's study of female felons in fourteenth-century England dating from the late 1970s. She argued that women primarily stole grain, clothing and household goods of low value,

101 Van der Heijden, *Women and crime*, 71-72; M. Vanbellinghen, 'Diefstal en heling van kleding en textiel: Antwerpen, 1775-1785,' *Tijdschrift voor sociale geschiedenis* 21:4 (1995) 387.

102 Lemire, 'The theft of clothes and popular consumerism,' 258, 265.

103 ASBO, Torrone, 7077-2, fasc. 1.

104 ASBO, Torrone, 7859-2, fasc. 51.

105 Beattie, 'The criminality of women,' 89-96; O. Ulbricht, 'Einleitung. Für eine Geschichte der weiblichen Kriminalität in der Frühen Neuzeit oder: Geslechtergeschichte, historische Kriminalitätsforschung und weibliche Kriminalität,' in O. Ulbricht (ed.), *Von Huren und Rabenmüttern. Weibliche Kriminalität in der Frühen Neuzeit* (Cologne/Weimar/Vienna: Böhlau, 1995) 19.

106 Spierenburg, 'How violent were women?,' 13; McEwan, 'Negotiating support,' 159; J. Philips and A.N. May, 'Female criminality in 18th-century Halifax,' *Acadiensis* 31:2 (2002), n.p. Retrieved from <https://journals.lib.unb.ca/index.php/Acadiensis/article/view/10721/11437>.

reflecting the economic interests of women since their preoccupation was with the home.[107] Since then, various scholars have challenged this binary distinction. Both Walker (for seventeenth-century Cheshire) and subsequently Dean (for late medieval Bologna) have suggested that men and women generally stole the same kinds of items and that the value of the goods stolen by women was not necessarily lower than those stolen by men.[108]

The types of goods that were stolen in seventeenth- and eighteenth-century Bologna support the notion that some of the patterns of theft were not as gender specific as was commonly believed. The criminal court records reveal that clothing, clothing accessories and textiles were among the most commonly stolen items (figure 8). The category of 'clothing' consisted of items such as aprons, capes, coats, busts, skirts, dresses, shirts, stockings and shoes and constituted the largest category of stolen items. The category of 'textiles' includes household linen, raw materials and assorted textiles such as silk and cotton found around houses and shops. Together, about 37 per cent of the theft cases brought before Bologna's criminal court concerned these kinds of textiles. In other towns in early modern Europe clothing also ranked high among the items that were stolen.[109]

Women were not the only ones with an eye for the value of linens and clothing. Historiographically the prevalence of these types of items among women's spoils is commonly portrayed as the outcome of their specific social and economic roles, their prominence in the less formal trading networks of second-hand domestic goods and pawnbroking and their subsequent knowledge about these types of goods.[110] However, the *Torrone*'s casebooks suggest that clothing, household linen and a variety of miscellaneous textiles were about as important for female defendants as for their male counterparts: about one-third were accused of stealing these types of goods. The situation laid out by the criminal court records thus provides little quantitative evidence for the

107 Hanawalt, 'The female felon in fourteenth-century England,' 262; Hanawalt. *Crime and conflict*, 122.

108 Walker, *Crime, gender and social order*, 159-209; G. Walker, 'Women, theft and the world of stolen goods,' in J.I. Kermode and G. Walker (eds.), *Women, crime and the courts in early modern England* (London 1994) 81-105; Dean, 'Theft and gender,' 399-415.

109 Hufton, *The poor in eighteenth-century France*, 259; Beattie, *Crime and the courts in England*, 187; J.A. Sharpe, *Crime in seventeenth-century England: a county study* (Cambridge: Cambridge University Press, 1983) 91-114.

110 Walker, 'Women, theft and the world of stolen goods,' 88-89, 94, 97; Gray, *Crime, prosecution and social relations*, 76, 89; L. MacKay, 'Why they stole. Women in the Old Bailey, 1779-1789,' *Journal of social history* 32:3 (1999) 629, 633; S. Howard, 'Investigating responses to theft in early modern Wales. Communities, thieves and the courts,' *Community and change* 19 (2004) 421; Kilday, '"Criminally poor?,"' 515.

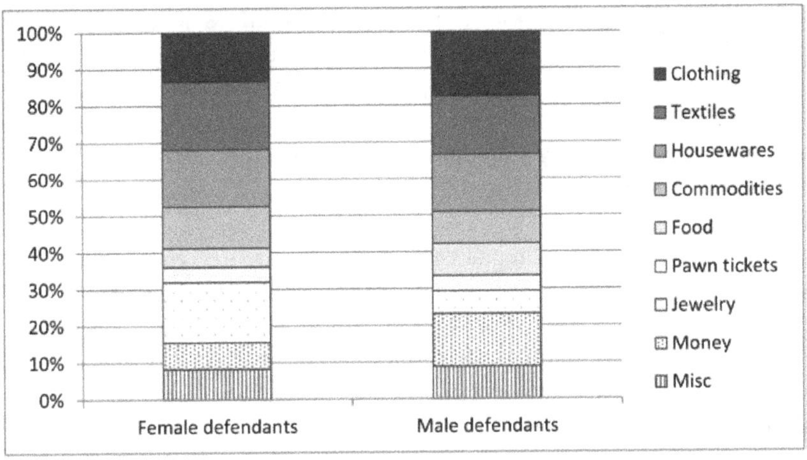

FIGURE 8 Stolen goods by gender of the offender, ca. 1655-1755
Calculations are based on the thefts captured in denunciations and *processi* with a total of 56 female defendants and 199 male defendants. Housewares: e.g. furniture, pots and pans, plates, vases, kettles. Commodities: e.g. raw materials, metals, building materials, tools and knives.
SOURCE: SAMPLES 2 AND 3 (SEE APPENDIX)

notion that the theft of clothing and household linen was a particularly gendered activity in early modern Bologna.

The general and pervasive theft of clothing and textiles speaks to the importance of these goods within the early modern material culture and plebeian commercial circuits.[111] Probate inventories from seventeenth-century Rome, for example, show that clothing formed the bulk of the possessions of both men and women.[112] Similarly, together with household linens, clothing consisted of the most important category of stolen goods Europe-wide.[113] They were relatively easy to steal and conceal, were very expensive and were among

111 Term coined by B. Lemire, 'Plebeian commercial circuits and everyday material exchange in England, c. 1600-1900,' in B. Blondé, P. Stabel, J. Stobart and I. van Damme (eds.), *Buyers & sellers. Retail circuits and practices in medieval and early modern Europe* (Turnhout: Brepols, 2006) 245; I. Cecchini, 'A world of small objects: Probate inventories, pawns and domestic life in early modern Venice,' *Renaissance and Reformation. Special issue: The material culture of debt* 35:3 (2012) 47.

112 R. Ago, 'Il linguaggio del corpo,' in C.M. Belfanti and F. Giusberti (eds.), *Storia d'Italia. Annali 19. La moda* (Turin: Enaudi, 2003) 120.

113 Van der Heijden, *Women and crime*, 71; Walker, 'Women, theft and the world of stolen goods,' 87.

the most sought-after and easily disposable commodities since people outside of the higher ranks largely depended on used garments to clothe themselves.[114] Second-hand clothing, whether acquired legally or illegally, therefore had guaranteed value and was assured of sale in early modern economies.[115] In a city like Bologna, in which a large group of its inhabitants worked in the textile industry, this value was apparently recognised by male and female thieves alike.

While the Bolognese criminal court records testify to a great demand for clothing and other textiles, they also reveal a significant demand for a range of other types of goods. Most of these goods were as important to female offenders as to their male counterparts. Domestic goods such as furniture, plates, vases and kettles made up about one-fifth of the goods stolen in Bologna and were of equal importance to offenders of both sexes. A range of work tools (hammers, knives, tailor's scissors and so forth), building materials, metals and raw materials are counted among the category of commodities and consisted of one-eighth of the total items pilfered in the city by men and women alike. Similarly, one in twenty thefts concerned pawn tickets for either jewellery, clothing or household linens. Pawns could be redeemed by bringing the funds of the loan and the interest and the copy of the pawn slip (*scrittarino*) to the *monte*. As the amount of the loans was usually one-half to two-thirds of the assessed value of the pawn, collecting and selling the pawned objects on the markets could be a lucrative endeavour.[116]

Some differences between the extent to which male and female offenders stole certain kinds of items are noticeable. Food was more commonly stolen by male offenders than by their female counterparts. This category consisted both of actual foodstuffs such as beans, meats, fish, bread, fruits and agricultural produce such as wheat and grain, and of a range of animals such as chickens, horses, cows, sheep, oxen, goats and donkeys. About one in ten of the male offenders were accused of stealing goods in this category, while this was only the case for one in twenty female thieves. Lastly, money and jewellery were also regularly stolen. Jewellery like gold, silver and coral necklaces rings and pearls figured more prominently among the loot of female thieves (16 per cent) than

114 Hohti, '"Conspicuous' consumption and popular consumers,' 666; Lemire, 'The theft of clothes and popular consumerism,' 256-257.

115 Lemire, 'The theft of clothes and popular consumerism,' 265.

116 M. Carboni, 'Converting goods into cash: An ethical approach to pawnbroking in early modern Bologna,' *Renaissance and Reformation. Special issue: The material culture of debt* 35:3 (2012) 71; M.G. Muzzarelli, 'From the closet to the wallet. Pawning clothes in Renaissance Italy,' *Renaissance and Reformation. Special issue: The material culture of debt* 35:3 (2012) 25.

men's (six per cent). The opposite is true for money, which made up 14 per cent of the goods pilfered by male defendants and only half that by their female counterparts.

The similarities between the pilfering propensities of men and women are significant and are indicative of a world of production and exchange in which both women and men played important roles. Some differences in what was stolen do emerge, notably regarding the theft of money and jewellery. A closer look at the court records suggests interesting contextual differences between these two types of cases. Jewellery and money were commonly taken from trunks and cupboards at home by the victims' neighbours or acquaintances, while money was also stolen from other types of places: pickpocketed while traversing night-time streets, from taverns and from shops, commonly by men whom the victims did not know or did not know well or not at all. While the difference between what men and women stole should not be overstated, it is imperative to examine the extent to which the spatial and social contexts of thieving were gendered.

5 The Geographies of Theft

Scholars generally agree that the criminal activities of men and women were shaped by the geographic and social boundaries of their everyday lives. By extension, it has been assumed that the geographies of theft must have been distinctly gendered because of the different opportunities that men and women had.[117] The importance of houses and the immediate neighbourhood as spaces for women's violence has already been discussed – not as a separate domestic sphere, but as sites where conflicts arose from their quotidian labour and social relations. Thieving also appears to have primarily occurred within the same environs.

Bologna's geography of theft entailed a broad range of locations: from homes and shared spaces within the apartment complexes, to workshops, markets, mills, granaries, theatres and churches. Theft from residential locations was the most prevalent (see table 23). This most commonly concerned apartments or rooms rented or owned by victims, and the variety of goods stolen from this residential environment was broad: ranging from clothing, household linen, jewellery and domestic commodities such as furniture, pans and pots, to foodstuffs, money and pawn tickets. Many of these thefts were highly opportunistic, as is illustrated by the case against Giuseppe Carboni, who was

117 MacKay, 'Why they stole,' 629-630, 633.

taken for questioning by the chief constable for his involvement in theft.[118] Giuseppe admitted that he had seized the opportunity to take away two copper vases when his neighbour Marina Landi had left the door to her house unlocked. Similarly, in 1675 Girolama Negrini, a married chestnut seller, had also stolen a large copper vase worth 9 *lire* when her neighbour Violanta had left her front door wide open.[119] To a lesser degree *bolognesi* also stole from the shared spaces within the apartment buildings, such as clothing hung to dry in courtyards and hallways.[120] All in all about one-third of accused male thieves and nearly three-quarters of their female counterparts are reported to have stolen from people's domiciles. For female offenders, the importance of houses was thus even more prominent than among reported acts of violence.

The aforementioned examples also speak to the important role of neighbours in theft from houses in early modern Bologna. Both in historiographical treatments of thieving and contemporary anxieties it was not this neighbour-persona that took centre stage, but the domestic servant.[121] Because domestic servants had access to every corner of the house and could easily incorporate thefts in their everyday work routines, their crimes were considered an important breach of trust. Due to this perceived betrayal, harsh sentences were prescribed for domestic theft (*furto domestico*) all over early modern Europe.[122] Indeed, when the *sbirri* in Bologna retrieved a bed sheet domestic servant Anna Leandri had stolen from her employer from underneath her mother's bed, it comes as no surprise that he described in his denunciation that he was wondering what else she might have taken from him in the past.[123] Yet, contrary to what both legislation and contemporary fears may suggest, domestic servants do not at all appear to have been in the majority among those stealing from houses: only one in six were employed as maidservants in these specific households. Instead, nearly half of the houses were pilfered by fellow tenants and neighbours, like Giuseppe and Girolama.

---

118 ASBO, Torrone, 7869-2, fasc. 26.

119 ASBO, Torrone, 7035, fasc. 3.

120 See, for example, ASBO, Torrone, 7044-2, fasc. 2.

121 For Germany, see Rublack, *The crimes of women in early modern Germany*, 93; for France: C.C. Fairchilds, *Women in early modern Europe, 1500-1700* (Harlow: Pearson Education, 2007) 289; for England: Gray, *Crime, prosecution and social relations*, 89; McEwan, 'Negotiating support,' 161, 164-165, 169.

122 M. Neale, 'Property crime in late eighteenth-century Bristol. Contexts of theft in the premodern city' (Unpublished PhD thesis, University of Leicester, 2012) 141; Rublack, *The crimes of women in early modern Germany*, 99-100; Fairchilds, *Women in early modern Europe*, 289; *Bando generale Serbelloni 1756*, 44-46.

123 ASBO, Torrone, 8171-2, fasc. 22.

TABLE 23 Locations of theft in denunciations and *processi* where known, ca. 1655-1755

	Female defendant		Male defendant		Total known		Unidentified offenders[c]	
House[a]	40	74%	62	33%	102	42%	84	41%
Shop	1	2%	51	27%	52	24%	72	35%
Tavern	1	2%	18	10%	19	8%	6	3%
Street/market	6	11%	37	20%	43	18%	26	13%
Public building[b]	6	11%	20	11%	26	11%	18	9%
Total	54	100	188	100%	242	100%	206	100%

SOURCES: DERIVED FROM SAMPLE 2A, 2B AND 3 (SEE APPENDIX), COUNTED BY DEFENDANT
a Also includes adjoining gardens, shared apartment hallways and courtyards
b Includes public buildings and structures such as churches, city gates, theatres, mills, granaries and stables
c Represents minimum counts; each case without suspect is counted here as one offender

Workshops, where goods were made and displayed to be sold, took second place among the most prominent locations of theft. At least a quarter of all reported thefts occurred in these places. Sometimes merchandise such as fabric, handkerchiefs, shoes, clocks and weapons were stolen from the display; a window that could be turned into a vending table. This happened on the 22nd of April 1705, when cobbler Appolinaro Guidi saw a carpenter's apprentice take off with a pair of shoes made from black cow leather he had placed in his shop's display.[124] Other times, money or tools were stolen from shopkeepers when they were not looking or had temporarily left the room. Baker Pietro Babina, for example, complained that the two brassmakers Gaetano Bovina and Gregorio Gamini had deceived his assistant Giuseppe by claiming that they had lost a buckle mesh in the cellar and asked him to assist Gregorio in finding it.[125] When Giuseppe left the shop to do so, Gaetano saw his chance to steal 10 to 12 *paoli*. Most common were night-time break-ins, resulting in the theft of anything from textiles, money, pottery, work tools such as hammers, scales and cooking utensils to pieces of furniture. Whether at night or during the day, stealing from shops was decidedly more common among male than for female defendants (27 compared to two per cent). This corresponds with

124 ASBO, Torrone, 7608-1, fol. 101.
125 ASBO, Torrone, 8171-1, fol. 265.

what is known for elsewhere in Europe, where cases concerning women's shoplifting only surged from the late-eighteenth century onwards under the influence of the so-called retailing revolution.[126]

A substantial part of the male thieves stole from other commercial spaces such as markets. Here a wide range of commodities – from foodstuffs and clothing to jewellery and tools – were stolen from the stalls displaying the market vendor's wares or from the baskets the street sellers used to transport their goods. Within this context, the victims were generally unacquainted with the thieves, who regularly only found out they were missing some of their merchandise some time after the fact. It was for example only by chance that market vendor Maria Annunziata, wife of Domenico Macchiavelli, found out who had stolen a brass scale from her market stall. She did not know who the men who stole from her were, but an acquaintance of hers had seen it happen and recognised local tailor Marco Boni and cobbler Angelo Nanni as the culprits.[127] While none of the female thieves in the sampled Bolognese court records were accused of stealing from markets, this example underlines that this does not mean that women were absent from these spaces. Aside from the examples of women's violent encounters in these marketplaces discussed in the previous chapter, their presence as buyers and sellers, as bystanders and victims of theft, was widely recorded in the criminal court records.

Places of sociability such as taverns also provided opportunities for theft. About one in ten of the thefts took place here. As spaces where people gathered to drink, eat and gamble, inebriated visitors commonly lost their capes, money and jewellery to thieving hands in these *osterie*.[128] They were also places where travellers received lodging. Because rooms and even beds were shared among strangers, personal items such as clothing and money were relatively easily misappropriated without the security of a locked room or trunk.[129] When a 65-year-old Franciscan friar spent the night in one of Bologna's taverns, he woke up to find his money missing.[130] He started complaining to the innkeeper that the foreigners in his room must have taken it. When interrogated by the criminal court's notary Agostino Grossi, a former servant from Modena who slept in the same bed as the friar, admitted that he had stolen the

126 S.G. Tickell, 'Shoplifting in eighteenth-century England' (Unpublished PhD thesis, University of Hertfordshire, 2015) 45-46; T.C. Whitlock, *Crime, gender and consumer culture in nineteenth-century England* (London/New York: Routledge 2016) 127-133.

127 ASBO, Torrone, 8171-2, fasc. 15.

128 ASBO, Torrone, 7869-1, fol. 154; 7869-1, fol. 256; 8171-1, fol. 43; 8171-1, fol. 244.

129 ASBO, Torrone, 6620, fol. 105; 7028, fol. 133.

130 ASBO, Torrone, 7028-2, fasc. 15.

money and had hidden it between the bed sheets to "serve his needs."[131] Guests furthermore stole goods that belonged to the tavern. On 22 August 1705, the proprietor of the *hosteria dei due Gamberi* located near to Bologna's largest square accused Antonio Romagnoli from Imola of stealing two bed sheets.[132] All in all, taverns featured more prominently as settings for thefts by men than for women (10 compared to two per cent). The normative and legal requirement of 'respectable' women to be accompanied to the tavern by male kin may have affected this outcome.[133] While this again does not mean that women were absent from taverns, their opportunities to steal in these spaces were likely circumscribed compared to men's.

Counted here among various public buildings in Bologna, about one in twenty thefts by both male and female offenders occurred in churches and other religious buildings. Here money, jewellery, clocks and clothing items were stolen from fellow churchgoers, but the theft of books, goblets, paintings and vases from churches and oratories themselves was more important. After climbing the wall of a convent in the inner-city parish of San Isaia, the unemployed Sabatino Stanzani had taken two water vases and a copper washbowl.[134] Similarly, Carlo Antonio Scagliarino stole a painting from the church of San Stefano after mass.[135] While everybody was leaving, he hid the painting under his coat and sold it to a seller of used goods for 40 *bolognini*. Finally, about one in twenty thefts had taken place in Bologna's mills, granaries and stables. On 21 November 1705 Giuseppe Guidazzoli, for example, was accused of entering the granary of Lazaro Sarti through a window during the night and taking away two sacks of wheat.[136] Other items that were reportedly taken from these places were such commodities as grain and flour, work tools, and animals such as horses, cows and chickens.

The landscape of theft in early modern Bologna was decidedly gendered. What stands out is the overwhelming importance of houses as locations for women's thefts. About two-thirds of the female defendants were accused of stealing from a room, apartment or within the apartment building in which the victim lived. While houses also featured prominently among men's geographies of theft, the proportional share of houses was less than half that of women's. Men were also much more likely than women to steal in a wide range of other spaces, such as the street, markets and taverns. It seems likely that this

131 "[...] *ad effetto di servirmene e di prevalentemente per li miei bisogni*"
132 ASBO, Torrone, 7608-1, fol. 99.
133 Angelozzi and Casanova, *Donne criminali*, 104.
134 ASBO, Torrone, 6620, fol. 285.
135 ASBO, Torrone, 6609, fol. 25.
136 ASBO, Torrone, 7606-1, fol. 279.

gendered pattern of thieving reflects the differences in legitimate social and economic opportunities. After all, both women's work and sociability were centred more in these spaces than men's, echoing the importance of the neighbourhood for women's everyday legitimate and illegitimate behaviours.

6 The Distribution of Stolen Goods

While the overwhelming majority of thieves who were brought under the criminal court's purview had no known criminal co-offenders, the redistribution of their stolen goods in society had nearly always involved a range of other actors. After all, despite associations between theft and poverty, registered thefts in which direct consumption played a role appear to have been rare. Most of the cases that came before the *Torrone* involved the reselling of goods. Even Maria Resonagli, who describes herself as a poor unfortunate person (*povera sventurata*) who sold her "body to survive," did not intend to consume the chickens she was accused of stealing. Instead, she had planned to sell them to an innkeeper through an intermediary.[137] On the other hand, just as foodstuffs could be sold rather than eaten, luxury items could be sold to buy bread and wine.[138] While the relationship between theft and economic hardship was complex, some form of commercial exchange played an important role in nearly all cases brought before the criminal court.

It is commonly assumed that there was significant overlap between illegal economic traffic and legal early modern markets.[139] Scholars have contended that goods were not only largely stolen from but were also redistributed through offenders' ordinary, legitimate social and economic networks.[140] Since the geographies of theft in early modern Bologna appear to have differed for male and female offenders, this raises the question of whether the redistribution of stolen goods was also distinctly gendered. To this end, table 24 shows the locations of the sale of stolen goods. Out of the enhanced sample of property offending, only the cases against 66 male and 17 female offenders

137 ASBO, Torrone, 8179-2, fasc. 25.

138 ASBO, Torrone, 6609, fol. 25; 6620, fasc. 1; 7044, fasc. 11.

139 Lemire, 'Plebeian commercial circuits,' 245, 254; Lemire, 'The theft of clothes and popular consumerism,' 256-257.

140 Walker, 'Women, theft and the world of stolen goods,' 81-105, MacKay, 'Why they stole,' 623-639, Callahan, 'On the receiving end,' 106-121; Howard, 'Investigating responses to theft,' 409-430.

shed light on the commercial journey of the goods that they were accused of stealing.[141] While the small sample size precludes us from drawing any statistically sound conclusions, these criminal court dossiers nevertheless provide an indication of how stolen goods found their way back into the urban economy of early modern Bologna.

For the mid-seventeenth to mid-eighteenth century, the Bolognese criminal court records suggest that workshops and tradesmen may have been the most important nodes in the redistribution of stolen goods. In about a third of the cases, stolen goods were disposed of through such shops and/or tradesmen. These stolen wares commonly were commodities they needed and used in their everyday occupation. As such, stolen fabric was turned over to tailors, silver and gold items to goldsmiths, flour to bakers and tin and copper pots and pans to tinsmiths.[142] The prominence of these businesses among illegal circuits has also been noted for eighteenth-century Bristol, where victuallers, carpenters, alehouse keepers, silversmiths, blacksmiths and other tradesmen readily (though purportedly unknowingly) purchased stolen property as part of their everyday business.[143]

In spite of their key roles in the distribution of stolen goods, it is unclear to what degree shopkeepers and tradesmen were aware of their unlawful origins. In order not to be treated and prosecuted as accomplices, the criminal bylaws stipulated that buyers should always inquire about the origins of both the seller and the goods.[144] In the sampled thefts there is only one example of a coppersmith who refused to buy two copper vases from two *contadini* (farmers) because he wanted to know who the two sellers were exactly as an assurance of good sale.[145] The court records indicate that it was fairly common to forgo persistent queries. Miller Domenico Ciapelli, for example, ground the grain that the temporarily unemployed bricklayer Gio Batta Consini had stolen, but excused his actions by saying he had not had a clue where Gio Batta had got the grain from because he simply had not asked him.[146] Gio Batta then sold the flour on to a baker for three *bolognini*. The baker in turn denied knowing that he had been offered stolen goods, although he also admitted never really in-

141 My sample includes another 211 theft cases for which it was entirely unknown who the offenders were. These are excluded from this examination as they never reveal information about what happened to the stolen goods.

142 ASBO, Torrone, 6653, fol. 276; 7869-2, fasc. 41; 7028, fasc. 12; 7055, fasc. 1; 7035, fasc. 3.

143 M. Neale, 'Making crime pay in late eighteenth-century Bristol: Stolen goods, the informal economy and the negotiation of risk,' *Continuity & change* 26:3 (2011) 445.

144 Angelozzi and Casanova, *Donne criminali*, 96; *Bando generale Serbelloni 1756*, 53-55.

145 ASBO, Torrone, 6620, fol. 285.

146 ASBO, Torrone, 6609, fasc. 2.

TABLE 24 Locations of sale of stolen goods by identified defendants, ca. 1655-1755

	(Work)shop/ tradesman	Reseller	Pawn bank	Unspecified individuals	Total
Male defendants	25	16	13	12	66
Female defendants	4	5	2	6	17
Total	29	21	15	18	83

SOURCE: DERIVED FROM SAMPLE 2A, 2B AND 3 (SEE APPENDIX)

quiring about it. Apparently the court officials were reluctant to convict tradesmen of malicious intent when performing their quotidian commercial activities, as only very few of the sampled Bolognese receivers were found guilty.[147]

Acquiring used goods was an essential part of the business of second-hand dealers, who made up the second most important role in the distribution of stolen goods. In Bologna, about a third of the female thieves and a quarter of their male counterparts disposed of stolen goods through such second-hand dealers. Because the vast majority of inhabitants lived a hand-to-mouth existence, the flourishing second-hand markets were pivotal in enabling ordinary people to obtain all kinds of domestic goods that would otherwise have been out of their reach.[148] Alongside local shopkeepers, a variety of second-hand dealers (*rigattieri, treccole or rivenditori/trici*) were key players in this kind of trade.[149] While these resellers sold a wide range of used goods, clothing and household linen figured prominently among the commercial journeys of stolen goods unearthed by the *Torrone*.

147 The sample includes 27 accused men and 7 women for whom it can be deduced from the sources that they played roles as 'receivers of stolen goods.' More buyers of stolen goods were mentioned and interrogated as part of the criminal records, but they were not formally accused. For five of the indicted receivers their fate was unknown, 13 were absolved and nine were bound to re-appear before the court if new information came up. Four men and one woman were pardoned (the original sentences were not always recorded: one man was originally sentenced to 5 years of imprisonment, and a woman to exile). Two men received guilty verdicts and were exiled.

148 Hohti, "Conspicuous' consumption and popular consumers,' 660. For an overview of scholarship on this topic from early modern England, France, and Scotland, see P. Allerston, 'Reconstructing the second-hand trade in sixteenth- and seventeenth-century Venice,' *Costume* 33:1 (1999) 46.

149 Hohti, "Conspicuous' consumption and popular consumers,' 659.

Women played vital roles in these second-hand markets. While the sampled criminal court cases do not suggest a vast difference between male and female offenders in their choice to dispose of goods via a second-hand dealer, their role as distributors appears to have been significant. Information about the share of women among second-hand dealers in early modern Bologna is scarce, not least because second-hand dealers' guilds in most Italian cities formally excluded women.[150] The repeated decrees of measures seeking to contain and control female sellers nevertheless speak to their constant presence in the fabric of urban life.[151] Remarkably, a close reading of the court records suggest that about half of the second-hand dealers that had handled the stolen goods investigated by the Bolognese criminal court had been women. Most of these female resellers are only known to us because they provided witness testimonies in the case, and a serious consideration of their possible malintent appears to be lacking. The significant role that these women played stands in stark contrast to the fact that they represented only one in five of the (admittedly few) receivers accused by the *Torrone*. The involvement of the other female resellers was limited to providing witness testimonies. This not only sheds light on the prevalence of female resellers in the urban economy of early modern Bologna, particularly in the second-hand clothes markets, but the fact that so many of them were not even indicted – let alone prosecuted – for their role may additionally reveal a certain judicial 'indulgence' towards women also observed for female thieves with co-offenders.

Another way to dispose of stolen goods was through pawn banks. Pawn banks emerged from the fifteenth century onwards in towns and cities across central and northern Italy.[152] Promoted by travelling preachers and run by lay religious groups, they provided low-cost credit to the working poor by allowing the poor to monetise the value stored in their moveable possessions. Bologna's *Monte di pietà* (literally a 'mountain of piety') opened in April of 1473, closed again the year after and, then backed by the ruling oligarchy, was revived in December 1504 as a civic bank with different agencies spread over the city's quarters and became one of the most successful pawn-broking institutions in Italy.[153] Based on the number of pledges, it has been calculated that there were

---

150 A. Meneghin, 'The trade of second-hand clothing in fifteenth-century Florence: Organisation, conflicts, and trends,' in G. Nigro (ed.) *Il commercio al minuto. Domanda e offerta tra economia formale e informale. Secc. XIII-XVIII. Selezione di ricerche* (Florence: Firenze University Press, 2015) 328.

151 Welch, *Shopping in the Renaissance*, 35-36.

152 N. Terpstra and M. Carboni, 'Introduction,' *Renaissance and Reformation. Special issue: The material culture of debt* 35:3 (2012) 6; Muzzarelli, 'From the closet to the wallet,' 23.

153 Carboni, 'Converting goods into cash,' 64-65.

nearly two pawns per inhabitant in Bologna by the mid-seventeenth century.[154] The majority of customers were artisans, shopkeepers and, above all, low-skilled (day) labourers.[155] While few households had many surpluses of goods, they nevertheless had many pawnables that functioned as a small, material reserve for times of need. As such, by lending on the security of pawns, the pawn banks performed a major countercyclical function in local economies.[156] They also constituted an important node in more illegal circuits of exchange. Between the mid-seventeenth and mid-eighteenth centuries, the *Torrone* was able to trace a little over one in six of the stolen wares back to Bologna's *monte*.

All in all, the criminal court records highlight the importance of ordinary and legitimate markets for the disposal of stolen goods. In early modern Bologna, workshops and their tradesmen, second-hand dealers and civic pawn banks played pivotal roles in both legal and illegal commercial activities for both male and female thieves. Unfortunately, the criminal court records often shed little light on the commercial journeys of these stolen goods, for example because the defendants kept denying involvement and there were no witnesses who reported having seen or heard about the stolen goods. It is therefore also difficult to ascertain if and to what extent the patterns of distribution were as distinctly gendered as the geography of theft appears to have been itself. While outside of the scope of this research, more in-depth examinations of the social networks of thieves may be fruitful. After all, there are important indications Italian women played vital roles in the distribution of stolen goods, yet by and large escaped scrutiny by the authorities. Gendered notions of culpability may well have clouded their appearance as criminal actors in property offences.

7 Conclusion: Judicial Paternalism and Women's Roles in Thieving

The pattern of reported crime in early modern Italian towns was extensively moulded by its everyday violence, rather than larcenous activities. Yet thefts were not infrequent occurrences and, importantly, were by no means considered futilities by either its victims or the authorities. While the criminal court records brim with acts of petty violence as part of conflict resolution strategies, thefts of all shapes and sizes were among the 'serious crimes' that the court

154 Ibidem, 66.

155 Ibidem, 78. The ledgers of Tuscan pawn banks paint a similar image, see P. Pinelli, '"Illegal" pawns for "immoral" loans; Testing the limits of the Monti di Pietà in late fifteenth-century Tuscany,' *Renaissance and Reformation. Special issue: The material culture of debt* 35:3 (2012) 14.

156 Carboni, 'Converting goods into cash,' 64; Terpstra and Carboni, 'Introduction,' 8.

sought to investigate and prosecute if in any way possible. This overall interest in prosecuting these kinds of crimes is not only apparent in the harsh sentences that the criminal bylaws prescribed, but also in the fact that thefts made up larger shares among the formal investigations (*processi*) than among the denunciations. This was especially true for women, who were above all subjected to a formal investigation not for their acts of violence but for theft.

Women's larcenous activities in early modern urban Bologna was distinct from men's in some ways but also shared many important characteristics. For one, both male and female offenders were by and large accused of committing the same type of offence – simple theft without resorting to violence – which was overwhelmingly committed by only one offender: rather than being confined to the role of accomplices, no less than two-thirds of the female Bolognese offenders committed thefts on their own. Male and female defendants also resembled each other in a socioeconomic sense: belonging to the large group of the labouring poor who, as textile workers, and market vendors, resorted to opportunistic theft to make shift. The *Torrone*'s casebooks furthermore suggest that what men and women stole – most commonly clothing, household linen and miscellaneous textiles – was not as distinctly gender specific as is often suggested. That the experiences of male and female offending were nevertheless gendered is above all apparent when scrutinising the geography of theft. Just as women's violence predominantly erupted between neighbours in their immediate neighbourhood vicinity, no fewer than eight out of ten of women's thefts (compared to 41 per cent of men's) were also committed from houses by neighbours and acquaintances. This echoes the importance of the neighbourhood for women's legitimate and illegitimate everyday behaviours.

For early modern Italian towns like Bologna it is furthermore important to highlight the impact of its legal culture on the judicial treatment of theft, and affected the proportion of women among thieves, which was significantly lower in Italy than it was in many other places in early modern Europe.[157] While crimes against property – however small in value – could rely on more judicial scrutiny than most acts of violence in early modern Italy, the criminal court records reveal that the culture of reconciliation also pervaded the ways thefts were dealt with. Renunciations and pardoning after peacemaking were less often achieved for property offences than for violent crimes, they were

157 Noordam, 'Strafrechtspleging en criminaliteit,' 228; *Old Bailey Proceedings Online* (<https://www.oldbailey online.org/>, version 7.2, March 2015), Tabulating offence category, between 1674 and 1800. Counting by defendant; Morgan. and Rushton, *Rogues, thieves and the rule of law*, 60; Schwerhoff, *Historische Kriminalitätsforschung*, 116.

nevertheless pivotal to the understanding of how crimes against property were dealt with in early modern Italy. Moreover, the judicial treatment of theft was also highly gendered. Emanating from a body of law that viewed male criminals as the norm, the gendered notions of appropriate and suitable punishments are a straightforward example of this. Where the galleys or torture via the *strappado* were deemed appropriate for offending men, confinement, exile or lashing was regarded as more suitable for their female counterparts. Importantly, a gender bias also led to women being treated more leniently in court. Particularly when women acted alongside male co-offenders, they could count on less harsh sentences or were not even indicted at all. The criminal court records furthermore suggest that by far most of the women involved in the distribution of stolen goods into the urban economy were never scrutinised as criminal actors in the first place.

Women's involvement in theft was both nebulous and pervasive. As criminal actors in a serious crime, the Bolognese criminal court records suggest significantly smaller shares of women among recorded property offenders than in many other regions in early modern Europe. While the evidence of women's everyday violent behaviours can be traced through the use of the criminal justice system as a forum for conflict resolution, our image of women's involvement in theft is contingent on the authorities' efforts to investigate and indict them. Alongside a range of factors such as the interlocking semi-charitable institutions for 'problematic' women and the social control exercised by the head of the family, the traces of judicial paternalism further uncover how women in early modern Italy were kept away from the law and the law away from women.[158] Rather than interpreting these silences as proof for early modern Italian women's lack of agency, they more than anything testify to the idea that these unusual suspects only represented a tip of the iceberg.

158 Sbriccoli, 'Deterior est condicio foeminarum,' 83-84.

Summary

This book started with Ursula Bagliardi's violent attack on her neighbour Barbara Lambertini in 1755. She was one of the many women and men whose transgressions filled the casebooks of Bologna's *Tribunale del Torrone* between the middle of the seventeenth and the eighteenth centuries, challenging oversimplified notions about Italian women's lives. Based on early modern didactic and prescriptive sources, images of seclusion and enclosure are often echoed in general and synthesising discussions about the divergence between the North and the more restrictive South. The criminal court records, however, reveal Italian women's involvement in property crimes, public order offences, and particularly violence to be more pervasive than was commonly been believed. But not all of these behaviours were subjected to a formal criminal investigation or prosecution. After all, recorded crime was not only the result of actual criminality, but also of decisions by both the authorities and communities on how to deal with certain behaviours by certain people.

The Bolognese case study reveals that the contours of women's urban criminality in the early modern period were more multifarious than commonly believed. The past decades a growing body of scholarship has demonstrated that historical patterns of female involvement in crime are far less static and uniform than was previously assumed. On the forefront of this revision were historians who observed significant disparities between urban and rural areas, and related them to the particular freedoms and vulnerabilities women experienced in urban environments. Based on the vast scholarly attention for England and the Dutch Republic, one could distil a kind of archetype of women's urban crime, featuring relatively high shares of women as criminal offenders, chiefly brought to justice for property offences. This would, however, do injustice to the women's diverging experiences with the law in the early modern period, since there is an increasing awareness that a generalised model of urban life does not account for disparities between different types of cities, nor for regional variations across Western Europe.

With its intermediate position on the scales of women's socioeconomic and legal rights, Bologna provides an admirable laboratory to test observations about women's everyday roles in criminal behaviours and their encounters with the criminal court system in a city in early modern Italy. It showcases an urban setting with a distinctly different urban crime pattern, featuring comparably low shares of women brought to justice, and a preoccupation with violent offences. On average, women made up less than ten per cent of the offenders in Italian criminal court records, a share that pales in comparison to those observed in cities across northern Europe. Yet the Bolognese casebooks also demonstrate that we cannot automatically equate these low shares with women's lack of agency, whether licit or illicit, because women themselves had an active hand in keeping the wheels of the court spinning through bottom-up processes of conflict resolution. Understanding women's roles in the judicial system helps to nuance our understanding of their quotidian scope of action. A closer examination of the structures and mechanisms producing these crime shares is thus imperative to understand urban women's involvement in criminal and deviant behaviour in a northern Italian town such as Bologna.

1 The Case of Bologna and Patterns of Female Crime

So far these divergent patterns of women's involvement in crime in Italy and their underlying causes have received only limited scholarly attention, especially for the so-called 'forgotten centuries' after the Renaissance. This book has sought to overcome this lacuna by providing an in-depth examination of the relationship between crime, criminal justice, and gender in seventeenth- and eighteenth-century Bologna. The comparably low share of women among investigated offenders is a striking feature of criminal prosecution in early modern Bologna: between the mid-seventeenth and mid-eighteenth centuries, women comprised about five per cent of those subject to formal criminal investigations (*processi*) in Bologna. The available data on other towns on the Italian peninsula reveal similarly low shares. While the early modern period marked a peak for women's involvement in crime in many cities across northern Europe, there is little evidence that this trend applied to the Italian peninsula.

To understand what engendered these comparatively low female crime shares in early modern Bologna, it is important to examine what crimes passed through the criminal court process. An important characteristic of premodern criminal justice in Italy is the proportional importance of violence among investigated crimes. As in Florence and Rome during earlier centuries, the dockets of Bologna's early modern *Tribunale del Torrone* brimmed with violent acts ranging from insults and blows to stabbings, shootings and murder. Making up 43 per cent of the total caseload of formal investigations at Bologna's criminal court, these predominantly physically violent offences were the most common reason for an encounter with the law. They were followed by a parity of offences against property and public order (just over a quarter of all cases), whereas criminal investigations concerning sexual offences were overall much more scarce. When viewed alongside of the available data from Spain, Portugal and South West France, the Bolognese case study provides further evidence for the existence of a southern European pattern of crime and criminal prosecution in which violent offences figured much more prominently than in the northern regions of Europe. This raises the question of the extent to which Italian women's lower share among criminal offenders can be attributed to an alleged culture of violence, which has commonly been linked to the enduring cultural importance of the masculine honour culture in which men frequently clashed over slights to reputation and status, in which women would have no place.[1]

Although the pattern of reported crime in the seventeenth and eighteenth centuries was to a large extent moulded by violence, thefts of all shapes and sizes belonged to the serious crimes for which women were predominantly subjected to a formal investigation. In general the authorities' interest in prosecuting these kinds of crimes was apparent in the fact that thefts made up significantly larger portions among these *processi* than among the phase of the initial denunciations. This was especially true for female transgressors, for whom property offences constituted the most important category of crime at the level of the *processi*. Property offenders of both sexes generally belonged to the large group of the labouring poor who opportunistically resorted to simple theft of items such as clothing, household linen and miscellaneous textiles without resorting to violence. However, thefts did not only figure so prominently among the criminal investigations against women because of the authorities' great interest in prosecuting crimes against property. After all there is significant evidence for the Bolognese magistrates' paternalistic attitude towards women's roles in theft. That property crimes such as theft constituted the largest proportion of crimes for which women were investigated was also highly contingent on the fact that other types of offences – such as their violent encounters – were not.

While both stringent gender norms and the ethics of honour meant that it was neither expected nor desirable for women to engage in aggressive acts, violent behaviour was in practice by no means the preserve of men. The one-third of the female defendants among the *processi* accused of committing serious physically violent affront already bears witness to this. However, the commonplaceness of women's violent altercations with male and female adversaries is above all apparent in the earlier stage of the denunciation – the moment when either local officials or the wronged individuals themselves denounced a crime

1 Ruff, *Violence in early modern Europe*, 75.

to the criminal court. With about nine denunciations to each formal investigation in Bologna, more than 80 per cent of the women and two-thirds of the men in these far more plentiful denunciations were denounced for violent behaviours. For both men and women, most of these altercations can be categorised as petty physical aggression that was by and large directed against members of their own sex and had erupted among their neighbours, fellow artisans, peddlers and porters during their daily social and economic affairs, arming themselves with whatever was at hand. Rather than relying solely on men for the defence of their reputation and interests – as prescribed by the ethics of honour – many Italian women took matters into their own hands. Clearly, while women's violent behaviour may have not found much cultural encouragement, it was far too common to be viewed as an anomaly.

To a certain extent these crime patterns reflected gendered socioeconomic realities. Importantly, the microcosm of the immediate neighbourhood bore greater importance for women as a site of violent conflict as well as for their larcenous activities than for their male counterparts. Both male and female fighters by and large settled their violent quarrels in public, urban space. Nevertheless, a substantial part of women's violence in Bologna took place just outside of houses: when entering or leaving the house, when using the shared spaces in apartment complexes, while standing in the doorway, leaning out of windows, or sitting on a doorstep under one of the city's many porticos. The close proximity and sharing of resources among commoners fuelled the bulk of women's neighbourly conflicts; aspects that were not only related to the daily rhythm not only of women's domestic chores, but also factored into their sociability and working lives through the concentration of these activities on houses – their own and those of their friends,' families' and employers.' The large majority of women accused of theft had also stolen from their neighbours' and acquaintances' houses, while the geography of men's thieving was much more diverse. Both the social profiles and motives of offenders underscore that women's broad socioeconomic roles in the urban economy should not be underestimated, yet the importance of the immediate neighbourhood for women's illicit behaviours reveals a gendered dynamic of women's everyday lives in early modern Bologna. While these dynamics may have in part been the result of a gender-appropriate judicial narrative, they also mirrored certain socioeconomic realities.

The significant discrepancy between 'crime patterns' at earlier and later stages of the criminal process, however, also illustrates the need to scrutinise how social and legal mechanisms affected the share of women in these records. After all, Italian women made up only five per cent of the accused offenders at the level of the formal investigation (*processi*), where property offences as well as serious violence constituted the majority of crimes. At the earlier stage of the denunciations, on the other hand, women constituted over 20 per cent of the offenders who were predominantly accused of petty violence – a figure much more similar to those found in other parts of Europe. This means that it is debatable whether Bologna's comparably low female crime shares can be explained away by its culture of violence. For the Bolognese context this book identifies three underlying mechanisms related to its legal culture that contributed to women's low share among the criminal court records: institutionalisation, judicial paternalism and peacemaking practices.

2 The Impact of Institutionalisation, Judicial Paternalism and Peacemaking Practices

Because women have often been overlooked in the study of crime in early modern Italy, the underlying mechanisms that obscured their criminal offending have also received little systematic scrutiny. One of Italy's most prominent legal historians convincingly argued that the legal system contributed to the low levels of women in recorded crime through its categorisation of women's behaviours as matters of sin, disorder, irregularity or censorable anomalies rather than a criminal offence subject to criminal justice.[2] Women's deviant behaviours could therefore largely be absorbed into a mesh of extrajudicial control ranging from the domestic sphere and the neighbourhood, to a range of ecclesiastical and civil institutions. While similar arguments regarding the importance of extrajudicial social control have been made for other parts of early modern Europe, what may set Italy apart is the important role played by a host of semi-public charitable institutions in connecting spheres of control for women at the fringes of society.[3]

Centuries before the better-known custodial institutions in Victorian England, integrated networks of semi-public charitable institutions emerged all over Italy from the sixteenth century onwards, seeking to correct, supervise and help 'problematic' women and girls.[4] This system consisted not only of orphanages, workhouses and conservatories, but also of dowry investment funds, institutions for mutual assistance and, importantly, a variety of enclosed shelters for women at the fringes of society. These institutions became increasingly purgative towards the women under their supervision and furthermore

2 Sbriccoli, 'Deterior est condicio foeminarum,' 81.
3 Woolf, *The poor in Western Europe*, 24; Terpstra, *Cultures of charity*, 17.
4 Cohen, *The evolution of women's asylums*, 3, 8.

increasingly housed a range of 'difficult women' admitted by their husband or kin or placed there by magistrates for punitive enclosure.[5] In early modern Bologna we also find that women were relatively more often incarcerated for theft – above all in the city's poor house – than their male counterparts. This stemmed from a broader, general notion that viewed confinement as particularly appropriate for all categories of problematic women. Based on some admission data of these institutions, it furthermore does not seem unlikely that women suspected of committing a crime were also placed in these institutions without a conviction. While the criminal women within these 'custodial warehouses' deserve further scrutiny, these traces suggest that these early modern welfare provisions may not have only reduced the need for women to engage in crime but also may have obscured their participation in it.

Gendered prosecution policies also profoundly affected early modern Bolognese women brought before the criminal court. Criminal prosecutions were and are always the result of political and institutional choices rather than a reflection of all of society's transgressions.[6] The Bolognese *processi* therefore represent the crimes for which the criminal court was willing and able to start an inquisitorial trial, but these cases constituted only a fraction of the crimes that were reported, let alone occurred. What crimes were prosecuted and in what way must therefore always be seen in relationship to the authorities' priorities and the discretion of the judges, who had a wide *arbitrium*, and weighed who to punish and how based on aspects of the crime itself as well as on the 'personal qualities' of the plaintiffs and defendants. Rooted in ideas about women's legal minority, and subordination in every social sphere, one's sex constituted one such quality. This is reflected in Bologna's criminal bylaws. In the mid-eighteenth-century bylaws the introductory remarks stress that the judge is free to impose judgement on women proportional to their sex, commuting punishments like the galleys and public *strappado* (pulls by the cord) to the more suitable options of confinement, exile, incarceration or lashing.[7]

Aside from receiving different types of punishments for their crimes, there were a range of circumstances under which the seriousness of women's involvement in crime was essentially called into question by the *Torrone*'s judges. Interestingly, this phenomenon is particularly evident among property offences; the type of crime for which most female offenders were subjected to a formal investigation. Particularly when women acted alongside male co-offenders in theft, regardless of their functional role, they could generally count

5 Ibidem, 17, 36, 79; Terpstra, *Cultures of charity*, 213; Cavina, *Nozze di sangue*, 48.
6 Dean and Lowe, 'Writing the history of crime,' 3.
7 *Bando generale Serbelloni 1756*, 3-4.

on less harsh sentences, or were not even indicted at all, often being absolved before even being formally interrogated. Furthermore, by far most of the women involved in the distribution of stolen goods into the urban economy were never scrutinised as criminal actors; an indulgence that should not be viewed as 'chivalry' but rather as paternalism rooted in ideas of women's minority and subordination in every social sphere.[8] Women's involvement in crime was often considered harmless or irrelevant, regardless of their actual role in the crime.

Early modern Italy's widespread culture of peacemaking furthermore contributed to the image emerging from Bologna's criminal court records. Although the participation of women remains understudied, the formal incorporation and continued importance of reconciliation in early modern Italy's criminal justice system is relatively well-documented.[9] In addition to exercising top-down control through the prosecution of crimes, early modern Italian criminal courts also encouraged their use as a site of bottom-up peacemaking and conflict resolution for a wide range of crimes, particularly (though by no means exclusively) for what were considered 'minor crimes' such as brawls and scuffles not resulting in life-threatening wounds. Most scholarly attention has been paid to the better-known petitions and notarised peace accords predominantly used for graver types of crimes such as homicide, but the most prevalent type of peacemaking took place at the level of the denunciation. Here victims and their close kin could halt any legal action through a simple juridical withdrawal of the complaint (*rinuncia*), often following a composition of some sort.[10] While some victims hoped to see those who wronged them punished by the authorities, many others used litigation as bargaining power within their communities. Interestingly, as the denunciations represented the earliest stages of the criminal court process, they included the petty grievances caused by and endured by significantly larger numbers and shares of women. These practices of conflict resolution, used by hundreds if not thousands Bolognese men and women each year, help explain why so many of these cases were never turned into a formal investigation.

An in-depth analysis of the different stages of the criminal court process nuances our understanding of the meaning of Italian women's comparatively low shares among formal criminal investigations. These shares do not simply point to women's marginal involvement in crime, but were engendered by the

8 Angelozzi and Casanova, *Donne criminali*, 239, 242; Casanova, 'Crimini di donne, giudici benevoli,' 1.

9 Bellabarba, 'Pace pubblica e pace privata,' 189-213.

10 Niccoli, 'Rinuncia, pace, perdono,' 226.

combination of a propensity to institutionalise 'problematic women,' a general judicial paternalism towards women, and a widespread and pervasive culture of institutionally-endorsed reconciliation. With over five times more female offenders at the level of the denunciations, it is furthermore evident that women were far less passive in their actual behaviours than is commonly suggested.

3 Crime and Italian Women's Agency

By their very nature these criminal court records attest to the discrepancy between norms and actual behaviour. As such they allow us to assess the scope of action of those that appeared before it as defendants and plaintiffs beyond what was normatively prescribed. Notwithstanding their modest presence among the *Torrone*'s formally investigated crimes, a significantly larger bulk of women's everyday behaviours were considered unwelcome acts worth denouncing to the criminal court – especially non-fatal, physical violence that did not result in life-endangering wounds. Women's lethal violence is believed to have centred around the domestic realm, while the judicial narratives from the earliest stages of the criminal justice process (the denunciations) shed light on the much more prevalent violence that erupted among neighbours, acquaintances and co-workers in the urban space. They indicate that Bolognese women fought with their fists as well as with the items they had at hand, in many similar kinds of spaces as men and, importantly, did so to a much larger extent than the formal investigation dossiers alone would ever suggest. Furthermore, both in violence and in their larcenous activities the majority of women acted alone, nuancing their image of mere accomplices in crime. While general discussions commonly suggest that the strict gender norms as well as Italy's honour culture left little space for women's agency, whether licit or illicit, the criminal court records reveal that women had a greater scope of action than is commonly believed.

Women's social and economic roles in the urban economy played important roles in shaping this leeway. Contrary to popular belief, women's labour force participation rates in Bologna (as in Turin) were as high as (or even higher than) those observed elsewhere in early modern Europe. As such the social profiles of the women and men whose offences came to the notice of the criminal court represented a broad dissection of predominantly lower- and lower-middle class society with a wide range of professions, albeit on-and-off or underemployed. An important share of the female offenders was active in the less-prestigious and poorly paid functions within the textile industry such as spinners, weavers, hosiers and seamstresses relying on the uncertainties of piecework. These working poor generally lived in close proximity to each other, shared resources with neighbours and attempted to maintain a livelihood through the household's combined labour efforts, occasional charity and, for some, opportunistic theft. For women as for men, the occasions, opportunities and setting for both thieving and violence were shaped by their legitimate socioeconomic roles in the urban environment. Especially in their neighbourhood surroundings but also on Bologna's markets, streets and in taverns women fought over neighbourly annoyances, resources and their economic interests within the capacities of their roles as neighbours, landlords and tenants, economic competitors, vendors and clients, and creditors and debtors. Female resellers' frequently documented though unprosecuted distribution of stolen goods furthermore suggests that their leeway may have been far more extensive than is currently known.

Another important way in which the sources reveal early modern Italian women's agency was through their litigation as plaintiffs. In general, the notion of women's inferior legal status derived from Roman law contributed to the idea that Italian women may have had limited legal agency, especially compared to northern European societies. However, the examination of seventeenth- and eighteenth-century criminal court records demonstrates that women, like men, were able to strategically employ justice to settle their conflicts. While inhabitants of even the most remote hamlets in the Bolognese territory could theoretically bring conflicts to the court, the reliance on male local officials in the countryside to relay cases to the *Torrone* created a structural impediment to women's ability to seek justice. Urban women could and did make their way to one of the court's eight notaries to lodge complaints in person. The petty grievances that they predominantly sought to pursue were rarely turned into a formal investigation, yet they found in the criminal court a forum through which they could wield and manipulate power and exert it over their community members. Here women were able to turn to litigation to mediate and settle their personal disputes, to establish boundaries, defend their reputations, and to make individual statements. For women the urban environment may not have only provided a more precarious context, but also better opportunities to resolve conflicts through the formal criminal justice system.

4 Avenues for Future Research

The juxtaposition of these fragments of individuals' lives derived from the criminal court records thus clearly reveals the ambiguity of women's position in early modern Bologna. On the one hand, both moral norms and early modern Italy's legal culture played important roles in obscuring and arguably even containing Bolognese women's illicit behaviours. This has resulted in relatively low female crime shares at the level of the criminal investigations. At the same time, the close-reading of these investigation dossiers reveal that the criminal involvement of women in, for example, larcenous activities often escaped the magistrates' scrutiny. The multitude of complaints concerning women's violent embroilments furthermore demonstrate that their agency as both criminals and litigants was far greater than a reading of the prescriptive literature, or their share among the *processi* alone, would suggest. Any social historical examination of women's gendered relation to crime and criminal justice needs to take the extent of women's scope of action amid a culture of constraint into account. In early modern Bologna both gender norms and the ethics of honour meant that women were not encouraged nor expected to engage in crime, but, at the same time, their public urban lives created the spatial and social latitude for licit and illicit activities beyond what the norms prescribed.

The city of Bologna has offered a fruitful setting for the historical analysis of the gender dynamics in crime and criminal justice. As one of Italy's many textile towns with one of the most long-term best-preserved criminal court archives both within and outside of Italy, the city has provided an opportune backdrop to trace women's involvement in criminal behaviour throughout the judicial process. Bologna was, however, only one city among many others. While this book has used this case study to theorise and nuance assumptions about the Italian peninsula and, by extension, southern Europe as a whole, it does not intend to infer uniformity across early modern Italy. For example, while interpretations of Roman law are assumed to have led to general constraints on Italian women's legal and socioeconomic agency, local statutes are known to have either moderated or exacerbated these effects. These local laws have placed Florence on one extreme of the balance of women's scope of action and towns such as Venice and Genoa on the – less restricted – other.[11] The existence of significant regional variations in these fields touching on women's agency is intuitively appealing, though its local implications remain obscure, also in relation to crime and criminal justice. How did women fare in the more restrictive Florence in the centuries after the Renaissance? And what was it like in other cities where women are assumed to have had more social and economic liberties, such as in Genoa? Can similar characteristics and mechanisms as those traced in the Bolognese case be observed, or were other local factors more decisive?

11 Kuehn, 'Gender and law in Milan,' 406-407.

Alongside of judicial paternalism and peacemaking practices, another factor of importance to the history of crime and gender in Italy is the institutionalisation of problematic women. Ranging from orphanages and conservatories to workhouses and enclosed shelters, they represented a double-edged sword of care and control for the women who either entered voluntarily or were placed there by their husband, kin or by local officials. That there were criminal women among the population of the increasingly purgative 'custodial warehouses' is commonly accepted. However, if the archival materials permit, it a closer examination of these women, their crimes and their pathways into these institutions would be useful to more fully understand the relationship between this general tendency towards the institutionalisation of women, their crimes and the criminal justice in early modern Italy.

Lastly, this book has examined the influence of gender on women's criminal behaviours and their judicial treatment in Bologna during the seventeenth and eighteenth centuries. It has largely done so through the lens of social history, examining how social actors moved within the socioeconomic and legal contours of the early modern city. In discussing the judicial narratives surrounding acts of violence brought before the criminal court, it did briefly touch upon more cultural interpretations of gender. A more extensive and systematic cultural historical examination of masculine and feminine narratives constructed in the criminal court record, of the differences and similarities that existed between them, has remained outside the scope of this book but would be an interesting avenue to unearth further knowledge about what it meant to engage with the law in the past.

This book, in its social historical approach to the history of women in crime, has focused on the 'forgotten' period between the mid-seventeenth and mid-eighteenth centuries. This was the period after the 1630s plague and its subsequent social unrest, and before the city experienced the full effects of the economic crisis. Delimiting the period under discussion has meant that various important societal transformations during the second half of the eighteenth century have remained unexplored. How women's criminal behaviour and their judicial treatment developed under the weight of the unfolding economic crisis, the increasing proletarisation of labour, and the assumed weakening of patriarchal control must consequently be answered in future research. The scrutiny in this book of the mechanisms affecting women's involvement in crime in the prior, relatively more tranquil period hopefully provides a fruitful point of departure.

APPENDIX

Information on Samples

The extensiveness of Bologna's unindexed criminal court archive has necessitated the taking of samples. The impact of the plague during the 1630s, the political turmoil of the early 1650s as well as the changing organisation of record keeping around the same time have been convincing arguments to select 1655 as a first sample year, followed by the less tumultuous years of 1675, 1705, 1725 and 1755, stopping just before the economic crisis fully impacted the city. For these sample years I have selected three datasets. The first dataset consists of 910 *processi* and represents all extant urban investigation dossiers for the five sample years. The data collected for these cases is less detailed than for the other samples and serves primarily to reveal representative, quantitative patterns of criminal prosecution and possible developments throughout time. The second dataset consists of one or more casebooks by a notary for each of the sample years. This resulted in a collection of 1,070 denunciations and 207 *processi* that were kept either in the back of these casebooks or later in its second, accompanying volume. The qualitative analyses in this book are based on these sources, as well as on a third data collection of 77 additional *processi*. These *processi* were selected at random for years surrounding the sample years, the only criteria being that a woman was named on the front sheet as one of the defendants.

1 Sample 1: Exhaustive and Representative Sample of Extant *Processi* for Urban Bologna for the Years 1655, 1675, 1705, 1725 and 1755

Archivio di Stato di Bologna, Tribunale del Torrone, Atti e processi, Book 6653 to 8179.

TABLE 25 Number of cases and defendants within the samples

	Type	Cases	Defendants			
			Women	Men	Total	Unidentified
Sample 1	*Processi*	910	70	1287	1357	62
Sample 2a	Denunciations	1070	241	903	1144	214
Sample 2b	*Processi*	204	20	287	307	7
Sample 3	*Processi*	77	91	61	152	–

This first dataset consists of 910 *processi* collected from 81 books and represents all extant urban investigation dossiers for the five sample years that I was able to locate in the archive. The data collected for these cases is less-detailed than for the other samples and serves primarily to reveal representative, quantitative patterns of criminal prosecution and possible developments throughout time.

2 Sample 2a: Non-exhaustive Sample of Urban Denunciations Derived from Several Notaries' Casebooks Centring around the Years 1655, 1675, 1705, 1725 and 1755

Archivio di Stato di Bologna, Tribunale del Torrone, Atti e processi, Book 6609, 6620, 6653, 7028, 7044, 7608-1, 7869-1, 8171-1.

The second dataset consists of a random sample of eight notaries' casebooks centring on the sample years. This has resulted in a collection of 1,070 denunciations. They have been examined in detail and have also been used for qualitative analyses of the sources.

3 Sample 2b: Non-exhaustive Sample of Urban *Processi* from Several Notaries' Casebooks Centring around the Years 1655, 1675, 1705, 1725 and 1755

Archivio di Stato di Bologna, Tribunale del Torrone, Atti e processi, Book 6596, 6609, 6620, 6653, 7028, 7044, 7055, 7077, 7608-2, 7869-2, 8171-2.

This second part of the second dataset consists of 204 *processi* found in the same notaries' casebooks as in sample 2a. They were either kept in the back of the casebooks in which the denunciations were written or were recorded in their accompanying, dedicated volumes (for example referred to as part 2). These *processi* have received the same treatment as the aforementioned denunciations, allowing for a qualitative analysis.

4 Sample 3: Non-exhaustive Sample of Additional Urban *Processi* from 1654 to 1757

Archivio di Stato di Bologna, Tribunale del Torrone, Atti e processi, Book 6526 to 8179-2.

The qualitative analyses in this book are also based on a third data collection of 77 additional *processi*. These *processi* were collected from 42 books for years surrounding the sample years, with the only criteria that a woman was named on the front sheet as one of the defendants. They were examined in the same in-depth way as sample 2.

Bibliography

Primary Sources

Archivio di Stato di Bologna, Tribunale del Torrone, Atti e processi.

Bando generale della legazione di Bologna e suo contado, fatto pubblicare li 12. ottobre 1756 dall'eminentiss., e reverendiss. sig. cardinale Fabrizio Serbelloni, legato a latere di detta città (Bologna 1756).

Bando generale dell'illustrissimo, e reverendissimo sig. Benedetto card. Giustiniano legato di Bologna, pubblicato alli 23. di Giugno, & reiterato alli 24. di Luglio 1610 (Bologna 1610).

Berlan, F., *Statuti Italiani. Saggio bibliografico* (Venice: Tipografia del commercio, 1858).

European sourcebook of crime and criminal justice statistics 2014 (Helsinki: Hakapaino Oy, 2014).

I Regolamenti penali di Papa Gregorio XVI per lo Stato Pontificio (1832), S. Vinciguerra ed. (Padua: CEDAM, 2000).

Mirogli, F., *Istruzzioni teorico-prattiche criminali di Filippo Mirogli Romano fiscal generale dedicate alla santita di nostro signore Clemente PP.XIII* (Rome 1758-1770).

Le chiese parrocchiali della diocesi di Bologna, ritratte e descritte (Bologna 1849).

Savelli, M.A., *Pratica universale del dottor Marc Antonio Savelli* (Parma 1717).

Secondary Literature

Abreu-Ferreira, D., *Women, crime and forgiveness in early modern Portugal* (Surrey-Burlington: Ashgate, 2015).

Ago, R., *Gusto for things. A history of objects in seventeenth-century Rome* (Chicago: University of Chicago Press, 2013).

Ago, R., 'Il linguaggio del corpo,' in C.M. Belfanti and F. Giusberti (eds.), *Storia d'Italia. Annali 19. La moda* (Turin: Enaudi, 2003) 117-148.

Allerston, P., 'Meeting demand: Retailing strategies in early modern Venice,' in B. Blondé, E. Briot. N. Coquery and L. van Aert (eds.), *Retailers and consumer changes in early modern Europe. England, France, Italy and the Low Countries* (Tours: Presses Universitaires François-Rabelais, 2005) 169-188.

Amussen, S., 'Punishment, discipline and power. The social meaning of violence in early modern England,' *Journal of British studies* 34:1 (1995) 1-34.

Amussen, S., '"Being stirred to much unquietness": Violence and domestic violence in early modern England,' *Journal of women's history* 6:2 (1994) 70-89.

Angelozzi, G. and Casanova, C., *Donne criminali. Il genere nella storia della giustizia* (Bologna: Pàtron Editore, 2014).

Angelozzi, G. and Casanova, C., 'Il tribunale criminale di Bologna,' in M. Cavina (ed.), *La giustizia criminale nell'Italia moderna* (*XVI-XVIII sec.*) (Bologna: Pàtron Editore, 2012) 247-260.

Angelozzi, G. and Casanova, C., *La giustizia criminale a Bologna nel XVIII secolo e le riforme di Benedetto XIV* (Bologna: CLUEB, 2010).

Angelozzi, G. and Casanova, C., *La giustizia in una città di antico regime. Il tribunale del Torrone di Bologna* (*secc. XVI-XVII*) (Bologna: CLUEB, 2008).

Angelozzi, G. and Casanova, C., *La nobiltà disciplinata. Violenza nobiliare, procedure di giustizia e scienza cavalleresca a Bologna nel XVII secolo* (Bologna: Patròn Editore, 2003).

Armelloni, E., 'Casa, famiglia e professione nel Milano di fine '700,' *Journal of the Lombard Society of history* 113 (1987) 164-187.

Arnade, P. and Colwill, E., 'Crime and testimony: Life narratives, pardon letters and microhistory,' *Journal of medieval and early modern studies* 47:1 (2017) 147-166.

Arnot, M.L. and Usborne, C. (eds.), *Crime and gender in modern Europe* (London: UCL Press, 1999).

Arnot, M.L. and Usborne, C., 'Why gender and crime? Aspects of an international debate,' in M.L. Arnot and C. Usborne (eds.), *Gender and crime in modern Europe* (London: UCL Press, 1999) 1-43.

Arrivo, G. 'Sposarsi in tribunale. Sessualità e matrimonio nella Toscana del settecento,' *Storicamente* 6 (2010), DOI: 10.147/stor84.

Arrivo, G., *Seduzioni, promesse, matrimoni. Il processo per stupro nella Toscana del settecento* (Rome: Edizioni di Storia e Letteratura, 2006).

Arru, A., 'The distinguishing features of domestic service in Italy,' *Journal of family history* 15:4 (1990) 547-566.

Asta, L., 'La violenza femminile nella Roma del primo ottocento,' *Rivista storica del Lazio* 13-14 (2000-2001) 17-45.

Barbagli, M., 'Three household formation systems in eighteenth and nineteenth-century Italy,' in D.J. Kertzer and R.P Saller (eds.), *The family in Italy from antiquity to the present* (New Haven: Yale University Press, 1991) 250-270.

Barbagli, M., *Sotto lo stesso tetto. Mutamenti della famiglia in Italia dal 15. al 20. secolo* (Bologna: Il Mulino, 1984).

Beattie, J.M., *Crime and the courts in England, 1660-1800* (Princeton: Princeton University Press, 1986).

Beattie, J.M., 'Violence and Society in Early Modern England,' in A.N. Doob and E.L. Greenspan (eds.), *Perspectives in criminal law : Essays in Honour of John L.J. Edwards* (Aurora: Canada Law Book, 1984) 36-60.

Beattie, J.M., 'The criminality of women in eighteenth-century England,' *Journal of social history* 8:4 (1975) 80-116.

Beattie, J.M., 'The pattern of crime in England 1660-1800,' *Past & present* 62 (1974) 47-95.

Becker, M.B., 'Changing patterns of violence and justice in fourteenth and fifteenth-century Florence,' *Comparative studies in society and history* 18:3 (1976) 281-296.

Belfanti, C.M. and Giusberti, F., 'Clothing and social inequality in early modern Europe: introductory remarks,' *Continuity and change* 15:3 (2000) 359-365.

Bellabarba, M., *La giustizia nell'Italia moderna* (Bari: Editori Laterza, 2008).

Bellabarba, M., 'Pace pubblica e pace privata. Linguaggi e istituzioni processuali nell'Italia moderna,' in M. Bellabarba, A. Zorzi and G. Schwerhoff (eds.), *Criminalità e giustizia in Germania e in Italia. Pratiche giudiziarie e linguaggi giuridici tra tardo medioevo e prima età moderna* (Bologna: Il Mulino, 2001) 189-213.

Bellavitis, A., *Il lavoro delle donne nelle città dell'Europa moderna* (Rome: Viella, 2016).

Bellavitis, A. and Zucca Micheletto, B., 'Introduction: North versus South – gender, law and economic well-being in the fifteenth to nineteenth centuries,' in A. Bellavitis and B. Zucca Micheletto (eds.), *Gender, law and economic well-being in Europe from the fifteenth to the nineteenth century: North versus South?* (Abingdon: Routledge, 2019) 1-27.

Bellettini, A., *La popolazione di Bologna dal secolo xv all'unificazione Italiana* (Bologna: Zanichelli, 1961).

Bellomo, M., *The common legal past of Europe, 1000-1800* (Washington: The Catholic University of America Press, 1995).

Bettoni, A., 'Fama, shame punishments and the history of justice in the sixteenth and seventeenth centuries,' in J. Rowbotham, M. Muravyeva and D. Nash (eds.), *Shame, blame and culpability. Crime and violence in the modern state* (London: Routledge, 2013) 32-42.

Bianchi, A., 'Madri e padri davanti al Tribunale arcivescovile,' in C. Grandi (ed.), *Benedetto chi ti porta, maledetto chi ti manda: l'infanzia abbandonata nel Triveneto* (Treviso: Canova, 1997) 58-73.

Bianchi, A. '"L'elemosina di un bambino": Practica e controllo dell'abbandono all'ospedale dei Bastardini (secc. XVI–XVIII),' *Sanità scienza e storia* 2 (1989) 35-54.

Black, C.F., *Early modern Italy. A social history* (London: Routledge, 2001).

Blanshei, S.R., 'Introduction,' in S.R. Blanshei (ed.), *Violence and justice in Bologna 1250-1700* (Lanham: Lexington Books, 2018) ix-xxxiii.

Blanshei, S.R., 'Homicide in a culture of hatred: Bologna 1352-1420,' in T. Dean and K. Lowe (eds.), *Murder in Renaissance Italy* (Cambridge: Cambridge University Press, 2017) 106-122.

Blanshei, S.R. and Cucini, S., 'Criminal justice and conflict resolution,' in S.R. Blanshei (ed.), *A companion to medieval and Renaissance Bologna* (Leiden: Brill, 2018) 335-360.

Blastenbrei, P., 'Violence, arms and criminal justice in Papal Rome, 1560-1600,' *Renaissance Studies* 20 (2006), 68-87.

Blastenbrei, P., *Kriminalität in Rom 1560-1585* (Tübingen: Niemeyer, 1995).

Boschi, D., 'Knife fighting in Rome, 1845-1914,' in P. Spierenburg (ed.), *Men and violence. Gender, honor and rituals in modern Europe and America* (Columbus: Ohio State University Press, 1998) 128-158.

Bosker, M., Brakman, S., Garretsen, H., Jong, H. de and Schramm, M., 'The development of cities in Italy 1300-1861,' *CESifo working paper* 1893, via <http://www.ehs.org.uk/dotAsset/491c2f80-6f0e-42c2-becb-228b23ef47b7.pdf>.

Brackett, J.K., 'The Florentine criminal underworld. The underside of the Renaissance,' in W.J. Connell (ed.), *Society and individual in Renaissance Florence* (Berkeley: University of California Press, 2002) 293-314.

Brackett, J.K., 'The Florentine Onestà and the control of prostitution, 1403-1680,' *The sixteenth century journal* 24:2 (1993) 273-300.

Brackett, J.K., *Criminal justice and crime in late Renaissance Florence, 1537-1609* (Cambridge: Cambridge University Press, 1992).

Broggio, P. and Caroll, S., 'Introduction. Violence and peacemaking in early modern Europe,' *Krypton* 3:5/6 (2015) 4-8.

Brown, J.C., 'Introduction,' in J.C. Brown and R.C. Davis (eds.), *Gender and society in Renaissance Italy* (London/New York: Longman 1998) 1-16.

Brown, J.C. and Goodman, J., 'Women and industry in Florence,' *The journal of economic history* 40:1 (1980) 73-80.

Burke, P. *The historical anthropology of early modern Italy* (Cambridge: Cambridge University Press, 1987).

Buttex, L., 'L'indulgence des juges? La femme incriminée à Genève au siècle des Lumières. Genre et répression pénale (1767-1792),' *Crime, history & societies* 19:1 (2015) 41-65.

Callahan, K., 'Women who kill: An analysis of cases in late eighteenth- and early nineteenth-century London,' *Journal of social history* 46-4 (2013) 1013-1038.

Callahan, K., 'On the receiving end. Women and stolen goods in London 1783-1815,' *The London journal* 37:2 (2012) 106-121.

Calzolari, M., 'Delitti e castighi,' in M. Calzolari, M. Di Sivo and E. Grantaliano (eds.), *Giustizia e criminalità nello stato pontificio* (Rome: Gangemi Editore, 2001) 39-75.

Cameron, I.A., *Crime and repression in the Auvergne and the Guyenne, 1720-1790* (Cambridge: Cambridge University Press, 2011).

Canepari, E., 'Civic identity, "juvenile" status and gender in sixteenth and seventeenth-century Italian towns,' in D. Simonton, *The Routledge history handbook of gender and the urban experience* (London/New York: Routledge, 2017) 182-194.

Carboni, M., 'Converting goods into cash: An ethical approach to pawnbroking in early modern Bologna,' *Renaissance and Reformation. Special issue: The material culture of debt* 35:3 (2012) 63-83.

Carpanetto, D. and Ricuperati, G., *L'Italia del settecento* (Rome: Laterza, 2008).

Carraway Vitiello, J., *Public justice and criminal trial in late medieval Italy* (Leiden: Brill, 2016).

Carroll, S., 'Revenge and reconciliation in early modern Italy,' *Past & present* 233 (2016) 101-142.

Carroll, S., 'Peace-making in early modern Europe. Towards a comparative history,' in P. Broggio and M.P. Paoli (eds.), *Stringere la pace. Teorie e pratiche della conciliazione nell'Europea moderna (secoli XV-XVIII)* (Rome: Viella, 2011) 75-92.

Carroll, S., 'Introduction,' in S. Carroll (ed.), *Cultures of violence. Interpersonal violence in historical perspective* (Basingstoke: Palgrave, 2007) 1-43.

Casanova, C., 'Crimini di donne, giudici benevoli (Bologna XVI-XVIII secolo,' *Historia et ius* 9 (2016) 1-11.

Casanova, C., *Crimini nascosti. La sanzione penale dei reati "senza vittima" e nelle relazioni private (Bologna, XVII secolo)* (Bologna: CLUEB, 2007).

Casanova, C., *La famiglia italiana in età moderna. Richerche e modelli* (Rome: Carocci, 1997).

Castan, N., *Les criminels de Languedoc. Les exigences d'ordre et les voies du ressentiment dans un société pré-révolutionnaire (1750-1790)* (Toulouse: Association des publications de l'université de Toulouse-Le Mirail, 1980).

Cavallo, S. and Cerutti, S., 'Female honor and the social control of reproduction in Piedmont between 1600 and 1800,' in E. Muir and G. Ruggiero (eds.), *Sex and gender in historical perspective* (Baltimore: Johns Hopkins University Press, 1990) 73-109.

Cavarzere, M., 'At the crossroads of feud and law: Settling disputes in early modern Tuscany,' in S. Cummins and L. Kounine (eds.), *Cultures of conflict resolution in early modern Europe* (Surrey: Ashgate, 2016) 51-74.

Cavaterra, A., 'Economia, povertà e consumi in età moderna,' in B. Coccia (ed.), *La quarta settimana: Storia dei bisogni e dei consumi degli italiani che oggi non arrivano alla fine del mese* (Rome: Editrice APES, 2009) 15-78.

Cavina, M., *Nozze di sangue. Storia della violenza coniugale* (Rome: Laterza, 2011).

Cavina, M., 'I luoghi della giustizia,' in A. Prosperi (ed.), *Bologna nell'età moderna (secoli XVI-XVIII). Tomo 1. Istituzioni, forme del potere, economia e società* (Bologna: Bononia University Press, 2008) 367-412.

Cecchini, I., 'A world of small objects: Probate inventories, pawns and domestic life in early modern Venice,' *Renaissance and Reformation. Special issue: The material culture of debt* 35:3 (2012) 39-61.

Chojnacka, M., 'Singlewomen in early modern Venice. Communities and opportunities,' in J.M. Bennett and A.M. Froide (eds.), *Singlewomen in the European past 1250-1800* (Philadelphia: University of Pennsylvania Press, 1999) 217-235.

Ciammitti, L., 'Fanciulle, monache, madre. Povertà femminile e previdenza a Bologna nei secoli XVI–XVIII,' in *Arte e Pietà: I patrimoni culturali delle Opere Pie* (Bologna: CLUEB, 1980) 435-520.

Clemente, A., 'Storiografie di confine? Consumo di beni durevoli e cultura del consumo nel XVIII secolo,' *Società e storia* 109 (2005) 569-598.

Cockburn, J.S., 'Patterns of violence in English society: homicide in Kent, 1560-1985,' *Past & Present* 130 (1991) 70-106.

Cohen, E.S., 'Open city. An introduction to gender in early modern Rome,' *I Tatti studies in the Italian Renaissance* 17:1 (2014) 35-54.

Cohen, E.S., 'To pray, to work, to hear, to speak: Women in Roman streets, c.1600,' *Journal of early modern history* 12 (2008) 289-311.

Cohen, E.S., 'Evolving the history of women in early modern Italy: Subordination and agency,' in T.J. Dandelet and J.A. Marino (eds.), *Spain in Italy. Politics, society and religion 1500-1700* (Leiden: Brill, 2007) 325-354.

Cohen, E.S., 'Seen and known. Prostitutes in the cityscape of late-sixteenth-century Rome,' *Renaissance studies* 12:3 (1998) 392-409.

Cohen, E.S., 'Honor and gender in the streets of early modern Rome,' *Journal of interdisciplinary history* 22:4 (1992) 597-625.

Cohen, E.S., '"Courtesans" and "whores." Words and behavior in Roman streets,' *Women's studies* 19 (1991) 201-208.

Cohen, E.S. and Cohen, T.V., 'Open and shut: The social meanings of the cinquecento Roman house,' *Studies in the decorative arts* 9 (2001-2002) 61-84.

Cohen, E.S. and Cohen, T.V., *Daily life in Renaissance Italy* (Westport/London: Greenwood Publishing Group, 2001).

Cohen, E.S. and Cohen, T.V., *Words and deeds in Renaissance Rome. Trials before the papal magistrates* (Toronto: University of Toronto Press, 1993).

Cohen, S., *The evolution of women's asylums since 1500. From refuges for ex-prostitutes to shelters for battered women* (Oxford: Oxford University Press, 1992).

Cohen, T.V., *Love and death in Renaissance Italy* (Chicago: University of Chicago Press, 2004).

Cohen, T.V., 'The lay liturgy of affront in sixteenth-century Italy,' *Journal of social history* 25:4 (1992) 857-877.

Cohn, S.K., *Women in the streets. Essays on sex and power in Renaissance Italy* (Baltimore: Johns Hopkins University Press, 1998).

Cohn, S.K., 'Women in the streets, women in the courts, in early Renaissance Florence,' in S.K. Cohn (ed.), *Women in the streets. Essays on sex and power in Renaissance Italy* (Baltimore: Johns Hopkins University Press, 1998) 16-38.

Cohn, S.K., 'Women and work in Renaissance Italy,' in J.C. Brown and R.C. Davis (eds.), *Gender and society in Renaissance Italy* (London and New York: Longman, 1998) 107-126.

Coletti, T., 'Did women have a Renaissance? A medievalist reads Joan Kelly and Aemilia Lanyer,' *Early modern women. An interdisciplinary journal* 8 (2013) 249-259.

Corley, C.R., 'On the threshold. Youth as arbiters of urban space in early modern France,' *Journal of social history* 43:1 (2009) 139-156.

Cowan, A., 'Gossip and street culture in early modern Venice,' *Journal of early modern history* 12 (2008) 313-333.

Crouzet-Pavan, E., 'Crimine e giustizia,' in G. Calvi (ed.), *Innesti. Donne e genere nella storia sociale* (Rome: Viella, 2004) 55-72.

Cucini, S., 'Législation statutaire et gouvernement pontifical en Italie centrale. Le cas de l'administration de la justice criminelle à Bologna, deuxième moitié du xve siècle' (Unpublished PhD thesis, Université Paul-Valéry, 2014).

Cummins, S. and Kounine, L., 'Introduction. Confronting conflict in early modern Europe,' in S. Cummins and L. Kounine (eds.), *Cultures of conflict resolution in early modern Europe* (Surrey: Ashgate, 2016) 1-16.

Cummins, S., 'Forgiving crimes in early modern Naples,' in S. Cummins and L. Kounine (eds.), *Cultures of conflict resolution in early modern Europe* (Surrey: Ashgate, 2016) 255-279.

D'Amelia, M., 'Scatole cinesi. Vedove e donne sole in una società d'ancien régime,' *Memoria* 18 (1986) 58-80.

D'Amico, S., 'Shameful mother. Poverty and prostitution in seventeenth century Milan,' *Journal of family history* 39:1 (2005) 109-120.

Davies, J., 'Introduction,' in J. Davies (ed.), *Aspects of violence in Renaissance Europe* (Surrey: Ashgate, 2013) 1-13.

Davis, R., 'Say it with stones. The language of rock-throwing in early modern Italy,' *Ludica* 10 (2004) 113-128.

D'Cruze, S., 'Unguarded passions. Violence, history and the everyday,' in S. D'Cruze (ed.), *Everyday violence in Britain, 1850-1950. Gender and class* (Harlow: Longman, 2000) 1-26.

Dean, T., 'Eight varieties of homicide. Bologna in the 1340s and 1440s,' in T. Dean and K. Lowe (eds.), *Murder in Renaissance Italy* (Cambridge: Cambridge University Press, 2017) 83-105.

Dean, T., 'Theft and gender in late medieval Bologna,' *Gender & History* 20:2 (2008) 399-415.

Dean, T., *Crime and justice in late medieval Italy* (Cambridge: Cambridge University Press, 2007).

Dean, T., 'Domestic violence in late-medieval Bologna,' *Renaissance studies* 18:4 (2004) 527-543.

Dean, T., 'Gender and insult in an Italian city: Bologna in the later Middle Ages,' *Social history* 29:2 (2004) 217-231.

Dean, T., *Crime in medieval Europe, 1200-1500* (Harlow: Longman, 2001).

Dean, T., 'Criminal justice in mid-fifteenth-century Bologna,' in T. Dean and K. Lowe (eds.), *Crime, society and the law in Renaissance Italy* (Cambridge: Cambridge University Press, 1994) 16-39.

Dean, T. and Lowe, K., 'Writing the history of crime,' in T. Dean and K. Lowe (eds.), *Crime, society and the law in Renaissance Italy* (Cambridge: Cambridge University Press, 1994) 1-15.

De Benedictis, A. 'Repubblica per contratto. Una città (Bologna) nello stato (Pontificio),' *Scienza & Politica* 2:4 (1990) 59-72.

Dinges, M., 'The uses of justice as a form of social control in early modern Europe,' in H. Roodenburg and P. Spierenburg (eds.), *Social control in Europe. Volume 1, 1500-1800* (Columbus: Ohio State University Press, 2004) 159-175.

Di Simplicio, O., *Peccato, penitenza, perdono: Siena 1575-1800. La formazione della coscienza dell'Italia moderna* (Milan: Franco Angeli Storia, 1994).

Di Sivo, M., 'Per via giustizia. Sul processo penale a Roma tra XVI e XIX secolo,' *Rivista storica del Lazio. Special issue: Giustizia e criminalità nello stato pontificio* 9:4 (2001) 13-35.

Dumont, D., 'Women and guilds in Bologna. The ambiguities of 'marginality,' *Radical History Review* 70 (1998) 4-25.

Edigati, D., 'La pace nel processo criminale. Il caso toscano in età moderna,' in P. Broggio and M.P. Paoli (eds.), *Stringere la pace. Teorie e pratiche della conciliazione nell'Europea moderna (secoli XV-XVIII)* (Rome: Viella, 2011) 369-409.

Eibach, J., 'Violence and masculinity,' in P. Knepper and A. Johansen (eds.), *The Oxford handbook of the history of crime and criminal justice* (Oxford: Oxford University Press, 2016) 229-249.

Eibach, J., 'Das offene Haus. Kommunikative Praxis im sozialen Nahraum der europäischen Frühen Neuzeit,' *History & Archaeology* 38:4 (2011) 621-664.

Eibach, J., *Frankfurter Verhöre: Städtische Lebenswelten und Kriminalität im 18. Jahrhundert* (Paderborn: Ferdinand Schöningh, 2003).

Eibach, J., 'Böse Weiber und grobe Kerle. Delinquenz, Geslecht und soziokulturelle Räume in der frühneuzeitlichen Stadt,' in A. Blauert and G. Schwerhoff (eds.), *Kriminalitätsgeschichte. Beiträge zur Sozial- und Kulturgeschichte der Vormoderne* (Konstanz: UVK Universitätsverlag Konstanz, 2000) 669-688.

Eisner, M., 'From swords to words. Does macro-level change in self-control predict long-term variation in levels of homicide?,' *Crime and justice* 43 (2014) 65-134.

Eisner, M., 'Long-term historical trends in violent crime,' *Crime and justice* 30 (2003) 83-142.

Eisner, M., 'Modernization, self-control and lethal violence. The long-term dynamics of European homicide rates in theoretical perspective,' *British journal of criminology* 41 (2001) 618-638.

Fairchilds, C.C., *Women in early modern Europe, 1500-1700* (Harlow: Longman, 2007).

Fanti, M., 'Bologna nell'età moderna (1506-1796),' in A. Ferri and G. Roversi (ed.), *Storia di Bologna* (Bologna: Bononia University Press, 2005) 185-256.

Farge, A. and Zysberg, A., 'Les théâtres de la violence à Paris au XVIIIe siècle,' *Annales. Économies, sociétés, civilisations* 34:5 (1979) 984-1015.

Farge, A., *Délinquance et criminalitè. Le vol d'aliments à Paris au XVIIIe siècle* (Paris: Plon, 1974).

Fazio, I., 'Storia delle donne e microstoria,' in M. Caffiero, M.P. Donato and G. Fiume (eds.), *Donne, potere, religione. Studi per Sara Cabibbo* (Milan: FrancoAngeli, 2017) 81-94.

Feeley, M.M. and Aviram, H., 'Social historical studies on women, crime and courts,' *Annual review of law and social science* 6 (2010) 151-171.

Feeley, M.M. and Little, D., 'The vanishing female: The decline of women in the criminal process, 1687-1912,' *Law & society review* 25:4 (1991) 719-757.

Ferrante, L., 'La sessualità come risorsa. Donne davanti al foro arcivescovile di Bologna (sec. XVII),' *Mélanges de l'École française de Rome* 99:2 (1987) 989-1016.

Ferrante, L., 'Malmaritate tra assistenza e punizione (Bologna secc. XVI-XVII),' in *Forme e soggetti dell'intervento assistenziale in una città di antico regime: Atti del IV colloquio (Bologna, 20-21 gennaio, 1984)* (Bologna: Istituto per la storia di Bologna, 1986) 65-110.

Ferrante, L., '"Tumulto di più persone per causa del calo del pane..." Saccheggi e repressione a Bologna (1671, 1677),' *Rivista storica italiana* 90 (1978) 770-809.

Ferraro, J.M., *Nefarious crimes, contested justice. Illicit sex and infanticide in the Republic of Venice, 1557-1789* (Baltimore: Johns Hopkins University Press, 2008).

Ferraro, J.M., 'The manufacture and movement of goods,' in J. Jeffries Martin (ed.), *The Renaissance world* (New York: Routledge, 2007) 87-100.

Ferraro, J.M., *Marriage wars in late Renaissance Venice* (Oxford: Oxford University Press, 2001).

Ferraro, J.M., 'The power to decide. Battered wives in early modern Venice,' *Renaissance Quarterly* 48:3 (1995) 492-512.

Fosi, I., *Papal justice. Subjects and the courts in the Papal State, 1500-1750* (Ann Arbor: Washington: Catholic University of America Press, 2011).

Gallée, B. and Ligthart, J., 'De remmende werking van huwelijk en arbeid op vermogensdelicten. Rotterdam, 1812-1820,' *Tijdschrift voor criminologie* 57:4 (2015) 353-367.

Gambier, M., 'La donna e la giustizia penale Veneziana nel XVIII secolo,' in G. Cozzi (ed.), *Stato, società e giustizia nella Repubblica Veneta (sec. XV-XVIII)* (Rome: Jouvenence, 1980) 531-575.

Garrioch, D., 'Verbal insults in eighteenth-century Paris,' in P. Burke and R. Porter (eds.), *The social history of language* (Cambridge: Cambridge University Press, 1987) 104-119.

Geltner, G., 'A cell of their own: The incarceration of women in late medieval Italy,' *Signs* 38:1 (2013) 27-51.

Geltner, G., 'No woman's land? On female crime and incarceration, past, present and future,' *Justice policy journal* 7:2 (2010) n.p.

Giusberti, G. 'La città assistenziale. Riflessioni su un sistema piramidale,' in M. Fanti (ed.), *Forme e soggetti dell'intervento assistenziale in una città di antico regime. Atti del IV colloquio, Volume II* (Bologna: Istituto per la storia di Bologna, 1984) 13-29.

Giusberti, F. and Roversi Monaco, F., 'Economy and demography,' in S.R. Blanshei (ed.), *A companion to medieval and Renaissance Bologna* (Leiden: Brill, 2018) 154-184.

Goldtwaithe, R., *Wealth and demand for art in Italy, 1300-1600* (Baltimore: Johns Hopkins University Press, 1993).

Gowing, L., *Domestic dangers. Women, words, and sex in early modern London* (Oxford: Clarendon Press, 1996).

Gray, D.D., *Crime, prosecution and social relations. The summary courts of the city of London in the late eighteenth century* (Basingstoke: Palgrave Macmillan, 2009).

Gray, D.D., 'The regulation of violence in the metropolis: The prosecution of assault in the summary courts, c.1780-1820,' *The London journal* 32:1 (2007) 75-87.

Graziosi, M., '"Fragilitas sexus." Alle origine della costruzione giuridica dell'inferiorità delle donne,' in N.M. Filippini, T. Plebani and A. Scattigno (eds.), *Corpi e storia. Donne e uomini dal mondo antico all'età contemporanea* (Rome: Viella, 2002) 19-38.

Graziosi, M., 'Women and criminal law. The notion of diminished responsibility in Prospero Farinaccio (1544-1618) and other Renaissance jurists,' in L. Panizza (ed.), *Women in Italian Renaissance culture and society* (Oxford: University of Oxford European Humanities Research Centre, 2000) 166-181.

Greenshields, M.R., *An economy of violence in early modern France. Crime and justice in the Haute Auvergne, 1587-1664* (Oxford: British Library, 1986).

Grendi, E., 'Sulla storia criminale: Risposta a Mario Sbriccoli,' *Quaderni Storici* 73 (1990) 269-275.

Grendi, E., 'Premessa,' *Quaderni Storici* 66:3 (1987) 695-700.

Groppi, A., 'A matter of fact rather than principle. Women, work and property in papal Rome (eighteenth-nineteenth centuries),' *Journal of modern Italian studies* 7:1 (2002) 37-55.

Groppi, A., 'Lavoro e proprietà delle donne in età moderna,' in R. Ago and A. Groppi (eds.), *Il lavoro delle donne* (Bari: Laterza, 1996) 119-163.

Guenzi, A., 'La tessitura femminile tra città e campagna. Bologna, secoli XVII-XVIII,' in S. Cavaciocchi (ed.), *La donna nell'economia secc. XIII-XVIII* (Florence: Le Monnier, 1990) 247-259.

Guenzi, A., 'L'identità industriale d'una città e del suo territorio,' in A. Prosperi (ed.), *Storia di Bologna nell'età moderna (secoli XVI-XVIII)* (Bologna: Bononia University Press, 2008) 449-524.

Guenzi, A., 'L'immigrazione urbana e rurale a Bologna in una fonte del secolo XV,' *Rassegna degli Archivi di Stato* 44 (1984) 149-163.

Hacke, D., *Women, sex and marriage in early modern Venice* (Aldershot: Ashgate 2004).

Hanawalt, B., *Crime and conflict in English communities: 1300-1348* (Cambridge: Harvard University Press, 1979).

Hanawalt, B., 'The female felon in fourteenth-century England,' *Viator* 5 (1974) 253-268.

Hanlon, G., 'The decline of violence in the West: From cultural to post-cultural history,' *English historical review* 128:531 (2013) 367-400.

Hanlon, G., 'Violence and its control in the late Renaissance: An Italian model,' in G. Ruggiero (ed.), *A companion to the worlds of the Renaissance* (Oxford: Blackwell, 2002) 139-155.

Hardwick, J., 'Between state and street: Witnesses and the family politics of litigation in early modern France,' in S. Desan and J. Merrick (eds.), *Family, gender and law in early modern France* (University Park: Pennsylvania State University Press, 2009) 101-136.

Heijden, M. van der, *Women and crime in early modern Holland* (Leiden: Brill, 2016).

Heijden, M. van der, 'Women and Crime 1750-2000,' in P. Knepper and A. Johansen (eds.), *The Oxford Handbook of the History of Crime and Criminal Justice* (Oxford: Oxford University Press, 2016) 251-267.

Heijden, M. van der, 'Women, violence and urban justice in Holland, 1600-1838,' *Crime, History & Societies* 17:2 (2013) 71-100.

Heijden, M. van der, 'Criminaliteit en sexe in 18e-eeuws Rotterdam,' *Tijdschrift voor sociale geschiedenis* 21:1 (1995) 1-36.

Heijden, M. van der and Muurling, S., 'Violence and gender in 18th-century Bologna and Rotterdam,' *Journal of social history* 51:4 (2018) 695-716.

Heijden, M. van der and Schmidt, A., 'Theorizing crime and gender in long term perspective,' in E.M. Dermineur, A.K. Sjögren and V. Langum (eds.), *Revisiting gender in European history, 1400-1800* (Routledge: New York, 2018) 52-77.

Herlihy, D. and Klapisch-Zuber, C., *Les Toscans et leur familles: Une etude du catasto florentin de 1427* (Paris: Éditions de l'École des hautes etudes en sciences sociales, 1978).

Herrup, C., 'New shoes and mutton pies: Investigative responses to theft in seventeenth-century East Sussex,' *The historical journal* 27:4 (1984) 811-830.

Hitchcock, T. and Shoemaker, R., *London lives. Poverty, crime and the making of the modern city, 1690-1800* (Cambridge: Cambridge University Press, 2015).

Hofman, E. 'Dikwijls bespied. Sociale controle onder buren in het achttiende-eeuwse Kortrijk,' *De Leiegouw* 55 (2013) 27-40.

Hohti, P., '"Conspicuous" consumption and popular consumers: Material culture and social status in sixteenth-century Siena,' *Renaissance studies* 24:5 (2010) 654-670.

Horodowich, E., *Language and statecraft in early modern Venice* (Cambridge: Cambridge University Press, 2008).

Howard, S., 'Investigating responses to theft in early modern Wales. Communities, thieves and the courts,' *Community and change* 19 (2004) 409-430.

Howard, S., 'Crime, communities and authority in early modern Wales: Denbighshire, 1660-1730' (Unpublished PhD thesis, University of Wales, 2003).

Howell, M., 'The problem of women's agency in late medieval and early modern Europe,' in S.J. Moran and A.C. Pipkin (eds.), *Women and gender in the early modern Low Countries, 1500-1750* (Leiden: Brill, 2019) 21-31.

Hufton, O., 'Women and violence in early modern Europe,' in F. Dieteren and E. Kloek (eds.), *Writing women into history* (Amsterdam: Historisch Seminarium van de Universiteit van Amsterdam, 1991) 75-95.

Hufton, O., *The poor in eighteenth-century France, 1750-1789* (Oxford: Clarendon Press, 1974).

Hughes, S., 'Fear and loathing in Bologna and Rome. The papal police in perspective,' *Journal of social history* 21 (1987) 97-116.

Humphries, J, and Sarasúa, C., 'Off the record. Reconstructing women's labor force participation in the European past,' *Feminist economics* 18:4 (2012) 39-67.

Hurl-Eamon, J., *Gender and petty violence in London, 1680-1720* (Columbus: Ohio State Press, 2005).

Jacobsen Schutte, A., 'Society and the sexes in the Venetian Republic,' in E.R. Dursteler (ed.), *A Companion to Venetian History, 1400-1797* (Leiden: Brill, 2013) 354-377.

Jansen, K.L., '"Pro bono pacis": Crime, conflict, and dispute resolution. The evidence of notarial peace contracts in late medieval Florence,' *Speculum* 88:2 (2013) 427-456.

Jones, K., *Gender and petty crime in late medieval England. The local courts in Kent, 1450-1560* (Suffolk: The Boydell Press, 2006).

Jütte, R., 'Geslechtsspezifische Kriminalität im Späten Mittelalter und in der Frühen Neuzeit,' *Zeitschrift der Savigny-Stiftung für Rechtsgeschichte* 108 (1991) 86-116.

Kamp, J., *Crime, gender and social control in early modern Frankfurt am Main* (Leiden: Brill, 2019).

Kamp, J., 'Female crime and household control in early modern Frankfurt am Main,' *The history of the family* 21:4 (2016) 531-550.

Kane, B. and Williamson, F., 'Introduction,' in B. Kane and F. Williamson (eds.), *Women, agency and the law, 1300-1700* (New York: Pickering & Chatto, 2013) 1-16.

Kelly, J., 'Did women have a Renaissance?,' in J. Kelly (ed.), *Women, history & theory: the essays of Joan Kelly* (Chicago: University of Chicago Press, 1984) 19-50.

Kilday, A.M., '"Criminally poor?"' Investigating the link between crime and poverty in eighteenth century England,' *Cultural and social history: The journal of the Social History Society* 11:4 (2015) 507-526.

Kilday, A.M., *Women and violent crime in Enlightenment Scotland* (Woodbridge: Boydell Press, 2007).

King, P., *Crime and law in England, 1750-1840* (Cambridge: Cambridge University Press, 2006).

King, P., 'The summary courts and social relations in eighteenth-century England,' *Past & Present* 183 (2004) 125-172.

King, P., 'Gender, crime and justice in late eighteenth and early nineteenth-century England,' in M. Arnot and C. Usborne (eds.), *Gender and crime in modern Europe* (London: UCL Press, 1999) 44-74.

King, P., 'Female offenders, work and life-cycle change in late-eighteenth-century London,' *Continuity and change* 11:1 (1996) 61-90.

Kirshner, J., *Marriage, dowry, and citizenship in late medieval and Renaissance Italy* (Toronto: University of Toronto Press, 2015).

Kirshner, J., 'Wives' claims against insolvent husbands in late medieval Italy,' in J. Kirshner and S.F. Wemple (eds.), *Women of the medieval world* (Oxford: Blackwell, 1985) 256-303.

Klapisch-Zuber, C., 'State and family in a Renaissance society: The Florentine Catasto of 1427-30,' in C. Klapisch-Zuber (ed.), *Women, family and ritual in Renaissance Italy* (Chicago: University of Chicago Press, 1987) 1-22.

Klapisch-Zuber, C., 'Women servants in Florence during the fourteenth and fifteenth centuries,' in B. Hanawalt (ed.), *Women and work in preindustrial Europe* (Bloomington: Indiana University Press, 1986) 56-80.

Knepper, P., *Writing the history of crime* (Bloomsbury: London/New York, 2016).

Kuehn, T., *Family and gender in Renaissance Italy, 1300-1600* (Cambridge: Cambridge University Press, 2017).

Kuehn, T., 'Gender and law in Milan,' in A. Gamberini (ed.), *A companion to late medieval and early modern Milan. The distinctive features of an Italian state* (Leiden: Brill, 2015) 406-431.

Kuehn, T., 'Daughters, mothers, wives and widows. Women as legal persons,' in A. Jacobson Schutte, T. Kuehn and S. Seidel Menchi (eds.), *Time, space and women's lives in early modern Europe* (Kirksville: Truman State University Press, 2001) 97-115.

Kuehn, T., 'Person and gender in the laws,' in J.C. Brown and R.C. Davis (eds.), *Gender and society in Renaissance Italy* (Longman: London/New York, 1998) 87-106.

Kuehn, T., 'Understanding gender inequality in Renaissance Florence. Personhood and gifts of maternal inheritance by women,' *Journal of women's history* 8:2 (1996) 58-80.

Kuehn, T., 'Law and arbitration in Renaissance Florence,' in T. Kuehn (ed.), *Law, family and women. Toward a legal anthropology of Renaissance Italy* (Chicago: University of Chicago Press, 1991) 19-74.

Kuehn, T., 'Reading microhistory: The example of Giovanni and Lusanna,' *The journal of modern history* 61 (1989) 512-534.

Lacché, L., *Latrocinium. Giustizia, scienza penale e repression del banditismo in antico regime* (Milan: Giuffrè Editore, 1988).

Lambert, K., *Itinéraires féminins de la deviance. Provence 1750-1850* (Aix-en-Provence: Presses Universitaires de Provence, 2012).

Lansing, C., 'Conflicts over gender in civic courts,' in J.M. Bennett and R. Mazo Karras (eds.), *The Oxford handbook of Women and gender in medieval Europe* (Oxford: Oxford University Press, 2013) 116-132.

Lansing, C., 'Concubines, lovers, prostitutes. Infamy and female identity in medieval Bologna,' in P. Findlen, M.M. Fontaine and D.J. Osheim (eds.), *Beyond Florence. The contours of medieval and early modern Italy* (Palo Alto: Stanford University Press, 2003) 85-100.

Lawrence, P., 'The historiography of crime and criminal justice,' in P. Knepper and A. Johansen (eds.), *The Oxford Handbook of the History of Crime and Criminal Justice* (Oxford: Oxford University Press, 2016) 17-37.

Lemire, B., 'Plebeian commercial circuits and everyday material exchange in England, c. 1600-1900,' in B. Blondé, P. Stabel, J. Stobart and I. van Damme (eds.), *Buyers & sellers. Retail circuits and practices in medieval and early modern Europe* (Turnhout: Brepols, 2006) 245-266.

Lemire, B., 'The theft of clothes and popular consumerism in early modern England,' *Journal of social history* 24:2 (1990) 255-276.

Lenman, B. and Parker, G., 'The state, the community and the criminal law in early modern Europe,' in V.A.C. Gatrell, B. Lenman and G. Parker (eds.), *Crime and the law. The social history of crime in Western Europe since 1500* (London: Europa Publications, 1980) 11-48.

Lesnick, D.R., 'Insults and threats in medieval Todi,' *Journal of medieval history* 17 (1991) 71-89.

Lipscomb, S., 'Crossing boundaries: Women's gossip, insults and violence in sixteenth-century France,' *French history* 25:4 (2011) 408-426.

Lombardi, D., 'Marriage in Italy,' in S. Seidel Menchi (ed.), *Marriage in Europe, 1400-1800* (Toronto: University of Toronto Press, 2016) 94-121.

Lombardi, D., 'Famiglie di antico regime,' in G. Calvi (ed.), *Innesti. Donne e genere nella storia sociale* (Rome: Viella, 2004) 199-222.

Lombardi, D., 'Giustizia ecclesiastica e composizione dei conflitti matrimoniali (Firenze, secoli XVI-XVIII),' in S. Seidel Menchi and D. Quaglioni (eds.), *I tribunali del matrimonio (secoli XV-XVIII)* (Bologna: Il Mulino, 2001) 577-608.

Lombardi, D. and Reggiani, F., 'Da assistita a serva. Circuiti di reclutamento delle serve attraverso le istituzioni assistenziali (Firenze-Milano, XVII-XVIII sec.),' in S. Cavaciocchi (ed.), *La donna nell'economia secc. XIII-XVIII* (Florence: Le Monnier, 1990) 301-319.

Lucassen, J., *Migrant labour in Europe 1600-1900* (London: Croom Helm, 1987).

Lynch, K., *Individuals, families and communities in Europe 1200-1800: The urban foundations of Western society* (Cambridge: Cambridge University Press, 2003).

MacKay, L., 'Why they stole. Women in the Old Bailey, 1779-1789,' *Journal of social history* 32:3 (1999) 623-639.

Mackkenney, R., *Tradesmen and traders. The world of guilds in Venice and Europe, c.1250-c.1650* (London: Croom Helm, 1987).

Malanima, P., 'Italian urban population 1300-1861 (The database)' (Last revised 2015, accessed via <http://www.paolomalanima.it/default_file/Italian%20Economy/Urban_Population.pdf>).

Malanima, P. and Pinchera, V., 'A puzzling relationship. Consumptions and incomes in early modern Europe,' *Histoire & mesure* 27:2 (2012) 197-222.

Malanima, P., 'I consumi in età moderna. Crescita o decline?,' in E. Sori and R. Giulianelli (eds.), *Consumi e dinamiche economiche in età moderna e contemporanea* (Napels: ESI, 2011) 43-68.

Malanima, P., 'An age of decline. Product and income in eighteenth-nineteenth century Italy,' *Rivista di storia economica* 12:1 (2006) 91-133.

Malanima, P., 'Urbanisation and the Italian economy during the last millennium,' *European review of economic history* 9 (2005) 97-122.

Malanima, P., *L'economia italiana. Dalla crescita medieval alla crescita contemporanea* (Bologna: Il Mulino, 2003).

Mantecón, T.A., 'The patterns of violence in early modern Spain,' *The journal of the historical society* 7:2 (2007) 229-264.

Mantini, S., 'Women's history in Italy: Cultural itineraries and new proposals in current historiographical trends,' *Journal of women's history* 12:2 (2000) 170-198.

Mariani, R., 'Criminalità e controllo sociale nella Crevalcore del seicento' (Unpublished Master thesis, Università degli studi di Bologna, 1991).

McCarthy, V.G., 'Prostitution, community and civic regulation in early modern Bologna' (Unpublished PhD thesis, University of Toronto, 2015).

McEwan, J., 'Negotiating support. Crime and women's networks in London and Middlesex, c.1730-1820' (Unpublished PhD thesis, University of Western Australia, 2008).

McMahon, R., Eibach, J. and Roth, R., 'Making sense of violence? Reflections on the history of interpersonal violence in Europe,' *Crime, history and societies* 17:2 (2013) 5-26.

Meek, C., 'Women between the law and social reality in early Renaissance Lucca,' in L. Panizza (ed.), *Women in Italian Renaissance culture and society* (Oxford: Legenda, 2000) 182-193.

Meneghin, A., 'The trade of second-hand clothing in fifteenth-century Florence: Organisation, conflicts, and trends,' in G. Nugro (ed.), *Il commercio al minuto. Domanda e offerta tra economia formale e informale. Secc. XIII-XVIII. Selezione di ricerche* (Florence: Firenze University Press, 2015) 319-336.

Misson, M., *Voyage d'Italie* (Amsterdam: Clousier, 1743).

Montenach, A. and Simonton, D., 'Introduction: Gender, agency and economy. Shaping the eighteenth-century European town,' in D. Simonton and A. Montenach (eds.), *Female agency in the urban economy. Gender in European towns, 1640-1830* (New York/London: Routledge, 2013) 1-16.

Moor, T. de and Zanden, J.L. van, 'Girl power: The European marriage pattern and labour markets in the North Sea region in the late medieval and early modern period,' *The economic history review* 63:1 (2010) 1-33.

Morgan, G. and Rushton, P., *Rogues, thieves and the rule of law. The problem of law enforcement in north-east England, 1718-1800* (London: UCL Press, 1998).

Muchembled, R., *A history of violence: From the end of the Middle Ages to the present* (Cambridge: Polity, 2012).

Muchembled, R., 'Anthropologie de la violence dans la France moderne (XVe-XVIIIe siècle),' *Revue de synthèse* 108 (1987) 31-55.

Muir, E., 'Italy in the no longer forgotten centuries,' *I Tatti Studies in the Italian Renaissance* 16:1/2 (2013) 5-11.

Muir, E. and Ruggiero, G. (eds.), *History from crime* (Baltimore: Johns Hopkins University Press, 1994).

Muir, E. and Ruggiero, G., 'Afterword. Crime and the writing of history,' in E. Muir and G. Ruggiero (eds.), *History from crime* (Baltimore: Johns Hopkins University Press, 1994) 226-236.

Muurling, S. and Pluskota, M. 'The gendered geography of violence in Bologna, 17-19th centuries," in D. Simonton (ed.), *Routledge history handbook of gender and the urban experience* (Abington: Routledge, 2017) 153-163.

Muzzarelli, M.G., 'From the closet to the wallet. Pawning clothes in Renaissance Italy,' *Renaissance and Reformation. Special issue: The material culture of debt* 35:3 (2012) 23-38.

Neale, M., 'Property crime in late eighteenth-century Bristol. Contexts of theft in the pre-modern city' (Unpublished PhD thesis, University of Leicester, 2012).

Neale, M., 'Making crime pay in late eighteenth-century Bristol: Stolen goods, the informal economy and the negotiation of risk,' *Continuity & change* 26:3 (2011) 439-459.

Nevola, F., 'Street life in early modern Europe,' *Renaissance Quarterly* 66:4 (2013) 1332-1345.

Niccoli, O., *Perdonare. Idee, pratiche, rituali in Italia tra cinque e seicento* (Rome: Editori Laterza, 2007).

Niccoli, O., *Storie di ogni giorno in una città del seicento* (Rome: Laterza, 2000).

Niccoli, O., 'Rinuncia, pace, perdono. Rituali di pacificazione della prima età moderna,' *Studi storici* 40:1 (1999) 219-261.

Noordam, D.J., 'Strafrechtspleging en criminaliteit in Delft in de vroeg-moderne tijd,' *Tijdschrift voor sociale geschiedenis* 15 (1989) 209-244.

Nubola, C., 'Giustizia, perdono, oblio. La grazia in Italia dall'età moderna ad oggi,' in K. Härter and C. Nubola (eds.), *Grazia e giustizia. Figure della clemenza fra tardo medioevo ad età contemporanea* (Bologna: Il Mulino, 2011) 11-42.

Nussdorfer, L., 'The politics of space in early modern Rome,' *Memoirs of the American Academy in Rome* 42 (1997) 161-186.

Palazzi, M., 'Economic autonomy and male authority. Female merchants in modern Italy,' *Journal of modern Italian studies* 7:1 (2002) 17-36.

Palazzi, M., 'Female solitude and patrilineage. Unmarried women and widows during the eighteenth and nineteenth Centuries,' *Journal of Family History* 15 (1990) 443-459.

Palazzi, M., 'Tessitrici, serve, treccole. Donne, lavoro e famiglia a Bologna nel settecento,' in S. Cavaciocchi (ed.), *La donna nell'economia secc. XIII-XVIII* (Florence: Le Monnier, 1990) 359-376.

Palk, D., *Gender, crime and judicial discretion, 1780-1830* (Woodbridge: Boydell Press, 2006).

Pastore, A., *Il medico in tribunale. La perizia medica nella procedura penale d'antico regime (secoli XVI-XVIII)* (Bellinzona: Edizioni Casagrande, 1998).

Pastore, A., *Crimine e giustizia in tempo di peste nell'Europea moderna* (Rome: Laterza, 1991).

Perego, N., *Homini de mala vita. Criminalità e giustizia a Lecco e in terra di Brianza tra cinque e seicento* (Lecco: Oggiono, 2001).

Philips, J. and May, A.N., 'Female criminality in 18th-century Halifax,' *Acadiensis* 31:2 (2002) n.p.

Pinelli, P., '"Illegal" pawns for "immoral" loans; Testing the limits of the Monti di Pietà in late fifteenth-century Tuscany,' *Renaissance and Reformation. Special issue: The material culture of debt* 35:3 (2012) 11-22.

Pluskota, M., 'Petty criminality, gender bias, and judicial practice in 19th-century Europe,' *Journal of social history* 51:4 (2018) 717-735.

Povolo, C., 'Aspetti e problem dell'amministrazione della giustizia penale nella repubblica di Venezia, secoli XVI-XVII,' in G. Cozzi (ed.), *Stato, società e giustizia nella Repubblica Veneta (sec. XV-XVIII)* (Rome: Jouvenence, 1980) 153-258.

Prior, M., 'Private spheres and public records. Reconstructing women's history for the early modern period,' in F. Dieteren and E. Kloek (eds.), *Writing women into history* (Amsterdam: Historisch seminarium van de Universiteit van Amsterdam, 1990) 55-74.

Prodi, P., *Settimo non rubare. Furto e mercato nella storia dell'Occidente* (Bologna: Il Mulino, 2009).

Prodi, P., *The papal prince. One body and two souls. The papal monarchy in early modern Europe* (Cambridge: Cambridge University Press, 1982).

Rapp, R.T., *Industry and economic decline in seventeenth century Venice* (Cambridge: Harvard University Press, 1976).

Rau, S., 'Public order in public space: Tavern conflict in early modern Lyon,' *Urban history* 34:1 (2007) 102-113.

Ricci, G., *Bologna: Storia di un'imagine* (Bologna: Arte Grafiche Emiliane, 1976).

Ricciardelli, F., 'Violence and repression in late medieval Italy,' in S.K. Cohn jr. and F. Ricciardelli (eds.), *The culture of violence in Renaissance Italy* (Florence: Le Lettere, 2012) 55-80.

Riebe, M.S., '*Sotto i portici*: Life in seventeenth-century Bologna through the games of Giuseppe Maria Mitelli (1634-1718)' (Unpublished PhD thesis, Bard College, New York, 2010).

Rizzo, V., 'Donne e criminalità a Viterbo nel XV secolo,' *Rivista storica del Lazio* 12 (2000) 11-27.

Rizzo, V., 'Giustizia e società a Viterbo nel XV secolo (da una ricerca sui registri dei malefici),' *Biblioteca e società* 3-4 (1999) 47-50.

Roberts, G.G., 'Vendetta, violence, and police power in thirteenth-century Bologna,' in S.R. Blanshei (ed.), *Violence and justice in Bologna: 1250-1700* (Lanham: Lexington Books, 2018) 3-25.

Rolla, N., 'Per strada e in giustizia. Strategie di difesa dentro e fuori il tribunale (Torino, XVIII secolo),' *Quaderni storici* 141:3 (2012) 637-667.

Romani, M.A., 'Criminalità e giustizia nel Ducato di Mantova alla fine del cinquecento,' *Rivista storica Italiana* 92 (1980) 679-706.

Romano, D., 'Gender and the urban geography of Renaissance Venice,' *Journal of social history* 23 (1989) 339-350.

Rose, C.S., *A renaissance of violence. Homicide in early modern Italy* (Cambridge: Cambridge University Press, 2019).

Rose, C.S., 'Violence and the centralization of criminal justice in early modern Bologna,' in S.R. Blanshei (ed.), *Violence and justice in Bologna: 1250-1700* (Lanham: Lexington Books, 2018) 101-122.

Rose, C.S., 'Homicide in North Italy: Bologna, 1600-1700' (Unpublished PhD thesis, University of Toronto, 2016).

Rose, C.S., '"To be remedied of any vendetta": Petitions and the avoidance of violence in early modern Parma,' *Crime, history & societies* 16:2 (2012) 5-27.

Roussel, D., 'La description des violences féminines dans les archives criminelles au XVIe siècle,' *Tracés. Revue de Sciences humaines* 19 (2010) 65-81.

Rublack, U., *The crimes of women in early modern Germany* (Oxford: Oxford University Press, 1999).

Ruff, J.R., *Violence in early modern Europe, 1500-1800* (Cambridge: Cambridge University Press, 2001).

Ruff, J.R., *Crime, justice and public order in old regime France* (London: Croom Helm, 1984).

Ruggiero, G., *Violence in early Renaissance Venice* (New Brunswick: Rutgers University Press, 1980).

Ruitenbeek, O., 'Niet zonder kleerscheuren. Criminaliteitspatroon, eergevoel en het gebruik van fysiek geweld door Amsterdamse volksvrouwen, 1811-1838,' *Jaarboek Amstelodamum* 102 (2010) 62-85.

Sandri, L., 'Matrimoni mancati. "Pericolate" e "gravide occulte" dell'ospizio di Orbatello di Firenze nel XVIII e XIX secolo,' in M. Lanzinger and R. Sarti (eds.), *Nubili e celibi. Tra scelta e costrizione (secoli XVI-XX)* (Florence: Udine, 2006) 71-91.

Sanfilippo, M., 'Il fenomeno migratorio italiano: storia e storiografia,' in A. Miranda and A. Signorelli (eds.), *Pensare e ripensare le migrazioni* (Palermo: Sellerio, 2011) 245-272.

Sardi, L.C., 'Analisi statistica sulla criminalità nel 1700 (reati e pene) con riguardo allo Stato senese,' in L. Berlinguer and F. Colao (eds.), *Criminalità e società in età moderna* (Milan: Giuffrè, 1991) 327-476.

Sarti, R., 'The true servant: Self-definition of male domestics in an Italian city (Bologna, 17th-19th centuries),' *The history of the family* 10 (2005) 407-433.

Sarti, R., 'Notes on the feminization of domestic service: Bologna as a case study (18th-19th centuries),' *Acta demographica* 13 (1997) 125-163.

Sbriccoli, M., '"Deterior est condicio foeminarum." La storia della giustizia penale alla prova dell'approccio di genere,' in G. Calvi (ed.), *Innesti. Donne e genere nella storia sociale* (Rome: Viella, 2004) 73-91.

Sbriccoli, M., 'Fonti giudiziarie e fonti giuridiche. Riflessioni sulla fase attuale degli studi di storia del crimine e delle giustizia criminale,' *Studi storici* 29:2 (1988) 491-501.

Schmidt, A., *Prosecuting women. A comparative perspective on crime and gender* (Leiden: Brill, 2020).

Schmidt, A. and Heijden, M. van der, 'Women alone in early modern Dutch towns: opportunities and strategies to survive,' *Journal of urban history* 42:1 (2016) 21-38.

Schmidt, A. and Pluskota, M., 'Gevaarlijke vrouwen, gewelddadige mannen? Een review van het historisch onderzoek naar criminaliteit en gender in Europese steden, 1600-1900,' *Stadsgeschiedenis* 8:1 (2013) 60-77.

Schmidt, H.R., 'Hausväter vor Gericht. Der Patriarchalismus als zweischneidiges Schwert,' in M. Dinges (ed.), *Hausväter, Priester, Kastraten. Zur Konstruktion von Männlichkeit in Spätmittelalter und Früher Neuzeit* (Göttingen: Vandenhoeck & Ruprecht, 1998) 213-236.

Schneider, Z.A., 'Women before the bench: Female litigants in early modern Normandy,' *French historical studies* 23:1 (2000) 1-32.

Schwerhoff, G., *Historische Kriminalitätsforschung* (Frankfurt/New York: Campus Verlag, 2011).

Schwerhoff, G., 'Social control of violence, violence as social control: The case of early modern Germany,' in H. Roodenburg and P. Spierenburg (eds.), *Social control in Europe. Volume 1, 1500-1800* (Columbus: The Ohio State University Press, 2004) 220-246.

Schwerhoff, G., *Köln im Kreuzverhör: Kriminalität, Herrschaft und Gesellschaft in einer frühneuzeitlichen Stadt* (Bonn: Bouvier, 1991).

Seidel Menchi, S., 'I processi matrimoniali come fonte storica,' in S. Seidel Menchi and D. Quaglioni (eds.), *Coniugi nemici. La separazione in Italia dal XII al XVIII secolo* (Bologna: Il Mulino, 2000) 15-94.

Sharpe, J.A., *Crime in seventeenth-century England: a county study* (Cambridge: Cambridge University Press, 1983).

Sharpe, J.A., *Defamation and sexual slander in early modern England: The church courts at York* (York: University of York, 1972).

Shaw, J.E., *The justices of Venice. Authorities and liberties in the urban economy, 1550-1700* (Oxford: Oxford University Press, 2006).

Shemek, D., *Ladies errant. Wayward women and social order in early modern Italy* (Durham: Duke University Press, 1998).

Shoemaker, R.B., *Gender in English society 1650-1850. The emergence of separate spheres?* (London: Longman, 1998).

Shoemaker, R.B., *Prosecution and punishment. Petty crime and the law in London and rural Middlesex, c.1660-1725* (Cambridge: Cambridge University Press, 1991).

Sovič, S., Thane, P. and Viazzo, P.P., 'The history of European families: Old and new directions,' in S. Sovič, P. Thane and P.P. Viazzo (eds.), *The history of families and households. Comparative European dimensions* (Leiden: Brill, 2016) 1-19.

Sperling, J., 'Dowry or inheritance? Kinship, property, and women's agency in Lisbon, Venice, and Florence (1572),' *Journal of early modern history* 11:3 (2007) 197-238.

Spierenburg, P., *Violence and punishment. Civilizing the body through time* (Cambridge: Cambridge University Press, 2013).

Spierenburg, P., *A history of murder. Personal violence in Europe from the middle ages to the present* (Cambridge: Polity, 2008).

Spierenburg, P., 'Knife fighting and popular codes of honor in early modern Amsterdam,' in P. Spierenburg (ed.), *Men and violence. Gender, honor and rituals in modern Europe and America.* (Columbus: Ohio State University Press, 1998) 103-127.

Spierenburg, P., 'Masculinity, violence, and honor: An introduction,' in P. Spierenburg (ed.), *Men and violence. Gender, honor and rituals in modern Europe and America* (Columbus: Ohio State University Press, 1998) 1-29.

Spierenburg, P., 'How violent were women? Court cases in Amsterdam, 1650-1810,' *Crime, histoire & sociétés* 1 (1997) 9-28.

Storey, T., *Carnal commerce in Counter-Reformation Rome* (Cambridge: Cambridge University Press, 2008).

Strocchia, S.T., 'Gender and the rites of honour in Italian Renaissance cities,' in J.C. Brown and R.C. Davis (eds.), *Gender and society in Renaissance Italy* (London: Longman, 1998) 53-54.

Taylor, S.K., *Honor and violence in golden age Spain* (New Haven & London: Yale University Press, 2008).

Taylor, S.K., 'Women, honor, and violence in a Castilian town, 1600-1650,' *The sixteenth century journal* 35:4 (2004) 1079-1097.

Tedoldi, L., *La spada e la bilancia. La giustizia penale nell'Europa moderna (secc. XVI-XVIII)* (Rome: Carocci editore, 2008).

Terpstra, N., 'Sex and the sacred. Negotiating spatial and sensory boundaries in Renaissance Florence,' *Radical history review* 121 (2015) 71-90.

Terpstra, N., *Cultures of charity. Women, politics and the reform of poor relief in Renaissance Italy* (Cambridge: Harvard University Press, 2013).

Terpstra, N., 'Working the cocoon. Gendered charitable enclosures and the silk industry in early modern Europe,' in K. Kippen and L. Woods (eds.), *Worth and repute. Valuing gender in late medieval and early modern Europe. Essays in honour of Barbara Todd* (Toronto: Center for Reformation and Renaissance studies, 2011) 39-72.

Terpstra, N., "Republics by contract': Civil society in the Papal State,' in N.A. Eckstein and N. Terpstra (eds.), *Sociability and its Discontents: Civil society, social capital, and their alternatives in late Medieval and early modern Europe* (Turnhout: Brepols, 2009) 293-311.

Terpstra, N., 'Theory into practice: Executions, comforting, and comforters in Renaissance Italy,' in N. Terpstra (ed.), *The art of executing well. Rituals of execution in Renaissance Italy* (Kirksville: Truman State University Press, 2008) 118-159.

Terpstra, N. and Carboni, M., 'Introduction,' *Renaissance and Reformation. Special issue: The material culture of debt* 35:3 (2012) 5-9.

Tickell, S.G., 'Shoplifting in eighteenth-century England' (Unpublished PhD thesis, University of Hertfordshire, 2015).

Tomkins, A. and King, S., 'Introduction,' in S. King and A. Tomkins (eds.), *The poor in England 1700-1850. An economy of makeshifts* (Manchester: Manchester University Press, 2003) 1-38.

Troilo, M., 'Popolazione e proprietà attraverso le fonti fiscali bolognesi nell'età moderna,' *Popolazione e storia* 12:1 (2011) 23-41.

Tsakiri, R.N., 'Deviance and morals. A study of sixteenth-century Crete under Venetian rule. An initial exploration,' *Crimes and misdemeanor* 1:2 (2007) 154-174.

Turner, J., 'Summary justice for women. Stafford Borough, 1880-1905,' *Crime, history & societies* 16:2 (2012) 55-77.

Ulbricht, O., 'Einleitung. Für eine Geschichte der weiblichen Kriminalität in der Frühen Neuzeit oder: Geslechtergeschichte, historische Kriminalitätsforschung und weibliche Kriminalität,' in O. Ulbricht (ed.), *Von Huren und Rabenmüttern. Weibliche Kriminalität in der Frühen Neuzeit* (Cologne: Böhlau, 1995) 1-37.

Vallerani, M., *Medieval public justice* (Washington: The Catholic University of America Press, 2012).

Vanbellinghen, M., 'Diefstal en heling van kleding en textiel: Antwerpen, 1775-1785,' *Tijdschrift voor sociale geschiedenis* 21:4 (1995) 385-405.

Vasta, C., 'Per una topografia della violenza femminile (Roma, secoli XVI-XVII),' *Genesis* 14:2 (2015) 59-81.

Vasta, C., 'Criminal women. Women's violence in sixteenth and seventeenth-century Rome' (Unpublished Conference paper 61th Annual Meeting of the RSA, Berlin, 26-28 March 2015).

Vermeesch, G., 'Reflections on the relative accessibility of law courts in early modern Europe,' *Crime, history & societies* 19:2 (2015) 53-76.

Viazzo, P.P., 'What's so special about the Mediterranean? Thirty years of research on household and family in Italy,' *Continuity and change* 18:1 (2003) 111-137.

Vickery, A., 'Golden Age to separate spheres? A review of the categories and chronology of English women's history,' *The Historical Journal* 36 (1993) 383-414.

Walker, G., *Crime, gender and social order in early modern England* (Cambridge: Cambridge University Press, 2003).

Walker, G., 'Women, theft and the world of stolen goods,' in J. Kermode and G. Walker (eds.), *Women, crime and the courts in early modern England* (London: UCL Press, 1994) 81-105.

Walker, G. and Kermode, J., 'Introduction,' in J. Kermode and G. Walker (eds.), *Women, crime and the courts in early modern England* (London: UCL Press, 1994) 1-22.

Warner, J., Riviere, J. and Graham, K., 'Women behaving badly. Gender and aggression in a military town, 1653-1781,' *Sex roles* 52 (2005) 289-298.

Welch, E., *Shopping in the Renaissance. Consumer cultures in Italy 1400-1600* (New Haven: Yale University Press, 2005).

Wettmann-Jungblut, P., '"Stelen inn rechter hungersnodtt." Diebstahl, Eigentumsschutz und strafrechtliche Kontrolle im vorindustriellen Baden 1600-1850,' in R. van Dülmen (ed.), *Verbrechen, Strafen und soziale Kontrolle. Studien zur historischen Kulturforschung* (Frankfurt am Main: Fischer Taschenbuch Verlag, 1990) 133-177.

Whitlock, T.C., *Crime, gender and consumer culture in nineteenth-century England* (London/New York: Routledge 2016).

Wiener, M., 'The Victorian criminalization of men,' in P. Spierenburg (ed.), *Men and Violence: Gender, Honor, and Rituals in Modern Europe and America* (Columbus: Ohio State University Press, 1998) 197-212.

Wood, J.C., 'Conceptualizing cultures of violence and cultural change,' in S. Carroll (ed.), *Cultures of violence. Interpersonal violence in historical perspective* (Basingstoke: Palgrave, 2007) 79-96.

Woolf, S., *The poor in Western Europe in the eighteenth and nineteenth centuries* (London/New York: Methuen, 1986).

Worden, N., 'Public brawling, masculinity and honour,' in N. Worden (ed.), *Cape town. Between East and West* (Hilversum: Verloren, 2012) 194-211.

Wray, S.K., *Communities in crisis. Bologna during the Black Death* (Brill: Leiden, 2009).

Wray, S.K., 'Instruments of concord. Making peace and settling disputes through a notary in the city and contado of late medieval Bologna,' *Journal of social history* 42:3 (2009) 733-760.

Zedner, L., *Women, crime and custody in Victorian England* (Oxford: Clarendon Press, 1991).

Zemon Davis, N., *Fiction in the archives. Pardon tales and their tellers in sixteenth-century France* (Stanford: Stanford University Press, 1987).

Zorzi, A., 'Legitimation and legal sanction of vendetta in Italian cities from the twelfth to the fourteenth centuries,' in S.K. Cohn jr. and F. Ricciardelli (eds.), *The culture of violence in Renaissance Italy* (Florence: Le Lettere, 2012), 27-54.

Zorzi, A., 'La pena di morte in Italia nel Tardo Medioevo,' *Clio & Crimen* 4 (2007) 47-62.

Zorzi, A., 'Aspetti e problemi dell'amministrazione della giustizia penale nella repubblica fiorentina I. La transizione dal XIV al XV secolo,' *Archivio storico italiano* 145 (1987) 391-453.

Zucca Micheletto, B., 'Reconsidering women's labor force participation rates in eighteenth-century Turin,' *Feminist economics* 19:4 (2013) 200-223.

Zucca Micheletto, B., 'Reconsidering the southern Europe model: Dowry, women's work and marriage patterns in pre-industrial urban Italy (Turin, second half of the 18th century),' *The history of the family* 16 (2011) 354-370.

Zuliani, D., 'Reati e pene nel vicariato di Prato prima e dopo la «Leopoldina» (1781-1790),' in L. Berlinguer and F. Colao (eds.), *Criminalità e società in età moderna* (Milan: Giuffrè, 1991) 307-327.

Permissions

All chapters in this book were first published in ECCJGEMB, by Brill by Sanne Muurling; hereby published with permission under the Creative Commons Attribution License or equivalent. Every chapter published in this book has been scrutinized by our experts. Their significance has been extensively debated. The topics covered herein carry significant information for a comprehensive understanding. They may even be implemented as practical applications or may be referred to as a beginning point for further studies.

We would like to thank the editorial team for lending their expertise to make the book truly unique. They have played a crucial role in the development of this book. Without their invaluable contributions this book wouldn't have been possible. They have made vital efforts to compile up to date information on the varied aspects of this subject to make this book a valuable addition to the collection of many professionals and students.

This book was conceptualized with the vision of imparting up-to-date and integrated information in this field. To ensure the same, a matchless editorial board was set up. Every individual on the board went through rigorous rounds of assessment to prove their worth. After which they invested a large part of their time researching and compiling the most relevant data for our readers.

The editorial board has been involved in producing this book since its inception. They have spent rigorous hours researching and exploring the diverse topics which have resulted in the successful publishing of this book. They have passed on their knowledge of decades through this book. To expedite this challenging task, the publisher supported the team at every step. A small team of assistant editors was also appointed to further simplify the editing procedure and attain best results for the readers.

Apart from the editorial board, the designing team has also invested a significant amount of their time in understanding the subject and creating the most relevant covers. They scrutinized every image to scout for the most suitable representation of the subject and create an appropriate cover for the book.

The publishing team has been an ardent support to the editorial, designing and production team. Their endless efforts to recruit the best for this project, has resulted in the accomplishment of this book. They are a veteran in the field of academics and their pool of knowledge is as vast as their experience in printing. Their expertise and guidance has proved useful at every step. Their uncompromising quality standards have made this book an exceptional effort. Their encouragement from time to time has been an inspiration for everyone.

The publisher and the editorial board hope that this book will prove to be a valuable piece of knowledge for students, practitioners and scholars across the globe.

Index

H

I

J

L

M

N

P

R

S

U

www.ingramcontent.com/pod-product-compliance
Lightning Source LLC
LaVergne TN
LVHW011515200926
848484LV00001B/45